TRANSFORMATION OF ECONOMY AS A REAL PROCESS

For my parents, with love

Transformation of Economy as a Real Process

An insider's perspective

DANIEL DAIANU

Ashgate

Aldershot • Brookfield USA • Singapore • Sydney

Published by
Ashgate Publishing Limited
Gower House
Croft Road
Aldershot
Hampshire GU11 3HR
England

Ashgate Publishing Company
Old Post Road
Brookfield
Vermont 05036
USA

British Library Cataloguing in Publication Data
Daianu, Daniel
   Transformation of economy as a real process : an insider's
   perspective
   1.Romania - Economic conditions 2.Romania - Economic policy
   I.Title
   330.9'498'032

Library of Congress Cataloging-in-Publication Data
Daianu, Daniel
    Transformation of economy as a real process : an
   insider's perspective / Daniel Daianu
       p. cm.
   Includes index.
   ISBN 1-84014-475-0 (hardcover)
    1. Structural adjustment (Economic policy)--Romania.
   2. Romania--Economic policy--1989- 3. Romania-
   -Economic conditions--1989- I. Title.
   HC405.D3 1998
   338.9498--dc21   98-34300
                                                                     CIP

ISBN 1 84014 475 0

Printed and bound by Athenaeum Press, Ltd.,
Gateshead, Tyne & Wear.

Contents

PART III: TRANSFORMATION AND EXTERNAL ENVIRONMENT

List of Figures

List of Tables

Foreword

There is a big academic industry nowadays on the economics and politics of post-communist transformation and many intellectual heavyweights are involved in it. There is even a circuit, like in tennis, where people accumulate points by producing state of the art papers in this new field; and attending the 'tournaments' (conferences) of the circuit helps tremendously by creating personal research momentum and a sense of belonging to the circle of connoisseurs. The output of this industry has been increasing exponentially in recent years and, consequently, the risk of being redundant or insignificant is considerable unless one finds a 'niche' of scholarly relevance.

What prompted me, then, to construct this book? For a long period of time I felt the compulsion to bring together in a structured manner several papers of mine which, I feel, have a common message; to come up with my thinking on the actual process of economic transformation and present the 'Romanian story' in a broader context, as viewed by an *insider*. By the latter, I mean an Eastern European economist, who has been watching closely the transformation in Romania not as a singular process, on the staff of the Ministry of Finance and the Central Bank. My thinking has been devoted extensively to issues like: the role of institutional change in societal transformation and the impossibility of compressing time at will; the intense *strain* in the systems undergoing radical change owing to the legacy of resource misallocation and institutional fragility, and the influence of *strain* on stabilisation; and the impact of the 'new age' of globalisation and information technologies on transformation.

To say the least, I found a lot of comfort when *The Wall Street Journal*, in a review article, highlighted the role of institutional change in post-communist transformation ('Market growth stalls in Eastern Europe', 25 August 1997, p.4). Or, as I would put it, the structurality of change in a post-communist setting explains the complexity and the complicated nature of the process. I very much hope that my perception of the embeddedness of the Romanian situation in the wider story of transformation in Europe will not leave readers unrewarded.

This book contains twelve chapters. There is thus an introductory chapter, which presents the philosophy of the text and some of its leading arguments.

The other chapters cover three major topics: institutional change; macroeconomic stabilisation and restructuring, and transformation and the international environment. This sequence was considered more suitable under the circumstances.

I should say that most of the chapters are revised versions of papers presented at international conferences where I was the beneficiary of the clash of ideas and the wisdom of many of the participants; I thank all of them for the privilege I had to attend those events. I am also grateful to the publications in which I had initial versions of my papers printed. Of invaluable usefulness were the fellowships I had at the Russian Research Centre of Harvard University, the Woodrow Wilson Centre in Washington DC, the Research Department of the International Monetary Fund, and the NATO Defense College in Rome, in the last few years.

The fellows of the Romanian Economic Society (SOREC) and the Romanian Institute for Free Enterprise (IRLI) have been a constant intellectual stimulus in writing the papers and completing the book; I am heavily indebted to all of them. I am grateful to Lucian Albu, with whom I co-authored the paper on the underground economy, and who was particularly kind to allow me to include it in the book.

My assistants, Corina Andricenco-Luca and Valentina Radu, who helped prepare the manuscript for publication, deserve my deepest appreciation.

Last but not least, I wish to thank the publisher, for nudging me to persist in my endeavour and for the support in bringing this manuscript to light.

Introduction

1 The Path of Transformation

It is a truism to say that post-communist transformation is liberal in spirit and action (in the European sense) as history goes, in the countries concerned, from the command (totalitarian) system to economic and political democracy – to what Karl Popper called the *open society*. The Zeitgeist of the eighties only accentuated the liberal spirit, but did not determine it! A simple intellectual exercise can be used in order to verify this assertion. Let us imagine that the domino effect of the collapse of communism in Europe had occurred in the 60s, which means in the years of paradigmatic supremacy of Keynesism in economic policy. Would that have meant an alteration of the liberal essence of transformation? The obvious answer is NO. How is the *path of transformation* and how would post-communist societies look after a longer period of time are, however, questions which are still begging answers.

One of the major lessons of the last years regarding transformation is the necessity of being open minded and of considering various hypotheses and viewpoints, of not becoming the prisoners of clichés and taboos, of understanding that there can be no perfect blueprints as there cannot be a perfect world. In this respect, I cannot help recalling Keynes' famous dictum that we, all, are, one way or another, the prisoners of some famous theories. In addition, this intellectual 'serfdom' is part of how science evolves, of its incremental development as well (aside from revolutionary changes) and of its 'internal burning'. Nonetheless, each scientific demarche needs to strive for authenticity and openness vis-à-vis the world of existing ideas. Additionally, the need of lucidity and pragmatism should compel us to keep our eyes open and confront a reality, which can be overwhelming by its complexity and the dimension of changes.

Let us remember how, some years ago, those who were prone to emphasise the *structural nature* of the problems facing post-communist countries made up a minority in the chorus of upbeat voices; they warned about the lack of realism of the theses and conceptions which smelled of the possibility of compressing time at will, of practising a sort of 'hocus pocus economics'. Currently, the majority of those who are frequent travellers of the circuit of conferences dealing with transformation reveal a different, significantly more poised stance. Quite tellingly, Alan Gelb, who headed the World Bank

Division conducting policy research on post-communist transformation, remarked that one should judge a policy on its own merits by skewing intellectual prejudices (1996, p.2).

An increasing number of professionals emphasise the role of institutions in economic development,[1] the burden of history, and the intensity of what Francois Perroux named 'emprise de la structure' (the power of structure), with the latter including the legacy of resource misallocation and the *strain* it entails in the system. Here one can talk about the structural (social) embeddedness of economic phenomena (Marc Granovetter, 1985), which is an approach having as illustrious precursors Max Weber and Emile Durkheim. Such a broad analytical perspective lends to transformation a much richer meaning and content, which go beyond what is implied by the generic notions of price liberalisation, macrostabilisation, and privatisation.

Among professionals it is increasingly accepted that an adequate understanding of the deep processes of transformation involves the scrutiny of aspects which can easily overstretch the analytical capabilities of economists; such aspects are the dynamics of institutions (seen as *social norms*[2] as well), corporate governance, the build up of human capital as an educational effort, etc. In order to overcome this analytical overstretch economists' investigations need to be intertwined with those performed by other social scientist fellows – sociologists, social psychologists and political scientists.[3] Those who ignore the fact that transformation involves modernisation and catching-up, on a road littered with structural traps, show naiveté and conceptual myopia.

What complicates further the scrutiny of transformation is the need to place the process into a world-wide context, which means the world at the end of this century. Unfortunately, there are many that seem to overlook what is happening on the European continent as well as major processes in the world space. In a way, this is not surprising since people have a natural temptation to be self-centred – Romaniancentric, or Europeancentric. However, this type of conceptual narrowness can lie at the origin of flawed analyses.

When highlighting the need for global embeddedness I have in mind an apparent loss of vitality by Western European countries, the crisis of the welfare state, the 'economic rise' of East Asia (which cannot be annulled by the recent major financial crisis) and shifting comparative advantages under the impact of the 'new information age' and of economic globalisation, etc. I think also of the pressure the globalisation of financial markets imposes on national economic policies, and the related increasing marginal cost of imprudent and inconsistent measures over time. Embeddedness into a wide context[4] helps detect both the expected and the new sources of difficulties encountered by post-communist countries, and what may lie ahead for them.

This introduction is an encapsulation of some of the main ideas underlying the chapters that follow; it is also a presentation of the philosophy which guided the construction of the book. Although most of these chapters deal with Romania they rely on working assumptions and draw inferences of wider bearing.

Getting rid of clichés, illusions and stereotypes

Transformation, as an analytical process is not devoid of clichés, illusions, and intellectual stereotypes. Let us start with semantics and the way we portray performances comparatively. Thus, the members of what is called the Visegrad Group and a few other countries (such as Slovenia) evince remarkably better transformation results; this is the main reason why these countries are called fast-reformers. Obviously, the rest of the pack is made up of so-called slow-reformers. This definition however needs qualifications. On one hand, it does obscure important differences among the countries which are grouped together. On the other hand, it downplays the importance of structural factors and of *history* in explaining performances. In this respect it seems to me that there has been an excessive temptation to lump countries together, in various groups, by assuming a pretty much deterministic (mechanical) relationship between preordained results and policies implied by a conventional wisdom in the making. In the vein of the old Latin saying 'post hoc, ergo propter hoc' close performances were ascribed more to presumed similar policies than to commonalties in initial circumstances, the power of structural factors and policy peculiarities.

It suffices to look carefully at concrete policies, at the fine print of reforms among the countries of the Visegrad Group to support such a thesis – for example Hungary vs. Poland. The latter country became the 'classical example' of shock therapy regarding price liberalisation. At the same time, Hungary, in spite of a remarkable policy consistency can be viewed as an example of gradualism,[5] and its economic performances are due also to reforms initiated before 1989. As to the Czech Republic, the fact that it could not avert a banking crisis in 1996, and that the lack of regulations of capital markets was heavily criticised by many cannot change the overall picture.

The sense of direction and consistency forms the basic ingredient that secures the credibility and the success of reforms. In my view, this factor has been at fault in Romania, which is a fact largely proven by the way the political cycle influenced the economy in the election years.

One can submit, therefore, the hypothesis that certain traits of politics and social life, of the local (national) industrial and political culture, and other structural factors have strong explanatory power for understanding policymaking. It may be the case that culture (the burden of the past), geography and structural factors explain to a large extent why certain policies (like macroeconomic stabilisation) were more likely to be undertaken and were more successful in certain countries than in others.

Likewise, the start of economic recovery in the transforming economies can be linked significantly with structural factors (such as the bottoming out of economies and the accumulation of a critical mass of *organisational* and *institutional capital* – Olivier Blanchard, 1996, P. Murrell), as with macroeconomic stabilisation. For instance, Romania's start of recovery in 1993 – at the peak of inflation (ca. 300%) – should give food for thought in this respect. That macroeconomic policy blunders in 1995 and 1996, together with the feeble pace of privatisation and the modesty of capital inflows, jeopardised sustainable recovery is another matter, certainly of no less significance. Macroeconomic stabilisation is unquestionably good for growth but it seems to me that the implied causality is sometimes overemphasised and structural factors are underestimated.

If a line of reasoning which emphasises the role of structural factors, of the burden of the past and their impact on policy is well considered then one may need to broaden the focus of analysis: instead of being absorbed by preferred clichés and ideal frameworks one should pay more attention to closer-to-reality second-best scenarios. This logic would have to apply to both first round as well as n-round (feedback) policy measures. Frequently and with surprising nonchalance, those who pass judgement or provide advice equate non-adherence to a 'first-best' policy-package to lack of political will. Political determination is clearly an essential ingredient of policy formulation and implementation, but far from sufficient in order to gain credibility and achieve success.

Janos Kornai was very much to the point when he remarked that 'Those who attach intrinsic value to democratic institutions must consider in their proposals the existing power relations and the rules of parliamentary democracy. We are not going to achieve much if we rely on advice of this kind: it is our job to advise you about what is good for your country and your job to take advice. If you do not take it, that is your problem. We cannot help it if your politicians are stupid or malicious' (p. 5). This is a strong prodding to consider the political economy of reform in the post-communist countries.

Relatedly, one has to ask whether the advocated 'first-best' policies are actually realistic, irrespective of circumstances. For example, can one really believe that not paying wages and salaries to many people, who are still employed, is a sustainable policy which can durably defeat high inflation? Alternatively, what is the meaning of a small-consolidated budget deficit if arrears as well as the quasi-fiscal deficit are growing? In addition, is the non-inflationary financing of the budget deficit sustainable when its service is skyrocketing because of very high positive real interest rates? It appears that, sometimes, some pundits disconnect what is desirable – from a results oriented perspective – from what is achievable, in terms of policy, under the circumstances. Let us remember how vigorously Jeffrey Sachs pointed out the need of external aid in order to get out of a vicious circle; for such aid would condition the credibility of reform policies and the preservation of a modicum of social stability under certain circumstances.

On this line of reasoning, one can try to understand the sources of *policy credibility* in the transforming economies. Again, aside from vision and the very quality of policy itself, I would highlight the initial conditions (including the legacy of resource misallocation), the history of partial reforms (which made certain environments more 'market-friendly'), and the role of foreign capital in triggering a virtuous circle. Particularly the last factor seems to have played a very significant role in the front-runner economies; this role is better understood bearing in mind the extreme complexity and complicated nature (the very high cost) of deep restructuring of economy. In Poland, where political commitment to reforms has been impeccable, the policy thrust was accompanied by a substantial write-off of the external liabilities of the country and by a stabilisation fund; these two elements helped greatly macroeconomic stabilisation.[6]

Without massive capital inflows, economies that bear the brunt of the legacy of tremendous resource misallocation run the risk of boiling in their own steam, of stagnating. It is likely that even high savings ratios would not change for the better the consequences of the legacy of resource misallocation other favourable conditions missing. One can argue that some of the fast growing economies of Asia relied less on foreign capital and that, in their case, the essential factor was the very high savings ratios (35-40%). Undoubtedly, such ratios are good for economic growth and economic policy should strive to stimulate them. Nonetheless, I dare to say that geographic and historical circumstances[7] make foreign capital play a special role in the post-communist countries. In addition, a clear indication of these circumstances is the intensity of structural strain in those countries.

The state of post-command economies makes the variable represented by capital inflows – as technology, managerial know how, financial resources, etc – a critical venue for seeing the light at the end of the transformation tunnel. By applying this logic, the lack of foreign capital helps explain Romania's track record and the fragility of its attempts at macroeconomic stabilisation.

Policy credibility, itself, depends on how much structural adjustment the system can undergo in a period covered by the respective policy; and the capacity to adjust depends, basically, on *structure,* on the dimension of required resource reallocation, and on the quality of institutions as premises for policymaking. A 'credibility paradox' seems to be at play here: those who need to be more credible are not (cannot be) because of the magnitude of required resource reallocation and of overall institutional change, and their related costs – what I called *strain* in the system; whereas those who can afford not to undertake similarly painful changes (e.g. Hungary) enjoy more credibility due to the, relatively, smaller scale of needed structural adjustment. Obviously, a political element has to be factored in as well, which includes the *reputation* of policymakers.

It is understood that credibility and the boldness of policy can be much enhanced by political climate and various sui generis anchors. The prospects for joining the EU and NATO have provided powerful policy-anchors to most of the countries, which signed Association agreements with Brussels. This also explains why, where there has been a political backlash at the polls no major policy reversals occurred in most of the reforming countries. Nonetheless the question which automatically comes to one's mind is what would happen if policy and social fatigue combine with receding prospects (for some, or most of the countries) to join the two institutions in the near future. This kind of anchor is non-existent for most of the former Soviet republics and its lack gives more degrees of freedom for policy to go astray.

As to the political climate, it can be judged on two grounds. One is related to timing; it is better to initiate reforms when people are still highly enthusiastic and would put up with assumed temporary discomfort. The longer policy lingers the worse it is for policy consistency and coherence. The other ground regards the overall context including the Zeitgeist; the latter enhanced a certain policy thrust and vision in most of the transforming countries, which was accentuated by the effects of globalisation and the advent of new information technologies. For instance, internal convertibility of the currency was used as a weapon for systemic transformation, which was not the case in the West in the aftermath of the Second World War.

When mentioning post-war western governments it is worthwhile to notice a growing similarity between their then obsession for dealing with high unemployment and their current policy worries regarding the size of structural unemployment. What I wish to imply is that post-communist countries' governments may not be in a better position in this regard and structural unemployment could very likely become very burdensome for their policies – a *hysteresis* phenomenon may develop quite disturbingly in this respect unless proper labour markets policies are developed.

Likewise, it is striking how the need for western countries to reform their welfare systems compares with the post-communist countries' need to restructure their public budgets. This is part of a dual challenge for Europe as a whole: Western Europe's quest to revitalise its economies combined with post-communist countries quest to build viable economies.

In the framework sketched above one should consider also the dynamic of wealth distribution in the transforming economies. As the experience of Latin America and East Asia amply shows, widely diverging wealth discrepancies are not conducive to social stability and long-term growth.[8] The idea here is that even a rapidly growing social pie may not be sufficient for maintaining (improving) the social fabric of society. The implied policy requirement is more than challenging since it needs to fit into the general pattern of market-based reforms which involve income differentiation; it also needs to help the transforming economies become more flexible (adaptable) instead of being mired into social rigidities – which would be fatal in a world increasingly subjected to the pressures of globalisation. In any case this is a domain which may critically test the governance capabilities of the elites in the transforming economies in the years to come; these elites would have to solve what Arthur Okun coined as the 'Big Trade-off' more than two decades ago.

Because of their major structural distortions (including resource misallocation) and the *fragility* of their institutions, the transforming economies have an almost in-built mechanism for subjecting themselves to intense *strain*. Not even the front-runners (except Poland, probably) have made big strides as far as deep restructuring is concerned and much of the potential *strain* has been mitigated by the effects of heavy capital inflows.[9] It can be submitted that feeble deep restructuring maintains a high degree of actual and potential *strain* in the system. This issue needs to be emphasised since the resumption of growth on a large area may have caused more optimism than is actually warranted. One should not overlook that what is happening now is more economic recovery from an extremely depressed level of production – even if correction is made for formerly useless production – and that this was helped by relatively easily obtained efficiency gains; that, over time, unless investment ratios are high, unless there is constant upgrading of the quality of output (tradeables), and there is a good functioning of institutions, growth will stall. Moreover, some of the post-communist countries may face dangerous stagnation against the background of intensifying social tensions.

The implosion of the Mexican economy at the end of 1994, the financial crisis in East Asia which started in the second half of 1997, in an indirect way, and the chaos in Albania in 1996, in a direct way, suggest how fragile and vulnerable post-communist economies are; they also show how deceptive macroeconomic figures can be when they are not supported by the strength of real economy and solid institutions.[10] One should not forget that Mexico was hailed in the early 90s as a role-model all over the world; and a few years ago Albania was considered a success story for its macroeconomic stabilisation and other reforms.

The *fragility* and *vulnerability* of the transforming economies should be judged against the background of globalising financial markets. Again, the East Asian crisis, the Mexican crisis, and also the hard times the Argentinean policymakers had in managing the 'tequila effect' (the currency board did not make the economy soundproof and IMF money had to be asked for!) come to one's mind. There are several aspects to think about here. One regards the link between the development of financial markets and the progress made in the real economy. It can be submitted that the degree of volatility of domestic financial markets would be exceedingly high unless there is sufficient restructuring of the economy. Conversely, it can be argued that capital markets do enhance restructuring which may suggest that one faces a chicken and egg problem in this respect.

There is here a policy conundrum, which outlines a multi-question one needs to answer: how would financial markets better serve the transforming economies and, implicitly, how should be they developed? Do financial markets influence the nature of capital inflows (when real interest rates are high and induce speculative inflows) and if that is the case what are policy implications? Another aspect is linked with the acute need for much prudence and wisdom in macroeconomic policy. The experience of Romania indicates clearly, what happens when economic recovery is not backed by changes in the real economy and is driven by domestic absorption in the main. A last aspect to be highlighted is the urgent need to strengthen the supervision of the banking industry; since many banks are congenitally fragile, quite prone to poor lending, and heavily fraught by conflicts of interest; it goes without saying that better supervision should be exerted on financial institutions as well.[11]

The role of institutions has been stressed herein several times. It seems to me that economists are insufficiently equipped to analyse institutional change in the transforming economies, which is so wide-ranging and deeply going. This fact is quite unfortunate since, as many of us would agree, the quality of institutions is what counts, ultimately, for the long-term growth differentials of national societies and for their varied lots. Recent studies by R. Barro, L. Summers, P. Romer, etc. reconfirmed the role of capital build-up, of human capital, for economic growth but this result did not surprise the profession; what needs to be elucidated is what makes a society accumulate more and invest more productively than others, what is the role played by wealth distribution in the process, and why a society can achieve dynamic efficiency gains over time whereas others may be plagued by substantial diminishing returns or secular decline.

One should think that the post-communist countries are in a period when the basic constructs of the future systems are being put in place and this can be seen as an historical opportunity for designing viable societal aggregates. For example, the future dynamics of the consolidated public budget will very much depend on how its structure is being built now, on reforming the pension systems, etc. At the same time, due to the pace of events and the complexity of the whole process big mistakes can be made. These mistakes may put the evolving systems on a less convenient path; they can create bad 'path dependency'. This is like saying that the institutional 'QWERTY keyboard layout' of the transforming economies is now being established and one needs to be very careful about which path the lock-in occurs.

Therefore, the fact that economic decline stopped and economic recovery was ushered into most of the European post-communist countries should not be overplayed unless one penetrates the very 'soft' portion of society; what I have in mind are its *institutions*. Only in this way can one scrutinise what lies ahead for the post-communist countries, what would be the nature of capitalism in those countries and, implicitly, their more likely political, social and economic performances.

Two major underplayed issues

What puzzled me during all these years of transformation has been the relative neglect of two issues, which in my view, are of utmost importance for coming to grips analytically and operationally with the reality of post-communist transformation. One issue regards the relative backwardness of the former command systems; the other issue refers to the magnitude of required resource reallocation in relation to the new relative prices dictated by liberalisation and opening of the economy.

The legacy of backwardness

If the system-related dimension of transition is of paramount importance, one can detect another meaning, which has defined the evolution of these societies through this century; it is 'the quest for catching-up with the West'. Today, this quest is reflected by the ardent desire to join the European Union and Euroatlantic structures. Why is the quest for catching-up emphasised? For knowledgeable professionals can often be heard making judgements on the transformation process, while seeming to neglect the legacy of backwardness of most of these societies – a state of affairs which goes back deeply into history.

A note of caution is nevertheless required. The post-communist societies of Europe are societal entities that show common (structural) traits, but also major discrepancies; the latter can be linked with the different pre-communist legacies (the former Czechoslovakia, as a leading industrial country during the inter-war period, is the most conspicuous example) and the different brands of national central planning, in terms of relaxation of direct controls and economic policy choices. The different histories explain widely different incomes per capita (with Romania as one of the poorest post-communist countries in Europe), why market institutions vary qualitatively among the national environments and why macro and micro-disequilibria differed among them on the eve of 1989. Undoubtedly, Hungary, the former Czechoslovakia and Poland had a substantial competitive edge in starting the process of managing transition. Unsurprisingly, all these countries have fared better than the rest in their stabilisation programmes, although their recipes were not similar, as some would argue.

Backwardness should be seen as bearing considerably on the potential for overcoming the performance deficit of societies with poor institutional arrangements; it points, on one hand, at the lack of specific knowledge of individuals and of society as a whole and at the constraints for genuine institutional change and, on the other hand, it suggests that there is much scope for a system to get outside what can be conceived as an ideal tunnel of evolution. The stress put on the burden of the past is meant to warn against its dragging effects and an unfavourable *path dependency*, from which it may not be easy to break away.

Backwardness makes it harder to overcome the fragility of the emerging market institutions and enhances the potential for the dynamics of change to get out of control. Institutional fragility was much underestimated by policymakers and their advisers. As Peter Rutland rightly points out 'in a travesty of Hayekian logic, it was assumed that market institutions would be self-generating' (1994/95, p.11).

Similarly inadequate is the neglect of the extreme complexity of the process under way. Gross oversimplifications and reductionism of the type 'black vs. white' (with no shades in-between), and the lack of understanding of how interests are socially articulated – particularly in a transition period – cannot but obscure real processes and lead to hasty and inadequate decisions. As G. Schopflin aptly noted, 'The elite failed to understand that society was a far more complex organism than what they had thought, that simple, well-meaning declarations were not effective in politics, that ideas and programmes would have to be sold to the public, and that institutions were necessary for the routinised exercise of power' (1994, p. 130).

There are some people who have a very rudimentary view of what a modern market-based system means, and who do not realise that there are variants of real capitalism – that a 'pure' market economy as such does not exist in reality and that the concept is meaningless without proper qualifications. Besides, 'Imperfect and costly information, imperfect capital markets, imperfect competition: these are the realities of market economies – aspects that must be taken into account by those countries embarking on the choice of an economic system'.[12] The implication is clear in the sense of the stringent need to consider how market economies actually function.

Many people are opaque to the reality that it is high time to deal seriously with the *fine print* of reforms, and that this involves much more than simple ideological statements and exhortations; that this involves unavoidable pragmatism and making hard policy choices based on solid theoretical and empirical knowledge, when one cannot escape facing painful trade-offs and dilemmas. For instance, one issue that badly needs serious debate is the structure of *corporate governance*; it is ever more clear that one needs to go beyond the general statement regarding the necessity of privatisation, and that it is not at all clear what are the best formulae for corporate governance in the transforming economies. On a more general level it is high time to take cognisance of an extremely important fact: the post-communist countries are in a period when the basic constructs of the future systems are put in place and this can be seen as an historical opportunity for designing viable societal aggregates.

The sintagma of *institutional fragility* has already been implied. Apart from the insufficient analytical attention paid to the institutional build-up in the transforming societies in Europe, one has to consider the seeds of instability produced by this fragility. The poor capacity of immature institutions to perform needs to be mentioned in this context. For example, the debate on universal vs. narrow banks (on whether and how banks should be involved in resource allocation) is quite relevant for the concern immature market institutions create in terms of enhancing instability and uncertainty in the system.[13]

From a broader perspective one can pose the issue of the *governance capabilities* of the political and economic elites of these countries – to what extent these elites are capable to induce and manage change (transformation) when so much fuzziness, volatility and uncertainty is prevailing. One can also assume that institutional fragility will bear significantly on the nature of capitalism in the region.

The magnitude of resource reallocation: the emergence of strain

Another issue which is not sufficiently highlighted in the professional and public debate is the dimension of the inherited misallocation of resources in Eastern Europe – i.e. the sheer scale of disequilibria, at the new relative prices, that indicates the magnitude of required restructuring as compared to the ability of the system to undergo wide-ranging and quick change.

In Eastern Europe, the structure of the economy and the legacy of resource misallocation, have put the system under exceptional *strain* once the combination of the internal shocks (engineered by reforms, or, simply, triggered by the uncontrolled processes of system dissolution) and external shocks occurred. When one sees Western governments – and their social constituencies – vacillating and deeply reluctant to undertake relatively minor adjustments, the *strain* under which the former command economies operate becomes understandable.

What are the major implications of this *strain*? One is that these economies can easily become exceedingly unstable and that their capacity to absorb shocks is quite low; these economies have a high degree of vulnerability! Another implication is that policymakers face extremely painful trade-offs and that, in most cases, unless policy is clever and sufficient external support is available, the room for manoeuvre is in practice, quite limited. Finally, macroeconomic stabilisation in certain countries hides deeply seated tensions which, sooner or later, come into the open unless deep restructuring takes place.

Current unemployment rates in the transforming economies are not exceedingly high in comparison with the European levels of the mid-nineties and this could assuage the perception of *strain*. However, several factors provide cause for concern. One is that the yardstick used is itself questionable taking into account the unemployment problem in Western Europe. A second factor is the weakness of safety nets; this problem acquires particular significance in the poorer post-communist countries, where the consequences of a 'new type' of poverty could be extremely serious.[14] And another factor is the fact that restructuring of large companies – which mostly need to shed labour in order to become profitable – is very slow, or, in practice, not taking place; this means that potential unemployment increases are still very significant.

One should also mention an increasingly intense *distribution struggle*, and an erosion of the consensus for societal change when many individuals appear as losers – once market forces start to reward people in accordance with merit, effort, good ideas, and inspiration, but also as a result of some workers' misfortune to have jobs in bad (unprofitable) enterprises. These two processes are not a good omen for securing consistency of and support for economic policy-making. This also explains why some governments see inflation as a redistribution device when *strain* is extreme.

There is another dimension to this distribution struggle which needs to be highlighted for its exceptional character in human history, and for its effects on system transformation. It is the process of privatisation, which means a massive (total) redistribution of state assets. As we know, economic textbooks take as a *given* the initial distribution of assets among individual private owners; this distribution is almost God given, and it underpins the whole reasoning on how best to allocate resources and achieve Pareto optimality (highest welfare). In the case of post-communist countries, 'God' has decided to come down from heaven – for what we are witnessing currently is an extraordinary process, without precedent in the history of mankind. In the next few years, much of the fate of tens, if not hundreds, of millions of living individuals (and of their descendants) is going to be shaped by the mechanics and dynamics of privatisation. What took many hundreds of years in the advanced capitalist countries is supposed to occur, through various procedures (more or less legal), in the post-communist countries, in a snapshot on the scale of history. It is not, therefore, surprising that everything surrounding this process is so highly charged emotionally – why so many hopes, dreams, reckless and ruthless actions, misbehaviour, and delusions are linked to it. All individuals want to be on the winning side, but markets cannot make them all happy.

The nature of capitalism in the post-communist countries will be decisively influenced by the actual results of privatisation as a process. If privatisation results in the development of a strong middle class as the social backbone of the new economic system, stability and vigour will be secured, and democratic institutions will develop. Otherwise, the new system in the making will be inherently unstable – like the bad Latin American model – with politics quite likely to take an authoritarian route.

There is a feature of communism that needs to be emphasised in order to understand better the social tension engendered by post-communist transformation, and the intensity of the distribution struggle. Communism – as an economic system – functioned as a kind of poor and steadily declining (suffering from *economic euthanasia*) but, nonetheless, 'welfare state'. Janos Kornai, called the former command system in Hungary a 'premature welfare system'.[15] The post-communist countries maintain among the most generous social welfare budgets in the world when calculated as a share of GDP; social spending budgets are between 15-30% of GDP as compared to 5-10% in the case of East Asian countries at similar income levels, for similar social programmes.[16] As in Western countries, where there exist powerful vested interests which oppose economic adjustment, in post-communist countries those who cannot compete on the markets have turned into a strong coalition of interests which can slow down, or even arrest reforms. This mass of individuals is most likely to fall prey to populist slogans and is obviously inclined to support left-oriented parties. Robert Gilpin's observation, that adjustment is very difficult in welfare states, applies *mutatis mutandis* in the case of post-communist countries.

Institutional change and economic performance: some linkages

The post-communist countries underwent a quick collapse of much of the old institutional framework and of the previous administratively upheld links among enterprises – what Calvo and Coricelli called 'trade implosion' (1992) and this author named 'network deconstruction' (1994). That was a spontaneous process, which distinguishes post-communist transformation of reforms 'controlled from above', as is the case in China, for example. In Romania, a very intense form of spontaneous change was land privatisation since the distribution of land titles followed the actual process. The emergence of the private economy (including the second economy) at the grass root level, and the creation of sui generis forms of financial intermediaries, occurred spontaneously in all the post-communist countries. However, there is another side of the process, which refers to institutional change by design; the latter can have a heavy dosage of imitation, or can present novel features.

It can be said, therefore, that institutional change is the result of the interaction between spontaneous change and large scale reengineering. Here one can see the tension between the work of organicist and constructivist forces.

Institutional change by design: are there any guiding principles?

There are several ingredients of the melting pot which produce policy in a transforming economy and it is worthwhile to make a presentation of them with reference to the issue of institutional change; in this way policy options and constraints can be better explored.

Firstly, the interaction between the realm of ideas and policy is to be mentioned; what I have in mind is the clash of paradigms. The neo-classical paradigm would consider the quick reallocation of resources and the maximisation procedures of agents. Simultaneously, a frictionless environment is taken as the standard and adjustment processes are viewed as being quickly triggered by price liberalisation. Rigidities are largely discounted which, further, would suggest that public intervention in managing adjustment is thought unnecessary. As to the question of picking winners, of creating comparative advantages, the *parti pris* is clearly against something which goes against the complete (undisturbed) operation of market forces. This equilibrium-focused paradigm pays less attention to the 'innovation moment', to the entrepreneurial drive of agents which create new circumstances in the economy via disequlibria, as does the Neo-Austrian School. Since releasing 'entrepreneurial energy' is essential for the transformation of the former command systems this fact, too, hints to the need to go beyond the boundaries of the equilibrium based paradigm. The neo-classical approach also underestimates the time-consuming nature of building up institutions and their impact on economic performance.

Two other competing paradigms exist which provide a rationale for public intervention in the economy. One is the Neo-keynesian approach which takes for granted the imperfection of markets; information and transaction costs, rigidities all compound in portraying an economy in which adjustments cannot be frictionless and in which there can appear large externalities (positive and negative). Whereas some Neo-keynesians are quite ambivalent whether public intervention can be effective (Gregory Mankiw), others – like Joseph Stiglitz

– are in favour of selective intervention. There are, also, economists (Alice Amsden etc.) who point the finger at the East Asian experience and emphasise that – in that case – public intervention went farther and constructed comparative advantages against the background of the operation of market forces.

A third paradigm, neo-structuralism (Lance Taylor, Sweder van Wijnbergen, etc.) looks at the tremendous structural distortions of the less advanced economies and stresses the 'power of structure' and its consequences – the inability of price adjustments to trigger quick resource reallocation and the time-consuming nature of institutional change.

Applying the paradigms highlighted above demands understanding the reality of post-communism; huge resource misallocation, the precariousness of institutions, and the collapse of Eastern markets indicate the existence of much friction in the system and explain why production imploded. Structural factors have significant explanatory power with respect to the evolution of output in the post-communist countries after 1989, and the resumption of growth in several economies appears to be due, to a large extent, to the build-up of *organisational* and *institutional capital*.

What all these paradigms need to incorporate nowadays are the effects of technological progress and of globalisation; namely, the need for flexible markets, for higher adaptability, has to be reconciled with the demands of building up human capital and of creating public goods as positive externalities. This is why the debate on the capitalism in the making in post-communist countries is justified and highly relevant for policymaking.

Obviously, the paradigm embraced by policymakers cannot leave policy unaffected, be it stabilisation, trade, or industrial policy. Let me give a simple example to show why industrial policy of a special kind is badly needed under the circumstances. If a big gap between exit and entry – caused by market forces – is accepted and, further, this imbalance is seen as affecting the size of the budget deficit, the development of the private sector, and social stability, the need for an industrial policy viewed as a damage-control device becomes quite clear. This means that, when exit cannot proceed but gradually, the downsizing and the restructuring of enterprises involves government policy as well; in this situation, public intervention aims at managing change (possibly as crisis management) by processing market information. The magnitude of required resource reallocation asks for a restructuring process, which combines market forces with the entrepreneurial activity of the state. To claim otherwise and to deny any role for the state is to live in a fantasy world, especially when liquidating very large plants means political decisions. In fact, this policy reality was imposed on policy-makers in several post-communist countries.

When viewed in relationship with institutional change and structural rigidities the dispute shock therapy vs. gradualism loses much of its relevance for change cannot take place via a 'big bang'. At the same time, gradualism is out of touch with reality when it ignores the institutional dissolution of the former command system, the collapse of external markets, and, consequently, the inability to control change from above.

Another ingredient of the 'melting pot' underlying policymaking regards the competition between different brands of capitalism: the Continental vs. the Anglo-Saxon view. It is true that globalisation brings the variants of capitalism nearer and this is pertinently exemplified by the debate on corporate governance and labour markets. However, differences among the variants are still substantial and rooted in institutional specificity, which predetermines economic and social performance. This competition affects policy-formulation in the transforming economies in domains like the role of capital markets (vs. banks) in allocating resources, the size of the public sector, the role and the nature of state intervention in the economy, the content of the welfare state, etc.

The competition mentioned above takes place via several channels. One channel is the scholarly debate, which always has some impact on policy. A second channel is the advice of the international financial organisations. Thirdly, national states, as suppliers of financial assistance, come in the picture themselves. Clearly, Europeans (Brussels included) favour certain solutions whereas Americans propound their own model; I use generic terms since in both the USA and Western Europe one can find a wide range of opinions. Ultimately, real life itself makes a verdict, with feedbacks becoming an input of policy or even shaping the latter. A telling example in this respect is what happened with the mass privatisation programme in the Czech Republic and the role played by banks in the whole process. One would have expected a big surge in the role of capital markets and a corresponding diminution in the role of banks as resource allocators. It appears that history, a certain cultural background, the involvement of European banks, and the design of the institutional big bang (represented by the privatisation scheme) did not give way to the Anglo-Saxon model; this explains why many foreign business people complain about the lack of transparency (insider-trading) and the very close intertwinment among banks, local investment funds, and enterprises.

The need for public policies

The magic words of transformation are liberalisation, privatisation, stabilisation, and opening. Nonetheless, it would be hard for someone to dispute on solid grounds the need for public policy in the transforming economies. As J. Stiglitz and Nicholas Stern, the chief economists of the World Bank and the EBRD, respectively, stressed 'A well functioning economy requires a mix of government and markets. The balance, structure and functioning of that mix is at the heart of a development strategy' (1997, p.1). The real issue at stake is, therefore, the nature and the scope of public policy. For instance, after the events of recent years, in most of the transforming economies, can one deny the need of strict regulations regarding banking industry and capital markets?

Clarifications regarding public policy are more than welcome in the case of post-communist economies, bearing in mind where they come from and where they intend to go to. Such clarifications are also needed because some people may find arguments in favour of public policy as being strange – in the historical circumstances of the transformation of the former totalitarian systems.[17] Moreover, such arguments may tempt some to capitalise on them in a direction opposed to market-based transformation. Nonetheless, such a risk should not deter a serious debate on how to formulate an intelligent public policy, wisely calibrated in order to serve transformation and modernisation.

Let us be more explicit by making reference to economic globalisation. For example, some – such as Kenichi Ohmae – would argue that economic globalisation destroys the effectiveness of national economic policy, implicitly, of public intervention; moreover, the relevance of the nation-state, as a relevant economic entity, is strongly questioned. However, what economists call the 'one price law' does function as a tendency and imperfectly; and the claimed mobility of factors of production is much too incomplete and asymmetric in the contemporary world. Let us think only of the 'mobility' of labour and of technological progress – the latter seen as an outcome of 'clusters' of technologies (Michael Porter). Can one realistically assert that the genesis of technological clustering is to be explained by the work of hazard only?

In the world, there are powerful factors at work, which push globalisation. Moreover, values and norms specific to industrial civilisation are to be highlighted, aside from the integration of financial markets. Such factors have a strong impact on the formulation and the effectiveness of national policies. Nonetheless, globalisation should not be equated with uniformisation and, particularly, equalisation of conditions; globalisation can coexist with and even deepen, economic gaps.[18] Additionally, if attention is directed to the soft portion of a societal aggregate – that which ensures social cohesion, and which makes individuals become members of a community (*Gemeinschaft*) – things get more complicated for analysis. National societies, as aggregates which are economically structured and politically articulated, have *cultural identities* with strong emotional content; human beings are not androids, and the need of identification is felt at the level of both family and community. Identification (the need of icons) and its linkages with public policy do affect the long-term performances of national communities (nation states).

Related to the ideas mentioned above it is worthwhile recalling Ernest Gellner's thesis that nation states can be a driving force behind modernisation. The fact is that the world is made up of national aggregates which reveal different economic dynamics. If the world were atomised, and borders (not only geographic) were irrelevant, no major economic discrepancies would be detectable among regions. This is why it makes sense to think in terms of the quality of national institutional settings and of national economic policies. If this line of reasoning is accepted, public policy gains its rationale as macroeconomic policy, industrial policy in a broad sense – including foreign investment, education and development of infrastructure – trade policy, social policy, and last but not least, the working out (or the preservation) of a societal model hypostasised by values, principles and a 'social glue'. An explicit or an implicit 'social contract' between the citizenry and government is also to be included.

Public policy refers to *norms* and *procedures* as well; without them policy could easily degenerate into malignant authoritarianism.

In history one hardly finds examples of successful economic catching-up which did not involve exceptional vision and effective public policy. Therefore, the question is not whether public authorities should intervene in the economy; it is how and how much they should.

The capitalist world is multicoloured with respect to the quality of public policies. Thus, past decades in Latin America show how not to practise public intervention. Exacerbated populism in economic policy, large budget deficits (which were financed inflationarily), overbloated public sectors, extreme import substitution and heavy subsidisation of unperforming industries, social and political clienteles, huge income inequalities, etc, are features of the ill famed Latin American model. A glaring example of what bad public policies do is Argentina of thirty years ago, which changed from a prosperous country before the Second World War into an economic mess during the years of Peronist policies. Likewise, Venezuela, in spite of its enormous riches showed very poor public management in recent decades. In addition, there are examples in Southeast Asia where public policy proved successful. The results of the Asian Tigers in the seventies and the eighties were due, essentially, to sound macroeconomic fundamentals, high savings ratios, and clever public intervention in the economy. Their experience teaches the importance of export orientation, of educational build-up, and of infrastructure development.

At the same time, the recent very severe and prolonged financial crisis in East Asia highlights the economic merits of transparency, self-restraint, and strong institutions including healthy financial entities.

A conclusion is easy to infer: although there is a demand for it, the construction of a wise and effective public policy is a hard task for policymakers bearing in mind the risk of committing major errors. Moreover, it can be argued that, in the case of post-communist countries one is faced with an almost innate lack of capacity (including the mindset) to formulate and implement public policies – which is due to the legacy of communism.[19] But this state of affairs cannot obliterate the need for public policy, for rallying efforts for the sake of modernization.[20] The big question is therefore: how to work out and implement clever public policies, which, on the one hand, should unleash the forces of creativity and the energy of individuals, and on the other hand, should solve problems which require state intervention – without bringing the demons of totalitarian thinking and practice back to life.

Three major challenges

I would submit that post-communist countries face three historical challenges:

a)   institutional construction (transformation);
b)   economic catching-up;
c)   ensuring social stability. In what follows, several initial remarks are made on these challenges.

Firstly, the special historical and political context has to be underlined, namely, the transformation of the former command systems into market based democratic polities. The *political dimension* of the 'Great Transformation' started in 1989,[21] implies the conquest – by citizens – of political freedoms and the build-up of political democracy. Therefore, the thesis can be advanced that, in Central and Eastern Europe, authoritarian[22] forms of government, of managing transformation, would be rejected by citizens and would cause themselves instability.[23] This thesis should be judged from the perspective of other modernisation efforts – like in Asia where authoritarianism has been conspicuous for decades now.

Secondly, a distinction should be made between modernisation and economic growth, though, in a broad sense, the first notion comprehends the latter as an expression of the dynamic performance of institutions. Simultaneously, dealing with structural *strain* and macroeconomic stabilisation are put under the umbrella of sustainable fast growth since they condition the latter.

Finally, the conventional analytical matrix represented by notions such as price liberalisation, stabilisation, and privatisation cannot capture each of the three major challenges.

Institutional change has not been neglected in debates but the burden of the past and the 'path-dependency' issues need to be given more attention. In this respect, two important aspects deserve to be underlined. One refers to the impact of institutions on overall economic performance; poor institutions explain, inter alia, low yields in agriculture, the fragility of the banking sector, or the malfunctioning of democracy. Institutions can also explain why the entrenched patterns of corporate governance make the use of resources inefficient. The second aspect regards the existence of two types of fragility: one linked with the infant nature of institutions; and another type related to the extraordinary magnitude of the changes under way (*structural strain*).

It can be inferred that both pre-communist and communist histories influence a post-communist country's transformation. Thereby, a modernisation strategy – where it does exist – needs to consider the difficulties of institutional build up and the available options; on one hand, 'natura non facit saltus', on the other hand, the 'making of history' (as against the mere presence in history) and the overcoming of structural traps asks for big 'historical jumps', which imply vision and wise choices in the realm of institutional construction and modernisation strategy.

Rapid economic growth is not easy to achieve for there are no easy blueprints. Although conventional theory suggests that any economy that possesses cheap labour has the potential for catching up, ultimately what matters is the quality of institutions and of human capital. Again one can see the importance of institutions which determine the way resources are combined and used, and the overall performance of society. It should also be mentioned that institutions explain the size of savings ratios (as a premise for fast economic growth) and the attractiveness of a national space for foreign capital.

Ensuring social stability is going to be a major challenge in the years ahead. The lessons of history teach that distribution tensions in production and consumption affects the homeostasis and performance of societies (economies). Globalisation of trade and financial markets puts societies under much *strain* and enhances social fragmentation. The latter can be detected all over the world, including the most economically advanced countries. Therefore, in the transforming societies, wherein market reforms (including possibly ill conceived privatisation schemes) are likely to lead to rapidly increasing economic status differentiation, and against the background of citizens' expectations (who all expected from revolutions to be better off soon), even fast economic growth can be accompanied by social tension if wealth discrepancies are perceived as too large. Social instability becomes an unavoidable phenomenon in an environment which produces marginalised people – or what the current French political terminology calls 'les exclus' – systematically and on a large scale.

From this perspective can be assessed the dire need in the post-communist countries to reform what Kornai named 'premature welfare states' since their total dismantlement hardly seems a realistic policy option (much like in Western Europe). In this context should be judged the importance of human capital build up, and of public education, as a means to ensure equal opportunities to all citizens.

It may be that capitalism finds itself in a stage, on the secular cycle, which explains the symptoms of fatigue, or the loss of economic vitality, in a series of Western countries. At the same time, tenacious modernisation efforts in emerging countries, the new information age, and globalisation explain the redistribution of economic power in the world. This stage of capitalism would suggest the need for institutional readjustments. It appears that, in the age of large organisations, social aggregates (societies), even when they are market-based and rely on ubiquitous hard budget constraints, do not seem to have 'institutional adapters' – which could ensure spontaneity of large scale adjustments when needed. This state of being can explain the development of rigidities and inertia in large systems and lends additional meaning to Schumacher's 'small is beautiful' sintagma. A *policy of adjustment* – which implies public policy in order to trigger, or smooth adjustment – demonstrates ipso facto this reality. Even the appearance of elements of the welfare state took place before Keynes's Magnum Opus, for it was asked for by social and economic dynamics.[24] The fact that it is high time today, in many advanced capitalist countries, to eliminate rigidities and institutional bottlenecks does not mean necessarily going back to the Victorian capitalism of the last century. It would be practically impossible. Moreover, the debate has to be carried on in terms of variants of capitalism and the direction world capitalism is heading.[25]

The dilemma underlined above has a double long-term meaning for a transforming economy: in the sense of imagining the systems in the making as a response to two sets of pressures, domestic and external. This assertion is made for its implications in both conceptual and policy terms. For it is one thing to view transformation, in a post-communist country, as a simple automatic by-product of world evolution after 1989; and it is something else if transformation is viewed as a modernisation process that has a powerful domestic engine. Does it make sense to talk about a project of society for what we are building in post-communist countries? I think it does. Talking about markets and democracy in an oversimplified way is insufficient analytically and cannot help to identity solutions to the acute problems confronting economic policy in the short and the long run.

The role of institutional capital

High savings ratios and the formation of human capital are essential for promoting rapid and sustainable economic growth. This is what both conventional and more recent growth theory underline. However, as this book espouses as one of its main arguments, the primary determinants of growth and modernisation are to be sought elsewhere, namely, in the realm of institutions; the latter determine the quality of policies and the overall performance of economy. This conclusion is extremely important when applied to the case of transforming economies, which face extraordinary challenges, particularly in the field of institutional build-up.

In this introduction, it may be of interest to present this author's visualisation of the role played by institutions in driving post-communist transformation. An attempt to capture institutions conceptually would pin attention on four forms of institutional capital: *social capital*, *civic capital*, *leadership capital*, and *cohesion capital*. Among these forms of institutional capital, there are visible linkages; their analytical separation is, however, useful.

Social capital refers directly to the norms which govern interactions among individuals, groups, and organisations. Kenneth Arrow (1974), Robert Putnam (1993), and, lately, Francis Fukuyama (1996) stressed the importance of social norms – as a form of social capital – for economic development. The difficulty for economic analysis is linked not necessarily with the fuzzy nature of the concept, but with the way institutions develop – in an incremental way, but without a mechanical determination. The import or the imitation of institutions can be practised without, nonetheless, ensuring their required organic assimilation and social embeddedness.

Civic capital regards several elements. Among them an essential role is played by the system of institutionalised checks and balances, which is supposed to control power (those mandated to run public affairs). Another element is represented by civic organisations. Civic capital implies a generalised state of mind, of civic behaviour. As in the case of social capital, civic capital poses a critical question: are not these two forms of institutional capital – when seen as sources and resources of transformation (modernisation) – themselves, a product of an advanced degree of societal development. Namely, do we not have here a vicious circle? This question indicates the tension between organicism and constructivism as approaches to transformation (modernisation). In the post-communist countries, during extraordinary times,[26] decision-makers are almost condemned to be constructivists. Their actions need however to be wise and consistent in order to avoid major historical blunders.

Leadership capital becomes an issue whenever it is acutely needed. The real world of the life of organisations shows that leadership comes to the fore especially during hard times, when critical decisions are to be made. Wouldn't it be better that decisions, themselves, be subject to optimisations which should rid us of uncertainty, 'artistry', and arbitrariness? On the one hand, this is practically impossible; on the other hand, it may be quite undesirable since optimisation algorithms are likely to impede creativity and breakthroughs, which lead to competitive edges, to progress in general. Moreover, transformation as a led-process involves more than the impersonal forces (mechanisms) of markets at work. Leadership, which involves vision and determination, cannot and should not be downsized to mere co-ordination.

Do post-communist countries have a significant stock of leadership capital? A pessimist would answer that a country's economic and political elites are, themselves, an 'infant industry', and that spectacular results should not be expected. An optimist would stress the lack of homogeneity of humans, the existence, always, of exceptional individuals who can rise to the challenge of history, provide a sense of direction, and run organisations (social aggregates). In any case, since post-communist transformation is going to be a lasting process the performance of post-communist countries' political and economic elites must have a high common denominator along a longer period of time – even if some of these countries have the chance to use NATO, the EU, and other international structures as institutional and policy anchors.

Cohesion capital is a form of institutional capital, which may sound esoteric to some. I thought it useful to introduce it within the quadrangle by taking into account the importance of social stability for the long-term evolution of society. Here, as well, one encounters the dilemma: is social stability a prerequisite or a product of the process? In the same equivocal way, the answer springs into the open: social cohesion helps development, or going through difficult times, but is, itself, influenced by the process. It should be mentioned relatedly that the stock and the flow of social cohesion depend on the functioning of institutions. Therefore, a lot depends on the choice of institutional constructs, which lend regularities to and give birth to norms in the overall functioning of society. From this perspective, it is fully justified to ask which kind of capitalism is more likely to ensure a higher degree of social cohesion concurrently with sustainable economic growth. Clearly, this is a question, which has significant policy implications.

*

*   *

Globalisation and the new information age, the quest to join the European Union, and the redistribution of economic power in the world, pose enormous challenges to the transforming economies of Central and Eastern Europe. These economies need to 'learn to race' when time cannot be compressed at will; they need to reconcile the exigencies of economic efficiency with those that demand coping with social fragmentation and with increasing interdependencies, or what Geoff Mulgan named *connexity* (1997); they will have to focus on human capital build up as the main tool for securing long term economic growth in a period of severe public budget retrenchment. How they will find solutions to these and other challenges and, primarily, the quality of their institutions will make, in the long run, the difference between success and failure.

Notes

1   Mancur Olson emphasised the role of institutions in economic development in a superb article in the *Journal of Economic Perspectives* (1996).
2   Douglas North, The Nobel Prize winner, has exceptional contributions in this field.
3   See Stephen Haggard and Robert R. Kaufman (1995), or Adam Przeworski (1991). See also the volume edited by John Williamson on the political economy of reform (1994).
4   See my work on 'Vitality and Viability' (1996).
5   The gradualism practised by Hungary does not justify what, in the case of Romania, Costea Munteanu named *pathological gradualism* (1995), since circumstances were different.

6   Jeffrey Sachs (1996, p.130).
7   The Asian countries did not have to deal with the legacy of resource misallocation, which is specific to former command systems. For them, the challenge consisted in saving and investing much. China, and more recently, Vietnam, seem to be exceptions because they still have communist regimes. However, one should not forget that, at the start of market reforms, both China and Vietnam had predominantly rural economies, which mitigated the structural *strain* due to resource misallocation.
8   See also the remarks of the late Michael Bruno, quoted by William Pfaff (1996).
9   Attracted by the big undervaluation of assets; this undervaluation is reflected by the low P/E ratios in the post-communist countries where there are stock exchanges and over-the-counter markets (R. Bonte-Friedheim, 1996, pp.1 and 8).
10 Although one has to admit that the remarkable manner in which Hungarian policy-makers were capable of weathering the fallout of the Mexican crisis is a proof that things may not get implacably worse. However, it is worth repeating that Hungary is the country with the best track record of partial reforms before 1989; these partial reforms are at the roots of relatively better functioning institutions.
11 Although financial liberalisation is a worthy policy goal, it does not have to be pursued with the neglect of the need to build 'proper institutional structures of supervision and regulation', in order to avoid financial disasters; this would imply a controlled pace of financial liberalisation (Frederic Mishkin, 1996, p.41).
12 Joseph Stiglitz, 1994, p.267.
13 Jacek Rostowski, 1993, p.5. Similarly sceptical is Ronald McKinnon (1991).
14 Including the potential for the appearance of aggressive extreme-left groups, liable to engage in domestic and international terrorism. The existence of extreme-right (fascist) groups would compound the danger.
15 Janos Kornai, 1994, p.16.
16 Jeffrey Sachs, 1995b, p.2. Though I agree with the main point made by Sachs I think he underestimates the importance of distributional effects entailed by market reforms. Living standards may increase overall and, nonetheless, people may vote against the government if the number of losers in society is high.
17 'Today's Russia makes excruciatingly plain that liberal values are threatened just as thoroughly by state incapacity as by despotic power' (Stephen Holmes, 1997, p. 32).
18 See also William Greider (1997).
19 Marek Dabrowski, the deputy minister of finance in the first Polish post-communist government, stressed this aspect to me persistently.
20 Apart from the situation when modernisation can be viewed as a 'dissolution' in a modernising transnational space - such as the EU in idealistic terms. But is such a vision realistic taking into account that accession implies having achieved already a certain level of development which conditions performance, and that

even the EU is facing some deep structural economic difficulties?

21 I say 'in general' since partial reforms were undertaken in Hungary and Poland before 1989 whereas Romanian communist leaders practised late Stalinism until that year.

22 *Authoritarianism* is not to be equated necessarily with *paternalism*.

23 I should admit that another logic could be applied as well: reforms can bring about a certain instability and the inability of authorities to administer them would favour the accession to power of authoritarian governments. Russia and other former Soviet republics – but not only them – can easily fall into this pattern. For this reason, analysis needs to be differentiated and consider various circumstances, changes, which can consolidate, or not, democratic processes.

24 Bismarck introduced first elements of a welfare state in order to prevent the ascendancy of the socialist movement in Germany.

25 In this subject, see also Robert Barrio (1996), Zbignew Brzezinsky, Daniel Cohen, Will Hutton, Paul Kennedy, Paul Krugman, Jeffrey Madrick, Geoff Mulgan, Lester Thurow, J.D. Davidson and W. Rees-Mogg (1997), etc.

26 Leszek Balcerowicz remarked that extraordinary times demand extraordinary policies.

References

Amsden, A. (1989), 'The Next Asia's Giant', Oxford University Press, New York.

Arrow, J. K. (1974), 'The Limits of Organisation', Norton, New York.

Arthur, B. (1994), 'Increasing Returns and the Path Dependency in the Economy', Ann Arbor, The University of Michigan Press.

Barro, R. (1991), 'Economic Growth in a Cross-section of Countries', *Quarterly Journal of Economics*, vol. I, 106, no. 2, pp. 407-443.

Barro, R. (1996), 'Getting it Right. Markets & Choices in a Free Society', MIT Press, Cambridge.

Berend, I. (Winter 1994), 'Annus Mirabilis. Anni Mirabiles', *Contention*, no.8.

Blanchard, O. (May 1996), 'Theoretical Aspects of Transition', *American Economic Review*, vol. 86, no. 2, pp. 117-123.

Bonte-Friedheim, R. (20 August 1996), 'Rising Stock Markets in Central Europe Stir Comparisons to Asia', *Wall Street Journal*.

Brzezinsky, Z. (1993), 'Out of Control', Charles Scribner's Sons, New York.

Chirot, D. (1989), 'The Origins of Backwardness in Eastern Europe', University of California Press, Berkeley.

Cohen, D. (1995), 'The Misfortunes of Prosperity', MIT Press, Boston.

Daianu, D. (1996), 'Economic Vitality and Viability. A Dual Challenge for European Security', Frankfurt am Main, Peter Lang.

Daianu, D. (1996), 'A Dual Challenge for Europe' in M. Landesmann and R. Dobrinsky (eds.), *Transforming Economies and European Integration*, Edward Elgar,

Aldershot, UK.

David, P. (1985), 'Clio and the Economics of QWERTY', *American Economic Review*, vol. 75.

Davidson, J.D. and Rees-Mogg, W. (1997), 'The Sovereign Individual. The Coming Economic Revolution', Macmillan, London.

Fukuyama, F. (1995), 'Trust. The Social Virtues and the Creation of Prosperity', Simon and Schuster, New York.

Gelb, A. (1996), 'From Plan to Market: a Twentyeight Country Adventure', *Transition*, vol. 7, no. 5-6.

Gellner, E. (1983), 'Nations and Nationalism', Blackwell, Oxford.

Gilpin, R. (1987), 'The Political Economy of International Relations', Princeton University Press, Princeton.

Granovetter, M. (1985), 'Economic Action and Social Structure: The Problem of Embeddedness', *American Journal of Sociology*, 19 (3), pp. 481-510.

Greider, W. (1997), 'One World. Ready or Not. The Manic Logic of Capitalism', Simon and Schuster, New York.

Haggard, S. and Kaufman, R. R. (1995), 'The Political Economy of Democratic Transitions', Princeton University Press, Princeton.

Hayek, F. (1972), 'The Use of Knowledge in Society' (1948) reprinted in *Individualism and Economic Order*, Henry Regnery Co, Chicago.

Holmes, S. (July-August 1997), 'What Russia Teaches us Now?', *The American Prospect*, pp. 30-39.

Huntington, S. (1991), 'The Third Wave. Democratisation in the Twentieth Century', Oklahoma University Press, Norman.

Hutton, W. (second edition 1996), 'The State We're In', Random House, London.

Kornai, J. (1994), 'Lasting Growth as a Top Priority', *Discussion paper* no.7, Institute for Advanced Study, Budapest.

Kornai, J. (May-June 1995), 'Painful Trade-offs in Postsocialism', *Transition*, vol. 5.

Krugman, P. (1994), 'The Age of Diminished Expectations', MIT Press, Cambridge.

Lucas, R. (1988), 'On the Mechanics of Economic Development', *Journal of Monetary Economics*, vol.22, pp. 3-42.

Lucas, R. (1990), 'Why Doesn't Capital Flow from Rich to Poor Countries', *American Economic Review*, vol. 80, pp. 92-96.

Madrick, J. (1995), 'The End of Affluence', Random House, New York.

Mishkin, F. (1996), 'Understanding Financial Crises. A Developing Country Perspective', National Bureau of Economic Research, *Working Paper Series*, no. 500.

Mulgan, G. (1997), 'Connexity. How to Live in a Connected World', Chatto and Windus, London.

Munteanu, C. (1995), 'Reform Policy in Romania between 1990-1993. A Case of Pathologycal Gradualism' (in Romanian), *Oeconomica*, no. 1.

North, D. (1981), 'Structure and Change in Economic History', Norton, New

York.

Ohmae, K. (1995), 'The End of the Nation-State – The Rise of Regional Economies', Free Press, New York.

Okun, A. (1975), 'Equality and Efficiency. The Big Trade-off', Brookings Institution, Washington DC.

Olson, M. Jr. (1996), 'Big Bills Left on the Sidewalk: Why some Nations are Rich, and Others Poor?', *Journal of Economic Perspectives*, vol. 10, no.2.

Perroux, F. (1969), 'Independence de la Nation', Aubier-Montaigne, Paris.

Pfaff, W. (1996), 'The Voter isn't Getting a Chance to Choose', *International Herald Tribune*, August 6th.

Pilat, V. (1993), 'On Transition' (in Romanian), *Oeconomica*, no. 5.

Porter, M. (1990), 'The Competitive Advantage of Nations', Free Press, New York.

Przeworsky, A. (1991), 'Democracy and the Market. Political and Economic Reforms in Eastern Europe and Latin America', Cambridge University Press, New York.

Putnam, R. (1993), 'Making Democracy Work', Princeton University Press, Princeton.

Rodrik, D. (March 1996), 'Understanding Economic Policy Reform', *Journal of Economic Literature*, vol. XXXIV, pp. 9-41.

Romer, P. (1986), 'Increasing Returns and Long Run Growth', *Journal of Political Economy*, vol. 94, pp. 1002-1037.

Rutland, P. (1994-1995), 'Has Democracy Failed Russia?', *The National Interest*, Winter.

Sachs, J. (May 1996), 'The Transition at Mid Decade', *American Economic Review*, vol. 86, no.2, pp. 128-133.

Schumacher, E. F. (1973), 'Small is Beautiful. Economics as if People Mattered', Harper and Row, New York.

Schumpeter, J. (1934), 'Theory of Economic Development', Harvard University Press, Cambridge.

Stern, N. and Stiglitz, J. (April 1997), 'A Framework for a Development Strategy in a Market Economy: Objectives, Scope, Institutions, and Instruments', London, EBRD *Working Paper*, no. 20.

Stiglitz, J. (1995), 'Whither Socialism', MIT Press, Cambridge.

Thurow, L. (1996), 'The Future of Capitalism', Morrow, New York.

Williamson, J. (1994), 'The Political Economy of Policy Reform', Institute of International Economics, Washington DC.

Part I

Institutional
Change

2 Transformation[1] and the Legacy of Backwardness[*]

Transition: new and old connotations

If the system-related (institutional) dimension of transition[2] is of paramount importance, one can detect another meaning, which transgresses ideological borders and has defined the evolution of these societies through this century. I refer to what can be named 'the quest for catching-up with the West', an idea which obsessed national politicians during the inter-war period and also the communist leaderships bent on proving the alleged superiority of their system and which, today, is reflected in the ardent desire to join the European Union. For example, in pre-communist Romania both the Liberal Party and the Peasant Party wanted to get the country moving, to get it away from her economically peripheral position in Europe; to this end they propounded different policies. The Liberals favoured protection of industry and state involvement in the economy, thinking more in terms of what one, today, would call dynamic comparative advantages and strategic industrial policy.[3] They feared foreign encroachment on the emerging Romanian industrial sectors and the marginalisation of the national entrepreneurial class, whereas the Peasants espoused an 'open doors' policy.[4] This conceptual and policy divide was not uncommon in the region at that time and was made more clear by the consequences of the Great Depression. As for the Romanian communist leadership, it viewed the catching-up issue in relation to both the main capitalist countries and the more advanced economies of the Moscow-led Bloc. The industrialisation drive in the post-war period was justified not only in ideological terms, but was also linked to national assertiveness among fellow communist countries, in particular, and among the other nations of the world, in general.

It is ironic then, that part of the legacy of Communism in Romania is represented by the effects of the self-imposed insulation from the winds of institutional change and reform, which were blowing in some neighbouring countries after 1956. This anti-reformist stance made it impossible for the national environment to evolve into something more conducive to the current

35

transformation efforts and it encouraged a sequence of irrational industrial policy choices, which ran counter to the stated ultimate goal of reducing development gaps.

It is relevant that in present-day Romania the debate on how to integrate faster into the European economic space evinces an underlying concern with the country's image in the West, as compared to 'the golden triangle' of Hungary, Poland and the Czech Republic. And there is no doubt that Romania's poorer image can also be directly linked with the track record of – or better said, the lack of – reforms under local communism, which can be summed up as a scarcity of market ingredients. Later I will return to this issue when talking about the economics of transition as applied to 'frontrunners' as against 'laggards'. By the latter, I denominate countries like Romania, Bulgaria and the former Soviet republics, which have not shown good credentials with respect to attempted reforms before 'the Big Bang' of 1989.

Why do I emphasise this quest for catching-up? Because not infrequently one can see presumably knowledgeable professionals making judgements on the transformation process, while seeming oblivious to the heavy legacy of backwardness of these societies, a state of affairs which goes back deeply into history.[5] As a keen student of the area remarked '... Eastern Europe was in some sense economically backward long before it was absorbed into the broader Western world market. This backwardness has roots in the very distant past...' (D. Chirot, 1989, p. 3). Backwardness should be seen as bearing considerably on the potential for overcoming the performance deficit of institutionally poorly arranged societies; it points, on the one hand, to the lack of knowledge of individuals and of society as a whole and at the constraints for institutional change and, on the other hand, it suggests that there is much scope for a system to be led astray from what could be conceived as an ideal 'corridor'[6] of evolution (which involves and is dependent on institutional reconstruction or, as in the case of post-communist societies, system transformation). I remember in this respect how baffled were some of my colleagues when Ken Jowitt, a political scientist from Berkeley and an astute observer of Romania, said that 'Latin American countries have been in transition for more than a century'.[7] He referred not only to mistaken economic policies (Argentina comes easily into one's mind for it belonged to the group of advanced economies – in terms of per capita income – before the second world war) but also, to institutional bottlenecks rooted in a certain level of development.

The stress put on the legacy of backwardness is not meant to dilute in any way the importance of institutional reconstruction; it aims, nonetheless, at cautioning against the dragging effects of this legacy and an unfavourable path dependency which is not easy to break away from. Against this background, the relationship between the economic system of communism and the legacy of backwardness (for the post communist societies) can be the object of further analytical scrutiny. The former Czechoslovakia – a leading industrial economy in inter-war Europe – provides a conspicuous example of the negative impact of the command system on the performance of the economy. This performance deficit can be judged in both static and dynamic terms; statically, as the distance from a level of output resulting from a full and efficient utilisation of resources (which presupposes adequate institutional arrangements) and dynamically, as the damage caused over time to the quality (performance potential) and quantity of the set of factors of production, as well as the lack of viability of the economic system – doomed to fail because of its inner laws of motion.

The command system had a logic of self-destruction, prophetically anticipated by L. Von Mises and Fr. Von Hayek in the much celebrated *Calculation* debate, which finds only partial explanation in the process of institutional obsolescence (decay) and fading away of an 'all encompassing interest' (M. Olson and P. Murrell, 1991). Communism, despite its aberrant nature, brought about huge social mobility and turned predominantly agrarian societies (exceptions being the former Czechoslovakia and the former East Germany) into semi-industrial societies with most of the active workforce consisting of industrial workers;[8] it practically eliminated illiteracy, and contributed decisively to the secularisation of these societies.[9] This endeavour to modernise, which was accompanied by terror and violence as state policy in action (forced collectivisation is a telling example), could not alter the logic of the historical demise of the system; moreover, it sowed new seeds of social, political, and economic decomposition. Outbursts like 1953 in the former East Germany, 1956 in Hungary and Poland, 1968 in Czechoslovakia, 1970, 1976 and 1980 in Poland, and 1977 in Romania are proofs of how people, at large, felt about the nature of the system. The fact remains that at the end of the eighties – in spite of the high literacy rate of the population and highly skilled segments of the labour force – Central and Eastern Europe were falling increasingly behind the developed market economies, unable to compete with even developing market economies (the new industrialised countries, in particular), possessing oversized and glowingly obsolete industrial facilities and projecting the image of a looming ecological disaster.

How does the cultural factor fit in the whole picture since backwardness has a cultural dimension? It is obvious that Transformation and, in a broader sense, catching-up with the West, implies cultural change as well. I am not a cultural anthropologist. However, I take the liberty to pinpoint two aspects that seem relevant in this respect. One is linked with historical cultural differences between the Western world and the whole, or part, of Central and Eastern Europe.[10] The other aspect regards the cultural legacy of communism, a certain ethos that shapes the behaviour and expectations of large masses of people and can play havoc with Transformation seen as an intended process (strategy). A further question can be raised as to what extent the cultural peculiarities which precede Communism and the cultural legacy of the latter, on the one hand, constrain the process of transformation and, on the other hand, ask for certain adaptations of the newly sought for institutional arrangements. The question can be formulated thus: which western economic model better fits the post-communist area?[11]

The challenges facing post-communist leaders are enormous and overwhelming if one thinks that progress is pursued simultaneously on several tracks: creating viable (market-based) economic entities, setting up pluralist democratic polities, re-entering a path of economic growth and achieving modernisation (including cultural change). Since Transformation as a real process cannot be decoupled from a concrete context, which itself is the product of both remote and recent history, I will deal next with specifics of the evolution of the Romanian economy under Communism.

The grand economic failure in Romania

Looking for legitimacy at home and espousing a specific brand of economic nationalism,[12] the communist leaders – Ceausescu, in particular – strove to turn Romania into an industrial stronghold; forced industrialisation, hyper centralisation of decision-making and the shunning of the 'socialist international division of labour' are keywords for describing the strategy of economic policy over the whole period of communist rule. The outcome is well-known; aside from all that defines a command economy the country ended up with an overdiversified, oversized and technologically obsolete industry, huge imbalances among economic sectors, a backward agriculture and one of the lowest living standards in Europe. Most of these features sound very common, but they are valid even when looked at according to the yardsticks of comparative analysis one applies to the former communist Bloc.

It would be redundant to produce an overview of the economic history of the last forty years;[13] all I wish to do is to point out several aspects which, I think, make Romania's experience 'remarkable'. These aspects, on one hand, can shed light on some developmental matters and, on the other hand, can help explain the peculiar economic situation of the country in December 1989.

Romania, under Communism, stands out for its unflinching adherence to Stalinist precepts of economic policy, its isolationism, its industrial policy choices which blatantly ignored the reality of comparative advantages, its trade policy choices that ran counter to the very logic of functioning of the domestic economy and a sui generis 'shock-therapy' in the eighties. If I were asked to put this abysmal record into a conceptual nutshell, I would resort to a function that links the performance deficit of the economic entity with its mode of functioning (the set of institutional arrangements[14]), with the economic policy, and with the surrounding environment.[15] On all these accounts, Romanian policymakers fared miserably.

At the end the eighties the Romanian economy was probably the most centralised in the former Soviet-led Bloc. The history of reform in Romania is, comparatively, an almost blank territory; what was attempted in 1967 and 1978 aborted quickly either for the political frailty of those championing real change,[16] or for the lack of genuine intentions.[17] What are some of the main consequences of this stunning rigidity and ideological immobilism? I would mention, first, the relative scarcity of market ingredients,[18] which finds expression in the lack of institutional prerequisites for facilitating system transformation now, and the lack of a business culture (embodied by an entrepreneurial class). Obviously, the economic doctrine of the Party and, related to it, the mode of functioning of the economy (with extreme centralisation of power, no checks and balances), made possible the degree of arbitrariness in economic and industrial policy, with so much disregard for endowment with factors of production and the ability to compete in world markets.

That the mode of functioning of the economy (the economic mechanism) is essential in explaining its performance is an obvious statement. What I believe still needs to be stressed is the damage caused to the economy in a dynamic sense, to its performance potential. Otherwise said, institutional rearrangements (turning the system into a market-based economy) would not lead to that increase of performance which might be suggested by the past flows of inputs (accumulated capital and human stock) and the macrostructural changes. One should recall that Romanian communist leaders boasted frequently about the 'statistical' achievements of the economy; they liked to talk about a 'Romanian economic miracle' and wanted to emulate the East Asian growth rates. To this end, they excessively forced the pace of accumulation in the sixties and the seventies.[19]

The Stalinist model was fatal also for the 'turning away from the CMEA' orientation that was initiated in the 60s.[20] Functionally extremely rigid, protectionistic and increasingly unreliable owing to its growing complexity[21] the Romanian economy could not capitalise on the opportunities opened by the attempt to extricate itself from the trade diversion and efficiency effects of the CMEA grip. This outward orientation (to the world markets) was like a programmed failure because of the inappropriate domestic base, the lack of supporting internal markets. What Japan, South Korea, Taiwan, or Singapore could achieve was out of reach for a command economy of the worst sort; the highly interventionist policies of the East Asian governments (less in Taiwan) do not change the fundamental truth that theirs are essentially market economies.

Though the way of functioning of the economy predetermines the nature of and the realm of choice for economic policy, policymakers have substantial leeway in influencing policy outcomes. A command economy, as a supply constrained system, reproduces shortages on a steady basis, but the size of imbalances depends on what planners do; the latter, for example, can pay more, or less attention to the comparative advantages of the country, even if the irrationality of domestic prices obscures them. The scope for major blunders in economic policy is immense under command planning, and Romania provides ample evidence in this regard. Thus, the former communist countries face dissimilar energy and food problems. Amazingly, Romania, which used to be the grain-basket of the sub-region and has a huge potential in agriculture and, furthermore, has a considerable natural resources base (as compared to her neighbours) has had a very precarious food situation for years now and became heavily dependent on foreign sources for raw materials and energy. One could argue that such a dependency should not be necessarily of concern and this is perfectly true if the economy runs efficiently. But Romania was not like Japan, where what goes as an imported input into the 'black-box' of the economy comes out as a high value-added output with the highest likelihood of being an exportable good.

Romania provides an interesting and instructive case of 'immiserising growth' caused by the logic of motion of the system, in the main, the rush to speed up industrial growth,[22] and to increase ties with market economies on a very weak functional basis. In the literature, this phenomenon is explained by the existence of various price distortions, which harm resource allocation, worsen the terms of trade and lower the welfare level.[23] However, one can think of the very mode of functioning of the economy (including the genesis of wrong industrial choices) as the distortion, which leads to immisering growth. It can be shown that the inner dynamics of the system – incapacity to cope with increasing complexity and inability to assimilate and generate technological progress – lead to a 'softening' of output, to its expansion with a large bias toward industrial soft goods, which entails a steady deterioration of terms of trade. This is what happened in Romania where forced industrialisation gave precedence to uncompetitive steel, chemical and machine-building industries, and agriculture was terribly squeezed. The unhealthy nature of such growth can be explained succinctly. The biased expansion of the production of soft goods – which belies the comparative advantages of the economy – demands a quantity of hard inputs which would either be provided only by disrupting domestic production, or not be achieved – for many export-destined goods are unsaleable.[24] Actual exports of soft goods are hence smaller than the level programmed and the remaining necessary inputs are obtained through an international exchange of hard goods. This means that the country has to forgo consuming certain kinds of hard goods (consumer goods which are in high demand from ordinary citizens) in favour of acquiring other types of hard goods, such as energy, raw materials and spare parts; the welfare loss for the population is tremendous and it, in turn, triggers a supply-multiplier on the part of consumers seen as labour-suppliers.

Apart from the fatal consequences of having been embedded in, and the product of, a non-market environment the strategy of industrialisation in Romania (and, naturally, in the other command systems as well) teaches several lessons, that I will try to summarise as follows:

- a development programme needs to be based on a realistic assessment of the economy's capabilities and potential;
- technological and economic possibilities are within the bounds given by the overall development level of the economy; these bounds cannot be pushed limitlessly outwards by capital and technology imports;
- a speed limit of raising the technological sophistication of the productive apparatus can be conceived, which is determined by the 'learning curve' of labour, the stock of managerial resources, and the qualitative structure of factors of production. This speed-limit suggests the objective need to go through necessary successive stages (processing levels) in the industrialisation process;
- meeting the basic needs of the population is necessary for both social and economic reasons. When consumers' preferences are grossly neglected, labour dissatisfaction and contraction (the labour supply multiplier,[25] which operates both quantitatively and qualitatively) have grave repercussions;

-   when a country is poor it does not make sense 'to put up with the burden of preventable waste that arises even within the static framework of given wants, techniques and resources' (H. Myint, 1971, p. 16). Support given to agriculture and to the development of infrastructure, and the stimulation of entrepreneurship (which means not emasculating market forces) are essential ingredients in a self-sustained growth process;
-   for the less developed economies, with a supposedly low innovative capacity, the static factors (the cost of labour, of raw materials procurement) are essential for making good use of comparative advantages. The more costly is the procurement of primary resources, the higher would have to be the processing level of goods in order to compensate for the loss in terms of the 'static production function'; therefore, the smaller is the probability for an economy that does not innovate and evinces a hard goods supply constraint (like the command economies) to be competitive;
-   by combining the static and dynamic time perspectives one can speak of an ideal (optimal) sequence of stages of climbing up the ladder of development which would minimise the costs of catching-up in a certain period of time.[26]

Returning to factual history, the start of the eighties highlighted the grand economic failure; the external shocks (like the rise in the oil price, or the sharp increase of world real interest rates), which were mitigated by external financing for a while only, speeded up the downward motion of the economy. Ceausescu rejected any suggestion of market inspired reform that could have improved the performance of the economy and its export capacity. In order to cope with the burden of debt repayments, he commanded an unprecedented – in the whole world – policy of paying back the entire external debt as soon as possible by means of its 'internalisation' (Daianu, 1984). He succeeded in enforcing this extraordinary 'shock-therapy' by means of a dramatic squeeze on domestic absorption; there occurred a substantial drop in consumption and the long-term growth possibilities were impaired by an unusual curtailment of imports of machinery and equipment from the western countries.[27] This policy relied on strengthening the isolation of the country and on suppression of any dissenting views.

At the end of the eighties the Romanian economy, the country, the people presented more than a desolate image. After more than four decades of forced industrialisation, the competitiveness of the economy was at the bottom of the communist League, disequilibria among sectors and shortages were increasing, the people's plight was beyond imagination;[28] the country was imploding. Romania was a laggard among her neighbours as to the institutional prerequisites for helping post-communist transition, the psychological preparedness of the population for abrupt change, and the social base for market reforms. Moreover, the 'shock-therapy' of the eighties created among people very high expectations for an immediate and substantial improvement of material conditions after a change of the rulers (of the regime), which signalled a high degree of intolerance for new austerity measures. The legacy of Communism made the spectre of economic and institutional backwardness hover with more intensity now, when the country entered the post-communist transition.

On the economics of transition. Frontrunners vs. Laggards

The early euphoria and high expectations after the chain reaction collapse of communist regimes have been replaced by sobriety, cautiousness and even anxiety. Both professionals and laymen realise that the process of transformation is much more complicated and complex than was initially anticipated. For example, shock treatment, which is so much debated nowadays, and can be met in various parts of the world, where it means, basically, macroeconomic stabilisation (control of hyper inflation) gets a different connotation in the case of post-communist economies. The latter are characterised – in general – by extreme rigidity of resource movement, ignorant agents as to the functioning of organised markets, the lack of a proper institutional set-up, a supporting ethos, and necessary cultural backup. Under such circumstances, shock therapy should be related to the transformation of the societal body that means institutional change, cultural change, and material reconstruction. Going further with this reasoning one can consider theoretical underpinnings of the advocated policies of transformation, beyond intuitions suchlike: that there is a tolerance limit of social sacrifice, that time cannot be compressed at will. Development economists in particular seem to be quite unhappy with oversimplifications regarding the economics of transition.[29]

A way to proceed is to link stylised theoretical explanation with the two competing visions within the paradigm provided by neo-classical analytics – equilibrium economics. One of them, that is best represented by the new classical macroeconomics, rejects any state intervention in the economy since agents – it is argued – optimise using all available information (in contrast, for example, with agents' 'bounded rationality' exposed by H. Simon (1958)), which secures full price flexibility and, thereby, sufficiently fast allocation of resources. According to this vision, any rate of unemployment is natural since it expresses agents' preferences. The other vision starts from the assumption that prices are rigid to an extent that induces adjustments through quantities as well, so that aggregate demand equilibrates aggregate supply below full employment; there is talk then of a non-Walrasian equilibrium, which would invalidate Walras' Law. The two visions look at the functioning of a market economy.

If the command system is viewed as a pathological form of market economy, wherein structural disfunctionalities are extreme, a hypothesis can be submitted: implementation of shock treatments would lead to a significant drop in production, in a first phase. In this stage of the process of transformation the entrenched structures have to be broken and changed, which means that the quantity of *friction*[30] inside the system goes up considerably and important energies (resources) are consumed in order to accommodate, adjust, change; a lot boils down to a change of the organisational behaviour of economic actors (P. Murrell, 1991). In this phase of the transition there exists a territory over which both commands and markets – as regulatory mechanisms – do not function according to their logic, and to the congenital inefficiency of the old (to a large extent, still existing) system is added the inefficiency caused by friction.[31] This perspective gets interesting insights from 'structuralist macroeconomics' (L. Taylor, 1991a, 1991b) which can help highlight perverse effects of 'orthodox' policies undertaken during transition.[32]

Within such a framework hysteresis phenomena can and should be tackled. Let us only think about the anticipated rising unemployment and the lasting effects of an overly open (unprotected) economy in an environment with imperfect markets. This is why many people meet shock therapy with reluctance and why it asks for a lot of political courage and popular support to be applied. The sooner net costs turn into net benefits, the better for the political leadership – whose stock of political capital would, otherwise, be rapidly wiped out – not to mention for the population at large. One could argue that a gradualist policy could not stop the decline of output (living standards) as well. There is nonetheless a difference which explains why gradualist policies enjoy appeal with many political leaders and large segments of the population: when processes are under control a less brutal initial drop of output is likely to occur as compared to a shock treatment.

However, can processes be under control? This is a crucial question to answer by considering the symptoms of system dissolution; when there is a collapse of the old institutional order and citizens rebel against any kind of authority,[33] and when, consequently, a 'free fall' syndrome is in full swing, gradualism presents pitfalls and can hardly be implemented effectively. Therefore, in many areas, the choice of speed can no longer be a realistic policy option.

Another track of analysis would contrast the equilibrium approach with the evolutionary approach. Neo-classical economists pay less attention to social, behaviour-related and cultural aspects; for them the transformation of the system seems to be concerned, almost exclusively, with institutional rearrangements (reconstruction), the fundamental assumption being that economic agents are rational – they optimise – and would act accordingly should the environment be changed. It can be argued that the transformation under way in the former communist economies is a process with a pronounced social and cultural dimension. This process involves overcoming inertia and ideological barriers, changing mentalities and psychologies[34] (the creation of a new social ethos adequate for a market economy), a fierce struggle among 'coalitions of interests' (M. Olson, 1982), some of which support change whereas others wish to preserve the texture of concentration of political and economic power. The clash of various interests in society during transition raises the degree of autonomy of the process in the sense of reducing the room to manoeuvre of decision-makers in terms of deciding upon the actual pace of change.

A sociological (institutional) approach to the process of change tells us that in order to have a fair chance of progressing smoothly, the process needs to be backed by a strong coalition of interests. A social basis in favour of change is necessary for it to occur, and this 'reform constituency' cannot be built overnight. In the more backward post-communist societies, this social constituency is still pretty weak. Which means that conservative forces are strong and can oppose change quite effectively. Seen under this light transformation should not be conceived as a sort of 'one stroke policy'; since as a real process change cannot be but evolutionary, policy has to be shaped appropriately.

There is an additional factor that helps explain why shock treatments are harder to implement in the laggard countries, like Romania and the former Soviet republics; it is what I call a 'socially lived own experience', that compels people to think that 'there is no other way'. As long as people - the largest, or the most politically vocal segments of the populace – tend to choose what they think involves smaller immediate costs –, a shock treatment is less likely to be actually undertaken, or sustained for a longer period of time (even if there is political goodwill). A muddling through process is more likely. In this case the inconsistencies of the policy of transition – and the resultant muddling through of the process – is to be related to the weakness of the social basis of change, which aggravates the very weaknesses of the policy itself (which are due to our limited knowledge).

An evolutionary (sociological) approach to understanding the dynamics of change and the likelihood of various policies to be applied would suggest a reconsideration of the partial reforms in Hungary and Poland. If one takes into account the process of 'learning' that these societies have been undergoing, including the acquisition of the mentioned 'socially lived own experience', and the formation of a social basis (an entrepreneurial class as well) for change, it is not hard to see the handicaps which latecomers in the process face.

The 'learning process' for society as a whole has to be linked with a 'limit rate for absorption of change', that notifies us of the danger of societies' intoxication with information. Here intervenes a big paradox of Eastern European societies – especially of the more backward among them – namely, the huge (practically limitless) thirst for information (novelty/change) coexisting with a limited capacity (both mental and infrastructural) to process this resource. A facet of this limitation is the fear expressed by many experts that the region has a limited capacity to absorb foreign capital productively, an issue different from that of conceiving foreign assistance as helping to create a 'safety net' during transition. When foreign assistance shifts the 'learning curve' of a society upwards, the capacity of society for absorbing change is automatically increased. It is clear that the limit rate of absorption of change puts a further brake on the desire to speed up change.

Another big paradox refers to the conditions which enhance rapid transformation. Thus, the more ingredients of the market environment are to be found within the national space – which is the comparative advantage of those who have started reforms earlier – and the more favourable political prerequisites are, the easier it is to move at a faster rate with the policy of transformation. On the other hand, the worse the state of the economy is and the more wanting the national space is, in terms of political and social prerequisites,[35] a radical treatment is both more urgent and harder to apply. Urgency as an economically defined need cannot lead to wise measures if social and political factors are overlooked. It would seem that there is a time schedule according to which the 'jump into the unknown' follows a curve so that we can image a point of least cumulated risk. This point would raise to a maximum the likelihood for the transformation policy to succeed. If it is assumed that, sooner or later, a radical treatment will be applied – for gradualism can only postpone some harsh measures – this point signals the moment to start shock therapy. This kind of reasoning may appear too speculative. Nevertheless, it hints at a paradoxical situation and at various trade-offs decision-makers have to make in order to identify the best route.

Decision-makers (political leaders) overshoot, or undershoot, as markets do – which means that they can rush things above the 'natural rate of adjustment'[36] of society, or underestimate the potential for change of the social body. Since policy over (under)-shooting is practically unavoidable, the problem lies with reducing the deviation as much as possible. Another interesting question to answer is on which side policy erring is to be preferred assuming that the goal of keeping the deviation at a minimum is kept in sight. Here one deals with both objective and subjective elements for making a judgement.

The optimisation implied above, which sounds very much neo-classical, could be attacked on the ground that the very actions of policymakers generate and assimilate new information and, more significantly, change the environment.[37] Otherwise said, the difference is between discovering the best route before starting the journey, or by finding it in action, by 'creating it'. Neo-Austrians can help us in this respect. I believe the two approaches can be reconciled, bearing in mind that corrections 'sur le terrain' are easier to make the more knowledgeable, and better equipped the travellers are.

There is also another factor that brings closer policies derived from different approaches; it is the time pressure exerted by the disintegration of old institutional structures, by the previously mentioned 'rebellion of citizens' (who defy any authority). This pressure induces the new power-holders, who have to cope with the 'free fall' syndrome (in economic activity) to try to resort to the presumed effectiveness of the impersonal disciplining power of market forces.

In my opinion, irrespective of the circumstances and the dominant vision espoused by policymakers, several priorities have to enter the scene. First comes the creation of a legal institutional set-up fitting a market environment (including the formation of a safety-net, which is indispensable if we think that people are accustomed to view job security and low and stable prices for basic consumer goods as major 'public goods' provided by the state). Second comes privatisation (particularly, at a grass roots level, for big privatisation takes more time), which has to be encouraged by all means available for both economic and social reasons. Economically, since it leads to higher efficiency (even if domestic prices are still not right and allocative efficiency does not improve dramatically). Socially, because it nurtures the entrepreneurial class as the main component of the social constituency favouring the transformation of the system. Thirdly, the price reform should be closely linked with income control within a policy-mix framework that proceeds from the major features of the environment; a system of industrial relations should be built upon the actual role which workers play as both labour-suppliers and (potential) enterprise owners, or 'managers-monitors'. Finally, an industrial policy should be devised in keeping with the need to maintain a balance between market-induced destruction and construction; this policy should enhance the positive effects of the operation of market forces.

The magnitude of intended change, the quantity of the unknown (uncertainty), and the lack of sufficient knowledge on how to respond to the myriad of unforeseen developments will most likely shape Transformation as a muddling-through process relying on trial and error procedures and showing a pattern of stop and go policies (including reversals).[38] Frontrunner countries will be able to have a less difficult time in maintaining the overall course of policy within a 'winning' corridor, whereas laggard countries will, more probably, experience larger zigzags. However, much will also depend on the quality of governance – the political and administrative elite.

I would also point out several fallacies, which seem to accompany the thinking of not a few ordinary people and even of fellow economists. One should not assume that a relatively well functioning market economy, ipso facto, would secure the prosperity enjoyed by Western nations; that prosperity relies on the high development level of the productive apparatus and the degree of homogeneity of the factors of production. Secondly, it would be a mistake to presume that Transformation would necessarily turn Eastern European economies into relatively well functioning market economies; the outcome for a foreseeable future is likely to be comparatively weak and less competitive (quasi) market economies. Thirdly, past policy mistakes have to be considered, for they make up a legacy to cope with; they can have a lasting impact and give shape to the course of events to come.

A further look ahead

What also makes the post-communist transition difficult is a legacy of pervasive moral crisis. It is hard to build new institutions when truth-telling, trust, loyalty are very scarce commodities. As J. K. Arrow said: 'They are goods they have real, practical, economic value; they increase the efficiency of the system, enable you to produce more goods or more of whatever value you hold in high esteem' (1974, p. 23). The events of 1989 and what has followed could not overcome this legacy and the scarcity of such public goods enhanced friction in society against the background of citizens' rebellion – its concrete forms being violence, all kind of crime (lawlessness), 'rent-seeking' and free-riding as increasingly widespread behaviour. Two major lessons can be drawn in this respect. First, that production of intangible goods – understood as moral reconstruction of society – is a must for helping a recovery of and boosting the output of material goods and services; the former 'crowds in' the latter. Secondly, trust, truth telling and loyalty can substitute tangible goods to a significant degree, which is particularly important, when recession is a dangerously lasting affair.

By admitting the hypothesis of the fundamental operational value of intangibles, the political and moral dimension of the process of transformation comes to the fore. Credibility and trust need carriers, and these can be only individuals of high moral and political standards, who can provide effective leadership and rally popular support behind the goals of transformation. When the moral legitimacy of new power-holders is questionable – as it occurred in Romania after Ceausescu's downfall – real institutional change is easily stalemated.

The historical circumstances in Central and Eastern Europe make it hard, almost impossible, to dissociate political change from economic change.[39] Romania's experience shows how entrenched vested interests connected with the old regime have slowed down or taken substance out of reforms under way, or have promoted wrong policies. For example, the first (provisional) government adopted populistic measures before the May elections of 1990; these measures helped the Salvation Front[40] win the elections, but worsened the state of the economy and compounded a stunning discrepancy between the electoral platform of the Front and the 'New Economic Policy' ushered in by prime-minister Petre Roman and his 'young turks' after the tragic events of June 1990 (culminating with the miners' rampage in Bucharest).[41]

There is a growing feeling in all the countries of the region that a complete 'hands-off' reform policy on the part of the governments is unjustified not only by the lack of institutional prerequisites for market forces to operate effectively, but also, by the simple fact that these forces alone would impose unbearable costs on the social body. In Central and Eastern Europe we deal with markets in their infancy, which need to be nurtured and even protected in a world of imperfect information and competition. There is need and scope for industrial policy which should aim at helping restructuring as it is suggested by market signals, and at protecting the main asset of these societies which is made up of segments of highly skilled labour and a large pool of scientific and technical intelligentsia. A paradox of these societies is that striking ignorance coexists with tremendous intellectual and labour capabilities; this combination obscures potentialities for progress by an apparent across the board depreciation of the factors of production. Capital and technology inflows as well as the functional opening of the economies would counteract this depreciation but they could impose undue hardship on the economy, which creates room for an industrial policy to play a role.

Industrial policy is critical for bridging the gap between the effectiveness of controlling demand and that of stimulating supply. Supply responsiveness is so low that stabilisation is hardly sustainable. When I mention industrial policy I refer to a mix that correlates income-control measures with industrial restructuring undertaken by public authorities which process information provided by the emerging markets. The goals would be to put a lid on inflation, alleviate unemployment (to cope with hysteresis phenomena) and promote exports. Such a policy is more urgently needed when the social pie is considerably smaller, redistribution effects exert a negative impact on many people, and safety nets are not in place.

A possible scheme would link incomes with the dynamics of saleable output, in the vein of what M. Weitzman proposed in a well-known book (1984). Thus, assuming that market-clearing prices operate (and that optimal sizes for producing units are observable, or can be estimated) enterprises can be split into three categories: negative value-added units, unprofitable (but positive value-added producing) units, and profitable enterprises. Negative value-added units should be closed down without any delay; it is less costly to pay workers unemployment benefits and retrain them than to keep these enterprises running. Profitable units do not present any problem since they are good business. The zone of concern for policymakers is represented by unprofitable enterprises which, under normal conditions (with sufficient flexibility of resources), would have to be done away with. The idea is to resort to a phased in elimination according to a timetable that pursues reducing the costs of adjustment. There are two essential variables in the whole scheme; one is the unemployment benefit and the other is the additional income provided by the state to workers so that they have an incentive to continue working in an enterprise instead of preferring to accept unemployment benefits. Unprofitable enterprises would be targeted for a gradual phasing-out so that unemployment is attenuated and its cost redistributed over time. At the same time, public authorities would have an easier time in securing resources for a safety net and for facilitating labour reallocation through training programmes.

The crux of the matter lies in convincing workers about the benefits of this scheme for the economy as a whole and for each and every one of the targeted enterprises. This can be achieved as part of social compact within the framework of an industrial relations agreement that sees workers as an active voice in the management of transformation. It can be argued that this scheme may slow restructuring, which is a valid statement if social and political constraints are dismissed. However, for the sake of process sustainability there are reasons for advocating an industrial policy.

In Romania (and in the former Soviet Union) another critical issue is turning around agriculture. Yields are very low which means that there is much room for improvement. People devote more than 60% of their incomes for getting essentials of life, so that a drastic boost of agricultural output – with a corresponding drop in the relative prices of agricultural products – would raise living standards dramatically and help transformation. The major stumbling block is that land reform, by itself, creates friction till new property rights get established and, additionally, price liberalisation produces a shock to the urban population by turning the terms of trade against it.[42] However, the stake is too high to not focus attention on a sector, which could lead the recovery of the economy.

If I were asked about Romania's long-term prospect, I would answer that its economy is like an underrated stock at a world stock exchange. Warren Buffett's philosophy about investment – that one should think in terms of fundamentals – is very much my way of thinking. But I also remember a discussion I had with Thomas Gibbons, an American diplomat, who listening to me and agreeing basically with my view made a meaningful remark: 'In that region all countries are like underrated stocks'. The implication is that the governance issue is of paramount importance for long-term dynamics. In addition, since the quality of governance, seen as a common denominator of succeeding government teams and of the structures underneath them, is a big unknown variable in the equation of transformation, predictions about long-term prospects are more than risky business. What is nevertheless highly certain is that those who will be able to practise good (healthy) politics will find it much easier to practise good (successful) economics.

A final say regards the involvement of the developed West in the whole process. In the last few years, academics and mass media in the USA have been debating on the causes of the evolution of the American economy in the eighties. Thus, much ink was shed on paper related to the stakeholder vs. shareholder issue in order to throw light on what secures highly performing governance at corporate level. One can make an analogy and view the ex-communist countries as bankrupt entities, which need to be restructured and turned into efficient economic systems. Since the West is vitally interested in the recovery of these entities, it has to act like a stakeholder – with a deep moral, political and economic commitment – and not like a simple shareholder. Such an attitude would considerably help solve the governance issue (both at macro and micro-economic levels) in Central and Eastern Europe and make the transition easier.

Notes

*   This paper was the subject of a presentation in front of the 1992 Pew Fellows at the School of Foreign Service, Georgetown University, January 29, 1992. It was also published by Économies et Sociétiés, no. 4-5-6, 1992, pp. 182-206, and in Alice Teichova (ed.).

1   J. Kornai is, I believe, the first who argued in favour of using the notion of 'transformation', as against 'reform', in order to convey the magnitude and complexity of the process.

2   It is noteworthy that Nobel prizewinners among economists, apart from rare interviews, do not seem to be engaged in the close scrutiny of transition, a fact that is quite puzzling.

3   The undisputed theoretical 'guru' was M.Manoilescu (1929, 1934) who advocated industrial protectionism and corporatism. Interestingly enough, after P. Schmitter (1974) drew attention to Manoilescu's seemingly lasting ideas about social development in this century, some are construing 'Neo-corporatism' as a way out of the malaise of industrial societies and, implicitly, as a venue for institutional reconstruction in Central and Eastern Europe (J. Lallement, 1991).

4   V. Axenciuc (1991) recently made a survey of the inter-war evolution of the Romania economy available.

5   According to A. Solimano, in 1937, nominal income per capita was estimated at $440 in Great Britain, and $400, $340, $330, $306, $265, and $190 in Sweden, Germany, Belgium, Netherlands, France and Austria, respectively. The corresponding estimates for Czechoslovakia, Hungary, Poland, Romania, Yugoslavia and Bulgaria were $170, $120, $100, $81, $80 and $75, respectively (A. Gelb and Cheryl Gray, 1991, p.65). See also A. Benner and J.M. Montias (1991, p. 163).

6   It can be likened to A. Leijonhufud's corridor within which 'the system's homeostatic mechanisms work well' (1973, p. 32).

7   Remark made during the Romanian-American economic roundtable, held in Bucharest, April 16-17, 1991.

8   By creating 'Big industry', Communism produced an oversized working class which, ironically, helped bring about its collapse. However, workers can slow down, or derail Transformation because of entrenched vested interests (see also J. Kochanowicz, 1990 on the preparedness of workers to accept Capitalism).

9   Thus, 'Russia is no longer the undifferentiated peasant country it was when Stalin embarked on his crash-course communism. In 1939, only 32% of the Russian population lived in town and cities. Now it is 74%. 'It has 99% literacy rate, 96% enrolment in secondary education, and a large educated scientific and managerial

elite' (*The Economist*, December 7th, 1991, p. 28).

10   The role of religion in the West, as compared to the East, can be talked about in this matter.

11   The German and the Japanese models can be juxtaposed to the Anglo-Saxon model; the former two show a higher degree of co-operation among government, business leaders and trade unions, and also a sense of solidarity (communitarian values) that might be quite attractive to many Central and Eastern Europeans.

12   Romanian communist leaders could be viewed as having been very nationalistic since they steadfastly opposed Moscow's wishes for close economic integration. However, I submit that the clever nationalists were those who succeeded in distancing their economies from the traditional (Stalinist) model of functioning. In this vein, Hungarian, Polish and others can be considered as not having been less nationalistic. Thus, nationalism in policy gets a more subtle meaning, which goes beyond the simple acts of defying the Superpower and relates to an understanding of the overall functioning of society. This is what made possible in Hungary the existence and development of a 'second economy' and a 'second society' (E. Hankiss, 1989). In this respect I remember an article in the Italian communist weekly *Rinascita*, in the late eighties, which decried the intellectual dwarfness of those commanding the heights of the Romanian Communist Party (not only the two Ceausescus). I wonder what would have been the evolution of the quality of the Party apparatus should L. Patrascanu (an outstanding intellectual and a leader of the Party, who was purged and, subsequently, murdered, in the early fifties) and not Gh. Gheorghiu Dej (Ceausescu's predecessor and the one responsible for Patrascanu's death) had been at its helm. One can think in terms of both doctrine and policy. I assume that Patrascanu – had he been able to stay in power, which is questionable for various reasons – would not have allowed Ceausescu-like minded people to surround him (for a brief but excellent analysis of 'National Stalinism' see V. Tismaneanu, 1990).

13   For a good coverage of the whole period see, for instance, R. H. Linden (1989), J. M. Montias (1991), P. Rönnas (1990), A. Smith (1990), A. Teodorescu (1990) etc.

14   By institutional arrangements I understand also 'the rules of game' enjoying wide social acceptability; it is a broad sense which can be found in the works of D. North (1981).

15   Th. Koopmans and J.M. Montias used such a function in a seminal paper (1971). I also used it in order to deal with the 'performance deficit' of supply-constrained economies (D. Daianu, 1984, 1987).

16   By the end of the sixties Ceausescu was getting a firm grip on the leadership of the Party and felt no more need for 'renewal' gestures. Moreover, the events in Czechoslovakia in 1968 convinced him that relaxation of control endangered his supremacy by loosening reform forces within society and by tainting his image as a staunch upholder of ideological 'purity' (which was a bargaining chip in his conflict with Moscow).

17   As M. Shafir nicely put it, it was an example of 'simulated change' (1985).

18   Market relations operate in any kind of environment; I have in mind officially sanctioned market transactions and corresponding institutions like those encouraged by partial reforms in Hungary and Poland.

19   The average annual share of accumulation (in current prices) in the net material product was stated to be 25.5% for 1961-1965; 29.5% for 1966-1970; 33.7% for 1971-1975; and 35.3% for 1976-1980 (Statistical Yearbook, Bucharest, 1986, p.60).

20   The share of CMEA countries in the overall trade went from just over 80% in the 50s to 34.6% in 1980 (CMEA data).

21   Command economies are cybernetic systems based on chain links, as compared to market economies that use, prevailingly, parallel connections. With growing complexity, the reliability of command economies is increasingly inferior to that of market-based systems.

22   What G. Offer aptly named 'haste' (1990).

23   See J. Bhagwati (1985, 1968) and H. Jonhnson (1967), especially. For the case of centrally planned economy and of Romania, in particular, see Daianu (1984).

24   Fr. Holzman talked about 'the saleability illusion' (1979).

25   R. Barro, H. Grossman (1974); for a command economy see J. Brada, A. King (1986).

26   S. Hirsch named it as a 'sequence of industrialisation' (1977).

27   The imports of machinery and equipment from the developed market economies were only 1/3 in the late 80s as compared to the level at the beginning of the decade.

28   Efficiency-wage models (G. Akerloff, J. Yelen, 1987) can be used for explaining the impact of the decline of the living standards on labour supply, particularly when the drop is extremely drastic.

29   For instance, D. Perkins, the Director of the Harvard Institute of International Development, expressing his misgivings about the big bang approach (1991, pp. 6-7).

30   A. Etzioni (1991) has an interesting elaboration on friction during transition.

31   J. Winiecki considers that much of the loss of output is benefactor, not to be seen as additional inefficiency (1991).

32   Analysing 'stagflationary effects of stabilisation policies' in reforming economies G.A. Calvo and F. Coricelli (1992) emphasise the similarities between the 'enterprise-side' and the neo-structuralist approaches.

33   This happened in Romania after December 1989.

34   Murrell (1991a, 1991b) is a leading advocate of an evolutionary approach to the economics of transition. For the general framework of this approach, see R. Nelson and D. Winter (1982). Among Eastern European economists, L. Csaba, a refined analyst and a well-known observer of the whole region, seems to hold similar views (1991).

35   The feasibility (sustainability) of a shock treatment depends on a series of critical

social, political and cultural components of the fabric of society. For such a treatment to be initiated, the goodwill of the political leadership needs to meet the goodwill of the population (the latter involving the existence of charismatic and trustworthy leaders, who can shape the public mood and energise individual and collective actions). This occurred in Poland, which still looks like an exceptional case. The therapy applied in Hungary is clearly of a milder sort, and the same can be said of what is being attempted in the Federal Czech and Slovak Republic. I stress this because however determined to start radical change a governmental team is, its ultimate decision will be a function of the responsiveness of the population. A policy that does not meet such requirements – running also counter to the preparedness of people to accept sacrifices – will inexorably bog down, will be emasculated.

36   The 'natural rate of adjustment' of society can be defined as an imagined optimal speed of change that maximises society's preference (welfare) function.

37   In a programmatic article in Financial Times, V. Klaus and T. Jezek, approvingly, cite A. Brzeski: 'just as the optimal allocation of resources cannot be achieved outside the market process, because the process itself generates the necessary information, so in the overhaul of an entire system, only the actual steps taken can disclose the acceptable path' (1989, p. 15).

38   A distinction has to be made between reform as a *real process* and reform *as policy*; the real process can move forward even when reform as a policy might experience setbacks. This is the point made by A. Wood when distinguishing between 'nominal pause' and 'real progress' (1990, p. 19).

39   As compared to China, where reforms initiated from above have been tightly maintained within an economic tunnel.

40   The political formation which appeared after the overnight collapse of the Communist Party.

41   'The New Economic Policy' highlighted an increasing influence of the liberal (in the European sense) wing within the ruling strata of the Salvation Front together with the desire to gain credibility abroad after the unfortunate events of June of that year. This policy would get a new radical twist in September of 1990 as the economy was getting ever more out of control.

42   Actually the shock is smaller if it is considered that a large part of the urban population is closely linked with the countryside, that many city dwellers stand with one of their legs in villages where they might own a house and a plot. The inference is that a substantial amount of what gets out of one-pocket gets into the other pocket. Nonetheless, there are people – like retired persons, some of those with fixed incomes – who are badly hurt by price liberalisation should they not be able to enter, or reenter the labour market by converting their additional available time (previously used as search and queuing time) into an attractive labour supply.

References

Akerloff, G.A. and Yellen J. (eds.) (1987), 'Efficiency Wage Models of the Labour Market', Cambridge University Press, Cambridge.

Arrow, J.K. (1974), 'The Limits of Organisation', Norton, New York.

Axenciuc, V., 'The Romanian Economy in the First Half of the Twentieth Century' (in Romanian) in T. Postolache (ed.), *Romanian Economy in the Twentieth Century* (in Romanian), Editura Academiei, Bucharest, pp. 99-173.

Barro and Grossman, H. (1974), 'Suppressed Inflation and the Supply Multiplier', *Review of Economic Studies*, vol. 41(1), pp. 87-104.

Benner, A. and Montias, J.M. (1991), 'The Introduction of Markets in a Hypercentralised Economy – the Case of Romania', *Journal of Economic Perspective*, vol. 5(4), pp. 163-170.

Bhagwati, J. (1958), 'Immiserising Growth – a Geometrical Note', *Review of Economic Studies*, 25.

Bhagwati, J. (1968), 'Distortions and Immiserising Growth – a Generalisation', *Review of Economic Studies*, 35.

Brada, J. and King, A. (1986), 'Taut Plans, Repressed Inflation and the Supply of Effort in Centrally Planned Economies', *Economics of Planning*, vol. 20(3), pp. 162-178.

Calvo, G. and Coricelli, F. (1992), 'Stagflationary Effects of Stabilisation Programs in Reforming Socialist Countries: Enterprise-Side and Household-Side Factors', *World Bank Review*, vol. 6(1), pp. 71-90.

Chirot, D. (ed.) (1989), 'The Origins of Backwardness in Eastern Europe', University of California Press, Berkeley.

Csaba, L. (July 1991 manuscript), 'First Lessons of Transforming the Economic System In Central Europe', Budapest.

Daianu, D. (1984), 'External Equilibrium and the Type of Control of Domestic Absorption', *Revue Roumaine de Sciences Sociales-serie economique*, 2, pp. 115-136.

Daianu, D. (1985), 'A Model of Immiserising Growth. The Case of Command Economy' (in Romanian), *Revista Economica*, no. 20.

Daianu, D. (1987), 'On Aggregate (Dis)equilibrium and Performance: Supply vs. Demand-Constrained Economies', *Revue Roumaine de Science Sociales - serie économique*, 1, pp. 31-65.

Etzioni, A. (1991 manuscript), 'A Socio-economic Perspective on Friction', study prepared for the IAREP/SASE Conference.

Gelb, A. and Gray, C. (1991), 'The Transformation of Economies in Central and Eastern Europe', The World Bank, Washington DC.

Hankiss, E. (1988), 'The Second Society: Is there an Alternative Social Model Emerging in Hungary', *Occasional paper*, 16, Woodrow Wilson Center, Washington DC.

Hirsch, S. (1997), 'Rich Man's, Poor Man's and Every Man's Goods, Aspects of Industrialisation', Tübingen, J.B.C. Mohr (Paul Siebeck), Kieler Studien, 148.

Holzman, Fr. (1979), 'Some Theories of the Hard Currency Shortage of Centrally Planned Economies, in Soviet Economy in a Time of Change – a compendium of papers submitted to the JOC', US Congress, *USGPO*, Washington DC, pp.297-316.

Johnson, H. (1967), 'The Possibility of Income Losses from Increased Efficiency of Factor Accumulation in the Presence of Tariffs', *Economic Journal*.

Klaus, V. and Jezek, T. (December 13, 1989), 'The Evolutionary Approach', *Financial Times*, 1989, p. 15.

Kochanowitz, J. (1991 manuscript), 'Is Poland Unfit for Capitalism? Poland in the 1980s and the 1990s: Social Change In Historical Perspective', paper prepared for a Conference on 'Dilemmas of Transition in East Central Europe', Center for European Studies, Harvard University, March 15-17.

Koopmans, T.C., Montias, J.M. (1991), 'On the Description and Comparison of Economic Systems', in A. Eckstein (ed.), 'Comparison of Economic Systems. Theoretical and Methodological Approaches', University of California Press, Berkeley.

Lallement, J. (September 1991), 'Corporatisme Societal et Employ', CFDT Aujourd'hui.

Leijonhufvud, A. (1968), 'On Keynesian Economics and the Economics of Keynes', Oxford University Press, London.

Linden, R. (October 27, 1989), 'Romania: The Search for Economic Sovereignty', in 'Pressure for Reform in Eastern European Economies', vol. 12, JEC.

Manoilescu, M. (1929), 'Theorie du Protectionnisme et de l'Echange international', Paris.

Manoilescu, M. (1934), 'Le Siecle du Corporatisme', Giard, Paris.

Montias, J.M. (June, 1991), 'The Romanian Economy: a Survey of Current Economic Problems', *European Economy*, Special edition, pp.177-198.

Murrell, P. (1991), 'Can Neo-classical Economics Underpin the Reform of Centrally Planned Economies?', *Journal of Economic Perspectives*, vol. 5(4), pp. 59-76.

Murrell, P. (1991a), 'Evolution in Economics and in the Economic Reform of the Centrally Planned Economies', manuscript.

Myint, H. (1971), 'Economic Theory and Underdeveloped Countries', New York.

Nelson, R. R. and Winter, S. (1982), 'An Evolutionary Theory of Economic Change', Mass, Harvard University Press, Cambridge.

North, D. (1981), 'Structure and Change in Economic History', Norton, New York.

Offer, G. (February 1990, manuscript), 'Decelerating Growth under Socialism: The Soviet Case'.

Olson, M. (1982), 'The Rise and Decline of Nations. Economic Growth, Stagflation and Social Rigidities', Yale University Press, New Haven.

Olson, M. and Murrell, P. (January 1991), 'The Devolution of Centrally Planned Economies', manuscript.

Perkins, D. (July 26, 1991), 'Developing Nations Now Turn to the Market

Economy Concept', a conversation in *The Harvard Gazette*.

Rönnas, P. (1990), 'The Economic Legacy of Ceausescu', Stockholm Institute of Soviet and East European Economics, *Working paper*, No. 11.

Schmitter, Ph. (January 1974), 'Still The Century of Corporatism?', *Review of Politics*, pp. 85-131.

Shafir, M. (1985), 'Romania: Politics, Economics and Society', F. Pinter, London.

Simon, H. (1959), 'Theories of Decision-Making in Economics and Behavioural Sciences', *American Economic Review*, vol. 49(3), pp. 253-283.

Smith, A. (April 1990), 'The Romanian Economy: Policy and Prospects for the 1990s', paper prepared for a NATO colloquium, Brussels.

Taylor, L. (1983), 'Structuralist Macroeconomics', Basic Books, New York.

Taylor, L. (1988), 'Varieties of Stabilisation Experience', Clarendon Press, Oxford.

Taylor, L. (August 1991), 'The Post-Socialist Transition from a Development Economics Point of View', MIT, manuscript.

Taylor, L. (1991b), 'Income Distribution, Inflation and Growth', MIT, Cambridge MA.

Teichova, A. (1992), 'Interwar Capital Markets in Central and Southeastern Europe', in J. R. Lampe (ed.), *Creating Capital Markets in Eastern Europe*, The Woodrow Wilson Center Press, Washington DC, pp.7-17.

Teodorescu, A. (1991), 'The Romanian Economy: The future of a Failure', in O. Sjoberg and M. Wyzan (eds.), *Economic Change in the Balkan States*, St. Martin Press, New York.

Tismaneanu, V. (1990), 'Understanding National Stalinism: A Comparative Approach to the History of Romanian Communism', Woodrow Wilson Center, Washington DC, *Occasional Paper*, No. 25.

Weitzman, M. (1984), 'The Share Economy', Harvard University Press, Cambridge.

Winiecki, J. (1991), 'The Inevitability of a fall in Output in the Early Stages of Transition to the Market: Theoretical Underpinnings', *Soviet Studies*, No. 4, pp. 669-676.

Wood, A. (October 4, 1990), 'A Nominal Pause, But Some Real Progress', *Financial Times*, p.19.

3 Economic Policy in Public Debate[*]

Amid all the scrutiny and discussion of the post-communist transformation in Central and Eastern Europe, public policy debate has been a comparatively neglected topic. This is a little surprising, for in the 'Big Bang' of 1989 citizens were seeking not just relief from a collapsing economic system, but political freedom, which implies participation in public debate. On the other hand, sometimes the 'bang' was so explosive, and citizens in such a state of rebellion against institutional authority – to the point of outright violence in Romania – that sheer ventilation had to come first, with public debate as a kind of second wind.

At first, the temptation was to focus here on 'ideal' institutions that would enhance public policy debate, especially on economic affairs in emerging democracies. But soon I realised that my attention was drawn toward two more subtle issues: the *quality* of public debate, which requires some historical perspective; and the *nature* of economic policy debate, that is, how the dynamics of the actual economy affect and are affected by the rhetorical veil that surrounds conflicting interests in the society.

I arrived at these questions because I sense a sort of worldwide policymaking *malaise*, which can be linked to generally negative economic conditions and to an exacerbated degree of 'cognitive dissonance' between top public servants (government) and the citizenry. The fall of the communist systems in Europe is a logical denouement of their history. However, these events are also being played out amid other pan-European and global economic and political tensions.

Was there any debate on economic policy under communism?

It is generally agreed that the smaller and more open a market economy is, the more endogenous – self-creating, self-sustaining – becomes its money supply (with related processes). In addition, as that economy opens up, monetary policy increasingly slips from under the reins of central authority into the control of the market's participants instead. Analogously, I suggest, in an open society, in a democracy, economic policymaking (like policymaking in general) becomes similarly 'endogenized'. As citizens – individuals or groups – begin to take an active part in public debate, they become engaged in policy formulation: they become members, as it were, of an invisible extended government.[1] In one (rather narrow) sense, the resulting economic policy is endogenous both because of the intensity of debate that created it and the compromises and procedures that hammered out the ultimate details. In a broader sense, economic policy is endogenous because it widens the scope of market forces and of individual endeavour – through the empowerment of citizens. The more economic power people gain the more opportunities they have to express their views on the construction of public policy.[2]

Seen in this light, the varied experiences of the Central and Eastern European countries during the socialist (i.e., communist) era show that at least some (varying) degree of public policy debate was possible under such regimes, particularly at points where economic reforms were undertaken. This 'stock' of historical experience continues to influence the current flow of economic events and adds its overtones to current public debate on economic policy.

Different styles in different countries

Despite its rigid ideological prototype, communism (or socialism, if you prefer) in Central and Eastern Europe diversified in significant ways, by mere chance and by design. The Hungarian model – popularly termed 'goulash communism' – achieved relative prosperity and (to some onlookers) tolerated an amazingly lively and open public debate. In Poland, however, a certain openness of society contrasted dramatically with a series of stalled economic reforms. The Soviets themselves practised an 'island strategy' of fostering scientific inquiry in near or actual sequestration. At the far end of the spectrum, if we leave Hodja's Albania aside, sat Ceausescu's Romania, 'an aberration within an aberration'.

Poland's situation was hallmarked by the strong role of the Catholic Church there, the anti-communism among the population, the country's very active intelligentsia, and a very large Diaspora. It is thus not surprising that after Krushchev's speech in 1956, the Conference of Polish Economists – whose members included such internationally renowned figures as O. Lange and M. Kalecki – forthrightly discussed the need to drastically overhaul the imported Stalinist economic model. However, their commitment and that of others who followed in their footsteps was of little avail in influencing the communist apparatus over the succeeding years. In hindsight, this failed effort to change the course of economic policy, in 1956 and immediately afterward, seems to me as damaging as the bloody crushing of the Prague Spring in 1968.

By 1962, with W. Brus's intellectually solid indictment of the communist command system,[3] the rift between genuine public debate (still entertained by uncompromising scholars) and the faked debate enforced by party propagandists had become more apparent. The sad joke then circulating about the waste of Poland's tremendous intellectual resources was that the country 'has superb economists, but a wrecked economy'. Nevertheless, it was still possible to keep up minimum standards in the teaching of economics,[4] which at least promised good future professionals. Most of these economists stayed in Poland and went on defending their scientific beliefs on the domestic battlefield. However, many joined the distinguished ranks of Polish intellectuals in exile. Together they offered their society, and their colleagues in neighbouring countries, a brave example of intellectual ethics and stamina in adverse conditions. We could say that they enhanced the culture of public debate by demonstrating, as role models, a quasi-scientific community.[5]

It is widely assumed that economic reforms in Hungary began in the late 1960s, but I believe the seeds can be detected in the late 1950s. One good indicator of this would be Kornai's *Overcentralisation in the Textile Industry*, which appeared in 1957 (and in an English edition by 1959). The wide-ranging reforms of the later 1960s came as no surprise to a society already accustomed to an intense public debate on economic issues, which was already developing traits of what Hankiss (1988) termed a 'second society'. It is especially notable that these reforms proceeded despite the cold wind that blew through Eastern Europe after the military intervention in Czechoslovakia in 1968. This suggests to me that the rise of public debate and the spread of reformist ideas were accompanied, in this one case, by a crucial policy-linked factor: the inner determination of the core Party apparatus to phase in radical economic reforms. My reading of what happened during the decades of communist regime in Central and Eastern Europe is that that combination was decisive in putting economic reforms in Hungary on a solid footing, whatever fluctuations in policy ensued. The Czechoslovakian experience could be offered as a counter-argument, but their foreign policy and security matters were at the base of the military intervention. By maintaining a very low profile in the foreign policy sphere, Hungary was able to relieve Moscow's worries about any proposed economic reforms.

It is also often assumed that Hungary's economic reforms did not succeed. That is to consider only the empty half of the bottle. The reforms did create many institutional ingredients of a market environment: a vigorous entrepreneurial class that has become the backbone of current reforms, and a new ethos among the populace. Those early changes went so far that Hungarian policymakers are now in an enviable position: the national economic environment is sufficiently attuned to the requirements of well-functioning markets that it can withstand 'shock treatment' measures if necessary; on the other hand, this environment creates some leeway, some 'slack', for avoiding hasty and costly short-run decisions that might provoke social disruption. This is, I think, the explanation behind the country's current atmosphere of economic pragmatism.

By the end of the 1980s, communism was so 'benign' in Hungary – at least from the Romanian perspective – and real changes had gone so far, that crossing the political Rubicon was quite easy. The 'gentleness' of the transfer of political power in Hungary offers an instructive case study of how pervasive and far-reaching the prior reforms had been.[6] The history of public policy debate was very much in the hands of leading economists, who championed radical reforms and who, eventually entered the inner circles of power at higher echelons of governmental bureaucracy. The reforms in turn changed the economic scene by dispersing power and modifying inexorably the nature of subsequent economic policy.

The language of debate

Another fertile field for inquiry into the quality and intensity of economic public policy debate under the communist regimes is the language used in the professional journals and mass media. This language can be seen as a variable dependent on both the professionalism of the debaters and the ideological constraints of the environment. It can also be seen either statically or as a 'living' language, whose evolution followed the dynamics of the political, social, and economic environment. And in its own dynamics, that language has both an internal dimension, pertaining to the developments of science, and an external one, of cross-fertilisation between national cultural milieus and surrounding areas.

As with styles of communism, the language of public debate varied across a wide spectrum. Hungary and Poland can again be cited for standards attained and set for the rest of the region,[7] even though the Polish example is one of decoupling professional public debate from actual economic policy. The language of debate can show both progression (as in Hungary), or regression – more obvious in Czechoslovakia after the Prague Spring, when so many eminent scholars and writers fell (or were put) into near or complete oblivion.[8]

Much 'esotericism' was injected into the language to make ideas more palatable to power-holders. Sometimes this was also the natural, genuine result of using mathematics as an analytical tool, which only a few economists could then grasp. Some specialists (particularly at the School of Mathematical Economics in Moscow) were legendary in that respect, even in the very arcane and ideologised Soviet intellectual climate.[9] Others – like I. Nikolov in Bulgaria – very cleverly used cybernetics as stalking horses to talk about the market. Nevertheless, nowhere was the language of public debate more devoid of substance than in Ceausescu's Romania.

The Romanian experience

In the fall of 1989 I was dumbfounded to read in a national daily, that the estimated grain crop in the Olt county would be double that of the preceding year – though Mother Nature had not blessed Romania with exceptionally salubrious weather in the meanwhile. In a command system – as in a shortage economy (see Kornai 1980) – truth is a scarce commodity, whereas lies are abundant; and I was used to the preposterous official boasting about Romania's economic 'achievements'. However, those grains figures seemed to me to have 'gone beyond the mark' and surpassed the bearable limits of indecency in misinformation foisted on the public.

I cite this example to give a glimpse into Romanian exceptionalism as late Stalinism (see Tismaneanu 1990), which made a mockery of what was conceived as tolerance of public policy debate in the neighbouring communist countries, and indeed raised some eyebrows among their leaders. Genuine public policy debate was extremely low-key and of poor quality in Romania; in this, it mirrored the harshness of the regime and the severe suppression of views dissenting from the official Party line.

The impact of these conditions on the social science was catastrophic. With the exception of a short-lived relaxation between 1966 and 1971[10] the profession regressed steadily, and honest practitioners were worse than humiliated. Isolation from outside contacts and downsizing or destruction of the scientific infrastructure was frequently employed to stifle any questioning of public policy. A particularly telling blow was Ceausescu's order in 1973 for the country's only economic journal to cease publication – surely a 'first' in all Europe, and perhaps the whole world beyond![11] Some of the best brains in the economics profession were forced to leave the country or were marginalised, and witch hunts were still practised. Perhaps the most notorious instance was the expulsion of I. Lemnij from the Institute of Socialist Economics in the late 1970s. A very fine analyst and one of the very few Romanian economists to enjoy an international reputation, Lemnij was punished for saying (in effect) that the emperor wore no clothes, and was accused of spreading imperialist propaganda.

Esoteric language was a constant tool among those – few indeed – who attempted to raise real issues and stir genuine public debate. (Sometimes, admittedly, obscurity was the unintended result of speaking in plain (true) economics).[12] Another way to make a point was to 'whip the saddle so the horse will get the hint': developments in neighbouring communist countries, analyses made by economists in Hungary, or Poland, or the Soviet Union, and viewpoints from Italian and Spanish 'eurocommunists' became an arsenal of analogues used to convey messages about the state of the Romanian economy. Insightful analysts, unwilling to bow their heads – like Al. Olteanu and S. Covrig from the Institute of World Economy – were obliged by the early 1980s to seek other jobs. Others – like V. Pilat of the Institute of Socialist Economics, for more than twenty years a staunch fighter for truth and whose numerous studies testify to his analytical skills, knowledge, and vision – saw their research remain unpublished, or circulated only as semi-underground work.[13]

In this disaster area of public debate – even gauged against regional standards – a few tiny islands of relative freethinking managed to surface and (sometimes) to survive. There were similar islands in the Soviet Union as well, like the Institute of Research for Industrial Organisation in Novosibirsk, but central authorities promoted those for reasons I shall not go into here. In the Romanian case, the island organisations were set up and driven along by strong-willed and courageous individuals, who were clever enough to use their academic situation as rallying places. I can only mention those I was privileged to encounter.

One such individual was C. Pintilie, head (and inspirational engine) of the Management Workshop at the Academy of Economic Studies in Bucharest. At one of its meetings in the late 1970s, I met the mathematician M. Botez, a leading dissident who produced over the years such scathing criticism of Ceausescu's economic strategy that he was eventually forced to emigrate in the late 1980s. Professor Pintilie asked me to present several lectures on 'the economics of shortage' in 1985 and 1986. Unfortunately, but not surprisingly, the Workshop was ordered out of existence in 1988. Pintilie, old and much enfeebled, lived to see its resurrection immediately after Ceausescu's regime collapsed in December 1989, but not much longer.

The Academy of Economic Studies sheltered two other pockets of 'heretical thinking' and resistance, through the workshops on Product Research and Development (headed by B. Cotigaru) and Energy Conservation Research (headed by Gh. Preda, who was also among those forced to emigrate in the late 1980s). They shared Pintilie's views on the country's plight and organised (sometimes jointly) scientific events whose open and genuine character was a *rara avis* in a world of posturing, bigotry, and intellectual prostitution.

Another 'island' was the Association of Scientists, which drew scientists from various fields, including several economists.[14] A number of its members became involved in the country's political life after 1989 – among them the lawyer Dan Amedeo Lazarescu, one of the leading figures of the reborn National Liberal Party.

This cursory, incomplete view of rudiments of genuine public policy debate in Romania during the communist years does not capture the ups and downs along the way. It is biased towards life within the community of economists, for very little is known about the struggle of those who, however few they were, individually or jointly attempted to voice their opinions about the official economic doctrine and policy. However, even this sketch suggests the actuality of an atomised universe, an opaque culture of public debate, and a near absence of regard for professionalism and intellectual rigour.

A *linked past and present*

It should by now be clear that public (economic) policy debate in Central and Eastern Europe varied quite substantially under communism, over time and territory. This variety of experience did shape national economic and political environments differently.

Where economic reforms moved forward, despite temporary setbacks, public policy debate reached remarkable levels of intensity and quality – and economic policy fell at least partially under the control of various social actors. That is, its endogenous character increased: citizens became involved in the debate and the economy, began to 'make it their own', thus building strength for further developments. Vice versa, where actual reforms were rejected, or only simulated, and neo-Stalinism blossomed, public debate sank into near insignificance; public policy was totally removed from the hands of citizens – it was imposed 'exogenously' by state authority.[15]

I have emphasised all this because current public policy debate in the post-communist countries is deeply influenced by the communist legacy each uniquely retains. There are deep socio-cultural dimensions to the problem. Where some degree of public policy debate was condoned (or even encouraged) and institutional ingredients of a market environment were available, some portions of social memory could be preserved. Individuals from such environment have an easier time adjusting to the rush of transformation. People's reactions to change, the gap between their expectations and reality, their ability to accommodate change – what I call a society's 'natural rate of adjustment' [16] – depends greatly upon the culture of public (open) dialogue, or lack of it, to which they have already been accustomed.

This link between past and present can be seen in the field of economic policy. Where economists were able to voice genuine opinions and influence policies toward reform, the environment changed considerably. The enduring impact of that experience on current public policy debate is obvious, not only in the *nature* and *intensity* of the present debate, but also its *quality*, its ability to navigate the space between the inherited system and the perceived target of a market economy.

The differences in this 'space' – the gap between 'before' and 'target' varies considerably from country to country – have meant different starting points in the transformation process, an issue that has received insufficient attention in current public debate. This seems quite puzzling to me, as so many of the differences of content, and result, in present-day reforms can be traced to those dissimilar conditions at the pivotal moment. The different histories explain not only why available ingredients of a market economy vary, but also why macro and micro disequilibria varied among these countries on the eve of the chain-reaction collapse of the communist regimes. With its stubborn adherence to Stalinist economic precepts, its isolationism, its industrial policy that blatantly ignored the concept of comparative advantages, and its *sui generis* 'shock therapy' in the 1980s, Romania confronts a very big and empty 'space' indeed.

Public policy debate in a transforming environment

The collapse of communism across Central and Eastern Europe in 1989 was truly a watershed in human history. To my mind, the acid test that the transformation will succeed – in terms of public debate, policy transformation, and solid ideological change – is the reinstitution of private property as the foundation of a market-based economy. This is a valid test for both the frontrunners and the 'laggard' countries. Even in Hungary, full acceptance of the central role of private property in the structure of ownership rights occurred only after the communists fell from power. Similarly, in Poland, the shift from the 'three S' policy (self-management, self-governance, and self-financing) to the political internalisation of private property as the core institution, ultimately required the political demise of the communists. Russia was similarly divided on this issue, as the clash between Gorbachev's advisers and the Gaidar-Fyodorov platform well attested.

But the debate on the *destination* of the transformation is still lively: what kind of market economy is desired, what kind can be attained? The menu includes (1) an unqualified market economy (the Anglo-American model); (2) a social market economy (*soziale Marktwirtschaft*), with heavy redistribution of income; and (3) a mixed economy, with an important public sector (best known from the Austrian example).[17] Debate on destination is linked with that on the pace of reform; one approach recommends holism, stabilisation, and speed; the gradualist approach emphasises institutional change and a cautious policy development. Either way, or somewhere in between, controversy is apt to be clouded by political tensions and doubts among the citizenry.[18]

In my opinion, three factors may shape the intensity and nature of this debate. (1) The concrete results of reforms, in terms of people's standards of living and expectations, will condition their political behaviour and showing at the polls.[19] (2) The effects of the downward cycle in the world economy – the reversal of the boom of the 1980s – may usher in policy changes in a recession-plagued Europe, which seems unable to come to grips with its own structural problems. (3) The slow pace of large-scale privatisation (of state-owned enterprises) may require the state to exercise its attributes of ownership longer than expected, if only to insure some sort of governance and promote stable reforms.

A clash of visions

Post-communist economies, generally, are troubled by extreme rigidity of resource movement, agents who are ignorant about the functioning of organised markets, lack of proper supporting institutions and a sustaining ethos, and necessary cultural backup. Transformation will entail institutional change, cultural change, and material reconstruction. Most people recognise that the world will not pause to accommodate these adjustments, that there is a tolerance limit to social sacrifice, and that time cannot be compressed at will. Beneath such basic intuitions we may discern two conflicting visions – two sets of underpinnings – in currently advocated policies of transformation.

One way to describe these is in terms of the paradigm provided by neo-classical economic analysis – equilibrium theory. One side, best represented by the New classical macroeconomics, rejects any state intervention in the economy as agents – so it is argued – optimise by using all available information,[20] which insures full price flexibility and thereby sufficiently rapid allocation of resources. According to this view, any rate of unemployment is natural, as it expresses the agents' preferences. The other side begins with the assumption that prices are rigid to an extent that induces adjustments in quantities as well, so that aggregate demand equilibrates aggregate supply below full employment. That is to speak of a non-Walrasian equilibrium (which violates Walras' Law).

Both visions focus on the functioning of a market economy. If the command system is seen as a pathological form of market economy, ridden with extreme structural dysfunctions, the hypothesis can be made that 'shock treatments' would lead, in the first phase, to a significant drop in production – the so-called J-curve effect. In that phase of transformation the entrenched structures would have to be broken down and changed, with the result that friction would escalate within the system and substantial energy (resources) would be consumed to accommodate, adjust, and change. A lot would boil down to changing the organisational behaviour of economic actors. To the congenital inefficiencies still in place from the old system would be added the inefficiency caused by friction.[21]

To extend the friction metaphor: hysteresis phenomena – effects prolonged because of friction – will also be met and will have to be tackled. Consider, for instance, the anticipated rising unemployment and the lasting effects of too open (unprotected) an economy in a world of imperfect markets: this is why shock therapy policies are feared and why it takes great political courage and firm popular support to implement them. The sooner net costs turn into net benefits, the better for the political leadership (whose stock of political capital would otherwise be rapidly wiped out), not to mention for the public at large. It could be argued that a gradualist policy could not arrest the decline of output (living standards) either. There is, however, one factor that explains why gradualist policies appeal to many politicians and many citizens: if processes are under control, the initial drop of output may be less brutal than under shock treatment. However, where the old institutional order has collapsed, and citizens are in rebellion against any kind of authority – like in a 'free fall' situation – gradualism may be useless.

Another line of analysis might be to contrast the equilibrium approach with the evolutionary approach. Neo-classical economists pay less attention to social, behavioural, and cultural factors. The underlying assumption is that economic agents are rational – that is, they optimise – and would act accordingly if the environment changed. But the economic transformation underway in Central and Eastern Europe has important social and cultural dimensions, not the least being efforts to overcome inertia and ideological barriers, to change mentalities, and to fathom the psychology of the fierce struggle among 'coalitions of interests' (M. Olson, 1982). The clash of various interests, especially during transition, invests the process with a life of its own, especially insofar as it reduces decision-makers' room to manoeuvre.

A sociological or institutional approach would suggest that in order to have a fair chance of progressing smoothly, the transformation process would need support from a strong coalition of interests. That is, a social basis in favour of change, a 'reform constituency' would have to be in place. In the 'laggard' post-communist societies, that reform constituency is still feeble and the forces that oppose change remain strong. From this standpoint, transformation cannot be usefully construed as a 'one-stroke policy'. In any case, the *real* process of change can only be evolutionary, and policy has to be conceived accordingly. One further factor helps explain why shock treatments are harder to implement in laggard countries: a life experience that has compelled people to think that 'there is no other way'. Insofar as that mentality leads them to choose whatever they believe will involve the least immediate costs, shock therapies will be avoided or resisted, or will be difficult to sustain over the long run, even amid political goodwill. A muddling-through process is more likely to emerge. In that case, inconsistencies in transformation policy and resulting further muddling-through may certainly be attributed to weakness in the social basis of change, even where a broad constituency supports the ideal of change.

Enlisting popular support through public debate

The years since 1989 have seen a major shift in the general mood about transformation, as people have realised that the process is much more complicated than had been anticipated. This unease has been further fed by apprehensions about developments in Europe and world-wide, among them vanishing eastern markets, – 'beggar thy neighbour' – policies in both East and West (including rising protectionism), and lack of policy co-ordination among the G-7 countries and within the EU (including the disarray in the European monetary system). Recognising that this uncertainty could become a serious problem among other domestic 'transition pains', governments have begun to recruit popular support by all available means, including public debate.

In an established democratic society public policy debate is a fact of life. However, when starting from scratch, new democracies have to consider on pragmatic grounds just how policy debate can be rationalised and how policymakers should view it. There are several approaches to this.

Disciples of the Chicago school (or new classical macroeconomists) might argue that too much concern with enhancing public policy debate, for the sake of obtaining popular support, is superfluous, since 'homo oeconomicus' hypostasizes credibly human behaviour (see Mises 1949). Individuals optimise and market forces need only be unleashed. There is no need to enlist popular support, since such backing would come automatically.

Several flaws are apparent in this approach. First, when output drops dramatically, the losers will need to be persuaded that they have not been excluded from society, that they are still eligible to enter the ranks of the 'contended establishment' (Galbraith 1992) in the making. A drastic drop of output scarcely validates the vision of a frictionless emerging market economy. Second, society is perceived as atomised: where are Olson's (1982) 'coalitions of interests', that can slow, forestall, or promote transformation? Third, the cultural dimension of transformation is overlooked. Suppose homo oeconomicus has a mindset counter to the requirements of quick transition.

Another approach would focus on 'optimisation failures' on the part of individuals: why do they happen? This would require campaigns in the mass media, designed to correct 'distorted' public perceptions and preferences. In this case public debate on policy options, during which central authorities are joined by those who claim to articulate citizens' interests, may be perceived by the public at large as a kind of collusion, whether deliberate or inadvertent. It thus becomes crucial not only *who* represents the people in such instance, but also *how* it is done – the *quality of* the communication (as a two-way street).

Then there is the option of proceeding 'against the will of the many'. This could be the motto of policymakers who are highly sceptical that meaningful public support can be mustered through democratic channels. This is certainly an invitation to ironclad policy and to an authoritarian style that could slip again into dictatorship. The corollary assumption would be that open public debate is an unnecessary nuisance that could undermine the enforced social and political stability required for undertaking painful market reforms. Proponents of the 'Chilean solution' have that approach in mind.

Nevertheless, whatever the *rationale*, several underlying reasons for the importance of public policy debate cannot be denied. The collapse of communist regimes in Central and Eastern Europe meant that 'revolution (through evolution) from above' was thenceforth out of the question. Controlled change has given way to uncontrolled processes, a 'free fall' syndrome in the economy. The political and social explosions of 1989 and 1990 were the equivalent of a citizens' rebellion or civil war in which individuals defied authority and contested institutions and the rules of a game that had infringed on their individual rights for nearly half a century.[22] The paradox in these emerging democracies is that people now have a lot of power to exercise – both as individuals and as social beings – but may feel disarmed in face of the difficulties of transition. The frightened can easily fall prey to populist slogans and policies. Strengthening democratic institutions through public debate is one fundamental way of decreasing the temptation, among both the leadership and the public, to revert to authoritarian patterns.

Which brings us to the question of leadership. If empowerment of the individual seems a steady prospect, even in the laggard emerging democracies, the selection of leaders for the transformation is by no means as stable an issue. In post-communist societies, which have been deprived of genuine political life for decades, political leadership is itself an 'infant industry'. Identifying good democratic leaders is difficult, as the prior regimes obviously did not inculcate any such values through the educational system and, for that matter, impeded what underground educational opportunities there were (here again Romania offers an outstanding example).

Apart from clairvoyance and professionalism, a good leader needs the knack of evoking popular support when unpopular measures are to be enacted. A good leader also needs to combine the virtues of knowledge and high moral standards with a respect for consensus politics. This delicate balance is most easily achieved when large segments of the civil society are actively engaged in working out policies through public debate. These qualities are essential if leadership is to retain popular support when policies do not yield the expected results.

Transformation also means a reconstruction of morality, an educational area that virtually requires public debate. One topic that most needs dissection is the communist legacy of pervasive moral crisis: it is hard to build new, democratic institutions and have them function properly when truthfulness, trust, and loyalty are scarce commodities. As Arrow (1974, 23) has said, such ethical virtues 'are goods... they have real, practical economic value; they increase the efficiency of the system, enable you to produce more goods or more of whatever value you hold in high esteem'. Moral values are thus public goods, which can substitute for or crowd in tangible goods: this is a terribly important thing to recognise in the early stages of transition, when material output is in considerable decline. Those who conduct public debate and champion certain policies must be legitimate carriers of the required moral values. One could even speak (in Gramsci's sense) of a 'hegemony' in public debate exerted by morally credible individuals.

In addition to the requirements of democratic procedure and the need to gain or retain political support, there is one further good reason for promoting public debate: it creates checks and balances. In democracies with established civil societies and where public ministers are more or less truly public servants[23] rather than capricious power holders, systems of checks and balances are wide-ranging and pervasive. These systems may occasionally render decision-making cumbersome, but they succeed in institutionalising democratic procedures. Checks and balances are particularly essential for reducing recurrent, persistent errors in matters of public interest. They are crucial tools in transformational societies, where abuses of power can occur all too easily and opportunities for self-serving or wrong decisions are rife.

A case study in Romanian economic policy debate

In the last days of December 1989, immediately after Ceausescu's downfall, several leading professional economists came together to discuss the possibility of establishing an economic association to promote the culture of a market economy and free society. The idea 'started small', as the brainchild of enthusiasts who had for many years laboured to raise a flag of truth in a wide valley of deception. The first big step was the formal decision to found an organisation – the Romanian Free Enterprise Institute – and publish a journal that would spread economic knowledge and help restore the profession's reputation. Soon afterwards, a big meeting of economists under the auspices of the Academy of Economic Studies was convened, which established the General Association of Romanian Economists (AGER), as umbrella organisation.

The Romanian Free Enterprise Institute (IRLI) was established in March 1990 as a private economic think tank, and as an intellectual backbone of the struggle to transform the nation's economy; its journal, *Oeconomica*, began publication short thereafter. As a non-profit organisation, IRLI expressly avoided financial support from political organisations with a view to preserving its independence. IRLI remained a tiny organisation, made up of foremost reform-minded economists. Through its debates, it has become a rallying point for other radical reformers who are operating within political parties and civic organisations.

Leading members of AGER have been critical of radical transformation policy and they escalated their efforts after the elections of September 1992; these elections portrayed an electorate largely disenchanted with the results of reform, with a turnout for the left-oriented parties (the Democratic National

Salvation Front, FDSN, in particular). Members of IRLI and other reformers, felt the necessity for a joint public stance in those circumstances and so formed the Romanian Economic Society (SOREC) at the end of November 1992; soon thereafter they issued a public statement strongly in favour of reforms.[24] The Society's emergence in the arena was politically significant, for it came at a critical juncture in the dynamics of transformation and was signed by persons of diverse political affiliations.

The direction of policy under both the Roman and the Stolojan administrations was heavily criticised both from within the governing National Salvation Front (NSF) and by the opposition parties grouped within the Democratic Convention. Those who later split off into FDSN accused the government of betraying the party's economic platform; the opposition pointed out the various flaws in the measures that had been enacted. It was under such circumstances that Roman and his team were ousted in September 1991. Stolojan's performance in turn was impressive, considering that compared to Roman (who had emphasised legal construction), he was concerned with macroeconomic stabilisation, which involved austerity measures. Throughout his tenure as Prime Minister, he was the most popular politician in the country. But even so, he was a popular politician obliged to implement a policy with waning popular support. The results of the September 1992 elections confirmed the apparent mood of the people at large (a *social fatigue* on the rise) and allowed the FDSN to accede to power with its intentions of policy corrections. In terms of pursuing a steady course with policy reforms, a coalition government might have fared better.

Despite all these conflicts and pressures, economic policy has somehow slipped into a kind of straitjacket along the pattern of prevailing conventional wisdom. Nonetheless, some big dangers remain, primarily through insufficient attention paid to structural adjustment and industrial restructuring, as well as to the effects of the brutal drop of output – in a worsening international economic climate – against a backdrop of left-oriented party politics. In my opinion, most of Central and Eastern Europe is economically at the mercy of regional and continental dynamics. Individual countries may find themselves unable to accomplish desired reforms for at least partly external reasons. Yet, if the population at large loses further patience with reform policies that do not bring sufficiently tangible results, social and political stability will suffer, and scarcely any politician or party will be able to keep things under control. When average citizens lose hope, extremism (whether right or left) gains ground. Extremism already exists in Romania, and it can be found in neighbouring countries, as well as in Western Europe. This must be watched closely.

Political parties, other civic organisations, the mass media, and business elites (through control of various media) are now very active in public policy debate in Romania. However, what is impressive is how the trade unions have learned to flex their muscles and make their voices heard, frequently by joining forces. They strike, participate in open public discussion, negotiate with government, and make policy suggestions. They have the power to bring the economy to a standstill.

However, there is still too much noise and confusion in public policy debate.[25] If it is to remain a vital 'infant industry', it needs special protection so that it can genuinely serve the public interest.

Missing or obscured issues in public policy debate

Instead of conclusion, I prefer to list several issues that, I think, are being neglected or played down in public debate and that deserve more attention.

The temptation to dichotomise society. By this I mean the tendency to view all issues and phenomena through partisan lenses – 'democrats versus antidemocrats (neo-Communists)'. On these terms one could interpret Romania's election results of September 1992 as rejecting democracy by a simple majority of the people, which is clearly nonsensical.

Structural rigidities. The former centrally planned economies are structurally extremely rigid; they can be seen as pathological market economies. This means that stabilisation policy can lead to brutal drops in output. How can recovery be achieved rapidly and efficiently when institutional construction or restructuring is slow, and critical human resources are lacking?

External conditions. I recall M. Mussa, director of the IMF Research Department, once asking: Can we imagine what would happen if the United States were all of sudden to lose half its markets? We, in the transformational economies of Central and Eastern Europe, are now in a precisely analogous position. Our domestic problems (costs) are compounded by collapsing former markets in the eastern countries, as well as by increasingly protectionistic EU policies and a global recession. National strategies of *sauve qui peut* and 'shun thy neighbour' are shortsighted, especially in view of international economic policies and developments. It appears that the lessons of the 'beggar thy neighbour' style of the 1920s and 1930s have fallen from policymakers' memories.

Market mystique. The state remains the big owner. It does not make sense to adopt a complete hands-off policy for government, which leaves no one accountable for the conduct of public enterprises. For example, Romania's Law

15, 'Restructuring of State Economic Units', devolved power by creating confusion over the ownership of assets of enterprises – thus encouraging collusion and the avoidance of management contracts. In addition, structural adjustments need state intervention, for the 'unleashing of market forces' will not accomplish the job alone. I share the pervasive doubts about industrial policy, especially in the present economic climate of uncertainty and obfuscation. But it should be valued as a 'damage control' device, which can allow breathing room to cope with the fuzziness surrounding property rights and mitigate the costs of restructuring and resource reallocation.

The West. Western democracies have a strategic stake in the future of post-communist societies, and they need to become involved in them as *stakeholders*, not merely shareholders. Life after the Cold War is no less complicated and presents many new unknowns. It is troubling to see Western countries caught up in their own difficulties and losing sight of global dynamics. There seems to be a worldwide leadership crisis.

Notes

*   Paper presented at the Conference 'Extending Public Policy Debate in Emerging Democracies', Bellagio, February 1993; it was also published in the volume edited by Craufurd D. Goodwin and Michael Nacht: 'Beyond Government', Boulder, Westview Press, 1995, pp. 227-247.

1   Theorists of public choice and those acquainted with the intricacies of democratic governments and the reasons why their performance deviates from expectations will no doubt find my description very idealistic. But I use it as a measuring rod for judging public policy in nondemocratic societies.

2   Two further issues must be raised in this respect: What realm of action is left for public authority? Moreover, how are decisions to be reached? The first question relates to the provision of public goods in society, and to regulations concerning the economy. The second involves the entire policymaking edifice and prevailing patterns in the conduct of public policy. How much room should there be for discretionary use of power? How important are rules? The old debate 'discretion versus rules' in the conduct of monetary policy has wider applications that exceed the criteria of narrowly defined policy performance. It goes to the heart of governance in a democratic society.

3   See Brus 1972 (the English edition). This was followed by O. Sik's book in Czechoslovakia (1967); one may also mention Liberman's article in Pravda, 9 September 1962 (see Liberman 1972). Many reform-minded economists believed at that time that market socialism was feasible. Br. Horvath, then the leading economist in Yugoslavia, held similar opinions in his influential work on the

planned economy (1964).

4   The School of Planning and Statistics in Warsaw harboured many leading economists.

5   What I have in mind here is their intellectual status, the quality of their journals, and their scientific output and participation at international gatherings.

6   A good example of this 'gentleness' is the new career of Miklos Nemeth, the last communist premier of Hungary: he is currently vice president of the European Bank for Reconstruction and Development (EBRD) in London. Imagine a former Romanian communist premier vying for such a position!

7   Overall, of course, because ideology heavily encumbered the social sciences in the 'Soviet bloc', particularly economists were forced into an intellectual dependency on scientific developments in the Western world.

8   K. Dyba, minister of the economy in the Czech Republic in the early 90s, who was a very young advocate of reform in the late 1960s, confided to me (at a conference in Munich in 1990) his great and lasting sadness over this lost generation.

9   Mathematical economists were not necessarily the most innovative. The journal EKO, based in Novosibirsk (and headed by A. Agabengyian), produced remarkable pieces of analysis over many years. The well-known sociologist Tatyana Zaslavskaya was a frequent contributor.

10   Translations of a number of important works in economics appeared during that five-year thaw, including Romanian editions of Keynes's General Theory (1970), Allen's *Mathematical Analysis* (1971), and Lancaster's *Mathematical Economics* (1978). A freezing wind followed afterward.

11   This was the monthly *Probleme Economice* (Economic Problems), which had just published a lengthy debate on the country's economic strategy. Among the contributors were I. Lemnij, V. Pilat, T. Schatteles, who never wavered in their advocacy of reform.

12   A. Iancu's books (1972, 1974, etc.) were of exceptional value as quasitextbooks on microeconomics and the theory of economic growth. His work continued the endeavours of Schatteles, who had left the country. (Pilat had stayed on, but worked in comparative obscurity.)

13   Sometimes things got into print through sheer accident, against all odds. So it happened in 1984, when together with Pilat, I wrote a study on the crisis of socialist economies, arguing in favour of structural reforms. C. Bogdan, a former Romanian ambassador in Washington DC saw a draft copy and encouraged N. Fotino, editor-in-chief at *Revue Roumaine d'Etudes Internationales*, to publish it, which he succeeded more than surprisingly. The whole business did not attract much attention, I suppose, because that journal was intended mainly for foreign readership and had a very low circulation within Romania itself. Nonetheless, the Warsaw correspondent of the *Washington Post* came to interview us. As usual, I was not available ('out of town'); Pilat met him in the company of 'escorts'.

14   Including I. Lemnij, V. Pilat, A. Iancu, and C. Munteanu, the latter better known

for his interests in the epistemology of economics.

15   An interesting and related paradox is that though *intended* central control was on the rise, *actual* central control over the economy was increasingly remote from its targets. This gap made contributions of its own to the widening economic chaos and inefficiency.

16   The natural rate of adjustment of society can be defined as an imagined optimal speed of change that maximises the society's preference (welfare) function.

17   Thus it is that Austrian economists are among the few who still speak of 'the third way' *(der dritte Weg)*. Many in Central and Eastern Europe quip that it 'leads only into the Third World'.

18   It is naive to imagine that only the former nomenclature opposes market reforms. Large segments of industrial workers, who fear unemployment and rising prices, view reforms very fearfully. And, ironically, there are former members of the nomenclature who desire the reforms, since they are prepared to thrive in a market environment, where they can turn political and invisible economic capital into visible economic assets.

19   Apart from personal sentiment or rationale, voting behaviour is also influenced by public rhetoric. The strong showing of leftist parties at the polls in Albania, Lithuania, and Romania in 1992 – in the 'laggard' countries in general – is an ominous trend.

20   In contrast, for example, with agents' 'bounded rationality' (Simon 1958).

21   See Taylor's (1991) interesting insights on this from the viewpoint of 'structuralist macroeconomics'.

22   By this, I mean the ordinary citizens who bore the brunt under Communism, the underdogs who made up the majority of the population. After all, the collapse did not make everybody happy.

23   Here again I have indulged in a rather idealistic phase. I am of course quite aware that established democracies seem also disenchanted with the practices, or malpractices, of some of their public officials. That is in part what I meant when I said there is a global *malaise* in the sphere of public policy. In all fairness, though, I think it may be said that those democracies enjoy various traditions of open popular complaint about government, an ethos that functions in a recognised 'watchdog', checks-and-balances role – something the post-communist countries have still to gain.

24   Former Premier Stolojan also signed this statement.

25   There are several reasons for this noise and confusion. One is that, even supposedly knowledgeable persons, quickly reach the limits of their ability to offer sound advice. Another is the obvious shortage of domestic analytical expertise in social sciences, especially economics. Those who possess such skills, mostly foreign experts, are not intimately acquainted with the Romanian situation; native experts, by contrast, often have not had the opportunity to master analytical tools. Political figures also contribute to the problem when they adopt public stances, in response to perceived immediate interests, that in fact

contradict their avowed philosophies – for example, when right-wingers propound populist economic reforms. Such tactics can further muddy the waters in public debate, rather than clarifying anything. Which brings us back to the question I posed early on: what is the *quality* of public debate under the circumstances, that is, taking into account the legacy of communist rule? The 'external' debate, among Western social scientists and politicians, can also be very confusing to newcomers to democracy, who desperately want clear-cut responses, a patch of solid ground to tread. Some of the external debate is genuinely focused on the problems posed by the dramatic new situation in Central and Eastern Europe, with the desire to alleviate them. However, it is also true that old (and sometimes unrelated) disputes have been transported to this new field of action, without much concern for how they may impede consensus.

References

Though I have supplied only English titles, all works published in Bucharest are in Romanian.

Allen, R.G.D. (1971), 'Mathematical Analysis for Economists' (Romanian translation), Editura Stiintifica, Bucharest.

Arrow, J.K. (1974), 'The Limits of Organisation', Norton, New York.

Brus, W. (1972), 'The Market in a Socialist Economy', Routledge & Kegan Paul, London, first published in Polish, 1962.

Galbraith, J.K. (1992), 'The Contended Establishment', Houghton Mifflin, New York.

Hankiss, E. (1988), 'The Second Society', *Occasional Paper*, no. 16, Woodrow Wilson Center, Washington.

Horvath, B. (1964), 'Towards a Theory of Planned Economy', Institute of Economic Research, Belgrade.

Iancu, A. (1972), 'Maximal Economic Efficiency', Editura Politica, Bucharest.

Iancu, A. (1974), 'Economic Growth Theory', Editura Academiei, Bucharest.

Keynes, J.M. (1970), 'The General Theory of Employment, Interest and Money' (Romanian translation), Editura Stiintifica, Bucharest.

Kornai, J. (1959), 'Overcentralisation in Economic Administration', Oxford University Press, London, first published in Hungarian, 1957.

Kornai, J. (1980), 'Economics of Shortage', North-Holland, Amsterdam.

Lancaster, K. (1973), 'Mathematical Economics' (Romanian translation), Editura Stiintifica, Bucharest.

Liberman, E. (1962),'The Plan, Profit and Bonuses', first published in Russian, Pravda, 9 September 1962, English edition in *Socialist Economics*, edited by A. Nove and D. M. Nuti, 309-18, Penguin Books, London, 1972.

Mises, L. (1949), 'The Logic of Human Action', Yale University Press, New Haven.

Nikolov, I. (1974) 'Economy & Cybernetics', Editura Politica, Bucharest.

Olson, M. (1982), 'The Rise and Decline of Nations', Yale University Press, New Haven.

Pilat, V. and Daianu, D. (1984), 'The Crisis of Socialist Economies', *Revue Roumanie d'Etudes internationales* 3:245-61.

Schatteles, T. (1969), 'Econometric Models', Editura Stiintifica, Bucharest.

Schatteles, T. (1972), 'Econometric Forecasting', Editura Politica, Bucharest.

Sik, O. (1967), 'Planning the Market under Socialism', PASP, New York and Prague.

Simon, H. (1959), 'Theories of Decision-making in Economics and Behavioural Sciences', *American Economic Review* 49, no. 3, 253-83.

Taylor, L. (1992), 'The Post-socialist Transition from a Development Economics Point of View', MIT, August 1991, manuscript.

Tismaneanu, V. (1990), 'Understanding National Stalinism: A Comparative Approach to the History of Romanian Communism', *Occasional Paper* no. 25, Woodrow Wilson Center, Washington.

4 Finance in Romania's Quest for Modernisation - the interwar period and the present[*]

What is the relevance of the *past* – namely, of the inter-war period – for the transforming (post-communist) economies of Central and Eastern Europe, in general, and for Romania, in particular. There are at least two explanations for trying to answer such a question. One is the *exceptionalism* of the process of post-communist transformation in human history, which makes most of Eastern European economists – in an almost inescapable way – 'intellectual opportunists'. By the latter expression is meant the overwhelming and compelling intellectual appeal of contemporary events, which guide and almost program our research agenda.[1] The second reason is the teaching role of history. For, on one hand, the flow of historical events and their analytical interpretation lie at the roots of the growth of our hard core theoretical and policy-oriented knowledge. On the other hand, history has an influence on the flow of current events in the sense of what development theorists name *path-dependency*; where the latter refers to the burden of the past, and in the case of Central and Eastern Europe, to the legacy of its backwardness, which goes deeply into history. Consequently, apart from specifics of the period under scrutiny, this chapter tries to capture commonalties and discontinuities along the secular quest for modernisation in Romania. It tries also to suggest some of what may lie ahead in the light of the author's perceptions and, unavoidably, of his intellectual biases.

The focus herein is on the role of finance, particularly of banks, as an engine for modernisation, for catching-up with the West. From this perspective it is easy to see the extraordinary handicap the transforming economies are facing in this respect. Because of the long communist interregnum they start, basically, from scratch. Paradoxically, for them, what should have come under the terminological umbrella of institutional modernisation, appears – bearing in mind what has been left in the memory of society – as grand *institutional (societal) innovation*; a change that is more profound than what Trygvee Haavelmo had in mind when he highlighted the importance of institutional change in modern society.[2] Among the related issues which are dealt with underneath are: the congenital institutional fragility of the banking and financial system and of the economy, in general – which is due to backwardness; the nature of banks as institutions asked for and shaped by the dynamics of reality (well beyond the aims of institutional designers); the impact of shocks (of the international environment) and the weak response on the part of policymaking; peculiarities of stabilisation policies; the role of foreign capital (foreign banks) and its relationship with the domestic capital; and last, but not least, the 'war of ideas' as a source of either accelerating progress, or of inducing policy mistakes.

The burden of the past[3]

The last sentence of a leading student of the history of Eastern Europe, at a conference in Sofia, several years ago, sounded like: 'If a lesson is to be learned from the functioning of the region's inter-war capital markets, it would more likely be what to avoid rather than what to emulate' (Alice Teichova, 1992, p. 17). I share much of what prompted this message. Nonetheless, a related question can be posed. It can be that farsighted and innovative individuals (or groups) can shape events and institutions under certain circumstances – that they can be effective *constructivists,* as Fr. von Hayek would have said. But is not there also always, at work, the powerful and impersonal *power of structure*[4] – seen as the very product of history – that bears considerably on the evolution of large socio-economic aggregates? This evolution appears, therefore, to be bent according to a logic of motion embedded in and emerged out of the flow of previous history.

An important inference is that, inexorably, there is much in the dynamic of reality which is outside what political and institutional would-be wizards assume to be able to design and control. And here one encounters a haunting and daunting challenge for the official designers of transformation policy: how to construct (or reconstruct) institutions, seen also as rules (norms) which enjoy social acceptability (D. North, 1980); how to undertake 'societal reengineering'[5] when so much depends on structure. Otherwise put, how to escape the grip of history when there is such a unique case (window of opportunity) of societal reconstruction – which should, hopefully, usher in economic miracles. By the latter is meant something else than what we – Eastern Europeans – got used to understanding by the possibly misleading sintagma of 'recovering normalcy'.

The power of structure connotes the *burden of the past*. On one hand, it affects the way the institutional constructs function in a – as in our case – relatively less developed society; and, on the other hand, it affects the very choice of institutional devices, should decision-makers (both at macro- and micro- levels) be cognisant of what better fits the environment. For example, the current debate on universal vs. narrow banks (in the transforming economies) loses much of its relevance to the extent the reality of unfettered social and economic forces determines the pace and the quality of institutional change and imposes its own solutions.

More significant than the new formal institutional constructs is their *functioning*. Here the burden of the past, the legacy of backwardness, makes its presence heavily felt. For institutions cannot but reflect society and its overall level of development. For instance, since the second half of the past century, numerous prestigious Romanian intellectuals have recurrently decried the structural syndrome of 'form without substance' in all spheres of social and economic life. It should be acknowledged though, that this feeling of disenchantment was only partially warranted to the extent the role-model provided by western institutions could not have been replicated locally but very imperfectly, and not fully in tune with what would have been required in order to uplift entire social bodies.[6] It is noteworthy that this feeling of puzzlement vis-à-vis the difficulties of the post-communist societies to accommodate (absorb) change, is pervasive among intellectuals nowadays as well; and it leads to frustrations similar to those encountered by our grand- and great-grandfathers, if not even bigger due to the ardent desire to join the European Union.

The current quest for catching-up with the West – as post-communist transformation – therefore, has to be judged in the larger period of the secular quest for modernisation, and of the potential for society to learn. An astute observer of the region remarked once: 'Eastern Europe was in some sense economically backward long before it was absorbed into the broader Western world market. This backwardness has roots in the very distant past...' (Daniel Chirot, 1992, p. 3). Likewise, Ivan Berend pointed out that 'What is missing in most of these analyses is a deeper understanding of long-term historical trends in East-Central Europe' (1994, p. 110).[7]

It may turn out that, due to the *new information age* and the high degree of literacy in the European post-communist societies, an upward shift in their long-term learning curve may occur, a phenomenon which may facilitate transformation. Moreover, the gravitational power of Western Europe is very likely to have a positive impact in this respect as well. Yet, I would still submit that ignoring the legacy of backwardness is counterproductive for understanding and assessing the real dynamics of change in the region.

One needs to mention that the desire to close the economic gap against the West has long since fuelled intense doctrinal debates and has influenced economic policy.

The clash of ideas (doctrines) and its impact on policy

During the inter-war period one can detect two intricately intertwined tracks in the realm of economic thinking and of the policy of modernisation, with significant reverberations on the role of finance as an agent of societal change: a sui generis *structuralism*, which provided a vision, a set of basic presuppositions (J. Schumpeter, 1955, p. 42); and the attitude vis-à-vis state intervention in the economy (interventionism vs. *laissez-faire*).

Structuralism directed attention to *structure*, to the structural deformities and constraints afflicting an underdeveloped economy. What catches the eye is the emphasis put on the characteristics of an agrarian economy with a large rural overpopulation and subject to the vagaries of agricultural production. Two schools of thought confronted each other: the agrarians vs. the industrialists. The first group viewed the solution within the boundaries of agriculture, whereas the second sought the way out of underdevelopment via a drive for industrialisation.

As the main spokesman for the agrarians, V. Madgearu, who was one of the most prestigious economists of the inter-war Romania and the leading theoretician of the National Peasants Party,[8] questioned the validity of Sombart's scheme for explaining the advance of capitalism in the Eastern part of Europe; to this end he stressed the so-called 'agricultural question'[9] – on whose adequate tackling, it was argued, depended the progress of the whole economy. In this context, the agrarian economists favoured the setting up of specialised financial institutions, which should cater to the special needs of Romanian agriculture. This was a view that had a certain impact on the development of the financial system.[10] The agrarians supported an 'open doors' policy; a main reason being that Romania was a major exporter of grains. It is noteworthy that later, after his emigration to the United States, N. Georgescu Roegen[11] retook the theme of overpopulated agrarian economies and highlighted an arguably related misuse of neo-classical economics (1960).[12]

'The Agricultural question' has been revived after 1989, for the reform of property rights indicates that it alone is insufficient in order to turn to good account the huge potential of Romanian agriculture. Besides, one needs to consider the impact of agriculture on the conduct of monetary policy in a primitive financial environment. For instance, during 1990-1996, most of the refinancing needs of the banking system pertained to agriculture, since one of the worst debt portfolios was held by Banca Agricola (the Agricultural Bank). This compounds a situation already complicated should one think that Eastern Europe – Romania included – possesses large industrial facilities,[13] of which many are at the origin of the bad debts held by the banking sector.

In a different vein, industrialists emphasised the need to develop industry in order to change *structure* – as a means to do away with the legacy of backwardness. To this end, finance was asked to play a special role and banks were seen as carriers of the seeds of modernisation. Under the prodding of state policy, or as the sheer consequence of being in the whirls of the psychological boom following the unification of the country in 1918, banks either maintained, or acquired large equity shares of industrial companies.

It should be mentioned in this context the crucial role played by the Central Bank, the National Bank of Romania – which supported the drive for industrial development ever since it was created in 1880.[14] A family stood staunchly behind this drive: the Bratianus, who were the brains and the soul of the Liberal Party. The Bratianus had a lot of say in the policy formulation of the National Bank.[15] Likewise, they controlled Banca Romaneasca, which was the largest commercial bank in Romania[16] at that time and the most capable to compete with the large foreign banks operating in the country. When thinking about the role of this family[17] in the political and economic history of Romania I am tempted to make a comparison – however stretched it may be – with the role played by Dr. Hermann Abs, the former Chairman of Deutsche Bank, in the reconstruction of Germany after the second world war, or by the Wallenbergs in Sweden.

Industrialists promoted a vigorous industrial policy under the slogan 'Through Ourselves'. They emphasised the need for the strengthening of the Romanian entrepreneurial class and pushed for the creation of strong Romanian banks, which would back the drive for industrialisation.

Banks' involvement in the economy as large equity-holders was not unaccompanied by risks. Thus, in the early twenties, due especially to poor lending, the mushrooming banking industry witnessed a logical sequence of boom and bust. The plight of banks was much accentuated by the consequences of the Great Depression, and by capital flight, in particular. After 1934, a period of intense consolidation followed and banks embarked on a policy of partial divestiture from industry, aimed at improving the quality of their assets. Additionally, the National Bank introduced very strict regulations aimed at preventing banks from indulging in reckless lending behaviour.

Protectionism was very lively as a doctrine[18] and was given a further boost after the Great Depression, when the major economic powers of Europe started to fend off their markets to exports from the less developed countries.[19] Protectionism was closely intertwined with the idea of state intervention in the economy.

Interventionism vs. *laissez-faire*

What is noteworthy about that period is that the Liberal Party – which governed the country most of those years – and its main theoreticians were adamantly in favour of an activist public (state) policy which should foster industrial development. This policy thrust was reinforced by the Great Depression. M. Manoilescu's theoretical work[20] was not, therefore, an intellectual curiosity; it reflected an evolving collective train of thought which had direct operational (policy) consequences.[21] One could argue that that stance was a response to the protectionistic tendencies of Romania's main trading partners, of the continental powers mostly, tendencies which were grossly amplified after the Great Depression. Moreover, Keynesian-type ideas were spreading throughout Europe in those times, and their influence on policy may have been likely increased by the clouding skies announcing a new European military confrontation. However, while having sense, such arguments are oblivious to the long tradition, among the Liberals, of the views advocating a quasi-state industrial strategy.

I point out the stance of the Liberals of 'old vintage' since it contrasts markedly with the prevailing views among the Liberals of 'new vintage' (who appeared since 1990). Certainly, the peculiarities of post-communist transformation does explain much of this contrast; the ideological winds which have been blowing throughout the world during the eighties[22] have explanatory power as well, but the existence of the contrast can give plenty of food for thought notwithstanding.

An example of interventionism (regulation), which is in stark contrast with the current policy regime in Romania – as in the other post-communist countries – is the commercial policy enacted after the Great Depression.

Having in the background the desire to maintain the stability of the national currency under circumstances of a relative scarcity of foreign exchange,[23] that policy meant a very strict regulation of foreign trade via licences. What may sound strange to our ears is that the National Bank was the institution empowered to implement commercial policy. This implementation, surely plagued by a lot of 'rent-seeking' and inefficiencies, facilitated the functioning of the regime of foreign exchange surrender. I mention this since one of the most important reasons which prompted Romanian authorities to resort to a foreign exchange regime of full retention rights in the spring of 1992, was the very liberal trade regime which came into being in the aftermath of the explosion of December 1989. This motivation was strengthened by a policy credibility problem, which was evinced clearly by massive capital flight.

Banks as an engine of development

There are several issues which can help us judge the financial system and compare the inter-war period with the first years of post-communist transformation: the need for capital; the need for adequate financial institutions (banks) which should channel capital to most profitable use; and the links between banks and the real economy.

After the end of the First World War, Romania's shortage of capital was augmented by the needs of reconstruction (including the monetary unification) and of industrial development within a unified territory, and by the consequences of the rural reform. The economy was, apparently, 'underbanked' both in quantitative and qualitative terms;[24] this state of affairs was certainly accentuated by the kind of operations the major foreign banks were engaged in. Thus, according to *Enciclopedia Romana*, foreign banks were substantially less interested in providing investment credit,[25] though their contribution to the institutional modernisation of Romania was widely acknowledged. Stimulated by the euphoric climate of peacetime, banks indulged in a binge of expansion both numerically[26] and regarding lending and acquisition of equity stakes in industrial companies. The National Bank was involved into this frenzy by its readiness to cover large budget deficits and to refinance commercial banks.

The competition among banks for deposits became ferocious and their lending rates skyrocketed in spite of a discount rate of the National Bank which hovered around 6% during the 1920s. This level of the discount rate was totally ineffectual in arresting the tremendous rise in lending rates (which rose in the range of 20% for the prime clients of banks in the late twenties), since the same National Bank was restraining severely the flow of credit in the economy in order to revalue the national currency. It is understood that the very high lending rates were detrimental to investment in production and, very probably, encouraged *adverse selection*. The crunch came together with the Depression and the resulting consolidation of banks was accompanied by the setting up of specialised financial institutions.

Those years give the image of an intense learning experience for both banks and policymakers. It was mentioned that policymakers reacted vigorously to the effects of the decade of almost 'free banking' and of the Great Depression by imposing strong regulatory measures on the banking industry; this happened within the framework of a radical change of the policy regime – which meant a significantly heavier reliance on controls.

The massive capital flight triggered by the crash of several leading Western banks and the domino effect on Romanian banks[27] caused misgivings about the usefulness, under any circumstances, of foreign capital. An increasingly influential line of reasoning cautioned policymakers against too much reliance on short-term (portfolio) capital inflows, and stressed the need to increase domestic savings which should finance investment in production.[28] Domestic savings were seen as essential for fostering growth during a period of increasing uncertainty in the international environment. The way I read the events of that period suggest that, because of the bitter experience of the Great Depression, scepticism vis-à-vis the working of capital markets (including the Stock Exchange) was, too, on the rise.

Translated into the current debate over which system is better for corporate governance, the tendencies initiated by the effects of the Great Depression seem to provide conflicting signals. Anyhow, the answer to this dilemma became irrelevant because of the war and, afterwards, because of the advent of the all-encompassing command system.

Which type of banks - the current debate

A major paradox and challenge facing post-communist economies is the assumed status and functioning of banks as agents of change. Apart from *institutional construction* change means, essentially, the restructuring of economies characterised by huge misallocation of resources – as a legacy of the command system. It is beyond contention that restructuring is a prerequisite for durable stabilisation in these economies bearing in mind the existing massive cross-subsidisation and entrenched behavioural patterns and routines of enterprises. A crucial question therefore emerges: should and can banks be in the forefront of change, in the sense of providing the thrust and the technical back up for restructuring?

The immediate answer would be affirmative since the financial system is presumed to be the main vehicle for resource reallocation in a market environment. Because capital markets are very much in their infancy and non-bank financial institutions are so crude (or non-existent), banks would get a high profile in a compelling fashion.[29] A sceptical answer would, however, pay attention to the inherent primitiveness and fragility of the banking sector and would question the realism of vesting so much of a role (allocative function) in it.[30] One could talk about an enhanced 'financial instability hypothesis' (H. Minsky, 1977) as applicable to the dynamics of post-communist (transforming) economies. Moreover, the mass privatisation programmes can be brought into the picture as an argument. For, via a 'Big-Bang' approach to the creation of capital markets, they would seem to favour the Anglo-Saxon model of corporate governance.

The narrow vs. universal banks debate pertinently mirrors this concern. This theoretical debate is still in vogue and may present more operational relevance for Russia and other former Soviet republics. For Central and Eastern Europe its significance as institutional design has been much diminished under the flow of real events,[31] although the banking crises of recent years in the region seem to vindicate those who expressed misgivings about vesting too much in banks.

The real functioning of banks is clearly shaped more by the dynamics of the environment than by the intentions of policymakers. In this context, it can be submitted that the less attuned to a market environment the economy is, the more ineffective the would-be 'universal' banks are and the more inefficient resource allocation is.

The experience of post-communist Romania supports the last statement. The Romanian banking system is confronted with a shortage of human skills, with a retardedness of institutional reform and the lack of a 'banking culture', with the common problems of segmentation, concentration and an antiquated payments system. It faces also the extraordinary pressure exerted by the magnitude of required resource reallocation, which is amply illustrated by the steady reproduction of bad debts (and, implicitly, of much of the old resource allocation) and by the structural phenomenon of inter-enterprise arrears.[32]

However, banks learn and improve their skills. It seems to me that what banks do now is, comparatively, less related to the skills of their staff than to what was defined as the *power of structure* and government policy. Therefore, on the one hand banks need to pursue their liberation of the malign grip of *structure* and of non-banking constraints; on the other hand, because of their high fragility as financial institutions and the high risks they pose to the functioning of the entire system (the systemic risk), they need to be under the tight rein of prudential regulations and supervision.

Apart from the extraordinary pressure exerted by *structure*, if one assumes that skills can improve quite significantly and twinning with foreign banks can compensate (and complement) local resources, the *fuzziness* of the environment turns out to be a difficulty that is comparatively harder to overcome. As the experience of foreign banks operating in the area shows, even they can perform surprisingly poorly in a post-command economy. *Fuzziness* and uncertainty explain why banks show a very low propensity to provide long-term credit, a phenomenon enhanced by low domestic savings. All this indicates the need for steady and substantial foreign capital inflows – committed to the restructuring of the economy.

Current banking reform in Romania

To provide a pertinent analogy to what is happening in this industry in the transforming economies the answer would be: an all-encompassing *systemic financial innovation* which is undertaken via a 'Big Bang' approach. As financial innovations, all over the world, mean increased uncertainty and volatility, inferences are not hard to make.

The new rules of the game, the lack of proper skills, and of professional routines introduce an almost congenital institutional fragility in the banking entities in the making. This initial seed of weakness reinforces the train of thought of those who argued in favour of limiting the attributes of banks for a while. This statement is even more valid for those countries, which, like Romania, evince a very poor history of partial reforms under communism. From another perspective, it can be claimed that too many restraints hinder banks in their quest for learning and impede financial intermediation. In any case, actual dynamics can make the policy choice highly irrelevant to the extent policy design is overtaken by events and universal banking gets the upperhand, which was the case in Romania as well. Automatically, two questions arise: what is and what is not avoidable, as poor banking activity, under the circumstances; and, how should the banking industry be shaped (regulated) in order to minimise errors and losses – if one accepts policy design in this field?

Whatever is the attempted answer bank supervision gets a very high profile in this respect. It is no wonder therefore that more severe prudential regulations (than the usual BIS rules) are advocated for the post-communist economies.

The issue of institutional change acquires a special dimension bearing in mind the role institutions play in economic life. Institutions determine ultimately economic performance. Institutions, understood also as socially accepted rules and procedures, determine the quality of economic policy and of its choices as well. However, institutions cannot be created by 'hocus pocus economics'. Particularly in the case of post-communist economies, one can detect the tension between constructivism and organicism in fostering institutional change. Nonetheless, institutional change from above is inescapable in such an economy, in which the central bank and the policymakers, in general, have to be very 'entrepreneurial' in constructing the two-tiered banking system and in designing the financial system. This twofold mission is complicated by the very fact that the implied metamorphosis regards the central bank as well, and that it does not take place in a socially and politically insulated environment.

Romania's experience shows how the development of the banking sector has been hampered by the scarcity of institutional ingredients which fit a market environment, by the limited stock of knowledge (human capital), by a poor business culture, by inadequate structures of corporate governance, a misuse of policy instruments, and by political intrusion. These factors explain the noisy failure of two banks,[33] the inadequacy of the supervision function exerted by the National Bank, and the latter's recurrent lapse into inflationary refinancing of the banking system.

I wish to emphasise the issue of central bank *autonomy* in a post-command economy setting. It is my contention that the actual status and performance of the central bank depends, to a large extent, on the intensity of pressure represented by resource misallocation in the economy, and the institutional inadequacy and fragility of the evolving environment. The magnitude of required resource reallocation can put a very constraining boundary to the real autonomy of a central bank and to the aim of pursuing a sustainable low inflation rate[34] – especially if the lack of domestic capital markets, large and growing budget deficits (including the quasi-fiscal deficits), low savings ratios and meagre capital inflows are considered. In addition, unless there is a proper embeddedness of monetary policy within the overall policy-mix the *time inconsistency problem* is magnified.

Another inference is connected with the institutional texture of checks and balances, which is still at an early stage in its formation, and with the fact that one policy tool's effectiveness depends, essentially, on the accompanying support of the other components of the policy-mix; in this respect a possible overburdening of monetary policy should be mentioned. This is why one of the major complaints vis-à-vis policymaking in Romania in the last few years refers to its lack of coherence and consistency. The relative neglect of trade-offs (for example, economic growth vs. external balance) and of the role of privatisation for bringing about capital inflows (and enhancing, thereby, restructuring) is a main feature of the economic policy of recent years.

Therefore, it appears that a relevant topic for debate goes much beyond the legal status of the central bank; it regards its *policy embeddedness* (and the latter's *social embeddedness*), the expertise of and the professional empathy among key decision-makers, as well as the probability for the persistence of good measures over time. For as many would agree it is this persistence that matters for building up reputation and credibility, and not measures that cannot be sustained.

The central bank needs to do more than simply be responsive to the need to inform and practice transparency. In our context, the central bank has to try to 'educate' its partners and social interlocutors on major policy trade-offs and the dangers of relaxing anti-inflationary brakes. It is telling, in this respect, how time-consuming it was to convince people (including key decision-makers) of the need to attain positive real interest rates in order to subdue very high inflation. The educational exercise – which may sound presumptions to some – is essential bearing in mind the inexistence of a relevant history or of a sound track record.

In Romania, the formulation of the policy-mix, by overlooking the issue of structural change (restructuring), maintained tremendous pressure on the National Bank to continue subsidising indirectly (via cheap credits to commercial banks) the losses of agriculture and other unprofitable activities. Thus, the refinancing of banks from the National Bank was almost the equivalent of the monetary base at the end of 1996, and for most of the period covered (1990-1996) this ratio oscillated between 0.7 and 1. This fact is also a proof of the inadequate sort of remonetization of the economy in recent years, namely by injecting base money following the rise in money velocity and not by an increase of the net foreign assets of the banking system.

The Romanian experience is a glaring example of the importance of structural reforms, of reducing the structural distortions of the economy for durable macroeconomic stabilisation. Unless financial discipline (hard budget constraints) is (are) imposed, the pressure on the central bank and on the banking sector in general, becomes a constant feature of the way the system functions, which also proliferates into wide-ranging rent-seeking (demand for cheap credit). Here one sees the combination of the pressure exerted by those who cannot pay at the new relative prices with that of those who do not wish to pay for 'it pays not to pay' (the moral hazard issue). Another lesson of this experience is the link between privatisation, capital inflows, and restructuring. With the benefit of hindsight it can be asserted that the magnitude of required resource reallocation assigns a special role to foreign capital in helping reallocate resources and in imposing financial discipline in the system.

How can banks be liberated when the *power of structure* is so intense and, apparently, so overwhelming? Here policymakers need to move forward on several tracks including: the speeding up of privatisation and the inducement of foreign capital, the determination to deal resolutely with big loss-making enterprises, the stimulation of competition in banking industry, and the strengthening of bank supervision. A lot depends also on prudence and wisdom in economic policy, which have been largely missing in 1996 when populism affected the thrust of policy and critical policy trade-offs were blatantly overlooked.

Moving conjointly along the tracks mentioned above is a must taking into account the *financial fragility* and *vulnerability* of the banking industry in a transforming economy, which will be increasingly subjected to the impact of globalisation.

The role of structure

By distinguishing between the structure of the economy and the structure of the banking industry I would highlight a paradoxical outcome of the mutual captivity between banks and big domestic enterprises in the largely non-contestable markets of Romanian banking; it is the fact that many banks have been capable of extracting handsome monopoly rents (via big spreads) although their actual state as ongoing concerns (taking into account the health of their clients) remains very fragile, or even deteriorates.[35]

Elsewhere it was argued that the legacy of resource misallocation engenders tremendous *strain* in the system (Daianu, 1994). At the dramatically changed relative prices and should financial discipline be strictly imposed, many enterprises (the inefficient ones) would have to be out of the economic circuit; they may try to survive by reducing X-inefficiency but, in the end, should potential efficiency gains be evenly distributed (ubiquitous), they would have to bow out. To put it in short, the array of structurally inefficient enterprises forms a silent 'conspiracy' against change; they represent entrenched personal stakes, which oppose restructuring for obvious reasons. Together with other factors (including insufficient policy credibility) the lack of capacity to pay triggers a chain reaction of inter-enterprise debt, of arrears which can be seen as *temporary quasi-inside money*. Arrears undermine the effectiveness of monetary policy and reduce the relevance of low official budget deficits – since quasi-fiscal deficits are large. It should be said that quasi-fiscal deficits have been looming ominously over economic policy in Romania in the years of transformation.

Where policy is inconsistent, privatisation is slow, and foreign capital is non-significant, high *strain* persists; it undermines macroeconomic stabilisation and preserves the *flow problem* of the banking industry. Here a dangerous vicious circle can be at work between macroeconomic policy and the state of the banking system. Thus, unless there is deep restructuring of the economy, both tightening and expansionary policies can be ambivalent as to their impact on banks; expansions can be accompanied by poor lending and unsustainable trade imbalances (as it happened in the second half of 1995 and in 1996), whereas high real interest rates can damage the payment capacity of banks and enterprises and unleash mounting pressure for forgiveness.

The banks, which have substantial exposure to big loss-making companies, have a very hard time in improving their balance sheets. This is, for example, the situation of the Agricultural Bank, which is extremely overexposed to a whole sector, agriculture. In fact, agriculture exemplifies a major structural weakness of the Romanian economy. In spite of its tremendous potential (the size of arable soil) and the change of property rights (privatisation of 80% of the land), the situation of this sector is shabby; there is much inefficiency owing to unfavourable domestic terms of trade, capped procurement prices for agricultural products (cereals) until recently, the size of plots, and the poor endowment with technical implements. A large part of the active population (ca. 28%) works in agriculture and its share in GDP is about 25%. The large and intermittent financing needs of agriculture, and the way these needs have been covered until now have constantly crippled monetary policy. The National Bank has been systematically under pressure to lend to the Agricultural Bank at preferential rates, which means that base money was injected in the system concomitantly with providing implicit subsidies. This 'rule of the game' either fuels high inflation (as during 1990-1993), or can be managed, for a while, in a period of increasing money demand (as during 1994-1995); but, in the latter case, it cannot last long since money velocity would start rising again, as it was conspicuously shown by the events of 1996.

The structural weakness mentioned above creates a major challenge for economic policy in terms of macrostabilisation. The problem, here, is twofold: there is need to devise a new institutional mechanism for financing agriculture; and there is need for coping with the 'crowding-out effect' were agriculture to maintain a certain share of financing out of a limited pool of resources. Clearly, the renunciation at administered procurement prices would improve the terms of trade for agriculture and its prospects (with a corresponding reduction of requested subsidies); the Agricultural Bank would, presumably, more than welcome such a development.

A mirror image of inadequate structure, of resource misallocation, is the evolution of refinancing of banks by the National Bank in the last couple of years. The declared goal of raising the share of auction in refinancing directed credits became overwhelming in 1996. The directed credits not only involved subsidised lending, but reduced the scope of manoeuvre for monetary policy and slowed down the development of policy instruments – such as open market operations; it also treated differently banks, however dissimilar their situation was.

It can be asserted that banks have been perpetuating a pattern of resource allocation which goes against the professed and alleged mission of banks in restructuring. Although capital markets are very much in their infancy banks are quite remote from what could be expected from presumed active players in the process of restructuring.

If the fight against inflation does not abate, the level of positive real interest rates would continue to be quite high in the absence of substantial restructuring and of the reduction of the fuzziness of the environment. This state of affairs can be quite detrimental to long-term investments and would skew the composition of foreign capital inflows in favour of portfolio capital. It would also damage the longer-term prospects for banks since, as I have already emphasised, high spreads do not help their clients and may intensify the phenomenon of *adverse selection*.

More on the role of the Central Bank

Is there a common feature between the inter-war period and the first years of post-communist transformation, as far as the activity of the National Bank is concerned? One answer regards its role as an *institutional builder*. In both periods, the National Bank emerges as a large-scale designer.

On the one hand, this is not surprising when seen against the backwardness of the country. The vision and the drive of the people at the helm of policymaking made the National Bank the main pillar of the modernisation policy during the inter-war period; this hypostasis reinforced only a pre-war (pre-1914) policy commitment. On the other hand, one cannot help being amazed at the diversity of the tasks which the National Bank was asked to take over directly, or of the needs it was asked to be responsive to. The range of tasks went from a designed development of the financial system, to the extensive support of industry,[36] and – after the Great Depression – the management of commercial policy. One can, surely, question the wisdom behind placing so much weight on the National Bank and, thereby, running the risk of diverting its attention from its main task: that of defending the value and stability of the national currency. In fact, the policymakers of those times were conscious of this risk, and they constantly tried to relieve the National Bank of the 'borrowed' tasks[37] simultaneously with the evolving institutional framework of the financial system. At the same time, however, the difficulties facing the country aborted such attempts largely – particularly after 1934.

It seems that the main factor which impeded the normal streamlining of the tasks of the National Bank was the sequence of major and lasting shocks which rocked the national economy: the war financing, the needs of post-war reconstruction, the Great Depression, the needs of rearmament in the anticipation of a new war.

Similarly today, the National Bank is engaged in a tremendous drive for building the financial system. It is obvious that the current endeavour is of much more scope and depth than what happened in the inter-war period. Likewise, the inherited huge misallocation of resources has put the economy under a tremendous *strain*, which as a lasting and very burdensome pressure complicates very much the conduct of monetary policy and undermines the effectiveness of stabilisation measures – especially if the lack of capital markets, budget deficits, low domestic savings rates and meagre capital inflows are taken into account.

The creation of sound money and the stability of the financial system are closely interrelated tasks, which affect the functioning of commercial banks. I wish to stress the issue of the soundness of the banking system, since its importance for the stability of macroeconomic policy is frequently underestimated.

Unless the central bank can create and maintain a momentum of policy steadiness, its interventions are unlikely to mitigate the feeling of overall uncertainty and volatility. Although stop and go measures can hardly be avoided under the circumstances, large policy fluctuations are detrimental to economy; they entail large income transfers among economic sectors and groups of population, and unnerve expectations instead of stabilising them. Think only about the dynamic of inflation in recent years: from about 200% and 295% in 1992 and 1993, respectively, to ca. 62% in 1994, 28% in 1995, and 57% in 1996.[38] This dynamic was accompanied by dramatic shifts in interest rates – from highly negative, during 1990-1993, to highly positive levels in 1994, when a major macroeconomic policy breakthrough occurred.

Large policy fluctuations can easily lead to a *boom and bust* evolution of the economy. The economic dynamics in post-communist Romania show the difficulty the National Bank has had in setting a corridor of policy steadiness and its reactive stance most of the time. The strong reignition of inflation in 1996, together with menacingly growing current account imbalances are the result of blunders of macroeconomic policy and reflect its subjugation to political interests in an election year.

Closely linked with the thrust and consistency of policy is the issue of *rules versus discretion* in policy implementation. Apart from the incompleteness of the task of rule design (such as the inadequate rules for controlling hard currency denominated credits[39]), policy implementation has relied extensively on policy reversals (as in the realm of reserve requirements), which did not help nurture the relationship with commercial banks.

The incomplete regulatory framework has also been a source of policy fuzziness and indecision to the extent inaction is motivated by the lack of explicit regulations. For example, the delay in dealing with the ailing banks Credit Bank and Dacia Felix was motivated by the unsatisfactory legal framework (the non-existence of a scheme for depositors' insurance), although law has both a spirit and an adjustable body of regulations. Interestingly enough, the National Exchange and Securities Commission advanced a similar argument in defending its attitude (inaction) with respect to a mutual fund crisis.

Policy inconsistency and fluctuations deter banks from extending their time horizons and from undertaking longer-term investments; they raise risk premia, which further affects the real economy. Actually, this should worry us since the inability to bring down inflation durably predicates an environment which is not conducive to sustainable growth. Moreover, brutal exchange rate depreciation, which is likely to follow inconsistent macroeconomic policies,[40] can be a nuisance to companies that are not export-oriented but rely heavily on external borrowing.

Coping with the international environment

Several issues can dominate the discussion over the role of finance in an open economy when focusing on the impact of the international environment: the relative level of economic development as a determinant of the need for foreign capital; the mechanism of interaction with the international environment; the size of domestic disequilibria; and the dynamics of the international environment.

Let us take the Romanian economy during the inter-war period. Its level of development and insufficient domestic savings asked for substantial capital inflows. The Gold Exchange Standard[41] provided the functional channel for free interaction between the domestic economy and the international environment. It can be argued that this mechanism lent a deflationary bias to the conduct of monetary policy, which was supposed to be targeted on the exchange rate. The bias became obvious when the National Bank embarked upon a revaluation policy in 1925.[42] But this kind of interaction – which implied free capital movements – was put under doubt by the massive capital flight experienced by Romania during the Great Depression. After 1934, a new policy relying on foreign exchange and trade controls was enacted.

The capital flight came as a very severe blow since it occurred soon after Romania initiated its stabilisation program in 1929[43] – a programme, which relied on considerable foreign loans. Some questioned the timing and the preparation of the programme,[44] whereas others criticised the level chosen for the exchange rate. What is certain, however, is that the time proximity of the Great Depression had a decisive impact on the expected outcome of the programme.

What looms here as a policy issue is the *vulnerability* of the economy, which depends heavily on the nature of capital movements as well. *Vulnerability* is very much an issue for a post-command economy. The size of disequilibria and the ensuing *strain*, against the background of the scarcity of *organisational capital* and of domestic resources for investment (restructuring), pose a daunting dilemma for policymakers. On one hand, they need to mold an environment which should be attractive to foreign capital. On the other hand, under certain circumstances, large movements of portfolio capital can be very destabilising. One should not forget that this capital is short-term focused and extremely volatile. Therefore, the likelihood for this capital to be oversensitive in a post-command transforming environment is very high – for such an environment is perceived by investors as highly uncertain and risky.

Concluding remarks

The inter-war period and recent history can reveal interesting lessons for the designers of financial systems in post-communist economies. One such lesson is that *natura non-facit saltus,* that making institutions function properly takes time, that there is a grip of *structure* – the latter seen as a product of history – which is hard to get rid of.

One can detect a 'clash of visions' regarding the model of financial system, which would arguably, fit better the conditions of the European post-communist countries. In the end, the evolution of the financial systems will depend on real dynamics, which are not necessarily under the control of those who design the transformation policy.

It would be naive to assume that the institutions of post-communist economies can and will perform according to the standards of the role model; they need time to grow in order to perform. Realism is needed not only in order to work out proper design policies, but, also, in order to make balanced judgements as to 'what are good performances', and on 'what is to be done next'.

Another lesson is that institutions in the making are fragile, and that their *fragility* makes the economic system more vulnerable to both internal and external shocks. This institutional fragility magnifies the *strain* in the system caused by the resource misallocation inherited from the command economy.

All over the world financial innovation subjects economies to pressure, the advanced market economies as well.[45] In the case of post-communist countries, the creation of financial systems is the equivalent of a *large scale financial innovation.* Consequently, here one deals with a relatively high degree of systemic risk unless the monetary authorities enforce proper regulations and prudential rules.

There is much need for foreign capital as a powerful force for modernisation and restructuring. The more this capital will be committed long-term, the easier it will be for the post-communist economies to weather the inherent risks of a market environment. Policymakers in the post-communist countries constantly need to remind themselves that the competition for capital is intensified by the effects of the redistribution of economic power in the world.

The time constraint is increasingly biting for the Romanian economy and society. Although time cannot be compressed at will, one has to deal with what years of footdragging and indecisiveness complicated as a burdensome legacy; this legacy is indicated by the intensity of the foreign exchange constraint and the, still, high softness of budget constraints in the economy.

Overall, economic policy needs vision, commitment and resoluteness, an understanding of critical trade-offs, steadiness, and consistency. Economic policy has to get rid of a bad *path dependency* and populist temptations (as happened in 1995 and 1996) must be avoided; this would also help deal with the *time inconsistency problem*.

The independence (autonomy) of the National Bank has to be strengthened; to this end, the National Bank has to practise a more effective exercise in persuasion.

The structure of the economy has to be tackled firmly and industrial restructuring must be enhanced by privatisation and capital inflows. Substantial capital inflows and deep restructuring of the economy have to take place if real interest rates are to come down significantly. Otherwise, high real interest rates would maintain intense *strain* in the system and would make it prone to macroeconomic instability. High real interest rates would also maintain the fragility of banks, particularly of the domestic ones.[46]

Working out a new institutional mechanism for dealing with the financial needs of agriculture is going to be a very serious task for decision-makers. On one hand, the institutional base of agricultural financing needs to be broadened and, on the other hand, channels have to be devised so that credits reach those who actually need them.

The National Bank has to develop its policy instruments. Secondary markets must develop in order to make the T-bills (now held by banks) liquid, and to attract liquidity from individuals and enterprises. The functioning of secondary markets would make the financing of budget deficits much easier and would relieve banks of their current undesired burden.

Bank supervision needs to be strengthened and the National Bank has to adopt an active stance; it also needs to fend off political intrusion into its activity and that of the banks. In general, the supervision of financial markets has to be strengthened.

Competition in the banking system has to be stimulated and foreign banks have a major role to play to this end. Although competition increases the banks exposure to market risk, it would improve the quality of bank services. Additionally, assuming a significantly quicker pace of restructuring, banks' higher exposure to market risk would be more than counterbalanced by the improved overall functioning of the economy. This effect would improve the financial lot of clients and, thereby, their ability to service liabilities towards banks.

The nature of capital inflows needs to change. Currently, most of them are of an accommodating nature, as a reflection of the pattern of production and consumption in the Romanian economy. Structural reforms are urgently needed in order to put the economy on another *evolution path* and trigger autonomous capital inflows. Privatisation and the creation of proper structures of corporate governance would play a major role to this end.

The increase of the external indebtedness of the country needs to be closely monitored and checked by the National Bank. Although, foreign debt is still small its growth rate has been quite rapid. More worrisome is the use made of the attracted resources against the background of a very severe foreign exchange constraint. This is a further argument for achieving a turnaround in economic policy, which should induce capital inflows toward productive investment, preferably in export-oriented sectors.

Notes

*   A shorter version appeared in Philip L. Cottrell (ed.), 'Rebuilding the Financial System in Central and Eastern Europe, 1918-1994', Scolar Press, Aldershot, 1997, pp. 145-160.

1   Nearly three decades ago, N. Georgescu Roegen remarked that every economist who has won a place in the history of economic thought 'has been intellectually opportunistic in the sense that each has been exclusively preoccupied with the contemporary economic problems of the society in which he happened to live...the economic profession should take pride in being opportunistic in the above sense' (1965, reprinted in 1976, p. 200). In this way he replied to Bridgman, the Nobel laureate for physics, who argued that the major handicap of economics is the characteristic intellectual opportunism of its servants (1950, pp. 303-305).

2   Haavelmo recommends 'a little more of the "engineering approach" in the study of economic systems' (1968, reprinted in 1971, p. 5).

3   The line of reasoning advocated by this section can be found in Daianu (1992) as well.

4   *L'Emprise de la structure* (the grip of structure) is an important concept used by Fr.Perroux (1969), who applies it at the level of national economic entities. This concept is widely used by the students of business schools, who learn about the inertia and entrenched behavioural patterns of large structures – very much in the vein of what M. Granovetter named the 'embeddedness' of economic action (1985, pp. 481-482).

5   After reading Champy and Hammer (1993), I wondered why so many – presumably knowledgeable professionals – do not seem yet to grasp the complexity and the complicated nature of 'reengineering' a society.

6   The overall judgement can become even less harsh should one consider some remarkable instances of institutional modernisation in that period. Thus, due to Professor Joe Tropea from George Washington University, I came across a revealing excerpt regarding the development of accounting as a profession in Romania after the turn of the century: 'accountancy has grown rapidly, reaching great heights in 1921 when a law was passed restricting the practice of accountancy to legally qualified accountants. Romania is the only European country aside from Italy to have restrictive legislation. The law has been successfully applied there for almost ten years (to 1930) and it is hoped that other European nations will pass similar legislation based on Romania's excellent example' (W. L. Green, 1930, p. 68).

7   Similarly instructive, about the origin of the economic 'schism' between the West and the East of Europe, is Z. A. B. Zeman (1991).

8   The National Liberal Party and the National Peasants' Party were the main political formations during the inter-war period.

9   See, especially, the introductory chapter to his main work, 'Evolutia economiei romanesti' (1940).

10   The setting up of *Creditul Rural*, in 1934, is due, largely to this type of advocacy.

11   N. Georgescu-Roegen is world famous for the application of entropy law to economic processes as well.

12   Georgescu-Roegen says: '...an intuitive knowledge of the basic cultural traits of a community is indispensable for laying out the basis of its economic theory' (1960, reprinted in 1976, p. 107). This may explain the difficulties of many western economists in understanding the specifics of post-communist transformation.

13   Jeffrey Sachs talks about an 'overindustrialisation' of the region.

14   On the circumstances surrounding the creation of the National Bank of Romania see C. Kiritescu (1964).

15   The National Bank was only partially state-owned.

16   It may be of interest to mention that Banca Romaneasca, as a bastion of the Liberal Party, reappeared after December 1989. But it has a long way to go in order to regain its former status and glamour.

17   Vintila Bratianu, in particular, who was finance minister during the twenties.

18   The big guru was M. Manoilescu, whose 'Theory of Protectionism' was published in Paris in 1929.

19   It may be incongruous with the current *Zeitgeist* of post-communist economic transformation but the fact is that what historians describe as the best economic years and the biggest industrial advance were registered after 1934 – a period characterised by pronounced state intervention in the economy and protectionism.

20   I do not refer to Manoilescu's espousal (especially during the 1930s) of *corporatism* and *authoritarianism*.

21   C. Murgescu makes a remarkable analysis of the impact of Manoilescu's thinking

and of its intellectual extraction out of a certain social *prise de conscience* concerning modernisation via industrialisation (1987, chapter XIII in particular).

22   Starting with the so-called Thatcher revolution in the UK and the *supply-side economics* in the USA.

23   Due to the above mentioned protectionistic tendencies.

24   P.D.Gusti (ed.) (Chapter: Commercial Banks, p. 571).

25   If in 1919 the number of banks was 486 (including those of the reunited territories), by 1928 the figure jumped to 1122 (P. D. Gusti (ed.), *Enciclopedia Romana*, Chapter: Commercial Banks, p. 565). It should be mentioned that the number of big banks stayed the same.

26   An interesting question could be the following: assuming that the Great Depression could have been avoided, what would have been the, presumably, unavoidable intensity of the retrenchment process in the Romanian banking industry – after the years of reckless lending during the twenties?

27   The run on Romanian banks is clearly indicated by the following figure: they lost almost 43% of their deposits in 1931.

28   See, for example, *Enciclopedia Romaniei* (Chapter: 'Monetary Policy', p. 710).

29   Thus, it is argued that 'the objection that banks do not have the skills to do that right is less compelling than at first sight. The point is not that banks are good at doing this, but that they are likely to be better than anyone is' (S. van Wijnbergen, 1992, p. 14). J. Corbett and C. Mayer (1991) hold a similar view.

30   As J. Rostowski remarked, 'The lack of banking skills thus introduces a fundamental instability into their monetary systems. Until this problem is resolved, macroeconomic stability will remain hard to achieve' (1993, p. 5). A similar opinion is held by R. McKinnon (1991) and D. H. Scott (1993).

31   I. Szekely asserts that 'the model issue thus was in fact not a real issue from the very beginning' (1993, p. 26). Szekely continues: 'On the other hand, it is not an issue any more as the so far introduced legal regulations in each country in the region opted basically for universal banking, following the EC regulations, and the intentions in the remaining countries point to the same direction' (Ibid.).

32   Inter-enterprise arrears, as *temporary quasi-inside money*, reflect the extraordinary *strain* under which post-command economies function (Daianu, 1994).

33   Out of a relatively low number of 30 banks. This shows that prudence in licensing new banks is a necessary but far from sufficient condition for avoiding failures of banks.

34   In the vein of Adam Posen's argument that central banks will take strong anti-inflationary action only when there is a coalition of interests politically capable of protecting it (1993). Whereas in the industrialised democracies that role can be played by the financial sector and the political articulation of social memory (as in Germany), in the post-command economies the picture is altered radically since many banks are captives of a real sector plagued by huge inefficiencies. In these circumstances, the support can come from external actors, such as the

international financial organisations.

35   I would submit that some banks indulge in this situation to the extent they expect an easy bailout from the central bank should they need it.

36   This support was increased after the Great Depression. As it was appropriately remarked, 'after 1933 industrialisation proceeded at a much more rapid tempo and in a somewhat different direction. The private banks after the depression played a less important part in financing industry; the principal initiative was by the National Bank or the state itself, but through state-owned corporations and through the growing importance of the state as consumer of industrial products' (H. L. Roberts, 1953, p. 198).

37   Like the Convention of 1925, which foresaw the termination of the extensive financing by the National Bank of the state budget deficits.

38   Inflation rates are recorded at the end of the year.

39   Hard currency denominated credits fuelled the expansion of domestic demand in 1995 and 1996, worsened trade imbalances, and raised the spectre of heightened exchange rate risk for uncovered borrowers. This clearly affected negatively the portfolios of imprudent banks.

40   I have in mind a properly functioning foreign exchange market, which has not been the case for most of the time under review.

41   In 1931 the National Bank reintroduced the Gold bullion Standard, after large fluctuations (devaluation) in the value of the British pound. Gold was deemed as a more reliable reserve.

42   This policy, which meant a very strict control of credit, led to a high jump in the lending rates of commercial banks which were forced to compete ferociously for deposits; these rates moved in the range of 18-20% for prime borrowers, whereas the discount rate of the National Banks was about 6%.

43   As against other countries, Romania did not resort to the monitoring role of the Financial Committee of the League of Nations. The then finance minister, V. Bratianu, felt that the economic situation of the country allowed a direct negotiation with the creditors: The Banque of France, The Bank of England, and the Federal Reserve Bank of New York. For an interesting analysis of the Romanian stabilisation programme, see R. H. Meyer (1970).

44   V. Madgearu (1940, p. 305). For a different view see V. Slavescu (1932, pp. 336-376).

45   A good example is represented by financial derivatives against the background of increasingly interdependent capital markets.

46   This is because foreign banks cater less to the needs of Romanian companies and are less dependent on the vagaries of the local environment.

References

Berend, I. (1994), 'Annus Mirabilis – Anni Mirabiles?', *Contention*, Winter, no.8, pp. 109-128.

Bridgman, P.W. (1950), 'Reflections of a Physicist', Philosophical Library, New York, quoted by N. Georgescu Roegen.

Chirot, D. (ed.) (1989), 'The Origins of Backwardness in Eastern Europe', University of California Press, Berkeley.

Corbett, J. and Mayer, C. P. (1991), 'Financial Reform in Eastern Europe: Progress with the Wrong Model', *Discussion Paper*, no. 603, CEPR, London.

Daianu, D. (1992), 'Transformation and the Legacy of Backwardness', *Economies et Societes*, No. 44, May, pp. 181-206.

Daianu, D. (1994), 'Inter-enterprise Arrears in a Post-command Economy. Thoughts from a Romanian Perspective', *IMF Working Paper*, 94/54.

Georgescu-Roegen, N. (1960), 'Economic Theory and Agrarian Economics', reprinted in the same author: 'Energy and Economic Myths', Pergamon Press, 1976, New York, pp. 103-146.

Granovetter, M. (1985), 'Economic Action and Social Structure: the Problem of Embeddedness', *American Journal of Sociology*, 19, 3, pp. 481-510.

Green, W. L. (1930), 'History and Survey of Accountancy', Standard Text Press, New York.

Gusti, P.D. (ed.) (1940), 'Enciclopedia Romana', Bucharest.

Haavelmo, Tr. (1968), 'The Scope for Widening the Scope of Economics', reprinted in S. Mitra (ed.), *Dimensions of Macroeconomics*, Random House, New York, 1971.

Hammer, M. and Champy, J. (1993), 'Reengineering the Corporation', Harper, New York.

Kiritescu, C. (1964, 1972), 'Sistemul Banesc al Leului' (The Monetary System of the Leu), Editura Academiei, Bucharest.

Madgearu, V. (1940), 'Evolutia Economiei Romanesti' (The Evolution of the Romanian Economy), Independenta Economica, Bucharest.

Manoilescu, M. (1929), 'Theorie du Protectionnisme et de l'Echange International', Paris.

McKinnon, R. (1991), 'The Order of Economic Liberalisation', John Hopkins University, Baltimore.

Meyer, R.H. (1970), 'Bankers' Diplomacy. Monetary Stabilisation in the Twenties', Columbia University Press, New York.

Minsky, H. (1977), 'A Theory of Systemic Fragility', in E. I. Altman and A. W. Semetz (eds.), *Financial Crises: Institutions and Markets in a Fragile Environment*, John Wiley and Sons, New York.

Murgescu, C. (1987), 'Mersul Ideilor Economice la Romani' (The Evolution of Economic Ideas in Romania), Editura Stiintifica si Enclopedica, Bucharest.

North, D. (1981), 'Structure and Change in Economic History', Norton, New York.

Perroux, Fr. (1969), 'Independance de la Nation', Aubier Montaigne, Paris.

Roberts, H. L. (1951), 'Romania. Political Problems of an Agrarian State', Yale

University Press, New Haven.

Rostowski, J. (1993), 'Creating Stable Monetary Systems in Post-communist Economies', mimeo.

Schumpeter, J. (1955), 'History of Economic Analysis', Allen and Unwin, London.

Scott, D.H. (1992), 'Revising Financial Sector Policy in Transitional Socialist Economies. Will Universal Banks Prove Viable?', *WPS* 1034, The World Bank.

Slavescu, V. (1932), 'Curs de Moneda, Credit si Schimb' (Treatise on Money, Credit and Exchange), Editura Scrisul Romanesc, Craiova.

Szekely, I.P. (1993), 'Economic Transformation and the Reform of the Financial System in Central and Eastern Europe, *Discussion Paper*, no. 816, CEPR, London.

Teichova, A. (1992), 'Interwar Capital Markets in Central and Southeastern Europe', in J. R. Lampe (ed.), *Creating Capital Markets in Eastern Europe*, The Woodrow Wilson Center Press, Washington DC, pp.7-17.

Wijnbergen, S. van (1992), 'Enterprise Reform in Eastern Europe', *Discussion Paper*, no.738, CEPR, London.

Zeman, Z.A.B. (1991), 'The Making and Breaking of Communist Europe', Basil Blackwell, Cambridge.

5 Institutions, *Strain* and the Underground Economy[*]

This chapter attempts to interpret the dynamics of the underground economy in a transforming environment by emphasising the role of institutions in enforcing the *rules* of the game and the phenomenon of *strain*. A main idea is that an underground economy emerges as a means for the system to diffuse its internal *strain*. Thus, an underground economy operates as a homeostatic mechanism which helps the system survive temporarily – as in the case of the command economy – and affects the structure of output according to consumers' preferences, in general. In the same vein the emergence of unofficial activities can be judged in an overregulated system be it market-based.

The first part deals with the command economy and its specific institutions (and rules of the game) as a glaring example of neglect of consumers' preferences and as a system developing endemic shortages. In such a system, very intense *strain* emerges. Since the structural constraint of supply cannot be removed simply by freeing prices a total overhaul of the system is needed; this transformation would allow organised markets to function. The second part focuses on explaining *strain* during system transformation and its impact on the underground economy. In this case, the magnitude of *strain* is related to the dramatic changes in relative prices and the imbalance between exit and entry. Likewise, new institutions in the making (including regulations) and their role in the functioning of the underground sector in a transforming economy are under scrutiny. Still soft rules shape agents' behaviours and explain the resilience and the patterns of unofficial activities. Such is the case of *reputation* seen as an asset, and of the local standards of compliance with the legal framework. The last part tries to apply empirical analysis – a model – to the Romanian economy and to speculate on the dimension of local unofficial activities.

It is worth noticing that the last variant of the empirical analysis supports official data which assess the size of the underground economy in Romania. It can be stated that a major difficulty in applying conventional methodological tools to the case of transforming economies is related to the state (fuzziness) of property rights, i.e. its impact on productivity in the official sector – which traditionally is assumed to be superior to the one evidenced by the unofficial sector.

The structural constraint of supply and *strain*

Command economies, as institutionally arranged entities, are structurally supply-constrained systems, or what Kornai called shortage economies; they evince much *strain* as a manifestation of producers and consumers' efforts to cope with ubiquitous shortages. This *strain* brings about responses of the economy, as an aggregate, which defy planners' intentions and commands. The response of economy, as a living body, to control and command is made up of black markets – on which market-clearing prices operate – and unofficial activities; both these effects represent a homeostatic mechanism of adjustment. Whereas market-clearing prices affect, partly, the level of demand, unofficial activities mitigate the pressure on the supply side. A presentation of the syndrome of the structural constraint of supply is made below.

Strain in a supply-constrained economy

When rational economic calculation is impeded, there is centralised direct co-ordination of the interaction among economic agents and their motivational state is hardly conducive to better performances, the generalised syndrome of soft-budget and the genetically related phenomenon of 'the structural inelasticity of supply'[1] emerge as systemic features of the functioning of the economy. This mode of functioning reveals a *structural constraint of supply*,[2] which distinguishes it fundamentally from that of demand-constrained (market) economies.

The structural constraint of supply reflects itself in a series of tendencies and organically correlated processes, which determine the quantity of friction in the economy and its aggregate (dis)equilibrium.

Firstly, there is the immanent drive that leads to the formation of aggregate excess demand, which makes structural constraint appear in the already emphasised hypostasis of a constraint of resources. Several qualifications are to be made in this respect. Thus, the structural resource constraint does not imply that resources available are *fully* and efficiently used; for each agent (enterprise) the constraint is felt at the level of the least available resources (or of best quality resource), so that a shortage of *mobilisable* resources coexists with a surplus of *non-mobilisable* resources – 'in a supply-constrained economy shortage coexists with slack' (Kornai, 1980, p. 30-36). A second comment regards the level of input stocks considered as normal by the enterprise, which prove to be substantially higher than under the circumstances of a demand-constrained economy. A last qualification is linked with the appearance of an external *demand constraint* in an open economy, which intensifies both shortage and slack.

Secondly, there occurs a gradual decline in the efficacy of factors that can counteract a worsening of 'inefficiency norms' in the economy. This tendency can be looked at and analysed from the standpoint of both allocative and microeconomic efficiency. It has to be stressed that the impressive *cost-overrun* (relative inefficiency) exhibited by supply-constrained economies expresses a relative incapacity to make good use of the resources essential for an economic growth based on technical progress. In Figure 5.1, which tries to depict this incapacity Q denotes the level of output, R(K, L) refers to capital and labour, and (G) indicates the innovational and entrepreneurial potential of society. It can be seen that the same output can be obtained with different outlays of material resources (capital and labour) depending on how the mode of functioning of the economy makes use of the innovation potential and *entrepreneurship* – Q^2 (R_2(K, L), G_1) and Q^2(R_1(K, L),G_2) symbolise the same level of output, but R_2 indicates a higher consumption of capital and labour than R_1.

Thirdly, there are *massive forced substitutions* of intermediate and final goods in production and consumption. This process has deleterious effects on both the efficiency of production and consumers' welfare.

Let us take a closer look at the consumption zone, where a hard-budget constraint is in force. Against the background of aggregate excess demand (repressed inflation) the structural imbalance between the supply of and the demand for commodities triggers the labour supply multiplier as an adjustment mechanism, which can be reinforced by an effort supply adjustment on the part of labour; i.e., when there appears an ever higher discrepancy between the efforts made by consumers to get their goods and the *apparent* real consumption a quantitative and qualitative adjustment of labour supply takes place. This fact can be illustrated by a change of the traditional effective labour supply function as below:

$$\overline{L}^s = L\left(\frac{W}{P}; \frac{M}{P}; L^d\right) \quad \text{where} \quad \frac{\partial \overline{L}^s}{\partial \frac{W}{P}} > 0$$

turns into,

$$\overline{L}^s = L\,(\frac{W}{P};\frac{M}{P};\ \varphi;\phi), \quad \text{where} \quad \frac{\partial \overline{L}^s}{\partial \dfrac{W}{P}} > 0$$

$$\frac{\partial \overline{L}^s}{\partial \varphi} < 0, \quad \frac{\partial \overline{L}^s}{\partial \phi} < 0$$

the additional notations being (φ) for a variable that denotes 'the searching time' and 'the queuing time',[3] and (ϕ) indicates the utility (welfare) loss caused by forced substitutions in consumption.[4] In order to simplify the equation L^s defines also the actual effort supplied by labour in production.[5] It can be easily inferred that while the traditional effective labour supply function indicates a positive relationship between the evolution of the situation of a complete saturation of consumption needs, which is very unlikely, the influence of an apparent rise in real wages on L^s can be more than counterbalanced by an intensification of the action of φ and ϕ. The modified labour supply function does not include L^d as an argument, since we are dealing with supply-constrained economies – where the shortage of labour is very intense, in spite of a striking underutilisation of labour resources.

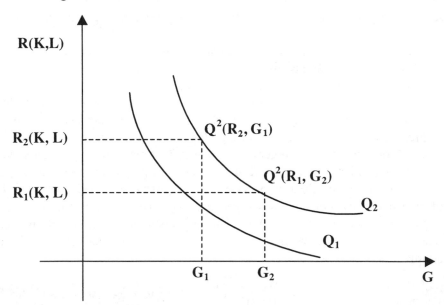

Figure 5.1   Factor combination and efficiency

As emphasised, the structural imbalance between the demand for and the supply of goods and services has a considerable negative effect on the quality (utility) of consumption. To serve the purpose an example is used in which, though – at the ruling fixed prices – the money value of aggregate supply exceeds the money value of aggregate demand, the level of utility of consumption can decrease should the structural imbalance get more acute.

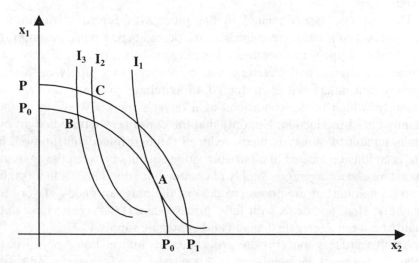

Figure 5.2   Structural disequilibrium and aggregate utility

In Figure 5.2 the level of utility given by the composition of output at $B(I_3)$ is inferior to the one at $A(I_1)$, which would reflect the structure of consumers' preferences. Even after production expands – the production possibility curve moves from P_0P_0 to P_1P_1 – the level of consumption utility at $C(I_2)$ stays further inferior to the one at A, though the money value of output at $C(q_{x1}, q_{x2})$ exceeds the one at $A(q_{x1}, q_{x2})$. At the ruling non-equilibrium prices (p_{x1}, p_{x2}) the following relation holds:

$$p_{x_1} q_{x_1}^c + p_{x_2} q_{x_2}^c > p_{x_1} q_{x_1}^a + p_{x_2} p_{x_2}^a$$

while, when equilibrium prices $(p^*{}_{x1}, p^*{}_{x2})$ are applied the sign of the relation is reversed:

$$p_{x_1}^* q_{x_1}^c + p_{x_2}^* q_{x_2}^c < p_{x_1}^* q_{x_1}^a + p_{x_2}^* q_{x_2}^a$$

Full flexibility of prices would not eliminate the structural constraint of supply in the zone of the economy where budget constraints are hard (consumption). Although the excess demand would tend to disappear – a tendency that can be slowed down or even annulled by the *sucking* performed by the agents (firms) facing soft-budget constraints – the structural inelasticity of supply would persist, so that producer's markets would continue to exist and, thereby, the seller's domination over the consumer would be felt no less strongly.

There is one aspect related to the process of forced substitution in consumption that needs more emphasis. In a demand-constrained economy, the play of relative prices mirrors the comparative values (utilities) of goods and services, the choices and preferences of consumers. In a supply-constrained economy consumers are even forced to purchase products of very low saleability, which in the conditions of a buyer's market would go almost instantly out of production. Not only that the consumers' utility bought by a certain amount of money is much reduced through forced substitution, but there is an illusion created of a possible value equality between the aggregate demand for and the aggregate supply of commodities through an administrative fixing (upholding) of the prices (values) of the range of goods of very low saleability. Here one deals with false prices (values) that create false value equality between aggregate demand and aggregate supply.

Another process concerns the generation of 'informational noise' in the system. Two aspects are significant in this respect. Firstly, a command system entails higher informational and transaction costs, which leads to a comparatively lower level of overall efficiency. Secondly, this system induces economic agents to 'process' (distort) information so that their performances look better to their superiors. It can be said that, in a chronic shortage environment, some externalities like trust, loyalty and truth-telling are in short supply as well.[6] Since 'They are goods... they have real, practical, economic value; they increase the efficiency of the system, enable you to produce more goods or more of whatever values you hold in high esteem' (K. Arrow, 1974, p. 23), their relative scarcity brings about an increase of the amount of friction (disequilibrium) in the economy as well as a reduction of its transparency, which makes peculiarly more difficult the evaluation of its aggregate performance.

Chronic shortage breeds the underground economy

The underground economy[7] is bred by chronic shortage. The luring force of the underground economy is given by the possibility to make a profit. As shown by S. Wellisz and R. Findlay, despite the handicap represented by 'factor acquisition constraints' – which reduce the technical efficiency of the 'parallel economy' – the possibility to make a profit exists provided the cost of production is lower than the (unofficial) market clearing price, and as long as turnover taxes do not apply to the product (1986, p. 650). They also point out that this condition holds *a fortiori* 'if we assume that the "second economy" is either the sole producer, or the more efficient producer in the technical sense, of consumer goods and services' (Ibid.).

The underground sector ambiguously affects the functioning of the economy, its aggregate performance. To the extent that higher gains can be obtained by undertaking unofficial activities (within the underground economy) resources will be diverted from the official economy; labour supply and working effort (both quantitatively and qualitatively) are reduced and various material inputs find their way to the underground economy, thereby causing a decrease of the output and efficiency of the official sphere of the national economy. On the other hand, activation by the 'parallel economy' of some non-mobilisable slack and of household resources can have a dampening influence on the decrease of output and of efficiency. The activation of parts of the non-mobilisable slack, especially, has a 'lubricating effect' on the official economy, which helps its functioning.

The underground economy, though assumedly less efficient than the official economy, has a positive impact on consumers' welfare by supplying goods in very high demand. Therefore, on one side the parallel sphere has an ambiguous effect on the overall productive efficiency while, on the other side it makes possible a rise in the efficiency of consumption (consumers' utility). This *self-regulatory device*[8] of the economy – understood as a living system made up of producing agents, who ask for what is due to them and act accordingly – points to a clear 'second best' situation.

Evaluating aggregate disequilibrium (the potential underground economy)

Aggregate equilibrium, conceptualised in a strict sense, means the equality between aggregate demand and aggregate supply. In this narrow sense then, the existence of permanent aggregate excess demand points to the existence of aggregate disequilibrium, under the specific circumstances when the structural resource constraint operates in the presence of a large amount of non-mobilisable slack; which also means that one of the conditions of aggregation under quantity rationing is not valid, since shortages and slacks coexist on the same market. The important thing to underline here is that the unutilised resources are 'frozen' (non-mobilisable in the short run), which makes the procedure of measuring net demand irrelevant by netting out surpluses and deficits of resources. For as J. Winiecki stresses 'there are no forces in the economy to produce equilibrium by reallocating excess supply to reduce excess demand' (1986, p. 201).

In a normative sense, in which it is construed as the loss of potential welfare for society[9] – or what can be called the 'aggregate performance deficit' – aggregate disequilibrium considers the degree of overall inefficiency of the system and the forced substitutions in consumption. It can be expressed as:

$$\Delta U = U^* - \overline{U} = U(Q(L^*)) - U(Q(L^*, \overline{e}), \phi)$$

where L^* includes the labour supply diverted to (by) the underground economy, e (the overall degree of inefficiency) regards the non-mobilisable slack and the quantitative and qualitative underutilisation of labour as well,[10] and ϕ regards forced substitutions in consumption. The expression above suggests, too, that in a command economy – viewed as a supply-constrained economy – the regulatory function of state authorities mainly affects the degree of shortage through the composition of output decided by central-planners and the programmed rate of economic growth (the investment rate);[11] it also influences the amount of labour force diverted to (by) the underground economy. This 'shortage regulation' by means of policymaking is supplemented by the activities of the underground economy, which acts as a self-regulatory device of the economy. Partial rearrangements within the institutional framework can influence (e), but its degree remains essentially determined by the systemic features of the economy.

'The UE in transition'; *strain*, the softness of rules (institutions) and *reputation as an asset*

With the benefit of hindsight, one can emphasise some main features of transition, which bear on the dynamics of the underground economy. These features are, inter alia: domestic supply adjusts slowly in spite of the stimulus provided by market incentives; shortages disappear quickly because of price liberalisation and imports; enacted rules are *soft*, which enhances the propensity of agents to ignore them, such as tax-evasion; and prohibited domains still exist.

Strain in a transforming economy

Intense *strain* does not disappear in a transforming economy. Its origin can be traced to two main sources: the fragility of institutions in the making and the magnitude of the required reallocation of resources (Diana, 1994, 1997). In what follows the focus is put on the second factor, namely, the ability of the system to react rapidly – via resource reallocation – to the new set of market-clearing prices.

Once prices are freed and start to operate at quasi-equilibrium (market-clearing) levels, the hidden inefficiency comes into the open and a massive resource reallocation would have to take place – from low onto high productivity areas. More precisely, the issue refers to the possible and probable intensity of resource reallocation in view of constraints like: the balance between exit and entry in the labour market, the size of the budget deficit and the means for its non-inflationary financing, social and political stability, etc.

Let us take the simplified case of a two-commodity economy. The initial production combination, (a_1, b_1), still reflects the central planners' preferences. Were consumers sovereign, the production combination would be (a_2, b_2). Should resource reallocation take place without friction – with no imbalance between exit and entry – there would be no *strain* in the system; the shift from (a_1, b_1) to (a_2, b_2) would proceed along the production possibilities curve.

In a real economy, friction is unavoidable. Furthermore, the imbalance between *exit* and *entry* can be considerable, and it can cause the production combination to be substantially inside the production possibilities curve – the fall of the output of (a) is not accompanied by a corresponding growth of the output of (b). This means a significant reduction of aggregate utility if the expansion of the unofficial economy does not offset it. Over time the production combination would have to come ever closer to (a_2, b_2).

The magnitude of the required resource reallocation can be illustrated by the ratio:

$$(1) \quad J = \frac{p_a^* \left| q_a^* - q_a \right| + p_b^* \left| q_b^* - q_b \right|}{p_a^* q_a^* + p_b^* q_b^*}$$

where (p^*) and (q^*) refer to equilibrium values, whereas (p) and (q) correspond to the current (distorted) resource allocation. J can be viewed as a measure of aggregate disequilibrium (in the system) as against the vector of equilibrium prices and quantities.[3] The general form of (1) is:

(2) $$J = \frac{\sum p_i^* \left| q_i^* - q_i \right|}{p_i^* q_i^*}$$

The size of the above ratio measures the *strain* within the system and reflects the magnitude of aggregate disequilibrium.

It can be assumed that the possible level of unemployment is related to the degree of *strain* in the system: the higher is *strain* (resource misallocation) the higher is the unemployment that would be brought about by the required resource reallocation. This is a major reason which lies behind the temptation to tolerate high inflation rates as a way to diffuse the tension within a system. Phenomena which can alleviate *strain* are: inter-enterprise arrears, monopoly pricing, explicit and implicit subsidies, spillover effects, the elimination of negative value-added activities, *learning*, and last, but not least, the efficiency reserves of producers (who operate within their production possibilities curves themselves).

The more numerous are those who would lose their jobs because of the needed resource reallocation the more intense would be the opposition against it, against restructuring. Paradoxically, but not surprisingly, *strain* and, relatedly, the acutely felt need to reduce it, can induce a logic of motion in the system that is liable to perpetuate flaws of the old mode of resource allocation.

For the open economy, there are several notable differences as compared to the closed economy model. The main one is the existence of comparative advantages, which, supposedly, orient – together with consumers' preferences – the allocation of resources. A second major difference is that domestic prices reflect the open character of the economy – the international exchanges. Since the economy is assumed a price-taker, world relative prices shape domestic relative prices. Another difference is that significant demand- and supply-related external shocks can lead to a compression (be it temporary) of the production possibilities curve. This compression amplifies both the reallocation problem and the related distributional struggle issue.

There are three phenomena specific to the open economy, which can alleviate the *strain* in the system. One is the possibility to export *strain*. This possibility is more likely to be present the more active and sizeable is an economy in the world space, and the more it operates as a price-maker. Another phenomenon refers to how comparative advantages have to be viewed in a world of global sourcing and procurement. By this is meant the non-negligible chances for activities which, presumably, would have to be discarded, to be saved by their getting into a worldwide network of interconnected operations under the aegis of global companies. Finally, possible positive external shocks need to be taken into account.

Another way of portraying *strain* is to focus on the scope of the required process of overall income (wage) readjustment, which should fit the new market-clearing prices. Under market equilibrium conditions wages equal the marginal productivity of labour: $w_i = q'(n) = dq(n_i)/dn_i$. For the declining and substantially overstaffed sectors the equilibrium wage is low – even below zero for negative value-added activities. The reverse is the situation for the sectors enjoying comparative advantages, or for which domestic demand is very high.

The modified form of J' that builds on wages is:

$$(3) \quad J' = \frac{\sum n_i \left| w_i^* - w_i \right|}{\sum n_i w_i}$$

where n denotes labour in sector (i), and w_i^* and w_i refer to equilibrium and actual wage, respectively, for the sector (i). $\Sigma n_i = N$, where N refers to all labour resources. For the inefficient, subsidised (explicitly, or implicitly) sectors actual wages exceed the marginal productivity of labour: $w_i > dq_i/dn_i$. The higher is J', i.e., the higher is *strain*, the more fierce would be the distributional struggle.

The difference between equilibrium and actual wages reflects the resource transfer (subsidies) practised by the system; the higher is this difference the stronger will be the forces that oppose change.

For the post-command (transforming) systems, the *distributional struggle*, which is related to the required resource reallocation, appears as a structural origin of *strain* and as a structuralist-type explanation of inflation. It can be submitted that, in the case of post-command economies, the *distributional conflict* gets a dimension which is given by the speed and, particularly, by the scope and magnitude of income redistribution entailed by the required resource reallocation. In many countries the distributional struggle takes place against the background of a pattern of income distribution which reflects a, relatively, stable allocation of resources. Therefore, individuals' expectations are relatively fulfilled. Differently, in the post-command economies a massive resource reallocation is under way, which considerably and brutally affects income distribution. Additionally, many individuals' expectations are profoundly unfulfilled. The frustration caused by unfulfilled expectations is magnified by exogenous shocks, which have led to a compression of production under circumstances when individuals are used to a certain pattern and level of consumption.

Strain is reduced by the underground economy. For example, can one believe that the current actual rate of unemployment in Spain is above 20%, or has one to correct this figure with what is meant by the underground economy? In the same vein can be judged the functioning of this sector in the transforming economies.

From supply-constraints to tax-evasion

It can be submitted that, the more regulated (and taxed) an economy is the more induced agents are to operate in the underground sector. It can be also admitted that there exists an optimal *structure* and *level* of regulation of the economy which maximises societal welfare; clearly, the optimal structure and level of regulation depend on social norms, values and principles which validate what people at large appreciate as being positive and, particularly, negative externalities.

Figure 5.3 tries to illustrate this optimality by dividing the economy into two sectors: the official and unofficial sectors, which, both, consume factors of production (labour and capital). Point A, which signals the optimal composition of the economy, is tangent to the highest welfare curve, W. Both overregulation and underregulation lead to inferior compositions of the economy in terms of societal welfare. Thus, overregulation means an expansion of the underground economy against the background of reduced overall efficiency; in figure 3 the effect of overregulation is indicated by the lower welfare curve, W_1, which goes through point B. Likewise, an underregulated system (as in the case of environmental protection) entails an 'official' expansion of socially pernicious activities, which also reduces societal welfare; point C indicates this lower welfare level, W_2. The shape of the combination curve indicates that both hyperregulation (as in a command system) and the lack of regulation (no rules) can lead to an implosion of the economy.[12]

When regulations (or taxes) rise (when the cost line of regulations moves from I to I_1) there is a shift of the price line in favour of the unofficial sector in the sense of stimulating its expansion – this happens because the goods produced in the official sector become more expensive. Another effect is an increase of the nominal prices of the goods and services in the underground economy – although they become relatively cheaper – which can be only partially mitigated by its expansion (which puts downward pressure on prices in the unofficial economy).

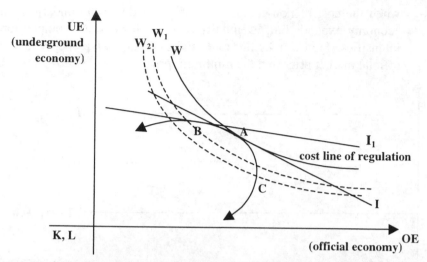

Figure 5.3   Overregulation (taxation) and the distribution of activities between the official and the underground sector

Understanding micro-behaviours

In a simplified way, agents' behaviour can be understood by comparing the benefits and costs of operating in the underground sector. The benefits are: the avoidance of the tax rate (t) and the cost of regulations compliance, (r). The cost is of non-compliance which means *inter alia*, the penalty fee, (c), adjusted by the probability of being caught, (b).

A variable whose size is most critical is the cost of non-compliance, cb. The thesis herein is that when standards of reputation are low in a local environment the cost of non-compliance is diminished, which enhances the functioning of the unofficial sector. To this issue, we come back when the emphasis is put on explaining reputation in a transforming economy.

What would be possible price dynamics in the underground sector? If p is the official market price, the minimum price acceptable in the unofficial sector can be defined as: $p - (t+r) + cb = \min(p)$.

Clearly, the price mentioned above is the minimum for not incurring losses. The equilibrium price in the underground sector depends on the intensity of competition, which further depends on the cost of non-compliance. Thus:

- when (cb) goes up, the underground economy shrinks and vice versa; likewise, the equilibrium price, p^*, rises

- when the cost of non-compliance, cb, goes down the underground economy expands but, eventually p^* goes down since competition intensifies. Figure 5.4. illustrates the operation of p^* between the official market price and the minimum price.

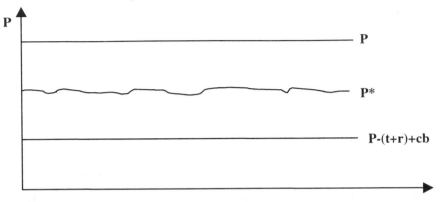

Figure 5.4 p^* between the official market price and the minimum price

It can be submitted that strong competition in the official economy and a rise of the cost of non-compliance, cb, would tend to bring together the values of p, the minimum price, and p^*. As it was emphasised, the cost of non-compliance depends essentially on the entrenched rules of the game in the local environment. To be more specific, the size of (b), which is the probability of being caught, depends on rule enforcement, social norms (D. North), and the local standards of reputation. It can also be assumed that the rules of the game depend on how agents (companies) view their reputation as an asset to be built up. This is why attention is focused next on the issue of reputation.

Reputation as an asset[13]

Why is the choice made for *reputation* bearing in mind that one may have thought about another intangible asset – such as *trust*, for example? It seems that this option can encapsulate conceptually well what is the source of other intangible assets, be they *trust, truth telling*, or *loyalty*. By accumulating *reputation*, individuals and communities increase the amount of all other intangible assets. Likewise, widespread better reputation (in a good sense) necessarily implies less corruption, which is a ubiquitous feature of underdevelopment.

Let us say a few words about possible ways to introduce *reputation* in the economic analysis of development (Daianu, 1996). One has to think about it in both static and dynamic terms. Thus, it should be very appealing to common sense to view higher reputation (and, consequently, trust and loyalty) as a means to reduce X-inefficiency at both micro- and macro- levels, or as an addition to the stock of overall capital. This means that higher stocks of reputation can be captured analytically in two ways: either by increasing the stock of overall capital (capital augmenting) and, therefore, output; or by enhancing efficiency and, concomitantly, output. In the latter case one can easily resort to the concept of transaction costs (Oliver Williamson) and conclude that higher reputation as an average trait of a system reduces transaction and information costs. This would be the static portion of analysis. Diagrammatically, this can be shown by an outward shift of the production possibilities curve, or by coming nearer the frontiers of the PPC when X-inefficiency is reduced.

What about dynamics? In this case, one can make an analogy with the role of human capital build-up, of education, in economic growth. Higher *reputation* has several implications. Firstly, by making agents more efficient this is very likely to raise their propensity to accumulate and invest over time. Secondly, higher reputation raises overall efficiency within the national environment and, thereby, it creates higher rates of return, which further may stimulate saving and investment. Summing up, one can draw an inference: higher reputation, seen as asset accumulation, is liable to make both individual agents and a national environment more efficient and competitive. On one hand, this shifts the production possibilities curve of economy outwards; on the other hand, it raises the growth path of the economy.

Viewing 'reputation' in transforming economies

Intangible goods such as *trust, truth-telling,* and *loyalty* were very scarce commodities in command economies. This legacy cannot be overcome instantaneously in the transforming economies. The explanation for this state of affairs is essentially twofold: institutional change is time-consuming; and society, the structure of property rights, is still too fuzzy in order to shape behaviours clearly and penalise misconducts. One can talk in this respect about a certain *ethos*, a business culture that reflects the quality of institutions; this business culture does not encourage high economic performances and enhances stagnation.

The shortage of ethical behaviour is a facet of the lack of *reputation*. In a normal society, where good rules of behaviour are the norm, reputation is highly valued; reputation can be built up, or destroyed, and this affects the evolution of individuals in society as well as their expected income streams. Normally, an individual who optimises for the long run would be much concerned about reputation and would not undertake actions inimical to it.[14] This type of behaviour is often neglected in transforming economies. There are several explanations in this respect. One, which was already alluded to, is linked with the fuzzy state of property rights. Another explanation can be connected with uncertainty, which reduces the time horizon used by individuals and organisations. These are, certainly, valid arguments. However, what frequently motivates people is the attraction of easy to obtain high gains by speculating legal loopholes and by overlooking the social consequences of their acts.

It should be borne in mind that such behaviour is not 'rara avis', including political life. Usually, a politician should be much concerned about deeds, which can harm reputation. In transforming economies, one can often see politicians' behaviour much focused on the short term, which can hardly be rationalised by the pressure of current events; significantly more seems to be related to an optimisation which involves the public position as a purveyor of *rents*. The public function is conceived as a good business, but not for a long time, and a *big discount is applied to reputation*. One could argue that this type of behaviour fits those who enter politics for extra-political (economic) reasons. On the other hand, since this behaviour is quite pervasive the resultant 'competition' leads to increasingly bigger discounts. In this way society as a whole is a loser and the 'rule of law' becomes a long distance image.[15]

How could biased behaviour in transforming economies be captured at a microlevel? A possible way is to use a utility function, which includes *reputation* as a variable. The analytical exercise, which follows, has a more heuristic than practical relevance and no computational implications are pursued.

The optimising (satisfying) behaviour implies the maximisation of a function U below,

$$(4) \quad \max U = \max \sum_{0}^{T} U_t(R_t...)e^{-at}dt$$

in which (U_t) is the utility stream, (R_t) refers to the stock of reputation at time t, (T) indicates the time horizon used by agents, and (a) is the discount applied to future utility flows. $T < \overline{T}$, where the latter refers to the potential active life of an agent. Obviously, the assumption is that higher reputation (R) implies higher utility:

$\partial U/\partial R > 0$

The dynamic of the stock of *reputation* can be illustrated by the function:

(5) $R_t = R_0 e^{g(t)}$

where (R_0) denotes the initial moment and g(t) is the function expressing the presumed evolution of the stock of reputation. In a normal environment, an agent would be interested in accumulating reputation and maximising her utility function in the long run.

(F) indicates the degree of *fuzziness* (including property rights) in the system. A relationship can be established between (F) and the time horizon used by economic and political agents. It thus makes sense to assume that the higher is (F), *ceteris paribus*, the bigger is the propensity to reduce the time horizon, T. This means that:

(6) $T = T(F)$, when $dT/dF<0$

An interesting aspect can be brought into analysis, which may throw light on and explain why relatively low standards of reputation and high corruption are resilient in many areas of the world. This would also illuminate why people seem to accommodate their habits and condone what one may consider to be unacceptable patterns of behaviour and, presumably, likely to change over time. Thus, it can be submitted that, when it is seen in relative terms, *reputation* depends on local standards of ethics and morality (corruption). This assumption is more realistic when globalisation of economic life, and of universally held standards of business ethics, has less of an impact. Therefore, a revised form of a reputation function takes into account what is perceived as 'normal' by the local environment. Thus,

(7) $R_i = R_i(R_l)$, when $dR_i/dR_l < 0$

The above formulation intends to say that the degree of corruption, or the moral (ethical) laxity in the system regarding the observance of normal (not local) standards of reputation affects the perception of agent (I)'s reputation. A state of affairs can be thought of when the spread of corruption is so wide and the interpretation of laws is so nonuniform that agents become indifferent to *reputation* as an asset.[16] Under such circumstances the growth rate of reputation, r, becomes insignificant, or even negative; it is the case of sacrificing any trace of reputation for the sake of realising exceptionally high material gains in the short run. In this case, the trade-off between *reputation* and other factors, which enter the utility function, does not favour the build up of reputation.

When short-term material gains get the upperhand vis-à-vis the accumulation of reputation one can complicate the optimisation process. Thus, the optimal stock of reputation can be seen as being dependent on the local rules of the game, and the specific 'weight' of the agent. In this case the utility function (6) is revised by making a distinction between reputation, R, as a goal in itself, and M(R) which denotes potential material gains to be made by using the 'rules of the game' and the knowledge of the local environment (inside information). The relationship (1) turns into,

$$(8) \quad \max U = \max \int_0^T U_t(R_t, M(R), ...) e^{-at} dt$$

with $M'(R) > 0$ and $M''(R) < 0$

Under sufficiently constraining conditions of the local 'rules of the games', or by very small incremental gains which induce agents not to care about reputation, a situation can be imagined when higher (R) is not accompanied by higher M(R) – dM/dR<0; it is like a point from which the marginal cost of 'puritanical' behaviour exceeds its marginal benefit – see Figure 5.5. This means that material gains prevail over the accumulation of reputation.

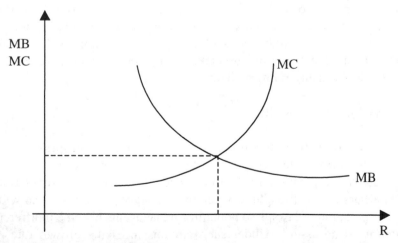

Figure 5.5   Optimal *reputation*

Why is the specific 'weight' of actors mentioned? For there are people, who, through their 'critical mass' (including reputation) can influence the rules of the game and the environment. For such individuals, whose dimension goes beyond the frontiers of the local environment, *reputation* acquires different parameters of definition and possible compromises they may get into have a different nature and other implications. Such individuals may develop the ability to lack 'flexibility' and not be forced to 'howl with the wolves'.[17]

There are cases when highly reputed individuals once taking over public positions, can improve the image of the public entity (the country) they represent. This can be the situation of a minister of finance, or of a governor of a central bank. Obviously, this reasoning can be extrapolated to a whole government. For such circumstances, a collective utility function includes as a variable the reputation of important public servants (ministers).

A few words concerning the discount rate (a): the latter depends also on the degree of uncertainty regarding the evolution of the legal environment. The less clear and more uncertain is this environment, against an ideal framework, the lower is (a).

An aspect needs to be stressed again. The initial drop of the output of tangible goods, which may be quite persistent, can strain social relations and diminish considerably the significance of the substitution relationship – both in consumption and production. Since the new norms are not rooted socially well enough and since a new moral order cannot emerge instantaneously, the role of 'moral models' acquires exceptional importance. Leaders of great charisma and moral probity, with vision and determination, are essential in making the mentioned substitutions operational. *Leadership* as an issue underlines the moral dimension of transformation. Ultimately, however, solid institutions have to come into being in order to make societies perform.

A global model based on the labour supply method

The national economy is considered as having two sectors: a visible (or official) sector and an invisible (or underground) sector. For the visible sector the registered GDP has the following components:

(9) $Yv = A + Sv + Bv$

where Yv is the GDP produced in the visible sector; A – consumption of fixed capital (only in the visible sector); Sv – wages of employees in the visible sector; Bv – profit of entrepreneurs (capitalists) in the visible sector. In the invisible sector the produced GDP will be:

(10) $Ya = Sa + Ba$

where Ya is the GDP produced in the underground sector; Sa – wages of employees in the invisible sector; Ba – profit of entrepreneurs (capitalists) in the invisible sector. In the invisible sector, it is supposed that there is only circulating capital.

Also, the available time fund and the total number of labour force is distributed between two components as follows:

(11) $F = Fv + Fa$

(12) $L = Lv + La$

where F is the total available time fund for work within a calendar year; L – number of total potential working persons; Fv – time used for work in the visible sector per year; Fa – potential available time used by the persons having status of employees in the visible sector for work as a double job in the underground sector; Lv – number of employees working in the visible sector; La – potential number of employees working in underground sector.

The available working time is taken as the average number of hours' value by a calendar year. For instance, the average number of hours worked by a person within a calendar year can be considered.

Now, the GDP created in the two sectors of a national economy is expressed as functions of productivity, which appear as linear functions:

(13) $Yv = Lv \cdot Fv \cdot wv$

(14) $Ya = (La \cdot F + Lv \cdot Fa) \cdot wa$

where wv and wa are the average productivity per person per hour in the visible sector and, respectively, in the invisible sector.

To obtain the total number of hours worked in a year in the underground sector two categories are considered. One includes persons who work full-time in the underground sector (persons having status of non-employees in the visible sector) (La F). The other category regards the persons having the status of employees in the visible sector, but working also in the underground sector during the supplementary work time as a second job (Lv·Fa).

What is important for agents or people is the level of disposable income or available GDP. In the two sectors of the economy the available income or GDP is given by the following relations:

(15) $Ydv = Yv - T = Yv \cdot (1 - t)$

and respectively

(16) $Yda = Ya$

which can be also written under the following forms:

(17) $Ydv = Lv \cdot Fv \cdot wv \cdot (1 - t)$

(18) $Yda = (Lv \cdot Fa + La \cdot F) \cdot wa$

where Ydv, Yda represent the available income in the visible sector and in the invisible sector, respectively; T is the total amount of taxes paid (or of obligatory levying); t - average tax rate relatively to Yv.

Taking into account the structural relations (17) and (18) we can write now the total available income as follows:

(19) $Yd = Lv \cdot Fv \cdot wv \cdot (1 - t) + [Lv \cdot (F - Fv) + (L - Lv) \cdot F] \cdot wa$

or

(20) $Yd = (L - La) \cdot (F - Fa) \cdot wv \cdot (1 - t) + [(L - La) \cdot Fa + La \cdot F] \cdot wa$

The first relation permits us to analyse the impact of the number of persons working in visible sector (Lv) and of their corresponding number of hours worked in this sector (Fv) on the total available income at national level. The second relation concerns the number of persons working in the invisible sector (La) and, respectively, the number of hours worked in the invisible sector by persons having the status of employees in the visible sector (Fa). We remember that in the case of persons actually having the status of non-employees in the visible sector (but having a potential to work by age and disposable free time criteria) it is supposed that they allocate their entire available working time to work in the invisible sector (F). At the same time, the persons actually having the status of employees in the visible sector are forced to divide the same entire disposable working time (F) between the work in the visible sector (Fv) and work in the invisible sector (Fa).

This total available income, greater than the available income in the visible sector, is responsible for some unexplainable macroeconomic non-correlation registered between some 'official' indicators.

What is defined as the following relation gives the yearly national potential GDP:

(21) $P = F \cdot L \cdot wv$

where P is the maximum level of annual GDP.

Since the productivity in the invisible sector is supposed to be lower than productivity in the visible sector it results the following non-equality:

(22) $Yv + Ya < P$

The actual total available income per year is:

(23) $Yd = P \cdot [m + lv \cdot fv \cdot (1 - t - m)]$

where m is the ratio between the productivity in the invisible sector and the productivity in the visible sector (wa / wv); lv – the share of employees in the visible sector in the total number of potential working persons (Lv/L); fv – the share of time used to work in the visible sector in the total available working time within a calendar year (Fv/F). On the other hand, if the entire activity were in the visible sector the maximum level of available GDP would be:

(24) $Yd^* = P \cdot (1 - t)$

Now, it is supposed that people choose the actual situation, that is the actual distribution of the total capacity to work between sectors. This produces an available income greater than or at least equal to that produced by the above hypothetical case. Thence appears the following restriction:

(25) $Yd > Yd^*$

After some technical algebraic operations the following equivalent restrictions are obtained:

(26) $m > 1 - t$

(27) $wa > wv \cdot (1 - t)$

It should be mentioned that the present model, as a simulation model, tries to determine the variance of interval thresholds of the underground sector based on the existing statistical data at macroeconomic level. The absolute values for the total potential number of working persons (L) and for the total number of potential working hours during a calendar year (F) are considered to this end. This could seem exaggerated compared with the real values registered in the case of the visible sector (Lv and Fv).

In the invisible sector, the levels of some indicators – productivity, profit rate – are considered smaller than, presumably, is the case in reality. This is partly because of the leisure component. For instance, the actual available income computed by our simulation model is greater than the level that would be obtained in the case of full-time work in the visible sector ($Yd > Yd^*$). The difference must be considered implicitly including the satisfaction of the leisure comprehension problem.

Now, it is important to evaluate the variation interval of the underground sector dimension. In this way, the share of the invisible sector in the national economy appears as:

(28) $ya (wa) = Ya (wa)/Y (wa)$

where Ya (wa) is given by the relation (31) and Y is the total yearly GDP:

(29) $Y (wa) = Yv + Ya (wa)$

For the productivity in the invisible sector the following extreme values are chosen:

(30) $wa_{min} = (1 - t) \cdot wv$

(31) $wa_{max} = wv$

to which correspond the following extreme values of the share of the invisible sector in the national economy:

(32) $ya_{min} = 1 - \{(lv \cdot fv)/[1 - t \cdot (1 - lv \cdot fv)]$

(33) $ya_{max} = 1 - lv \cdot fv$

Diverse alternatives regarding the average wages and profits in the underground sector relating to the situation registered in the visible sector are analysed within this interval.

In the visible sector, in order to evaluate the average wage and the average rate of profit, the following relations are posited:

(34) $sv = [Sv/(Lv \cdot Fv)] = [Yv - (T + Bv + A)]/(Lv \cdot Fv)$

(35) $bv = [Bv/(T + A + Sv)] = [Yv - (T + Sv + A)]/(T + A + Sv)$

where sv is the average wage per person per hour of work in the visible sector; bv – the average profit rate in the visible sector; Sv – the total amount of yearly salaries in the visible sector; Bv – total amount of yearly profits in the visible sector.

On the other hand, in the invisible sector the corresponding relations are:

(36) $sa = [Sa/(La \cdot F + Lv \cdot Fa)] = (Ya - Ba)/(La \cdot F + Lv \cdot Fa)$

(37) $ba = [Ba/Sa] = (Ya - Sa)/Sa = (wa - sa)/sa$

where sa is the average wage per person per hour of work in the invisible sector; ba – the average profit rate in the invisible sector; Sa – total amount of yearly salaries in the invisible sector; Ba – total amount of yearly profits in the invisible sector.

In the applications, the consumption of fixed capital (A) is replaced by investment. Moreover, the average wage in the invisible sector is comprised between the values 0.5 and 2 relating to the average wage in the visible sector. Here are presented some conclusions from the application of the model to Romania' economy.

For each year of the period 1989-1993, the number of employees in the visible sector (Yv) is from the available official statistical publications. To evaluate the yearly time of work in the visible sector weekend days and vacations diminished the number of days of the year. Then the result was multiplied by the legal time working per day (8 hours) and subsequently by an average coefficient that designates the average utilisation degree of total legal working time.

For the total potential numbers of employees, (L) and the total number of hours per year per person (F) three versions were designated as maximum (I), intermediary (II), and minimum (III). In the maximal version, L includes the employees in the visible sector (Lv), the official unemployed, the school population of age over 15 years, and the retired population of age less than 70 years. The intermediary version, adds to Lv the same number, as in the previous case, divided by two. In the minimal version, it adds to Lv only half of the unemployment number.

In the case of F, the maximal version was obtained by multiplying the calendar year number of days by eight (representing hours of work per day). In order to determine the intermediate value of F, 52 (representing the number of Saturdays per year) was added to the average number of days worked per year by a person in the visible sector (Fv). Moreover, half of the number of days used for vacations in the visible sector was added. Then, the result was multiplied by eight. In the minimal version the same number of days worked in the visible sector was chosen, and was multiplied by eight hours per day.

In the case of each variant (I, II, and III) two threshold values – minimum and maximum – of the underground economy were calculated by using formula (32) and (33). In addition, within this interval, a sub-interval was separated. This sub-interval covers, on the one hand, the intersection between the curve of salary in the underground sector and the value of salary in the official sector (inferior limit). On the other hand, it covers the intersection between the curve of profit rate in the underground sector and the value of profit rate in the official sector (superior limit). This sub-interval represents the most probable values of the underground economy share. A synthetic presentation of simulation results is in the following table. Figure 5.6 shows the dynamics of the underground economy in Romania in the period 1989-1993, according to the three variants.

Variant I, which is derived from the theoretical limits of the productive national potential, suggests the maximal values to which the underground sector could extend. This variant is useful for long run forecasts. Variant III produces estimates that are near the figures commonly used to gauge the size of the underground sector in the Romanian economy. One of the most difficult problems remains the separation between the preference of people to use their available time for work in the underground economy and the available time for leisure. In any case, variant I can produce a satisfactory estimate of the total available time (including both components).

Concluding remarks

The underground sector can be seen as a homeostatic device (mechanism) of an economy under *strain*. The latter, as a phenomenon, is caused either by inappropriate rules of the game – as in the command economy – or by dramatic changes in the parameters defining the functioning of an environment. *Strain* is also enhanced by institutional fragility.

Whereas the underground sector is an outstanding structural feature of the command system (which, as a hyperregulated entity, ignores consumers' and producers' preferences) it continues to exist in market economies as well. For, as this chapter argues, no real economy can escape *strain*. The issue, therefore, is the intensity of *strain* and its malign effects on the economy. An implication would be the need for policymaking to consider *strain* at both micro- and macro-levels. Reengineering enterprises and reforming economies can be scrutinised from this perspective.

Subjected to dramatic changes in relative prices, transforming economies – as market economies in the making – are under much *strain*. It is no surprise that transforming economies show substantial underground sectors. As it is our contention, the exceptional magnitude of the required resource reallocation and the fragility of the new institutions (the *softness* of formal rules) stimulate the 'development' of hidden sectors.

The globalisation of trade and financial markets, as well as the 'new information age' speed up the process of required change and add additional pressures on the transforming economies.

The formal model and the empirical analysis applied herein to the Romanian economy helps gauging the potential size of the underground sector. One should say that, a factor which affects some of the assumptions contained in the model is the fuzziness of property rights. This factor may change the presumed relative productivities in the two sectors of the economy without, however, modifying the main results of the analysis.

Variant I:

$Year_t :=$	$Iyamin_t :=$	$Iyamax_t :=$	$Iya\_sa_t :=$	$Iya\_ba_t :=$
1989	35.8	51.3	44.6	50.8
1990	48.4	59.4	54.5	56.8
1991	57.2	67.3	62.8	65.8
1992	62.3	71.3	67.5	69.4
1993	64.8	71.8	68.7	70.4

Variant II:

$Year_t :=$	$IIyamin_t :=$	$IIyamax_t :=$	$IIya\_sa_t :=$	$IIya\_ba_t :=$
1989	24.8	38.4	32.3	37.9
1990	33.3	43.7	38.9	41.2
1991	41.7	52.4	47.6	50.6
1992	47.4	57.6	53.0	55.4
1993	49.6	57.7	54.0	56.0

Variant III:

$Year_t :=$	$IIIyamin_t :=$	$IIIyamax_t :=$	$IIIya\_sa_t :=$	$IIIya\_ba_t :=$
1989	6.0	10.8	8.5	10.6
1990	10.7	15.8	13.3	14.4
1991	20.1	28.0	24.3	26.6
1992	26.7	35.4	31.3	33.4
1993	27.6	34.6	31.3	33.1

Figure 5.6(a)   Dynamics of the underground economy

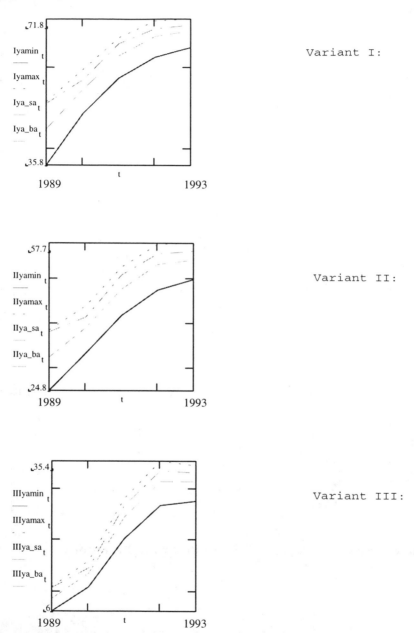

Figure 5.6(b)   Dynamics of the underground economy

Notes

* This is a revised version of a paper co-authored with Lucian Albu for the conference 'The Importance of the Underground Economy in Economic Transition', Zagreb, 15-17 May 1997. Many thanks to Ivo Bicanic, Roger Bowles, Krassen Stanchev, John Tedstrom, and particularly Edgar Feige, for their useful comments. It was published also as The William Davidson Institute Working Paper, no. 98/1997.

1 R. Hoch (1981) and, particularly, K.A. Soos (1985) are among those who pointed out that the *structural inelasticity of supply*, as a phenomenon, does not derive solely from chronic shortage.

2 Besides J. Kornai etc. outstanding contributions to the analytical investigation of *chronic shortage* were made by M. Kalecki, J. Goldmann and K. Kouba, Fr. Holzman, H. Levine, V. V. Novozhilov etc. The research was also enriched by the studies of T. Bauer, J Beksiak, J. Burkett, S. Gomulka, D. Kemme, R. Portes, K.A. Soos, J. Winiecki, etc. I. Kritsman (1925, 1929) seems to be the first to have spoken of 'general shortage' in an economy.

3 (φ) can be viewed as a factor that diminishes the real wage (W/P), taking into account the energy and time deployed for getting the goods in short supply.

4 How important (ϕ) is can also be seen from a remarkable paper by I. Lemnij (1984), that highlights *variety* as a collective use value of commodities.

5 The analysis can consider separately the effect on the effort in production and on labour supply. Thus J. Brada and A. King (1986) use a formal macroeconomic model of a centrally planned economy in order to determine the degree of 'plan tautness' which maximises output, when both the supply of effort and the supply of labour are influenced by 'plan tautness'. Differently, L. Podkaminer tries to explain investment cycles in centrally planned economies by invoking consumer markets disequilibrium and labour shortage (1985).

6 Concerning the 'informational noise' in supply-constrained economies see also N. Spulber, I. Horowitz (1976, chapter 2), and R. K. Sah, J. Stiglitz (1986).

7 For a many-sided discussion of this phenomenon in centrally planned economies, see G. Grossman (1981). See also M. Wisniewski (1985), and P. Galasi and G. Kertesi (1985).

8 In a supply-constrained economy the underground economy operates in conjunction with central decision-making bodies to create the economy's system of regulation ('through shortage').

9 Here it is considered a highest societal indifference curve when consumers (markets) decide on the composition of output. In the sense of the Lange-Lerner model the State is an agent that influences this composition through the rate of investment (rate of interest), taxation, etc.

10 The expression would be the same for an open economy that faces an external demand constraint, especially if the longer run is considered.

11 Investment cycles can be provoked by policy actions that respond to extreme

imbalances in consumer goods markets (J. Winiecki (1982), H. Olivera (1960), L. Podkamminer (1985), etc.), or to supply tensions (J. Goldmann and K. Kouba (1967), T. Bauer (1978), etc.).

12   This observation is due to Edgar Feige.

13   For various ways of dealing with reputation in formal models see the book edited by Daniel B. Klein (1997), particularly part three.

14   The dynamic of the accumulation of reputation is analogous to human capital build up, in the spirit of the models used by Gary Becker and Th. Schultz.

15   A fallacy of composition is involved here: what seems to be rational for individuals becomes detrimental for society. A negative externality thus emerges.

16   One can imagine situations of equilibria – good or bad – related to individuals' behaviours. An example is when people pay their due taxes, or they evade them. There are models, which try to portray such situations. Thus, it is assumed that the production of an individual firm is an increasing function of the public good provided by the state; the production function can be written as ($q_i=q+ag$) when taxes are paid, and $qi=q$ for the case of tax evasion. It is assumed now that (nt) gives the level of public good (g), where (t) indicates the degree of fiscality, and (n) denotes the number of firms that pay taxes. Different equilibria appear. Let us assume that a $<1<N$. The income after tax of the firm is ($q+ag-t$) if the firm pays taxes and (q) if the firm does not pay taxes. It seems that the decision is clear for the firm; it tries to avoid taxes as long as $t>ag=ant$, or $n<1/a$. If $n=1$ (which means that all firms practise tax evasion) the firm N is also stimulated to get into tax evasion since $n<1/a$ (according to the assumption made). If $n=N$, then the firm is interested in paying taxes since $n>1$ (see also J. Sachs, 1994, p.48). This reasoning can be applied to any kind of criminal, or illegal act.

17   Once, a banker confessed to me that the world of business 'does not like those who are more catholic than the Pope'. This would mean that one needs to be particularly heavyweight in order to be successful as a businessperson while being 'excessively puritanical' in behaviour.

References

Adair, P. (1995), 'Economie informelle et economies de marches industrialisees', Congress of AIELF, Bucharest, 29 June-2 July.

Albu, Lucian-Liviu (1995), 'La modelisation de l'economie souterraine et des politiques fiscales', CEPREMAP-Paris, ACE-PHARE, Aout.

Arrow, J. Kenneth (1974), 'The Limits of Organisation', W.W. Norton, New York.

Bauer, Tamas (1978), 'Investment Cycles in Planned Economies', *Acta Oeconomica*, vol. 21, 3, pp.243-260.

Beksiak, J. (1966), 'Inflation in the Socialist Economy' (in Polish), *Ekonomista*,

1, pp.91-107.

Brada, C.J., King, E.A. (1968), 'Taut Plans, Repressed Inflation and the Supply of Effort in Centrally Planned Economics', *Economics of Planning*, Vol. 20, 3, pp. 162-178.

Burkett, P.J. (1987), 'Slack, Shortage and Discouraged Consumers in Eastern Europe: Estimates Based on Smoothing by Aggregation', manuscript.

Daianu, D. (1987), 'Demand vs. Supply-constrained Economies', *Revue Roumaine de Sciences Sociales-serie economique*, no.1.

Daianu, D. (1994), 'Inter-enterprise arrears in a post-command economy', *IMF Working Paper*, 54/94.

Daianu, D. (1996), 'Reputation as an Asset', paper presented at the workshop of the European Association of Comparative Economic Studies, Budapest, December.

Daianu, D. (1997), 'An economic explanation of *strain*' in J. Backhaus (ed.), 'Issues in Transformation Theory', Metropolis, Marburg.

Daianu, D. and Albu, L. (1996), 'Strain and the Inflation-Unemployment Relationship: a conceptual and empirical investigation', *Research Memorandum* No.96/15, Centre for European Economic Studies, University of Leicester.

Galasi, P. and Kertesi, G. (1985), 'Second Economy, Competition, Inflation', *Acta Oeconomica*, Vol. 35, 3-4, pp.269-293.

Goldman, J., Kouba, K. (1967), 'Economic Growth in Czechoslovakia', Academia, Prague.

Gomulka, S. (1982), 'Kornai's Soft Budget Constraint and the Shortage Phenomenon: a Criticism and Restatement', in *Economics of Planning*, vol. 19,1.

Grossman, G. (1981), 'The Second Economy of the USSR' (Problems of Communism, 1977), reprinted in Bornstin, M. (ed.), 'The Soviet Economy: Continuity and Change', Westwiew, Boulder.

Hoch, R., Book, A. (1981), 'Review of J. Kornai's Economics of Shortage', Szigma, 1.

Holzman, Fr. (1960), 'Soviet Inflationary Pressures 1927-1958: Causes and Cures', *Quarterly J. Economics*, vol. 74, 2, pp. 167-188.

Kalecki, M. (1972), 'Selected Essays on the Economic Growth of the Socialist and Mixed Economies', Cambridge University Press, Cambridge.

Kemme, D. (1987), 'The Chronic Shortage Model', paper presented at the Conference on Disequilibrium Modelling, Birmingham (manuscript).

Klein, Daniel B. (1977), 'Reputation: Studies in the Voluntary Elicitation of Good Conduct', Michigan University Press, Ann Arbor.

Kritsman, I. (1929), 'Die heroische Periode der grossen russichen Revolution', Verlag fur Literatur und Politik, Viena.

Lemnij, I. (1984), 'Variety as a Collective Use Value of Commodities', *Revue Roumaine Science Sociale – Série Economique*, 2, pp. 91-100.

Levine, H. (1983), 'Book Review: Economics of Shortage by Janos Kornai', in *Journal of Economic Literature*, vol.21.

Novozhilov, V.V. (1926), 'Neodostatok Tovarov', Vestnik Finansov, 2.

Olivera, H.G. (1960), 'Cyclical Economic Growth under Collectivism', Kyklos, 2, pp. 229-232.

Podkamminer, L. (1985), 'Investment Cycles in Centrally Planned Economies: An Explanation Invoking Consumer Markets Disequilibrium and Labour Shortage', *Acta Oeconomica*, Vol. 35, 1-2, pp.133-144.

Portes, R. (1977), 'The Control of Inflation: Lessons from East European Experience', *Economica*, Vol.44, pp. 109-129.

Sachs, J. (1994), 'Russia's Struggle with Stabilisation. Conceptual Issues and Evidence', paper prepared for the World Bank's Annual Conference on Development Economics, 28-30 April.

Sah, R., Stiglitz, K., Joseph, E. (1986), 'The Architecture of Economic Systems: Hierarchies and Polyarchies', *American Economic Rewiev*, Vol.76, 4, pp. 716-727.

Soos, A. Kiraly (1984), 'A Propos the Explanation of Shortage Phenomena: Volume of Demand and Structural Inelasticity', *Acta Oeconomica*, Vol. 33, 3-4, pp. 305-320.

Spulber, N., Horowitz, I. (1976), 'Quantitative Economic Policy and Planning – Theory and Models of Economic Control', Norton, New York.

Wellisz, S. and Findlay, R. (1986), 'Central Planning and the Second Economy in Soviet-Type Systems', *The Economic Journal*, vol. 96.

Winiecki, J. (1982), 'Investment Cycles and Excess Demand Inflation in Planned Economies: Sources and Processes', *Acta Oeconomica*, Vol. 28, 1-2, pp.147-160.

Wisniewski, M. (1985), 'The Sources and Size of the Underground Economy in Poland' (in Polish), *Ekonomista*, 6, pp. 913-940.

Part II

Macroeconomic Stabilisation and Restructuring

6 The Changing Mix of Dis-equilibria during Transition – a Romanian background*

The legacy of the previous decade is a *sine qua non* starting point for analysis in order to get a firmer grasp of the main processes and phenomena occurring after December 1989 in Romania. The eighties offered an example of shock therapy – as a balance of payments adjustment – undertaken in a command economy. Direct controls were used to cut domestic absorption to the largest possible extent. This forced adjustment can be seen as an 'internalisation' of external disequilibria that entailed increased domestic disequilibria, both open and hidden. If one conceives an optimum degree of internalisation (which would indicate the composition of external and internal disequilibria that policymakers should aim at in order to minimise the cumulated costs of imbalances for the economy) an obvious overtaxation of domestic absorption took place during those years.

After December 1989, the abrupt change of the overall domestic environment consisted, among other things, of decentralisation of decision-making power (when soft budget constraints still operated!), a fading away of the direct control devices (including fear and hierarchical links), an increasing fuzziness concerning property rights with trade-unions turning into key-players and 'managers-monitors', introduction of a very liberal trade and foreign exchange regime. Macroeconomic policy was unable to contain growing and changing disequilibria because of the modifying domestic institutional and economic set-up (including the social and political climate) aggravated by unfavourable international environment (collapsing former CMEA, effects of the Gulf war, etc). One can talk of a reversed process: an 'externalisation' of domestic imbalances, which led to a surge of imports and a dramatic deterioration of the current account balance.

The stabilisation and transformation policy in Romania gives further food for rethinking issues like: how sustainable is stabilisation if financial discipline can scarcely be imposed? Furthermore, can the latter be imposed without clearly defined property rights (creating the micro-foundations of macroeconomic policy during transition)? Does industrial policy have a role to play in supporting enterprise reform and stabilisation? What is the impact of stabilisation policy on a 'free falling' economy? What is the effectiveness of income-control policy in an uncompetitive environment? What is the role of industrial relations policy (as part of industrial policy) in enhancing stabilisation under the prevailing circumstances related to the structure of property rights? What is the role of foreign direct investment in fostering industrial restructuring when domestic investment is more than insufficient? How to cope with *hysteresis* phenomena linked to unemployment brought about by austerity and foreign competition when factors of production have low mobility? If wage dynamics will not favour human capital build-up how will long-run growth potential be impaired?

Part one refers to (dis)equilibria, in general, and is followed by an attempt to define an optimal mix between external and internal disequilibrium, the latter seen in a broad sense. Part three presents the forced adjustment of the balance of payments in Romania in the 80s as a prologue to the analysis of transformation policy. Results and dilemmas of stabilisation policy during the first three years of transformation in post-communist Romania are presented in section four. The last part talks about (dis)equilibria in transforming economies by providing some insights into this issue. The chapter ends with concluding remarks.

On (dis)equilibria

Equilibrium can be seen as 'a state of balance among certain forces within the economic system', that is a simple and mechanical meaning. It can be illustrated, for instance, by the equality between market demand and supply, or by monetary equilibrium understood as a balance between money inflows and outflows. Another definition emphasises 'the state of rest of the system, or of its elements'. The Keynesian case of unemployment can be given as a mechanical understanding of this definition,[1] which is to be compared with an approach that tries to put under scrutiny the nature of relations among economic agents. In this respect, Fr. Perroux thinks that an economic system is in a state of general equilibrium when the net energy for change, resulted from the interaction among its economic agents, is nil (1975, p. 156). And F. Hahn (1976, p. 243) – by taking into account the relationship between available information and agents' actions – considers that an economy is in a state of equilibrium when the messages circulating inside the system do not induce agents to modify the precepts that guide their actions and the ends pursued. Another meaning, that stresses individual behaviour and the psychology of economic agents, views equilibrium as 'a state of perfect fulfilment of agents' *expectations* on the essential variables of the economic system'. Thus, equilibrium – seen as 'informational equilibrium' – denotes a state in which wage rates and other prices on average are found – over space and over time – to be what they were expected to be (E. Phelps, 1970, p. 8). When expectations are not fulfilled and agents' plans are not reciprocally compatible the economy would be in disequilibrium. Finally, a meaning offered by J. Kornai (1983, p. 150) takes equilibrium as a 'normal' state of the system, a state which reproduces itself as 'the deviating or even opposing internal forces compensate each other and their resultant is unable to shift the system from its equilibrium path'.

The second and third definitions are quite interesting since they point to the possible latency of a system, seemingly and temporarily in a state of rest, under conditions when the expectations of numerous agents are far from being fulfilled. Under such circumstances, the pressure for change – toward re-establishing equilibrium – is likely to increase. Consequently, a state of equilibrium (disequilibrium) is to be qualified in relation with the period of time considered. Common sense leads us to see the concept of equilibrium referring to the outcome of interactions among economic agents, and to the state of a system. However, the drive for change manifests at microlevels or at the level of economic agents.[2]

The behaviour of economic agents can be judged by taking into account a set of criteria, which help give a meaning to the state of (dis)equilibrium. It can be said that micro-equilibria exist when micro-units (individuals, firms) attain a balance between efforts and rewards (incomes), when their goals are reached and expectations are fulfilled. For the system equilibrium (disequilibrium) emerges as an aggregate state.

The evaluation of the state of a system requires the selection (identification) of aggregates to characterise it. While aggregate equilibrium does not exclude the existence of 'informational noise' and 'friction' within the system – caused by information and transaction costs – a state of general equilibrium precludes them. It is obvious that more informational noise and friction entail bigger micro-disequilibria, higher inefficiency, or a lower level of utilisation of factors of production.

Stricto sensu, the comparison between aggregate effective supply and aggregate effective demand gives a measure of aggregate (dis)equilibrium. In a normative sense – from the perspective of general equilibrium that maximises output and welfare in the system – the analysis has to take into account a series of parameters regarding the actual state of an economy: a) the level of unemployment of resources; b) the degree of allocative inefficiency and 'X – inefficiency'; c) the physical and moral depreciation of resources; d) the intensity of forced substitutions in production and consumption, which harms the quality of output and the welfare of consumers. As it can be seen, the broad (normative) sense of aggregate disequilibrium used herein comes very close in meaning to what could be called the aggregate performance deficit of the economy.

Therefore, in a normative sense, aggregate disequilibrium, which is equivalent to a deficit of utility (performance), means the distance to the level of output resulted from a full utilisation of resources in the system. In a formal manner, this relation is illustrated as:

$$dU = U^*\text{-}U =\ U(Q(L^*)) - U(Q(L; e),\ \theta)$$

where (U) is the utility function; U^* refers to the maximum level of utility attainable when there is full employment of resources; (Q) is the production function that depends on the level of employment of resources (labour, L) and the degree of inefficiency (e);[3] and (θ) denotes the intensity of forced substitutions.

External vs. internal disequilibrium - is there an optimal mix?

In a perfect world, there would be no external and internal disequilibria; economies would operate at full employment and there would be no performance deficits. But the real world is imperfect and since imbalances arise on a recurrent basis, one can imagine and aim at an assumed optimal composition of disequilibria. In fact, the trade-offs encountered by policymakers in working out economic policies are a telling proof in this respect. *The misery index* (the inflation rate + the unemployment rate) is a well-known, very simple, but suggestive way of trying to depict a macroeconomic situation. However, it does conceal a fundamental relationship, which has much relevance for governments, in the short-run at least.

Another fundamental relationship (trade-off) exists between aggregate external disequilibrium and aggregate internal disequilibrium, the latter being understood in a broad sense. The trade-off does not necessarily arise when internal disequilibrium is seen in a narrow sense as the equality between aggregate demand and aggregate supply. A proper use of macroeconomic policy tools would reduce both the external imbalance and the internal imbalance. For example in an economy confronted with large unsustainable current account deficits and high inflation, tight monetary and fiscal policies can be used to squeeze domestic absorption and would deal with both problems simultaneously.

When accommodating capital inflows are triggered by rises in real interest rates and foreign capital markets can be resorted to (by sales of bonds) authorities can have substantial room for influencing the required trade balance adjustments. This line of reasoning leads us to think of a composition of disequilibria which would, presumably, be most advantageous for the economy; costs, viewed as *foregone utility*, compared to the performance potential of the economy would be minimised over time. This potential can be judged for the short-run and the long-run. In the short-run it depends on structural constraints (that reduce supply-responsiveness), whereas, in the long-run, these constraints can be removed and the performance potential can be related to factor endowments. The costs (foregone welfare) can be thought of in absolute terms, or in relative terms – as a percentage of the flows of potential output. Figure 6.1 is an attempt to illustrate the optimal mix between external disequilibrium, ED, (the current account deficit – corrected by autonomous long term capital inflows – as per cent of GDP) and internal disequilibrium, ID (measured as the rate of unemployment). Point A denotes the optimal mix and is given by the least-cost line that touches tangentially the transformation curve between external and internal disequilibrium. Clearly, the marginal cost and the marginal benefit of internalising one unit of the current account deficit are equal in A. Outside point A the marginal cost of internalisation (or externalisation of the internal imbalance) increases steadily. Should A be available to the policymakers as an option, B and C indicate an *underreaction* and an *overreaction*, respectively, on their part.[4] Over time point A shifts according to the dynamics of the economy, one powerful reason being that an economy faces a hard-budget constraint in the long run; a nation cannot accumulate IOUs ad infinitum. Consequently, the optimal-mix of disequilibria has to be seen both statically and dynamically. In the latter case, dynamic optimisation can be used in order to identify a least-cost function, which bears in mind various constraints.

Further comments rely on the case of command economies. Internalisation of the external debt was the major feature of economic policy in Romania in the past decade and its legacy has much explanatory power for current events.

A distinction should be made between repayment of debt and

internalisation of an external imbalance. Obviously, not any repayment of external debt is an internalisation of external imbalances; one need only think of how these external debts emerge. Two major situations appear in this respect: the importation of foreign resources in order to increase domestic productive investment and, consequently, the growth rate of the economy, and the foreign financing of imports aimed at alleviating internal imbalances (the externalisation of these imbalances).

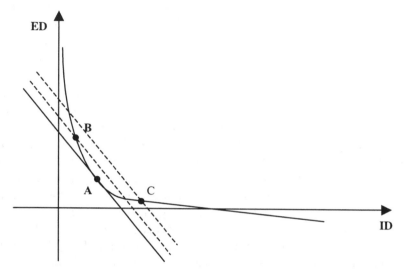

Figure 6.1   The optimal mix of disequilibria

Let us a look at the first situation. When efficient use is made of imported capital – which implies a satisfactory rate of return for the newly obtained externally tradable output – the repayment of the debt is made out of the surplus of utility. The smaller efficiency (external purchasing power) of the utilisation of the imported capital, the smaller becomes the net surplus of utility (which remains after disbursement). The internalisation process sets in when the cumulated net effect turns negative, i.e. when net utility turns into net disutility.[5] Should the productivity of imported capital put to work be low, then the case appears as if the country imported resources for consumption on credit. By assuming an economically insignificant productivity of imported capital, the second[6] situation is reached.

This situation implies the externalisation of internal imbalances, which sooner or later brings about the unavoidable internalisation process when net borrowing comes to a halt because of its prohibitive cost. The process of externalisation postpones bringing the economy towards a new motion path of aggregate effective demand, according to the actual dynamics of internal supply. When it is not accompanied by positive changes in the functional structure of the economy and when the external environment does not produce 'windfall gains' (such as a dramatic and resilient improvement of the terms of trade) the externalisation of internal imbalances complicates the delayed and enforced adjustments.

As pointed out, internalisation can be subject to optimisation. By assuming a minimum cost (disutility) of disequilibria for the economy – which is given by their composition between internal and external imbalances – it can be inferred that internalisation should not exceed a certain degree. This degree is related to an optimum period of repayment of the external debt; a period that minimises the adjustment costs, *ceteris paribus*, by presuming no change in the quality of functioning of the economy. The minimisation of costs and the optimum degree of internalisation are thus seen in an inter-temporal perspective.

The costs of internalisation are temporary and durable. The temporary, immediate costs, regard the curtailment of absorption (consumption) while the durable costs are reflected by a fall in the growth rate of domestic absorption (consumption) following the reduction of investment as a result of the forced cut in imports – capital goods[7] included. Since the process of internalisation, as gradual repayment of the debt, entails also benefits for the economy under the form of a reduced debt service,[8] the analysis deals with net costs.

An *overreaction* signifies a larger and a speedier internalisation as compared to the size and pace indicated by the optimum process. In the case of overreaction policymakers put a higher value on the reduction of the external debt than on the need to cushion against growing internal imbalances. Their perception of economic difficulties is biased towards the presumably (on their part) more visible and pressuring side of overall disequilibria. An *underreaction*, i.e. a too slow and too small internalisation, also increases the costs of forced adjustment in comparison with the optimum situation. When policymakers underreact there is an underestimation of the later costs of forced adjustment. The cases of overreaction and underreaction throw light on major interrelated problems of internalisation: dimension, speed, and structure.

The *dimension* and *speed* of internalisation, on which the repayment period[9] depends, determine the extent to which domestic absorption is curtailed. The *structure* of internalisation refers to how the two basic components of domestic absorption are hit by its programmed reduction. Thus, deeper cuts in consumption can protect its future levels by maintaining investment above a reasonable level. And vice versa, a drastic and persistent reduction of investment, though it facilitates the task for policymakers of not touching the current consumption of population, negatively affects the development of the productive apparatus of the economy and, further, the future growth rates of consumption, since the latter is a function of capital stock. The longer the period of disbursement the easier it is to make the choice concerning the structure of internalisation. Another factor that intervenes in the optimisation analysis is the level of the interest rate, the more so when it fluctuates and causes upward variations of the debt-service, which can hardly be borne by the economy. A high real interest rate favours a reduction of the repayment period, but its 'pressure' is to be judged in conjunction with the influences of other factors. Some restrictions for the process of internalisation must be considered as well. Curtailment of consumption cannot go below a critical level and the investment cannot be cut more than is absolutely necessary for the economy to continue running, which further gives the critical level of intermediate imports.

If the hypothesis regarding the invariability of the mode of the functioning of the economy is dropped, the optimum period of internalisation has to be correlated with the period of adjustment of the functional structure of the economy, and of its industrial structure (to bring about the required changes in the material structures of production).

The pre-transition shock-therapy

Initial conditions in transforming economies are often neglected. This is quite puzzling since differences in the content and results of the currently undertaken stabilisation policies can be related to dissimilar initial conditions. The countries in the region have different histories under command planning in terms of relaxation of direct controls and economic policy choices. The different histories explain why market institutions vary among the national environments and why macro- and micro-disequilibria differed among them on the eve of 1989.

Thus, Hungary is the classical example for reforms evolving within the system and the former Czechoslovakia is conspicuous for the ability of central planners to keep macro-disequilibria under relative control though, for the latter country, dynamic losses (measured as against the pre-communist legacy and the investment rates during the last four decades) are much higher.[10] Unsurprisingly, both countries have fared better than the rest in their stabilisation programmes.

Romania, under communism, stands out for its unflinching adherence to Stalinist precepts of economic policy, its isolationism, its industrial policy choices which blatantly ignored comparative advantages, its trade policy choices that ran counter to the very logic of the functioning of the domestic economy and a *sui generis* 'shock-therapy' in the eighties. At the end of that decade, the Romanian economy was 'one of the most tightly controlled and centralised in Eastern Europe'. The Ceausescu regime deprived the country of the experience of any significant economic reform, leaving the administration tied to a Stalinist model that had been abandoned by almost all other countries in the region. In addition, the economic policies of the regime further distorted the economic system (D. G. Demekas and M. S. Khan, 1991, p. 8).

Romania provides an interesting and instructive case of 'immiserising-growth' caused by the logic of the motion of the system, in the main, by the rush to speed up industrial growth, and by the attempt to increase ties with market economies on a very weak functional basis. In the literature this phenomenon is explained by the existence of various price distortions, which harm resource allocation, worsen the terms of trade, and lower welfare.[11]

However, one can think of the very mode of functioning of the economy (including the genesis of wrong industrial choices) as the distortion, which leads to immisering growth. It can be shown that the inner dynamics of the system – incapacity to cope with increasing complexity and inability to assimilate and generate technological progress – lead to a 'softening' of output, to its expansion with a large bias toward industrial soft goods, which entails a steady deterioration of the terms of trade. This is what happened in Romania where, forced industrialisation gave precedence to steel, chemical and machine-building industries, and agriculture was terribly squeezed. The unhealthy nature of such growth can be explained succinctly. The biased expansion of the production of soft goods – which belies the factor endowments of the economy – demands a quantity of hard inputs which could either be provided only by disrupting domestic production, or not be achieved as many export-destined goods were unsaleable. Actual exports of soft goods were, hence, smaller than the level programmed and the remaining necessary inputs are obtained through an international exchange of hard goods. This means that the country has to forgo consuming certain kinds of hard goods (consumer goods which are in high demand by ordinary citizens) in favour of acquiring other types of hard goods, such as energy, raw materials and spare parts. The welfare loss for the population is tremendous and this, in turn, triggers a negative supply-multiplier on the part of consumers seen as labour suppliers.

The start of the eighties highlighted the grand economic debacle; the external shocks – like the brutal rise in oil prices, or the sharp increase in world interest rates – that were mitigated by external financing for a while, accelerated the decline of the economy. External debts stood at over 10 billion dollars. Ceausescu rejected any suggestion of market inspired reform that could have improved the performance of the economy and its export capacity. It makes sense to surmise that this attitude made any attempt to reschedule external debts very difficult. Getting rid of the whole external debt became the paramount goal of his economic policy. Moreover, it was decided that no effort be spared in order to reach this goal as soon as possible. How daunting the goal became is proved by the size of prepayments in the latter half of the decade: $0.5 billion in 1987, $2.9 billion in 1988, $1.2 billion in 1989. This is a clear case of overreaction in internalising the external debt, with deleterious effects over all the economy.

This extraordinary 'shock-therapy' was enforced through a considerable squeeze on domestic absorption, both consumption and investment.

Since 'immiserising' growth limited the potential to raise exports, targeted trade surpluses were achieved through very heavy cuts of hard currency imports – see Table 6.1.

Table 6.1   Current account balance in Romania, 1980-92 (in million $)

	1980	1983	1985	1987	1988	1989	1990	1991	1992
			Convertible currencies (in US $)						
Trade account	- 1.534	1.688	1.558	2.436	3.608	2.559	-1.743	-1.357	-1,420
Exports, fob	6.503	6.246	6.156	5.864	6.511	5.965	3.364	3.533	4,364
Imports, fob	8.037	4.558	4.598	3.428	2.903	3.406	+5.107	+4.890	5,784
Services balance	-0.865	-0.766	-0.450	-0.211	0.017	0.305	0.087	-0.012	-168
Current account	-2.399	0.922	1.118	2.225	3.625	2.864	-1.656	-1.369	-1.200

Source: National statistics

Apart from the reduced level of investment, growth possibilities were also impaired by an unusual curtailment of imports of machinery and equipment from the Western countries.[12] By using a Laffer-curve-analogy it can be said that a heavy *overtaxation* of domestic absorption took place during those years which showed up in lower growth rates of production, lower welfare (consumption), bigger domestic disequilibria; shortages were on the rise in both production and consumption.

Official figures do not convey the extent of the harm done by this overtaxation. Table 6.2, for instance, shows the dynamic of GDP growth rates.

However, these figures do not capture the effect of the decline on the quality of resources used – partially, as a result of import substitution and import switching (from CMEA countries). The actual loss of output was obscured considerably by rising costs of production that transferred into higher nominal values of goods and, thereby, artificially inflated the nominal GDP.[13] It is quite possible and probable that the growth of nominal national income represented a drop of real national wealth valued in international terms. The labour-supply multiplier compounded this effect: workers who adjusted the real performance to their real income.

Table 6.2   GDP dynamics in Romania, 1978-92

(percentage change per annum)

1978-1981	1982-1985	1985	1986	1987	1988	1989	1990	1991	1992
4.5	4.0	-0.1	2.3	0.8	-0.5	-5.8	-5.6	-12.9	-8.8

Source: National statistics

The welfare effect of the shock-therapy, too, can hardly be captured by statistics for they express several interlinked phenomena including reduced available consumer goods because of net exports. The net foreign balance was 7% of GDP during 1985-1987 and attained 9.5% in 1988, the peak level for the decade, illustrating the loss of utility caused by the softening of certain goods (of output, in general), forced substitutions, and forced delays in consumption. The change in the utility preferences of the consumers, due to demonstration effects and changes in availabilities of goods, was enormous. The impact of the shock-therapy on the average citizen is indicated by the pattern of consumption in 1989: food expenditure, 50%; clothing and shoes, 13%; energy, 7% etc. Essentials of life held a disproportionately high share – in comparison with countries of similar income per capita levels – which cannot be attributed to spillovers caused by distortions in relative prices.[14] I assert it since real incomes (not 'measured' real incomes) went down and shortages of the mentioned items intensified over the period.

The eighties brought about a substantial increase of monetary overhang. Estimates that use the income velocity of broad money held by households as a proxy for the degree of forced savings of the population suggest that up to one third of money balances were held involuntarily (E. R. Borensztein, D. G. Demekas, J. D. Ostry, 1992, p. 27). Relatedly, I wish to emphasise another phenomenon: the existence of a 'suppressed excess demand' under the guise of forced substitutions in consumption.[15] When 'demonstration effects' in consumption are strong, the supply-constraint is not absolute and the structure of consumers' preference is quite stable (the 'discouraged consumer effect' is much less significant than what might be presumed in conditions of intensified shortage over long periods of time) the elasticity of substitution in consumption is sufficiently low[16] for consumers' welfare losses to be considerable. The monetary overhang and the hidden excess demand formed a disequilibrium on the side of household demand (pent-up demand). This repressed demand put a tremendous pressure on the balance of payments after December 1989, when consumers were able to switch their preferences in favour of tradeables.[17] If excess demand is combined with the unaccepted drop in consumption, during the 80s, one realises the magnitude of the urge to return to 'normal' paths and patterns of consumption, which took concrete shape once the command system began to crumble. The ten years of debt internalisation accentuated the decline of competitiveness of the economy, disequilibria among sectors and shortages increased, the people's plight went beyond imagination; the country imploded. Romania was a laggard among her neighbours as to the institutional prerequisites for helping post-communist transition, the psychological preparedness of the population for abrupt change, and the social base for market reforms. Moreover, the 'shock-therapy' of the eighties created among people very high expectations for an immediate and substantial improvement of material conditions after a change of the rules (or of the regime), which signalled a high degree of intolerance for new austerity measures.

Stabilisation policy and disequilibria in Romania

Internalisation of external disequilibrium and the extreme overreaction of decision-makers were indicated as the major trait of economic policy in Romania in the 80s. Almost symmetrically, the most salient feature of economic life after December 1989 has been a major reversal of the above-mentioned phenomenon: an externalisation of domestic imbalances. What happened in Romania in a relatively short time (one year) is also unique among her neighbours: from a current account surplus in hard currency of $2.864 billion in 1989 the country moved to a deficit of $1.656 billion a year later – see Table 6.1. The turnaround is astonishing if the size of foreign trade is taken into account – in 1989 exports and imports in hard currency totalled slightly under $10 billion. Thus, the reversal equalled almost 45% of the foreign trade turnover in 1989.

I have already highlighted the roots of this situation, which go into the previous decade; there was a tremendous pressure from *below*[18] to consume tradables, and to reduce exports and boost imports of both consumer and intermediate goods. The switch in favour of tradables was almost instant and irresistible; it was strengthened by a 'shunning of domestic goods' syndrome (foreign goods, apart from quality attraction, still mean – for many – prestige, status). Having been starved for years, consumers and producers reacted immediately to the new environment and their reaction forms one side of the story. The new environment in the making consisted of: decentralisation of decision-making power (when soft budget constraints still operate!), a rapidly fading away of direct control devices (including fear and hierarchical links), an increasing fuzziness concerning property rights with trade unions turning into key players and 'managers-monitors', a very liberal trade and foreign exchange regime and a much overvalued exchange rate. External shocks, including the effects of the CMEA collapse[19] and the Gulf war (Iraq was a major trading partner and debtor of Romania), played a major part as well.

However, there is another side of the story that needs to be highlighted. The policymakers complicated the state of the economy by commission and omission. By commission, since they practised a brand of populist macroeconomics, faltering in the face of pressures from below, but lured also by the elections held in May 1990. This resulted in high laxity in conceding wage rises,[20] and introduction of the five day workweek. Meanwhile output was plummeting, wide-ranging price controls were maintained with the exchange rate much overvalued and foreign exchange reserves mismanaged. At the end of 1989 foreign exchange reserves stood at more than $1.7 billion; these went down to under $400 million at the end of 1990. By omission, for one can hardly talk about real attempts to stabilise the economy before November 1990. Trying to sum up one can say that both aggregate external disequilibrium and aggregate internal disequilibrium increased,[21] with micro-disequilibria partially alleviated by substantially increased imports. For policymakers much concern should have caused policymakers the fact that production was re-establishing an import-dependency unsustainable in the long run. This soon became obvious.

Events during that year showed a fundamental flaw of the system in transformation: the high degree of decision-making power of enterprises when they do not face hard-budget constraints and enjoy free access to hard currency. They also made clear the damage caused by an economic policy whose dimension of 'benign neglect' was very high profile. November signalled the beginning of intentions toward a stabilisation policy by a partial liberalisation of prices and a devaluation of the domestic currency (from Lei 20/$1 to Lei

35/$1). However, these measures, followed by another package in January 1991, proved to be too little and too late.

Confronted with a free-falling economy[22] and unable to contain growing disequilibria (unsustainable trade deficits,[23] rising prices, vanishing investment) an IMF supported stabilisation plan was introduced at the start of 1991.[24] The government had no choice but to resort to such a plan since looming trade deficits had became more than threatening. With the benefit of hindsight it can be said that, in view of the large external disequilibrium, policymakers were constantly *underreacting* to the dynamics of the economy.

Why did they underreact? The state of the economy in December 1989 and the high expectations of the populace after the 'shock-therapy' of the 80s, obviously, blunted the resoluteness of decision-makers to move swiftly with a comprehensive austerity programme and comprehensive freeing of prices. Another possible explanation is that the government underestimated the seriousness of the situation for quite a while. Finally, the lack of foreign financing, instead of stimulating boldness, increased caution.

A conceptually middle of-the-road (gradualist) stabilisation programme took shape which meant essentially: tightening of the fiscal and monetary policies[25] (though real interest rates remained highly negative), a tax-based income control policy, a new devaluation,[26] and a two-tier exchange rate system (through the introduction of an interbank foreign exchange auction system, in February 1991).

The programme was ineffective in stopping inflation – see Table 6.3. Moreover, the real credit squeeze, caused by the high jump in prices (after deregulation) followed by their steadily rising level (the price index reached 352,2% in October 1991 as compared to the moment of deregulation), did not help in moderating output decline. The volume of gross arrears increased exponentially reaching a figure approximating 50% of the GDP (measured in the prices of December 1991) by the end of the year. At the same time, the spread between the two exchange rates persisted, exports continued to be sluggish whereas the CMEA trade virtually disappeared.

The end of the year brought about a 'global compensation' as a means to reduce inter-enterprise arrears. Though the additional credit was mostly sterilised, the fact brought to the fore the *moral hazard* issue. The only achievement of the programme was the elimination of the monetary overhang.

At the end of 1991, growing tensions were building into the system: an overvalued official exchange rate and an excessively liberal trade regime, too low prices for energy and raw materials which favoured their overconsumption, and insufficient inflows of capital to compensate for low levels of saving and the feebleness of investment. The strategic move of November 1991, the unification of the exchange rate,[27] and the introduction of internal convertibility, became irrelevant in a short while, basically, for the lack of supporting foreign financing and, very likely, for the choice of an overvalued rate. For several months the exchange rate was stuck at the Lei 198/$1 rate which meant a growing imbalance between the supply of and the demand for foreign exchange;[28] thus an overhang of hard currency claims[29] was stockpiling. Many exporters and importers found a way out by practising barter deals, which introduced an *implicit* exchange rate into the functioning of the economy. This implicit exchange rate mitigated the pernicious effects of overvaluation. However, capital flight and insufficient exports caused much alarm. The whole policy was in need of a major overhaul which, among other goals, should restore actual internal convertibility.

Table 6.3   Inflation in Romania, 1991-92 (in per cent)

1991		1	2
	January	158.1	
	February	169.2	
	March	180.4	
	April	228.2	
	May	239.8	
	June	244.5	
	July	267.7	
	August	297.6	
	September	319.4	
	October	352.6	
	November	391.0	
	December	444.5	
1992			
	January	531.2	119.5
	February	624.4	112.5
	March	657.3	110.0
	April	688.0	104.7
	May	771.3	112.1
	June	804.1	104.3
	July	829.6	103.2
	August	857.6	103.4
	September	944.5	110.1
	October	1035.2	109.6
	November	1174.9	113.5

Note: 1 = Oct. 1990 = 100
            2 = consumer price index, previous month = 100
Source: National statistics

What came out of the decision-making process in the Spring of 1992 provides, in my opinion, a good case study for understanding critical choices faced by macroeconomic policy during transition. Basically, policymakers had to decide on an optimal mix of short-run disequilibria that should reduce the performance deficit and deal with the major constraints. The line of reasoning was that recessionary effects of the fight against inflation which involved austerity measures, could be counteracted by the pulling (multiplier) effect of a policy that would succeed in boosting exports and attracting capital inflows. Increasing exports and restoring internal convertibility appeared as a *must* since the economy was menaced by suffocation on the side of the external balance. The idea of creating an *export drive* was reinforced by the long-run requirements of reform policy: achieving an equilibrium exchange rate, attaining positive real interest rates (which should encourage saving and relieve the pressure on the exchange rate), adopting export promotion measures, and working out an industrial (restructuring) policy that should enable the imposition of financial discipline (the fight against arrears) by distinguishing between 'bad guys' and 'good guys'. Interest rates were raised considerably (the refinance rate of the National Bank reached 80%), the exchange rate was devalued substantially – see Table 6.4[30] – and exporters were granted full retention rights in order to cope with their distrust of policymakers and encourage capital return. The full retention measure was thought necessary since enterprises still had very vivid memories of what they considered the partial 'confiscation' of their hard-currency holdings at the end of 1991; for, after 'exchange-rate reunification', their claims for foreign exchange were not satisfied adequately by banks and a hard-currency overhang started to build up. At the same time, Law 76/1991, aimed at enforcing financial discipline and triggering restructuring, was passed by Parliament.

Two major debates revolved around the new package of measures introduced in May of 1992. One controversy related to interest rate policy. Some would argue that in a depressed (declining) economy in which the disinclination to save is on the rise – because of the shrinking household budgets – it is counterproductive to raise interest rates in real terms. On the other hand, in Romania's case, the foreign exchange constraint had become so threatening and the capacity for expanding exports was not so insignificant, that the choice favoured the attempt to achieve positive real rates of interest. In addition, an additional argument was at hand: domestic investment was so feeble (after 20% in 1990, it reached 12.3% of GDP in 1991, the lowest level since 1945) that bringing in foreign capital was also necessary in order to promote recovery and restructuring in industry.

The other controversy is a Romanian version of the much-celebrated confrontation between elasticity 'optimists' and 'pessimists'. The latter point out the structural rigidity and heavy import dependency of the economy. Thus, they fear that devaluation would only fuel inflation, without provoking a quick and significant improvement of the trade balance. On the other hand, they ignore an essential truth hovering over the functioning of the Romanian economy: the much-overvalued exchange rate, which has been discouraging exports and has been subsidising imports. That devaluation was the right move is proved by the dynamics of foreign trade which scored a succession of surpluses after June 1992. Moreover, temporary real unification of the exchange rate (and the disappearance of the black market for foreign exchange) – as a fundamental structural achievement in the mode of functioning of the economy – was obtained during the second half of 1992.

Table 6.4   Exchange rate Lei/USD

Period			End of period	
		Official	Interbank rate	Market rate
1991				
	January	34.74	-	-
	February	34.86	203.00	-
	March	36.97	200.00	-
	April	60.67	200.00	-
	May	60.35	190.00	-
	June	62.05	190.00	-
	July	60.77	270.00	-
	August	61.38	250.00	-
	September	59.77	230.00	-
	October	60.36	260.00	-
	November	-	-	184
	December	-	-	189
1992				
	January	-	-	198
	February	-	-	198
	March	-	-	198
	April	-	-	206
	May	-	-	226
	June	-	-	304
	July	-	-	365
	August	-	-	383
	September	-	-	430
	October	-	-	430
	November	-	-	430
	December	-	-	430

Source: National statistics

Unfortunately, political reasons connected with the elections of September 1992 stymied the determination of the government to pursue a consistent exchange rate policy. Once the official exchange rate was stuck again (at Lei 430/$1) trade imbalances reappeared (in October 1992) and the spread between the official rate and the black market rate resurfaced alarmingly at the end of 1992 (Lei 430/$1 vs. over Lei 600/$1 for the black market rate). In this case, one can see how easily politics can alter economic policy and eliminate a structural achievement acquired through a lot of effort. As far as the interest rate policy is concerned, it had little success since arrears – as a form of *quasi-money* – provided enterprises with very cheap credit and enabled them to continue putting pressure on the foreign exchange market and push prices upwards. In fact, arrears, which can be viewed as a defence reaction of the old system, *endogenise* money supply and largely emasculate monetary policy. They mirror structural and sectorial disequilibria within the economy and make up a *structural trap* for stabilisation policy.

The first three years of stabilisation policy in Romania encountered a major dilemma: how to reconcile the urgent need to address the external constraint with the aggregate internal disequilibrium (understood in a broad sense) against the background of the lack of restructuring and of financial (market) discipline caused, essentially, by unclear property rights.

Interpreting (dis)equilibria in transforming economies

New phenomena such as open inflation and open unemployment connote new forms of operating disequilibria in the emerging market economies. They still coexist with substantial hidden unemployment and price controls making up complex and intricate combinations of imbalances. We can think also of other genres of disequilibria, which go out of the strict realm of conventional economics, and which can help us in understanding better the functioning of economies (societies) in transition. I have in mind something that could be called 'organisational disequilibrium' meaning the shortage of market-required organisational capital. Another prime candidate for discussion can be the gap between people's expectations and what governments can deliver in the short run i.e. 'expectational disequilibrium' or excess expectations. The micro-foundations of macro-disequilibria should also be under close srutiny; the extent to which Say's principle operates and hard budget constraints are imposed.

Recently there has been a flurry of research activity obsessed with the brutal drop of economic activity in the region.[31] Why is so large and why so persistent 'aggregate disequilibrium' in the broad sense? To give an answer one needs first to define the potential performance under the circumstances.

It is often asked rhetorically 'why have we overestimated by so much the actual and potential performances of the former centrally planned economies'? If we admit this 'performance illusion' then, part of the fall in output can be seen as a normal *depreciation*, at world market prices, of production. 'The Midas-touch effect' in reverse[32] can explain the damage caused to the economy in a dynamic sense, and to its performance potential. Otherwise said, institutional rearrangements (turning the system into a market based economy) would not lead to that increase of performance which might be suggested by the past flows of inputs (accumulated capital and human stock) and macrostructural changes.[33] Another way of looking at this issue is by exploring missing factors in an extended (multifactor) production function. Here the finger could be put on 'organisational capital' (P. Murrel, 1991)[34] and on critical institutions[35] which cannot be built overnight. Moreover, let us not forget that imports are not a solution since the aforementioned factors, essentially, cannot be but home-grown. From this perspective, the proper set of property rights – which cannot be decreed and enforced by authorities at will – appears as a structural constraint affecting potential performance.

What about the rest, or the corrected – after depreciation – J-curve (or L-curve) effect mirroring aggregate disequilibrium in this broad sense? Taken as outcome, the performance deficit can be related to *structure, policy* and *environment* (Th. Koopmans, J. M. Montias, 1971).

Reform of property rights shows that drawing the conceptual dividing line is not an easy task. Where private property rights can be quickly enacted and enforced, and they actually drive individuals' actions and enhance efficiency (land reform and active privatisation are examples), structure is very much alive as a target for transformation policy. However, when the texture of property rights is harder to define and the governance issue clouds the sky, one easily trespasses into the territory of developmental matters. Nonetheless, it is clear that when fuzziness about property rights is policy-related action is urgently required. I will give an example from Romania's experience. Law 15 of August 1990 on 'Restructuring of State Economic Units' devolved power by creating confusion as to the owners of enterprise assets. In this way collusion phenomena are encouraged, management contracts (to monitor the performance of managers) were easily circumvented by managers and, ultimately, the prerogatives of the state (as the owner of the still unprivatised property) have become devoid of substance.

Admittedly, the fuzziness created by this law has been embedded in a climate of *'citizens' rebellion'* against any kind of authority, but the fact remains and gives much concern to policymakers. Together with 'citizens' rebellion', fuzziness about property rights can explain the rise in X-inefficiency and the non-profit centred objective function of enterprises, which strive to boost wages and preserve jobs. My contention is that as long as property rights will not be well defined and enforced, budget constraints will be soft enough to undermine efforts to stabilise the economy; *hardening the budget constraints represents the 'Achille's heel' of stabilisation policy.*

Underlining the weak micro-foundations of macroeconomic policy in transforming economies does not mean that the remedy is around the corner. Clamoring in favour of privatisation[36] does not help much when the real process is slow and cumbersome. Notwithstanding, all available means must be used in order to impose financial discipline.

Structure can help us in understanding why it is so hard to impose financial discipline – over and above the general climate in the economy and inadequate property rights. Let us focus on the given distribution of resources (assets)! Transformation sets in with an initial endowment of resources that spans the whole spectre of enterprises: negative value added, non-profitable, but still positive value-added, and profitable units. 'The power of the weak' (the loss-making enterprises) is the power of the structure over those which can make ends meet financially but are trapped into the network. Inter-enterprise arrears are, perhaps, the most telling embodiment of this phenomenon. The higher the deficits in real performances and the larger the share of total output held by giant loss-making units, the more overwhelming is the power. The events in Romania (e.g. 'the global compensation' of December 1991), in Russia, and in many other transforming economies fit this description. A way out of this mess would be to devise a sort of industrial policy that would buttress stabilisation by means of an effective income-control and *enterprise reform* (including restructuring).

The initial factor endowment, as a legacy of communist industrialisation, can bring fortune to some and misery to others. It lies at the roots of what can be construed as a *distributional struggle* within society between potential haves and have-nots. In so heavily monopolised and monopsonised economies inflation is resurgent and a vicious circle can emerge. Because of external and internal shocks the social pie shrinks, pressure groups demand and get higher wages to keep pace with rising prices, the wage-price spiral is given a further push, monetary and fiscal policy must be tightened, output shrinks further, and the vicious circle goes on – see Figure 6.2.

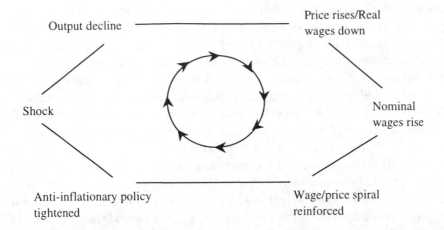

Figure 6.2   The vicious circle due to distributional struggle

This scenario is more plausible the less mobile resources are and the less competitive markets are, and when governments are weak and likely to give in to pressures.[37] The policy impact on aggregate disequilibrium (performance deficit) makes us automatically direct attention towards the efforts deployed to combat inflation – on stabilisation policy and its effects on aggregate supply and aggregate demand which show up as abrupt and seemingly persistent declines of output and slowly, but steadily, rising unemployment.

What could be the theoretical underpinnings of the macroeconomics of transition? A way to proceed is to link stylised theoretical explanations with the two competing visions within the paradigm provided by the neo-classical analytical frame. One of them, best represented by new classical macroeconomics, rejects any state intervention in the economy, since agents, as rational beings – it is argued – optimise using all available information, in contrast to agents' 'bounded rationality' (Simon H. 1958). Microeconomic optimisation would secure full price flexibility and, thereby, sufficiently rapid allocation of resources. According to this vision, any rate of unemployment is natural since it expresses agents' preferences. The other vision starts from the assumption that prices are rigid to an extent that induces adjustments through quantities as well, so that aggregate demand equilibrates aggregate supply below full employment. There is talk then of a non-Walrasian equilibrium, which would invalidate Walras' Law. Both visions look at the functioning of a market economy.

If the transforming system is viewed as a pathological form of market economy, wherein structural disfunctionalities and rigidities are extreme, some hypothesis can be submitted. Implementation of any shock treatment would lead to significant drops in production, at least in the first phase. In this stage of transformation, the entrenched structures are being broken and changed, which means that the quantity of *friction* inside the system goes up considerably and important energies (resources) are consumed in order to accommodate change. A lot boils down to a change of the organisational behaviour of economic actors, to the build-up of new organisational capital. In this phase of transition there exists a territory over which both commands and markets function according to their inherent logic. Over this territory, market co-ordination failures combine with the 'abandoned child' feeling of many enterprises, which are no longer able to rely on central allocation of both suppliers and customers. For these enterprises information and transaction costs skyrocket. This perspective can get interesting insights from 'structuralist macroeconomics' (L.Taylor, 1983, 1991) which can help highlight perverse effects of 'orthodox' policies undertaken during transition.[38]

What neither of the two visions can tackle adequately is the weak microfoundations of macroeconomic policy in a transforming system, wherein budget constraints are still soft and short-term economic rationality of many units and individuals clash with the need to reallocate resources. Monetary and fiscal policies can hardly be effective when market discipline is weak. The temporary quasi-money represented by arrears, as a symptom of weak market discipline, shows the relative ineffectiveness of tight monetary policy under the circumstances.

An issue that, in my opinion, has not been put under proper scrutiny is 'implementation of stabilisation policies in free-falling economies'. It is clear that much of the decline in output is due to what was named depreciation of potential performance, due to structure and external shocks (like the collapse of CMEA and foreign competition). The crux of the matter here is not apportioning the blame for the drop of output,[39] but realising the impact of stabilisation on rapidly falling aggregates. Another way of looking at the impact of policy on the dynamics of output is to consider the process of *market destruction* and *construction*. In this respect, I would use the term 'network deconstruction', which connotes delinkages produced in the system because of its functional opening. A command system relies on chain links whereas a market system is based on parallel connections. The opening of the economy perturbs entrenched relationships and it starts a process of delinking whose outcome is that a growing number of domestic players may be out of the game;

this process can be viewed as a short-run *market co-ordination failure* that leads to declines in aggregate effective supply and aggregate effective demand. For the delinked parties information and transaction costs are exceedingly high. It can be argued that delinking puts pressure on inefficient units and speeds up restructuring. However, this does not necessarily compensate the undesirable effects on aggregate domestic supply. Within such a framework *hysteresis* phenomena can and should be dealt with. Let us only think about rising unemployment and the effects of an overly open (too unprotected) economy in a world with imperfect markets and fierce competition.

The discussion can be broadened and led in terms of a 'dual economy', with a healthy and dynamic sector and a retrenching, declining sector. As long as the declining sector has the upper hand economic aggregates would follow downward-shaped curves. The recovery sets in when the growth sector goes over a threshold in its share of output held in GDP. Four essential variables can be thought of as influencing the dynamic of aggregate supply: the shares held initially by the two sectors, the speed of growth and that of decline, and the *metamorphosis* speed. The latter indicates the restructuring of parts of the declining sector (resource reallocation) which join the healthy sector. The speed of metamorphosis affects both other speeds, but cannot be identified with either of them. Manipulating the essential variables can suggest different situations. One situation can involve rapid and brutal downturn, quick recovery and intense metamorphosis, hopefully brought about by substantial inflows of foreign investments.[40] A J-curve like situation means less brutal decline than in the first case, but still impressive, whereas the upturn is not in immediate sight; metamorphosis is less strong. An L-curve like situation denotes strong imbalance between market destruction and market construction with the upturn remote. The intensity of metamorphosis (of resource reallocation) determines the scope of *hysteresis* phenomena and, broadly speaking, the dynamics of *social equilibrium*; the fewer the losers, the smoother the transformation will unfold.

Social equilibrium leads us to the *expectational shock* the transforming economies have undergone. People expect governments to deliver the goodies after decades of communism and, in the Romanian case, after a terrible shock therapy in the 80s. Expectations are high whereas output – even if corrected for the increase of variety, quality, and availability of goods – has been going down dramatically. A growing gap between aspiration and reality can easily perturb the fragile social and political equilibria and undermine stabilisation policy.

Expectations should be related also to moral goods seen as public goods.

What also makes the post-communist transition difficult is a legacy of pervasive moral crisis. It is hard to build new institutions when truth-telling, trust, loyalty are very scarce commodities. As K.Arrow (1974, p. 23) said: 'They are goods... they have real, practical, economic value; they increase the efficiency of the system, enable you to produce more goods or more of whatever value you hold in high esteem'. Two ideas can be put forward in this respect. First, production of intangible goods – understood as moral reconstruction of society – is a must for helping a recovery of the output of material goods and services; the former 'crowds in' the latter. Secondly, trust, truth telling, and loyalty can substitute tangible goods to a degree, which is particularly important when depression is a dangerously lengthy affair.

Concluding remarks

How to stabilise the economy – achieve aggregate equilibrium in the narrow sense – how to stop the fall of output and, eventually, resume growths are daunting tasks for policymakers in the transforming systems. When policy overshoots[41] and takes the economy outside a zone covering an assumed optimal state (mix) of disequilibria, at fault is not necessarily the decision-maker but the weaponry at his disposal. Policymakers always overshoot, or undershoot, as markets do – which means that they can rush things above the *natural rate of adjustment*[42] of society, or underestimate the potential for change of the social fabric. Since policy over(under)-shooting is practically unavoidable, the problem lies with reducing the deviation as much as possible. Another interesting question to answer is on which side policy erring is to be preferred assuming that the goal of keeping the deviation at a minimum is kept in sight. Here one deals with both objective and subjective elements for making a judgement.

In my opinion, in the transforming economies the policy-mix of stabilisation should not rely exclusively on classical tools. Fiscal and monetary policy, exchange rate policy, income policy, need to be complemented by an industrial policy that should help tackle the crucial issue of *enterprise reform* (S.Van Wijnbergen, 1992) and impose market discipline. Industrial policy linked with enterprise reform has been given a too low profile or neglected, which has crippled economic policy, in general, and stabilisation in particular. Industrial policy can reduce the costs of stabilisation, can help policymakers deal with the three major constraints (the foreign exchange gap, the budget deficit and the low level of savings) in making choices about the trade-off between external disequilibrium and internal disequilibrium, the latter with its many facets. It can also help dealing with the big trade-off (A. Okun, 1975) which has come into the open in post-communist societies: efficiency vs. equality. It is noteworthy that even the experience of frontrunner transforming economies suggests the need for such a policy (G. Szapary, 1992). I fully share reservations about industrial policy seen as a means to pick winners especially in an environment with so much uncertainty and lack of transparency. However, under the circumstances, industrial policy should rather be viewed as a *damage-control device,* aimed at allowing a breathing space needed to cope with the high degree of uncertainty and fuzziness about property rights, and to mitigate the costs of restructuring and resource reallocation. A complete 'hands-off' reform policy on the part of the governments is unjustified not only by the lack of institutional prerequisites for market forces to operate effectively, but also, by the simple fact that these forces alone would impose unbearable costs on societies. In Central and Eastern Europe we deal with markets in their infancy, which need to be nurtured in a world of imperfect information and competition. There is need and scope for industrial policy which should aim at helping restructuring along market signals, and at protecting the main asset of these societies which is made up of segments of highly skilled labour. A paradox in these societies is that striking ignorance coexists with tremendous intellectual and labour capabilities. This situation can lead to a possible across-the-board over-depreciation of the factors of production. Capital and technology inflows, as well as the functional opening of the economies, could counteract an over-depreciation of segments of the economy, but could also impose undue hardships on it and stalemate reforms.

Industrial policy is critical for bridging the gap between the effectiveness of controlling demand and that of stimulating supply. Supply responsiveness is so low that stabilisation seems to be hardly sustainable. When I mention industrial policy I refer to a combination that correlates income-control measures with industrial restructuring (including privatisation) initiated by public authorities which process information provided by markets. I have also in mind the introduction of a proper set of incentives for managers of state-owned enterprises, which should induce them to run these units efficiently. Slow privatisation makes the improvement of the management of state-owned enterprises urgent. The goals would be to put a lid on high inflation, alleviate unemployment (to cope with the hysteresis phenomena) and to promote exports. Such a policy is more urgently needed when the social pie is considerably smaller, redistribution effects impact negatively on many people, and safety nets are not adequate.[43]

Transformation is a process with a pronounced social and cultural dimension, that involves overcoming inertia, changing mentalities and psychologies (the creation of a new social ethos adequate for a market economy), a fierce struggle among 'coalitions of interests' (M. Olson, 1982), some of which support change whereas others withstand it. The clash of various interests in society, against the background of an evolving structure of ownership, raises the degree of autonomy of the process in the sense of reducing the room to manoeuvre of decision-makers. For smooth landing the process needs to be supported by a strong coalition of interests. This 'reform constituency' cannot be built overnight since privatisation is very slow. Since, as a *real* process, change cannot be but evolutionary policy would have to be shaped appropriately.

Stabilisation itself would have to be understood as a process most likely to follow a *stop and go* cycle. I submit that the control of disequilibria will feature a *stabilisation policy path* moving in tandem with the speed with which the economy will acquire more of the basic ingredients of an advanced market environment. In this vein the stabilisation policy, itself, could undergo a 'stabilisation process'.

The bottom line is: when can overall growth be resumed? The answer is not easy. A pessimist would point out the success story in Latin America – Chile, that needed over 15 years to embark on a sustainable growth path – and would doubt that people in Eastern Europe and the CIS would be so patient.[44] Additionally, the international environment, with worrying trends (beggar your neighbour policies, lastingly modest economic activity in Europe, etc.) would be pointed at. An optimist would, perhaps, stress the major comparative advantage of these economies – an abundance of highly trained labour and considerable R&D capabilities – which, from a 'neo-growth theory' perspective might bring about sizeable rates of growth in the not too distant future.

Notes

*   Many thanks to Laszlo Csaba and Joshua Greene for their helpful comments. As usual, I bear sole responsibility for the content of the paper. This material was presented at the Congress of the European Association of Comparative Economic Studies, Groeningen, September 1992; it was also published as IMF Working Paper, no.73/1994, and appeared in L. Csaba (ed.) (1994), 'Privatisation, Liberalisation and Destruction. Recreating the Market in Central and Eastern Europe', Dartmouth, Aldershot, pp. 189-212.

1   The Keynesian case of unemployment appears as a state of disequilibrium according to the first definition mentioned, if one bears in mind the existence of excess supply of labour at operating wages.

2   An economy where domestic absorption exceeds domestic output can be viewed as being in a stable state as long as the disequilibria of the current account balance are tolerated by the outer world. When adjustments can no longer be put off, they will take place at the level of individuals and economic organisations. For an application of the concept of equilibrium at the level of individuals (economic agents) see, for instance, F. M. Fisher (1985, particularly p.160).

3   The degree of inefficiency, (e), practically reduces labour productivity. In order to simplify analysis, only labour is considered in the production function.

4   Policymakers over(under)react according to their preference function, which does not fit a Paretian welfare function.

5   Internalisation is more intense the smaller is the efficiency of the utilisation of imported capital.

6   The general criteria for measuring internalisation in the first situation (the second situation speaks for itself) sounds like this: the extent to which repayment of the external debt creates a cumulated (over time) net disutility for the economy which translates itself into lower consumption and smaller economic growth rates.

7   The costs are felt on the supply-side of the economy in another way as well: prolonged containment of internal consumption with the inherent lack of new material incentives to producers and individuals would hardly stimulate innovative efforts. In a worst scenario, the consumption effect and the production effect would reinforce each other on a downward spiral. This point was made forcefully by L. Antal (1983) as well.

8   Benefits could accrue to the economy should a significant change occur in the attitude of the trading partners, following an improved financial standing of the debtor country.

9   In spite of the known term structure of the external debt, its period of repayment becomes variable in the optimisation analysis; the debt can be repaid faster than the period suggested by its maturities or it can be restructured and paid back over a longer period. In general, it is hard to think that the time variation of internalisation can enable a one-time process to take place since the critical floor levels of consumption and investment (obviously different for each national economy) act as restrictions.

10 The relative ease in subduing open inflation in Czechoslovakia would vindicate partially R.Portes (1977) – in particular, and others who pointed out that central planners can be quite effective in keeping macro-disequilibria under control. Relatedly, I would say: (a) traditionally, Czechoslovakia has had a 'comparative advantage' in this respect vis-à-vis her communist neighbours; (b) after the invasion of 1968 the new communist leaders entered into a kind of social contract with the populace: better and more consumer goods through an altered

investment policy; (c) though command economies generate shortages constantly and macro excess demand is a structural feature of the system, central planners can react and alleviate both micro and macro imbalances. When the assessment is made in terms of foregone efficiency (performance), due to the impact of the command system, the country finds itself at a tremendous loss after more than four decades of communist rule. One should recall that the former Czechoslovakia was a leading industrial power in Europe before the Second World War.

11   See J.Bhagwati (1958) and H. Johnson (1967), especially.

12   At the end of the 80s, these imports were ca. 10% of the level at the start of the decade (0.1 billion in 1989 as compared to 1.1 billion in 1990).

13   In two main instances import substitution entailed soaring costs of production that showed up in higher nominal values of output. First, it is the case of promoting very costly domestic production of technology and equipment. Secondly, rising costs accompanied inexorably the efforts deployed to increase the degree of procurement of energy and raw materials out of domestic sources.

14   In the case of Poland L. Podkamminer (1982) stresses the spillover effects in consumption due to distortions in relative prices.

15   There is yet another aspect about forced substitution in consumption that needs to be pointed out. Consumers are forced to purchase products of very low saleability, which in conditions of a buyers' market would go almost instantly out of production. Not only that the consumer's utility bought by a certain amount of money is reduced through forced substitution; there is an illusion created of a possible value equality between the aggregate demand for and the aggregate supply of goods through an administrative fixing of the prices (values) of the inferior goods. Here one deals with additional distortions in prices that can create false value equality between aggregate demand and aggregate supply.

16   'It is important to recognise that household behaviour, including the supply of labour and effort, is clearly determined by shortages faced in markets for individual goods, but unaffected by the existence of unsold inventories of other, overpriced goods' (J. Brada, A. King, 1986, p.174).

17   The switch was reinforced by a shunning of domestic goods in favour of imported goods (a phenomenon acutely felt in the former East Germany).

18   What my colleague E. Ghizari named *decompression.*

19   Exports to the former CMEA member countries fell by about 40% in 1990.

20   Some would link it with the elections of May 1990. Measured real wages rose by 11% over the period December 1989 – October 1990 while output was on the decline; price decontrol was initiated in November of that year.

21   The rising nominal wages against the background of declining output and price controls led to increased monetary holdings.

22   Real GDP fell by 5.6% in 1990, by 12.9% in 1991, and by 8.8% in 1992 (Table 6.2).

23   The trade deficit in hard currency was – $1.743 billion in 1990; it was followed

by – $1.357 billion in 1991 (Table 6.1).

24   In January 1992 P.Murrell asked me: 'why did Romania resort to an IMF supported plan in view of her excellent external account position at the start of the transition?'. I replied that: a) more important than the stock of external debt are the sustainable flows of imports; and b) under the prevailing social and political circumstances rejecting conditional support from the IMF would have forced authorities to try to reimpose direct controls, a path-policy scarcely desirable and, practically, unfeasible at the time. People too often tend to forget that the Chinese solution means 'change controlled from above'. In Romania, the social explosion triggered processes beyond any control.

25   Credit ceilings of 22% were imposed for the year and interest rates (though they remained negative in real terms) were liberalised in April of 1991.

26   From Lei 35/$1 to Lei 60/$1 (Table 6.4).

27   At the level of Lei 184/$1 (Table 6.4).

28   Caused by the increasing overvaluation of the domestic currency due to inflation differentials.

29   Because, officially, internal convertibility was enforced.

30   From Lei 206/$1 in April, it moved to Lei 226/$1 in May, Lei 304/$1 in June, Lei 365/$1 in July, Lei 383/$1 in August and Lei 430/$1 in September (figures are end of month).

31   The conference on 'The Macroeconomic situation in Eastern Europe', jointly organised by the IMF and the World Bank in June 1992, is an example.

32   Expression concocted by J.Winiecki several years ago. Winiecki referred to King Midas of Ancient Greece who turned into gold everything he put his fingers on, including his own food.

33   J.Rostowski (1991, p.191) is very much in my line of thought with his stress that in centrally administered economies the problem is not just that resources are allocated inefficiently, but the process of allocating them is inefficient.

34   The leading fountain of ideas can be found in R. Nelson and S.Winter (1982).

35   Rules enjoying wide social acceptability are also to be included (D. North,1982).

36   J.Sachs and D. Lipton (1991) voiced most strongly the need to privatise fast in order to avoid undermining stabilisation.

37   I owe to L.Csaba the observation that weak governments raise the probability for such a vicious circle to occur.

38   Analysing 'stagflationary effects of stabilisation policies' in reforming economies G.A.Calvo and F.Coricelli (1992) emphasise the similarities between the 'enterprise-side view' and the neo-structuralist approach.

39   Some of the drop – as rightly emphasised by J.Winiecki (1991) – is beneficial since it means doing away with useless production.

40   Like in the former East Germany.

41   This is, for instance, what Gr. Kolodko (1991) and D. M. Nuti (1992) claim has happened in Poland, where too much emphasis was put on reducing external imbalance by 'a too large devaluation of the zloty and too tight monetary and

fiscal policy'.

42   The *natural rate of adjustment* (of accommodating change) of society can be defined as an imagined optimal speed of change that maximises society's welfare function intertemporally; it, itself, is adjustable because of the learning capacity of society. L.Csaba talks about a *natural rate of ownership change* 'which is fairly difficult to bypass, or prevent from happening' (1992, p. 22).

43   A possible scheme would be to link income with the dynamics of saleable output, in the vein of what M.Weitzman proposed in a well-known book (1984). Thus, assuming that market-clearing prices operate (and that optimal sizes for producing units are observable, or can be estimated), enterprises can be split into: negative value-added units, unprofitable (but positive value-added) units, and profitable enterprises. Negative value-added should be closed down without any delay; it is less costly to pay workers unemployment benefits and retrain them than to keep these enterprises running. Profitable units do not pose any problem since they are in good business. The zone of concern for policymakers is represented by unprofitable enterprises which, under normal conditions (with sufficient flexibility of resources), would have to be done away with. The idea is to resort to a phased in elimination according to a timetable that pursues reducing the costs of adjustment. There are two essential variables in the whole scheme. One is the unemployment benefit and another is the additional income provided by the state to workers so that they have an incentive to continue working in an enterprise instead of preferring to accept unemployment benefits. Unprofitable enterprises would be targeted for a gradual phasing-out so that unemployment is attenuated and its cost redistributed over time. At the same time, public authorities would have an easier time in securing resources for a safety net and for facilitating labour reallocation through training programmes. The problem lies in convincing workers about the benefits of this scheme for the economy as a whole and for each one of the targeted enterprises. This can be achieved as part of a social compact within the framework of an industrial relations agreement that sees workers as an active voice in the management of transformation. It could be argued that this scheme may slow down restructuring, which is a valid statement if social and political constraints are dismissed. However, for the sake of process sustainability there are many reasons for advocating an industrial policy.

44   S. Edwards (1991).

References

Arrow, J. K. (1974), 'The Limits of Organisation', Norton, New York.

Bhagwati, J. (1958), 'Immiserising Growth – a geometrical note', *Review of Economic Studies*, 25 June, pp. 201-205.

Borensztein, E. R., et al (1992), 'The Output Decline in the Aftermath of Reform:

the Cases of Bulgaria, Czechoslovakia and Romania', IMF, Washington DC, *Manuscript.*

Brada, J. and King, A. (1986), 'Taut Plans, Repressed Inflation and the Supply of Effort in Centrally Planned Economies', *Economics of Planning*, vol.20, 3.

Calvo, G. and Coricelli, F. (1992), 'Stagflationary Effects of Stabilisation Programs in Reforming Socialist Countries: Enterprise-Side and Household-Side Factors', *World Bank Review*, vol.6, 1, pp. 71-90.

Csaba, L. (1992), 'After the Shock – Some Lessons of Transition Policies in Eastern Europe', Kopint-Datorg, *Discussion paper*, No.8, Budapest.

Demekas, D.G. and Khan, M. S. (1991), 'The Romanian Economic Reform Program', IMF *Occasional Paper*, No. 89, Washington DC.

Edwards, S. (1991), 'Stabilisation and Liberalisation Policies in Eastern Europe: Lessons from Latin America', Department of Economics, UCLA, *Manuscript*, Los Angeles.

Fisher, M. F. (1985), 'Disequilibrium Foundations of Equilibrium Economics', Cambridge University Press, London (second edition).

Hahn, F. (1976), 'On the Notion of Economic Equilibrium' (in French), *Economie appliquée*, 2.

Johnson, H. (1967), 'The Possibility of Income Losses from Increased Efficiency of Factor Accumulation in the Presence of Tariffs', *Economic Journal*, vol.77, pp. 151-154.

Kolodko, G. (1992), 'Structural Adjustment Policy in Poland', *Working Paper*, No.26, Institute of Finance, Warsaw.

Koopmans, T.C. and Montias, J.M. (1991), 'On the Description and Comparison of Economic Systems', in Eckstein. A (ed.), *Comparison of Economic Systems: Theoretical and Methodological Approaches*, University of California Press, Berkeley.

Kornai, J. (1983), 'Equilibrium as a Category of Economics', *Acta Oeconomica*, vol. 30, 2, pp. 145-159.

Lipton, D. and Sachs, J. (1990), 'Privatisation in Eastern Europe: The Case of Poland', *Brookings Papers on Economic Activity*, Washington DC.

Murrell, P. (1991), 'Evolution in Economics and in the Economic Reform of the Centrally Planned Economies', *Manuscript.*

Nelson, R.R. and Winter, S.G. (1982), 'An Evolutionary Theory of Economic Change', Harvard University Press, Cambridge.

North, D. (1981), 'Structure and Change in Economic History', Norton, New York.

Nuti, D.M. (1992), 'Lessons from the Stabilisation Programs 1989-1991', Brussels, *Manuscript.*

Okun, A. (1975), 'The Big Trade-off: Efficiency vs. Equality', Brookings Institution, Washington DC.

Olson, M. (1982), 'The Rise and Decline of Nations. Economic Growth, Stagflation and Social Rigidities', Yale University Press, New Haven.

Perroux, Fr. (1969), 'Independence de la Nation', Aubier Montaigne, Paris.

Perroux, Fr. (1975), 'Active Units and New Mathematics' (in French), Dunod, Paris.

Phelps, E. (ed.) (1972), 'Inflation Policy and Unemployment', Norton, New York.

Podkamminer, L. (1982), 'Estimates of the Disequilibria in Poland's Consumer Markets', *Review of Economics and Statistics*, vol. 64, pp. 423-431.

Portes, R. (1977), 'The Control of Inflation: Lessons from East European Experience', *Economica*, vol. 44, pp. 109-129.

Rostowski, J. (1991), 'Comments on Distortionary Policies and Growth in Socialist Economies' in V. Corbo, F. Coricelli, J. Bossak (ed.), *Reforming Central and Eastern European Economies*, Washington DC, The World Bank, pp. 191-193.

Simon, H. (1959), 'Theories of Decision-Making in Economics and Behavioural Sciences', *American Economic Review*, vol. 49, 3, pp. 253-283.

Szapary, G. (1992), 'Transition Issues: A Case Study of Hungary', IMF *Departmental Memoranda Series*, October 1992.

Taylor, L. (1983), 'Structuralist Macroeconomics', Basic Books, New York.

Taylor, L. (1991), 'Income Distribution, Inflation and Growth', MIT Press, Cambridge MA.

Weitzman, M. (1984), 'The Share Economy', Harvard University Press, Cambridge.

Wijnbergen, S. Van (1992), 'Enterprise Reform in Eastern Europe', *Discussion paper*, No.738, CEPR, London.

Winiecki, J. (1991), 'The Inevitability of a Fall in Output in the Early Stages of Transition to the Market: Theoretical Underpinnings', *Soviet Studies*, No.4, pp. 669-676.

7 Resource Misallocation and *Strain* - explaining shocks in post-command economies[*]

A fundamental tenet in economic theory – which was confirmed by reality – is that a command system allocates resources poorly because of the impossibility of economic calculation.[1] Therefore, once prices are freed and start to operate at quasi-equilibrium (market-clearing) levels, the hidden inefficiencies come into the open and a massive resource reallocation would have to take place – from low to high productivity areas.

More precisely, the issue refers to the possible and probable intensity of resource reallocation in view of constraints such as: the balance between exit and entry in the labour market, the size of the budget deficit and the means for its non-inflationary financing, social and political stability, etc.

A hypothesis I used in other studies[2] is that the magnitude of the process of resource reallocation – the imbalance between exit and entry – brings about tremendous *strain* in the system. Flemming (1992), Aghion and Blanchard (1993), Sachs and Woo (1993), and Gavin (1994) are among those who captured analytically implications of the magnitude of required resource reallocation in a post-command economy. Flemming, for example, focuses on the very shock caused by the brutal changes in relative prices which – as it is argued – would ask for temporary subsidies for the declining sectors. These analyses should be contrasted with Mussa (1982), who considered adjustment in a frictionless environment.

It can be submitted that when the expansion of the private sector is slow, the foreign support is insufficient, external (negative) shocks are powerful, and the underground economy is not effective enough in absorbing the labour shaded by the official economy, the *strain* in the system can lead to its growing destabilisation. Consequently, in spite of possibly vigorous efforts at macroeconomic stabilisation, *strain* should not leave decision-makers insensitive to how they evaluate macroeconomic linkages and work out the policy-mix.

By looking at post-command economies, mainly, this study attempts to show why *strain* emerges within an economic system and what are the implications for a stabilisation policy. Beginning with the closed economy, after which the open economy case is looked at, a possible formalised expression of *strain* is suggested. A distribution struggle, which accompanies resource reallocation, is highlighted. Next, and taken as an example, it is argued that inter-enterprise arrears are also a symptom of *strain*. The study concludes with final remarks. The annex mentions some empirical work done by Joaquim Oliveira Martins on the explanatory power of *strain*. The line of reasoning espoused herein can help in developing an economic explanation of shocks in post-command economies.

The closed economy case

The relevance of the closed economy framework could be questioned. I would argue that, apart from purely theoretical interest and the help it provides in scrutinising the open economy model, its features fit the case of a very large economy – like the Russian economy, even though, this economy suffered the impact of the collapse of Eastern markets.

Let us take the simplified case of a two-commodity economy – see Figure 7.1. The initial production combination, (a_1, b_1), still reflects the central planners' preferences; the latter are indicated by the price line P^1. Were consumers sovereign, the production combination would be (a_2, b_2) and the price line denoting equilibrium (market-clearing) prices would be P^2. Were resource reallocation without friction – with no imbalance between exit and entry – there would be no *strain* in the system; the shift from (a_1, b_1) to (a_2, b_2) would take place along the production possibilities curve.

In a real economy friction is unavoidable. Furthermore, the imbalance between *exit* and *entry* can be considerable, and it can cause the production combination A to be substantially inside the production possibilities curve – the fall of the output of (a) is not accompanied by a corresponding growth of the output of (b). This means a significant reduction of aggregate utility – from I_1 to I_2 – if the expansion of the unofficial economy does not offset it. Over time the production combination would have to come ever closer to (a_2, b_2). The thick arrow in figure 7.1 shows this process.

The magnitude of the required resource reallocation can be illustrated by the ratio:

$$(1) \quad J = \frac{p_a^*|q_a^*-q_a|+p_b^*|q_b^*-q_b|}{p_a^*q_a^*+p_b^*q_b^*}$$

where (p^*) and (q^*) refer to equilibrium values, whereas (p) and (q) correspond to the current (distorted) resource allocation. J can be viewed as a measure of aggregate disequilibrium (in the system) against the vector of equilibrium prices and quantities.[3] The general form of (1) is:

$$(2) \quad J = \frac{\sum p_i^* |q_i^* - q_i|}{\sum p_i^* q_i^*}$$

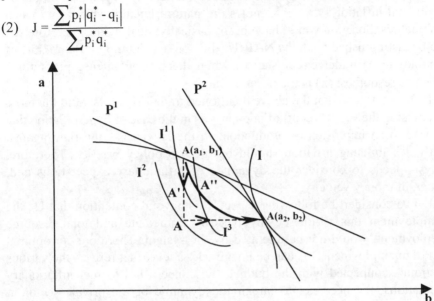

Figure 7.1   Reallocation in a closed economy

The size of the above ratio measures the *strain* within the system and reflects the magnitude of aggregate disequilibrium.

It can be assumed that the possible level of unemployment is related to the degree of *strain* in the system: the higher is *strain* (resource misallocation) the higher is the unemployment that would be brought about by the required resource reallocation. This is a major reason which lies behind the temptation to tolerate high inflation rates as a way to diffuse the tension within a system. Thus, in the social cost function:

$$Z(U, \pi) = (U - U^n) + \beta\pi^2$$

the weighting parameter (β) is lower the more pressuring is the unemployment level, or when inflation emerges as the only way for diffusing tension in the system. Thus, let us consider the Phillips curve relationship, $U=U_n - \alpha(\pi-\pi^e)$, where π^e is the expected inflation rate. The social cost function can be written as $Z(U, \pi)=(U^n- \alpha(\pi-\pi^e)-U^n)+ \beta\pi^2$, or $Z(U,\pi)= -\alpha(\pi-\pi)+ \beta\pi^2$. It can be seen that

Z is inversely linked with unexpected inflation, and directly linked with effective inflation. Minimisation of the social loss function implies: $Z'(\pi) = -\alpha + 2\beta\pi = 0$. Therefore, the optimum level of inflation is $\pi = \alpha/2\beta$. The smaller is (β) – i.e., the more disturbing is the unemployment level – the higher would be the optimal inflation rate. U^n denotes the natural unemployment rate when resource misallocation would have been, basically, dealt with. Therefore, U^n is to be distinguished from the NAIRU (the non-accelerating inflation rate of unemployment) under circumstances when there is an intense pressure to reallocate resources; (π) is the inflation rate.

It can be argued that the above mentioned trade-off is less valid the more destabilising the very level of inflation is – as in the case of hyperinflation that can lead to an implosion of production. In the latter case, the fight against highly destabilising inflation should be the top policy priority. Therefore, analysis needs to consider the dynamics of inflationary expectations and, further, of money velocity.

Let us consider the following aspect. It is beyond contention that U^j, the unemployment that would be involved by immediate and total resource redeployment, would not be tolerated by the system. Therefore, an optimal level of unemployment, U^*, can be imagined – a level that reflects the various constraints connected with the budget, the concern not to fuel inflationary expectations, the need not to impair the dynamic of the private sector in particular, and of the economy, in general, etc.[4] This optimal level implies a resource transfer via explicit and implicit subsidies. The transfer appears as a combination of non-inflationary and inflationary financing. The major inference is that, by presuming a limit to the volume of available non-inflationary financing, a higher *strain* makes more likely, and raises, the amount of unavoidable inflationary financing – either through deliberate money creation or through the growth of temporary quasi-inside money (inter-enterprise arrears[5]). It follows that the expected inflation, π^e depends on *strain*: $\pi^e = \pi^e (J)$. Figure 7.2 shows how *strain* (J) affects the trade-off between inflation and unemployment; a higher J leads to an outward shift of the curve. In Figure 7.2 $J_1 < J_2 < J_3$.

Are there any phenomena which can alleviate *strain*? Yes, and some of the most important are: inter-enterprise arrears,[6] monopoly pricing, explicit and implicit subsidies, spillover effects,[7] the elimination of negative value-added activities, *learning*, and last, but not least, the efficiency reserves of producers (who operate within their production possibilities curves themselves). In Figure 1 A' denotes the action of the mentioned phenomena, whereas A'' indicates the expansion of the production of (b) as well.

The more numerous are those who would lose their jobs because of the needed resource reallocation, the more intense would be the opposition against it, against restructuring. Paradoxically, but not surprisingly, *strain* and, relatedly, the acutely felt need to reduce it, can induce a logic of motion of the system that is liable to perpetuate flaws of the old mode of resource allocation.

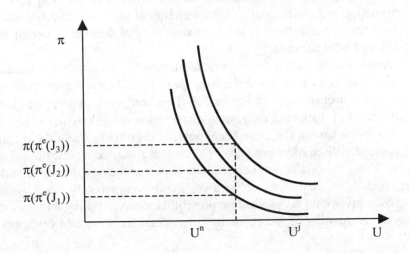

Figure 7.2   How *strain* affects expected inflation

The open economy

There are several notable differences as compared to the closed economy model. The main one is the existence of comparative advantages, which, supposedly, orient – together with consumers' preferences – the allocation of resources. As we know, under a complete specialisation of the economy comparative advantages – alone – would determine the structure of production, while consumption would be determined by the structure of demand and by foreign trade. However, no real economy evinces complete specialisation; comparative advantages are not fully transparent, or total specialisation is not possible (and desirable) – at least, because of the existence of non-tradeables. Besides, sometimes it pays to think in terms of dynamic comparative advantages.[8] It is noteworthy that, in the case of post-command economies, the structure of demand overlaps considerably with the structure of production suggested by comparative advantages – in the sense of the needed expansion of 'hard' goods. This is shown in Figure 7.3 where optimal production indicates the opportunities for specialisation (A_3). For the sake of simplification, Figure 7.3 overlooks non-tradeables.

A second major difference is that domestic prices reflect the open character of the economy – the international exchanges. Since the economy is assumed a price-taker, world relative prices shape domestic relative prices. In Figure 7.3 the world price line P^w shows this. It is obvious that the best production combination is A_3, which, through international trade would bring about the highest aggregate welfare; I_3 is higher than I_2 (that does make use of foreign trade), and both are superior to I_1.

Another difference is that significant demand – and supply-related external shocks[9] lead to a compression (be it temporary) of the production possibilities curve – the broken curve in Figure 7.3. This compression amplifies both the reallocation problem and the related distribution struggle issue.

As in the case of the closed economy, intense friction and the magnitude of aggregate disequilibrium make it such that resource reallocation does not occur along the production possibilities curve; at the new prices P, and were the inefficient activities done away with immediately, A_1 would be considerably within the production possibilities curve. Taking into account the functional opening of the economy, *strain* can be illustrated by a modified ratio:

$$(3) \quad J = \frac{\sum p_i^w \left| q_i^w - q_i \right|}{\sum p_i^w q_i^w}$$

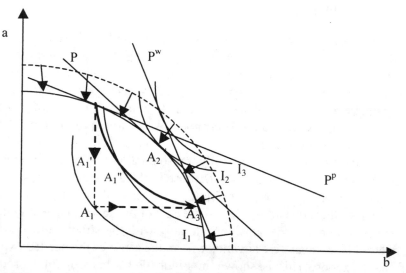

Figure 7.3   Resource reallocation in an open economy

As in the closed economy case, certain phenomena can alleviate the *strain* in the system. Additionally, there are three phenomena specific to the open economy. One is the possibility to export *strain*. The recent years provide a remarkable case study in this respect. Thus, after reunification, Germany exported *strain* to her neighbours, which led to the facto dismantling of the Exchange Rate Mechanism and other consequences. This possibility is more likely to be present the more active and sizeable an economy is in the world space, and the more it operates as a price-maker. For example, after the dramatic rise in the oil price in the seventies, the major industrialised countries experienced a lot of *strain* under the guise of stagflation. However, since these countries (the USA, in particular) operate as price-makers in the world economy, a partial transfer (diffusion) of this *strain* took place via increases of the prices of capital goods. Moreover, the USA, due to their role as provider of the main world currency, were able to pay their way out by simply printing money – by exporting inflation. Exporting *strain* can take the form of protectionism as well.

Another phenomenon refers to how comparative advantages have to be viewed in a world of global sourcing and procurement. By this is meant the non-negligible chances for activities which, presumably, would have to be discarded, to be saved by their getting into a worldwide network of interconnected operations under the aegis of global companies. Finally, possible positive external shocks need to be taken into account.

The thick arrow in Figure 7.3 indicates the path suggesting the probable dynamic of resource reallocation in the open economy.

The *distributional conflict*

Another way of portraying *strain* is to focus on the scope of the required process of overall income (wage) readjustment, which should fit the new market-clearing prices. Under market equilibrium conditions wages equal the marginal productivity of labour: $w_i = q'(n) = dq(n_i)/dn_i$. For the declining and substantially overstaffed sectors, the equilibrium wage is low – even below zero for negative value-added activities. The reverse is the situation for the sectors enjoying comparative advantages, or for which domestic demand is very high.

The modified form of J' that builds on wages is:

$$(4) \quad J' = \frac{\sum n_i \left| w_i^* - w_i \right|}{\sum n_i w_i}$$

where n denotes labour in sector (i), and w_i^* and w_i refer to equilibrium and actual wages, respectively, for the sector (i). $\Sigma n_i = N$, where N refers to all labour resources. For the inefficient, subsidised (explicitly, or implicitly) sectors, actual wages exceed the marginal productivity of labour: $w_i > dq_i/dn_i$. The higher is J', i.e., the higher is *strain*, the more fierce would be the distributional struggle.[10]

It is realistic to presume that the change of the regime of the functioning of the economy (the revolution) has led to high expectations concerning steadily increasing incomes (wages) all across the social spectrum. Therefore J' can be written as:

$$(5) \quad J' = \frac{\sum n_i \left| w_i^e - w_i^* \right|}{\sum n_i w_i^*}$$

where w_i^e denotes the expected income (wage) of agent (i) following the change of the functioning regime of the economy. It is very likely that the expectations adjusted J' is higher than the level that overlooks them.

One should consider a factor that mitigates the intensity of *strain* when expectations are factored into the analysis. In the old system there were informal channels of income redistribution; most of redistribution was caused by shortages (which forced people to pay premiums for acquiring goods in short supply), but also by perks and privileges enjoyed by the party and the bureaucracy nomenclature. The closer those channels brought the initial income distribution to that outlined by the required resource reallocation (at the equilibrium prices) the more significant the above-mentioned mitigation is.

The difference between equilibrium and actual wages reflects the resource transfer (subsidies) practised by the system. The higher is this difference, the stronger will be the forces that oppose change. When the actual (subsidised) wage is significantly more attractive than the unemployment benefit and the labour market has opportunities, the resistance to quit a job is heavy; therefore when:

$$(6) \quad w_i^* + \left| w_i - w_i^* \right| > \varrho \gamma d + (1-\rho) w_j^e$$

where $\left| w_i - w_i^* \right|$ measures the total subsidy, (ϱ) is the likelihood of becoming unemployed, (d) is the unemployment benefit, $(\gamma)\varepsilon(0,1)$ is a coefficient that corrects the utility of the unemployment benefit by a *psychological cost*, and $(1-\rho)$ refers to the likelihood of finding a job in a viable sector (j). The psychological cost can help explain the permanence of what was previously seen as temporary unemployment – the *hysteresis* phenomenon.

The distribution of income between labour and the other factors of production (capital) has an impact on the formation of coalitions of interests. In potentially expanding sectors wages should be lower than the marginal labour productivity: $w < q'(n)$ – this would suggest the room for labour reallocation until $w = q'(n)$; the equalisation would take place by decreasing marginal labour productivity. Nonetheless, to the extent workers behave as quasi-owners and wages equalise marginal labour productivity, or even average labour productivity[11] (for trade unions set wage rates) a bizarre situation can occur: workers in potentially expanding sectors, too, would oppose resource reallocation should the latter be seen as affecting the wage level which is equal to marginal labour productivity. Here one meets a wage *illusion* since the workers in efficient sectors do not realise that they make up the source for the subsidies granted to the inefficient sectors – the inflation tax included. They do not realise, too, that following an adequate restructuring of the economy, the dynamics of subsidies (their diminishing) would more than offset the tendency for the marginal labour productivity to be reduced because of new labour resources entering the expanding sectors. But this realisation would require workers in efficient sectors to optimise by comparing what they gain because of a diminished resource transfer – to subsidised sectors plus unemployment benefits – with the effect of a lower marginal labour productivity owing to labour reallocation.

Critical elements for judging the prospects for resource reallocation are the unemployment benefit (d) and the size of wages in the expanding sectors (w_j). The lower are these the more difficult is reallocation. In this respect Blanchard and Aghion talk about an optimal speed of restructuring, which should be evaluated in conjunction with the state of the budget deficit and, relatedly, the impact on the development of the private sector – for the latter finances, partially, the budget deficit. Sachs and Woo underline, implicitly, the distributional struggle issue when they stress the requirement of providing financial incentives to workers in the subsidised sectors in order to intensify job search and, consequently, to enhance labour mobility. To this end, they stress the importance of foreign aid as a means for breaking a vicious circle of macroeconomic stabilisation.

For post-command (transforming) systems, the *distributional struggle*, which is related to required resource reallocation, appears as a structural origin of *strain* and as a structuralist-type explanation of inflation. Though it is aimed at the Latin-American experience mostly, Williamson's remark is quite relevant in this respect: 'One can look beyond the Patinkinian vision of the economy as a Walrasian system plus a money demand equation, and ask whether it may be necessary to incorporate one important idea in the post-war history of inflation theory...This idea is the notion of inflation as the result of inconsistent claims for real income shares' (1994, pp. 68-69). He adds: '...stabilisation is not only a matter of fiscal probity plus a nominal anchor plus credibility: it may also demand a choice between social confrontation and achievement of a social consensus' (Ibid., p.72).

I would submit that in the case of post-command economies the *distribution conflict* gets a dimension which goes beyond Williamson's meaning; this dimension is given by 'the speed and, particularly, by the scope and magnitude of income redistribution entailed by the required resource reallocation'. In the countries Williamson[12] focuses on, the distributional struggle takes place against the background of a pattern of income distribution, which reflects a relatively stable allocation of resources. Therefore, individuals' expectations are relatively fulfilled. Differently, in the post-command economies a massive resource reallocation is under way, which affects considerably, and brutally, income distribution. Additionally, many individuals' expectations are profoundly unfulfilled. The frustration caused by unfulfilled expectations is magnified by exogenous shocks, which have led to a compression of production[13] under circumstances when individuals are used to a certain pattern and level of consumption.

A symptom of *systemic strain:* inter-enterprise arrears

Elsewhere I argued that inter-enterprise arrears reflect *strain* within a post-command economy (system); that they are a structural phenomenon[14] which will take time to solve as such. As *temporary quasi-inside money*, inter-enterprise arrears endogenize the money supply growth in a perverse way and emasculate monetary policy to a significant extent. This reinforces the train of thought of this study: because of *strain* the achievement of durable macroeconomic stabilisation and subduing inflation to a low level, in a post-command economy, cannot be a one-shot affair; it is a process that will overlap in time and reflect an evolving environment that will, eventually, acquire the critical mass of traits of a fully-fledged market system.

Concerning inter-enterprise arrears in post-command economies, there are other explanations to highlight: the fuzzy state of property rights (Khan and Clifton, 1993), the primitive state of the financial system (Ickes and Rytermann, 1992), the real credit squeeze (Calvo and Coricelli), and the lack of policy credibility (Rostowski, 1994). The latter explanation seems to be espoused by Balcerowicz and Gelb as well (1994, pp.18-19). In what follows I will use a very simple model[15] in order to underline *strain* in explaining inter-enterprise arrears.

Let us suppose that the output of an agent is an increasing function of market *discipline* visualised as a public good, or as a *positive externality* – as a means for easing the efficient allocation of resources. *Market (financial) discipline* emerges as a public good and as a *positive externality* because of collective (generalised) good behaviour. The state does not supply it, though it can influence its production by the enforcement of bankruptcy procedures and the provision of other institutional means. Nonetheless, the state action (policy) of enforcement becomes irrelevant when collective good behaviour is impossible for various reasons, and, as it is our contention, because of *strain* in the main.

Were market disciplines perfect and resource reallocation fast enough, inter-enterprise arrears would not exist; any inefficiency would be promptly penalised. Should inter-enterprise arrears arise however, they would harm creditors – a fact which would be reflected by their output. Taking as a working hypothesis *immediate resource reallocation*, it can be assumed that the production of agent (i) is:

$$q_i = q + c \cdot g \qquad \text{for the agents who do not cause arrears}$$
$$= q \qquad \text{for the agents who cause arrears}$$

Another assumption is that the level of *financial discipline* (g) – seen as a positive externality – is determined by $n \cdot t$, where (t) indicates whether agents pay their debts, and (n) refers to those who do not cause arrears. A final assumption is that $c < 1 < N$, where $N > 1/c$.

Multiple equilibrium situations can be imagined depending on agents' behaviour and the existence of financial discipline as a public good. If agents pay their debts in due time, their incomes show up as $q + c \cdot g - t$, whereas if they produce arrears, their earnings appear as simply (q). The decision for an enterprise is to cause arrears if $c \cdot g = c \cdot nt < t$ or, $n < 1/c$, i.e., when the number of those who pay in due time is low. A conclusion would follow: when policy credibility is low, and when financial discipline is widely disregarded, agents are tempted to produce arrears. Instead, if $n = N$ agent N is stimulated to pay debts since $n = N > 1/c$, as our assumption says.

It would seem that everything boils down to *policy credibility*, to the functioning of market discipline. However, a critical question arises. What is going to happen, and what can be done if the number of those who do not pay is high and, what is even more important, non-payment is the result of the lack of capacity to pay. This means that non-payment is not an opportunistic response to the existing circumstances concerning market (financial) discipline, or the low policy credibility.[16] Consequently, whichever is the determination of decision-makers to pursue a policy course, the sheer number of those who cannot pay makes n<1/c – and thus, the vicious circle of arrears comes into being.

Moreover, the working hypothesis should be made more realistic by assuming that resource reallocation is slow. In this case, a *complete exit* of the inefficient but, still, positive value-added enterprises would mean that output is substantially less than if arrears emerge in the system.[17] Consequently, the short-run production function of an agent could be redefined as:

$$q_i = q + c \cdot g$$ no arrears and immediate resource reallocation

$$= q$$ arrears and no, or very slow reallocation of resources

$$= q - k$$ no arrears and no, or very slow reallocation of resources – the case of an efficient agent

$$= 0$$ no arrears (full exit) and no resource reallocation - the case of an inefficient agent

where k indicates the fall of output when there is full *exit*. It is clear that, under the circumstances, the second situation (that includes arrears) appears as a preferred solution for the short term. It should be stressed that the choice of agents is influenced – in most cases – by their wage fund-centred goal function.

Therefore, when resource reallocation is very slow and when the number of those who cannot pay – because of the lack of capacity to pay – is high, *policy credibility* cannot be the main factor behind the growth of arrears;[18] the main factor is represented by the large number of enterprises which, at the new equilibrium prices, would have to get out of the economic circuit. In addition, since such a huge *exit* is impossible,[19] inter-enterprise arrears emerge as a symptom of *strain* in the system and as a way to diffuse *strain*.

Final comments

The working hypothesis of this study relies on the exceptional magnitude of the required resource reallocation in the former command economies; it aims at emphasising the extraordinary *strain* these systems are undergoing. Ignoring this *strain* would be tantamount to accepting a nonsensical proposition – that the command system was, eventually, capable of allocating resources satisfactorily.[20] One needs to highlight also another factor that enhances *strain*: the change of the regime of functioning of the economy and, relatedly, the scarcity of organisational and institutional capital, which explain high systemic fragility and vulnerability.

It can be argued that the degree of *strain* in post-command economies is the main impediment for the achievement of quick and durable macroeconomic stabilisation.

The assessment of realistic policy choices needs to consider various constraints: the size of the budget deficit and the available non-inflationary means for its financing,[21] the concern not to fuel inflationary expectations, the impact of restructuring on the dynamics of the private sector, the level of external aid (financing), the social consensus regarding the speed of restructuring,[22] the privatisation policy, etc.

Concerning the speed of restructuring, a hypothesis can be submitted. Thus, to the extent restructuring has a positive impact on 'organisational behaviour' and, further, on the efficiency of the overall economy, a virtuous circle can be imagined: restructuring speeds up the change of organisational behaviour, efficiency rises and, consequently, the parameters for judging the optimal speed of restructuring need to be revised. However, the functioning of this virtuous circle depends on the existence of a relationship whose practical validity is questionable. Moreover, a counter-interpretation can be put forward: under pressure, enterprises use their efficiency reserves in order to avoid restructuring – though, in such a case, restructuring can only be postponed, for efficiency reserves are, supposedly, ubiquitous.

Economic policy decisions are hard to make not only because of our limited knowledge, but also because they entail painful trade-offs, irrespective of choices. Viewed from this perspective, the attitude of those who relate failures to the lack of political will, only, is remote of what can be called the 'real political economy' of transformation. In this respect, I fully endorse Kornai's remarks that 'Those who attach intrinsic value to democratic institutions must consider in their proposals the existing political power relations and the rules of parliamentary democracy'. We are not going to achieve much if we rely on advice of this kind: It is our job to advise you about what is good for your country and your job to take our advice. If you do not take it, that is your problem. We cannot help it if your politicians are stupid or malicious' (1994, p. 5).

Aside from the attempt to decipher *strain,* this study has three main messages. Firstly, it does underline that what can be done quickly should be done accordingly; delays can bring about very damaging detours and can create a hard-to-escape 'path-dependency'. Secondly, it cautions against unavoidable trade-offs among policy goals and commends the need to understand what is possible and probable to achieve bearing in mind the complexity of transformation and the *strain* in the system. From this perspective, it is argued that durable macroeconomic stabilisation and bringing inflation to a one digit level takes time and depends on the evolving institutional body of the post-command economies and on the pace of restructuring (resource reallocation).[23] Finally, it is contended that the reasoning proposed herein can be applied to any socio-economic aggregate (economy) undergoing heavy shocks (external and internal) and, in which, consequently, an intense *strain* emerges.[24]

Annex

Strain and structural change[25]

As opposed to a command system, market economies are assumed to possess a high capacity for absorbing shocks due to their intrinsic flexibility and ongoing micro-adjustments.

When faced with a dramatic and sudden change in relative prices, as happened in the post-communist countries after 1989, an economy can adapt more or less easily. While the dynamics of such an adjustment process depends on many interactions (including non-economic factors) and therefore are difficult to measure, it is possible to provide an estimate of the *distance* between two states of an economy at two points in time. This distance conveys some information about the required adjustment.

Depending on the magnitude of this required structural change, an economy can be more or less under *strain* (in a temporary disequilibrium). For an economy (or any kind of organisation), *strain* may nevertheless act as a catalyst to concentrate resources, raise flexibility and thereby speed-up the transition; in other words, it can enhance adjustment. However, it may also produce unacceptable social costs. When faced with unbearable levels of *strain*, an economy can become unstable. In a nutshell, the fine art of a policymaker would be to find the feasible reduction of *strain* over time and manage the transition properly.

As proposed by Daianu, *strain* can be defined as the distance between two vectors of prices and quantities as follows:

$$J = \frac{\sum_i q_i \left| p_i - p_i^* \right|}{\sum_i p_i^* q_i^*}$$

where p_i and q_i refer to current prices and quantities (at the start of transition) for the sector (i) and the (*) denotes their level after the full adjustment takes place. The latter could be associated, for instance, with a shift towards international prices and an economic structure closer to a western country[26] (e.g. a lower share of employment in agriculture and in industry, and expansion of the service sector). A higher J means a higher *strain*, i.e. a larger required change in relative prices. Another way of portraying *strain* is to focus on quantity rather than price adjustment:

$$J' = \frac{\sum_i p_i^* |q_i - q_i^*|}{\sum_i p_i^* q_i^*}$$

These two indicators are dual measures of required structural change. Normally, one would expect the economy to adjust both prices and quantities at the same time. It may happen, however, that either the price or quantity adjustment proceeds more rapidly. In consequence, one should take into account the total level of *strain* in the economy, i.e. the aggregate distance of both price and quantity adjustments:

$$\bar{J} = \sqrt{J^2 + J'^2}$$

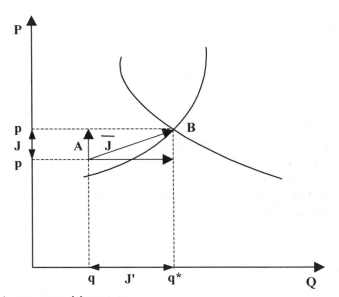

A: pre-transition state
B: post-transition state

Figure 7.4   Illustration of one *strain* indicator

The level of *strain* in labour market adjustment is compared with other countries in Table 7.1. The equilibrium level was defined, in a somewhat arbitrary way, as the structure of relative wages (on the price side) and employment (on the quantity side) in the U.K. for the year 1994 (latest data available). Another benchmark country could be used; the essential results do not change dramatically if, for example, France was chosen instead of the U.K. – see table 7.1.

The results suggest four main points:

i) As expected, the distance between the U.K. and the transition countries, in particular Romania, is much higher than the distance vis-à-vis a country like France. It is important to confirm this basic and intuitive result before pursuing further the interpretation of the indicator.

ii) The distance for the case of Romania is much higher for the employment structure than for relative wages. Somewhat surprisingly, Romania had by 1995 a much closer relative wage structure to the U.K. than other countries in transition. This suggests that prices have adjusted much faster than quantities.

iii) However, the overall required adjustment (combining the price and quantity sides) is the highest in Romania.

iv) Finally, without the agricultural sector, the structure of the Romanian economy would appear much closer to the other countries in transition.

This indicator confirms some of the features of the Romanian economy. Notably, the legacy of the previous economic structure appears to be particularly heavy in Romania at least when compared with other transition countries in Central and Eastern Europe. This may explain why there is so much resistance to structural change; and, also, why inflation and inter-enterprise arrears have become a way of diffusing the pressure in the system when unemployment was not allowed to exceed a certain upper limit (for political reason) and when non-inflationary means for financing the budget were hardly available.

Table 7.1   Levels of *strain* in labour market adjustment

	Romania		Hungary		Poland		Czech Rep.		Slovakia		Slovenia		France	Reference point: UK
	1990	1995	1992	1995	1992	1995	1991	1995	1991	1995	1993	1995	1992	1994
Relative wages (average monthly earnings = 100)[1]														
Agriculture and forestry	104.2	81.6	68.9	76.8	82.3	90.6	97.2	84.2	99.7	81.7	105.3	95.5	72.5	77.9
Industry	98.6	107.6	99.0	104.0	98.7	108.9	104.5	99.2	101.4	104.3	84.9	85.0	111.1	116.5
Construction	110.9	106.4	90.2	84.4	106.1	92.5	106.2	108.0	102.4	104.8	83.0	82.5	98.6	109.2
Trade, hotel and restaurant	86.1	78.2	97.0	90.0	90.3	88.9	85.8	88.2	89.3	94.0	102.2	99.8	90.9	69.9
Transport, communications	108.5	121.0	105.8	106.5	102.1	101.2	102.1	100.7	102.1	108.4	115.0	110.9	105.4	144.6
Financial banking and insurance, real estate and other services	109.3	126.8	144.7	137.4	147.7	137.3	99.9	130.7	103.9	131.4	143.8	124.6	128.0	136.8
Education, health and social assistance	96.5	85.3	93.5	86.5	86.9	81.7	93.2	91.2	97.6	87.2	111.8	109.6	75.8	53.0
Public adm. and defence, other branches	88.9	88.6	118.0	111.3	115.7	108.9	88.5	103.8	103.4	102.5	127.8	132.7	91.0	93.6
Index of "strain"[2] on prices (excluding agriculture)	23.0	9.8	24.1	19.7	18.3	17.0	21.1	19.1	23.8	17.2	33.9	33.1	11.7	
	21.2	12.9	26.0	21.3	22.9	18.1	21.2	20.0	24.0	18.6	34.5	34.8	12.0	
Employment shares (%)														
Agriculture and forestry	29.0	34.4	11.4	8.1	25.5	22.6	12.1	6.6	15.8	9.2	10.7	10.4	5.2	2.0
Industry	36.9	28.6	30.2	27.1	25.2	25.9	41.0	33.2	35.9	30.3	38.7	38.0	20.6	20.2
Construction	6.5	5.0	5.4	6.0	6.6	6.1	5.7	9.2	8.2	8.6	5.4	5.1	7.2	6.4
Trade, hotel and restaurant	6.7	10.4	14.8	15.9	10.7	13.6	7.8	15.7	8.1	13.1	14.6	15.4	17.4	20.8
Transport, communications	7.0	5.9	8.6	8.8	5.5	5.8	9.0	7.7	5.5	7.8	6.5	5.9	5.8	5.8
Financial banking and insurance, Real estate and other services	3.9	4.2	5.2	5.9	1.3	2.0	5.4	6.7	5.4	5.8	4.6	6.1	10.8	12.5
Education, health and social assistance	6.7	8.1	13.6	15.6	13.1	13.3	13.8	12.1	16.5	14.5	10.2	11.4	6.9	14.5
Public adm. and defence, other branches	3.1	3.4	10.6	12.5	12.1	10.7	5.1	8.8	4.6	10.7	9.2	7.6	26.2	17.9
Index of "strain" on quantities (excluding agriculture)	91.4	76.6	47.6	37.2	60.4	56.7	68.1	47.1	68.7	45.9	62.2	56.7	13.8	
	76.4	57.5	41.5	33.7	46.0	42.4	63.1	44.4	63.4	43.2	52.9	48.3	21.8	
Indicator of total "strain" (excluding agriculture)	94.2	77.2	53.3	42.1	63.1	59.2	71.3	50.8	72.6	49.0	70.9	65.6	18.1	
	79.3	59.0	49.0	39.9	51.4	46.1	66.6	48.7	67.8	47.0	63.2	59.5	24.9	

1) Gross monthly earnings, except for Romania, was net.
2) The *strain* indicator is computed as a distance between the structure of relative wages and employment vis-a-vis the UK in 1994.
Source: National Commission for Statistics and OECD

Notes

* Revised version of a paper presented at the annual meeting of the German Association of Political Economy, Frankfurt am Oder, October 1995 and at an economics workshop of the Central European University of Prague, in June, 1995. Many thanks to Fabrizio Coricelli, Laszlo Csaba, D. Mario Nuti for their useful comments. The paper was also published as 'An Economic Explanation of *Strain*: explaining shocks in post-command economies', in J. G. Backhaus (ed.), 'Issues in Transformation Theory', Metropol, Marburg, 1997.

1   Apart from the suppression, or diversion, of the entrepreneurial spirit, which – as best indicated by the Austrian School (Schumpeter, von Mises, Kirszner, Rothbard) – is vital for the dynamics of an economy.

2   See Daianu (1994a, 1994b).

3   See also Portes, 1986.

4   Aghion and Blanchard, or Sachs and Woo highlight such constraints, for example.

5   Inter-enterprise arrears, as a symptom of *strain*, partially endogenise the money supply dynamics and emasculate monetary policy.

6   Daianu (1994b).

7   When supply does not react sufficiently fast consumers may persist in using certain substitutes for a while.

8   I think, mainly, of segments of highly qualified labour.

9   Such as the collapse of Eastern European markets and the worsening of the terms of trade of most post-command economies in their trade with Russia.

10 Daianu (1994a, pp. 202-203).

11 When wages consume the whole product nothing is left for capital renewal or enlargement (for investment) – which is a paradoxical situation bearing in mind the potential for expansion of those sectors. An even worse case is when there is *asset stripping*, when wages are higher than average labour productivity.

12 Williamson glosses over what he considers a standard thinking on macroeconomic stabilisation – well exemplified by the book edited by Bruno, Fischer, Helpman, Liviatan and Meridor.

13 In the ratio (4) the denominator can be written as $(1-\phi) \Sigma n_i \cdot w_i$, $\phi \in [0,1)$, where $(1-\phi)$ illustrates the degree of reduction of the production possibilities curve (and, implicitly, of incomes) because of exogenous shocks. Clearly, J' increases and the *strain* in the system increases as well.

14 Daianu (1994b, especially section III).

15 Sachs makes use of such models in trying to depict the system (institutional) dissolution in the former Soviet Union (1994).

16 The very notion of *policy credibility* needs to be qualified in the case of post-command economies because of the 'thin' history of stabilisation attempts. Without such a history agents react according to entrenched behavioural norms, and not on the basis of learning from past policies and their eventual reversal.

Certainly, when wide-ranging bailouts make up a policy goal reversal stabilisation starts off on the wrong foot and policy credibility is impaired from the very beginning. However, still, a question can be posed: under what circumstances is policy credibility a realistic policy trait and what policy choice favours its attainment. This question suggests the link between *policy credibility* (choices) and *strain*.

17   In this case, the damaging effect of inter-enterprise arrears on efficiency is more than counterbalanced by their mitigating effect on the drop of output.

18   As Agenor says, 'It is the persistence over time that matters to establish reputation of policymakers, rather than the degree of restrictiveness of the policy measures implemented at the outset of a stabilisation programme. Macroeconomic adjustment measures that are not regarded as politically and economically sustainable (within the limits imposed by a democratic regime) cannot be credible' (1993, p.9).

19   Theoretically, a level of foreign aid (or external financing) which should enable a 'big bang' exit can be thought of. Practically, however, this is more than unrealistic as a policy option, and may not even be the best choice.

20   This proposition does not cover the problem of incentives (of microeconomic efficiency) as well. Besides, the poor intra-sectoral allocation of resources would have to be considered, for enterprises of disparate performance potentials can be met in the same sector.

21   See Tanzi (1993). By considering the available means for non-inflationary financing of the budget deficit, and an optimal misery index, one can try to identify an optimal inflation tax.

22   A social pact can be a very useful institutional device to this end.

23   This conclusion is in line with the train of thought defended by the author in two other studies (1994a, 1994b), including the need for an industrial policy, which should be construed as a 'damage-control' device.

24   Japan of the late seventies and early eighties – following the oil price shocks – is an example of a remarkably successful macro- and microadjustment to *strain*. By paraphrasing Hammer and Champy (1993) reengineering post-command economies is a gigantic endeavour, which has to deal with an extraordinary intensity of *strain* at both aggregate (system), and micro levels.

25   Research done by Joaquim Oliveira Martins from the Economics Department of the OECD (Paris); Ms. Anne Legendre assisted him.

26   This may give a justification for computing the *strain* indicator at a relatively aggregated level. At a detailed sectoral level, it would be much less meaningful to use a western country as a benchmark.

References

Agenor, P. R. (1993), 'Credible Disinflation Programmes', IMF PPAA/93/9.

Aghion, P. and Blanchard, O. (1993), 'On the Speed of Transition in Eastern Europe', Mimeo, March.

Balcerowicz, L. and Gelb, A. (1994), 'Macropolicies in Transition to a Market Economy: a three-year Perspective', paper prepared for the World Bank's Annual Conference on Development Economics, Washington DC, 28-30 April.

Bruno, M., Fischer, S., Helpman, E., Liviatan, N. and Meridor, L. R. (ed.) (1991), 'Lessons of Economic Stabilisation and its Aftermath', MIT Press, Cambridge.

Calvo, G. and Coricelli, F. (1992), 'Output Collapse in Eastern Europe - The Role of Credit', *IMF Working Paper*, August.

Cassell, M. (1993), 'The Dangers that Lurk in Delay', *Financial Times*, 23 February.

Daianu, D. (1994a), 'The Changing Mix of (Dis)equilibria in a Transforming Economy', in L. Csaba (ed.), *Privatisation, Liberalisation and Destruction. Recreating the Market in Central and Eastern Europe*, Dartmouth, Aldershot.

Daianu, D. (94/54, 1994b), 'Inter-enterprise Arrears in a Post-command Economy', *IMF Working Paper*.

Flemming, J. (September 1992), 'Relative Price Shocks and Unemployment: Arguments for Temporarily Reduced Payroll Taxes or Protection', Mimeo.

Gavin, M. (January 1994), 'Unemployment and the Economics of Gradualist Policy Reform', *manuscript*.

Hammer, M. and Champy J. (1993), 'Reengineering the Corporation', Harper, New York.

Ickes, B. and Rytermann, R. (September 1992), 'Inter-enterprise Arrears and Financial Underdevelopment in Russia', Mimeo.

Khan, M. S. and Clifton, E. (September 1993), 'Inter-enterprise Arrears in Transforming Economies - the Case of Romania', *IMF Staff Papers*, pp.680-696.

Kornai, J. (May-June, 1994), 'Painful trade-offs in Postsocialism', *Transition*, vol.5.

Mussa, M. (1983), 'Government Policy and the Adjustment Policy', in J. Bhagwati (ed.), *Import Competition and Response*, Chicago University Press, Chicago, pp.73-120.

Portes, R. (1986), 'The Theory and Measurement of Macroeconomic Disequilibrium in Centrally Planned Economies', *Discussion Paper*, no. 91, Centre for Economic Policy Research, London.

Rostowski, J. (August 1994), 'Inter-enterprise Debt Explosion in the Former Soviet Union; Causes, Consequences, Cures', *IMF Working Paper*.

Sachs, J. (28-30 April 1994), 'Russia's Struggle with Stabilisation. Conceptual Issues and Evidence', paper prepared for the World Bank's Annual Conference on Development Economics.

Sachs, J. and Wing, T. W. (October 1993), 'Structural Factors in the Economic Reforms of China, Eastern Europe and the Former Soviet Union', *manuscript*.

Tanzi, V. (September 1993), 'Fiscal Policy and the Economic Restructuring of Economies in Transition', *IMF Staff Papers*, pp. 697-707.

Williamson, J. (1994), 'The Analysis of Inflation Stabilisation (a review article)', *Journal of International and Comparative Economics*, vol.3, no.1, pp.65-72.

8 *Structure* and *Strain* in Explaining Inter-enterprise Arrears[*]

Because of their impact on stabilisation policy and on the transformation of post-command economies, inter-enterprise arrears have captured the attention of both theorists and decision-makers. However, the diagnosis and solutions which have been submitted so far do not directly address what this study considers to be the main source of arrears: *strain*, which itself, can be linked with the *structure* of the economy and the size of *resource misallocation*. Therefore, the study focus here is on the real side of the economy in explaining the growth of arrears and on exploring avenues for their reduction.

Section one deals with macroeconomic implications of arrears. Arrears 'soften' markets and influence the system, apparently, in an ambivalent way: they seem to operate as a self-protecting device against the pressure for change (against the need to proceed with swift and fundamental reforms); at the same time, they can dangerously slow down the speed of restructuring and adjustment by relaxing financial discipline. Arrears tend to preserve a soft-budget constraint syndrome. As *temporary quasi-inside money* arrears in fact fuel inflation: they enable firms to raise prices and wages without fearing immediate consequences. However, paradoxically, arrears can also have an anti-hyperinflationary potential. Since they are only a temporary substitute for real money, arrears work to 'endogenise' money supply dynamics in a perverse way.

Section two underlines that the systems undergoing transformation have been under tremendous *strain* because of internal reforms and external shocks. *Structure* and *magnitude* of *resource misallocation* are highlighted and it is argued that the system develops a logic of motion that entails inflation tax and real interest rates as implicit subsidies. Analogies are made with the adjustment of the industrialised countries following the oil price shock in the 1970s and early 1980s, as well as with that of the oil-importing developing countries to the real interest rate shock in the early 1970s. The dimension of the arrears problem in the various post-command economies is linked, basically, with their *capacity*

195

to adjust, which in turn depends on *structure* and the size of required structural change (adjustment). Relatedly, a paradox of policy credibility in undertaking structural adjustment is emphasised.

Section three uses the Romanian experience as a background in order to show exports as a possible side effect of arrears and as a constraining factor. Arrears tend to restrain the evolution of enterprises along a common denominator path, which explains why those that can grow try to escape the real liquidity constraint by pushing exports: even when exports seem unprofitable a *premium on liquidity* can more than compensate the value differential. Dollarization is mentioned in this regard and the size of the economy is seen as affecting the relationship between arrears and exports.

Section four tries to offer an operational framework for containing arrears. The areas for action include in particular:

- 'breaking up' *structure* by inducing a strategic alliance among creditors and insulating the big offenders (debtors);
- imposing a disciplining 'straitjacket' on *structure* by modifying the set of rewards and penalties so that agents optimise in congruence with the thrust of transformation;
- industrial policy, as part of the policy-mix of stabilisation and transformation, is viewed as a 'damage-control device' ('picking losers among losers') which allows a breathing space needed to cope with the high degree of uncertainty and fuzziness about property rights, and which can mitigate the costs of resource reallocation;
- targeted external assistance. Income-control policy is seen as an essential component of the 'straitjacket' in light of the heavily monopsonised labour markets.

The concluding remarks underline that the best one can hope in fighting inter-enterprise arrears is, essentially, to try to *contain* and reduce them. Containing arrears cannot be a one shot policy-drive. Here one deals with a process that will eventually overlap with the evolving environment.

Macroeconomic implications of arrears

Inter-enterprise credits are a normal way of doing business in a market economy and their existence should not, normally, be a cause of concern. In a mature market economy bank and non-bank credit are of roughly equal size (D. Begg and R. Portes, 1992, p. 9). When certain enterprises enjoy excess liquidity they lend it and, thus, non-bank credit emerges. Complications arise for both theory and policy when credits are not voluntary, or when overdue payments are, as a matter of fact, payments delayed *sine die* i.e., arrears with less than a very slim chance of being repaid.

Inter-enterprise arrears are a symptom of an economy under stress and it is conceivable that during recessions, the length of delays in making payments grows; the weaker, less competitive, firms try to survive by resorting to arrears and, thereby, they spread financial strain around. However, in a well functioning economy market (financial) discipline (see T. Lane, 1992) is a golden rule of the game and, ultimately, *exit* befalls those companies that cannot deliver accordingly.

Ever more attention has been paid to inter-enterprise arrears in the transforming (post-command) economies lately for two main reasons:

a) the peculiar nature of the phenomenon in these systems, with aggregate net arrears portraying congenital inefficiency (losses/incapacity to pay) and gross arrears reflecting the institutional primitiveness of the domestic market environment;

b) the impact of arrears, as *temporary quasi-inside money*, on monetary policy and, ultimately, on stabilisation policy. The evolution of arrears in the transforming economies, especially in those that have started reforms later, has thrown more light on the extreme structural rigidities of these systems and raised questions about the microfoundations of macroeconomic stabilisation policies during transition.

Arrears 'soften' markets

It can be assumed – and empirical evidence supports it – that the more rigid (inadequate) a system is, structurally and institutionally, the more intensely arrears show up as a structural problem. Arrears appear to influence the system in an ambivalent way:

- on one hand they seem to operate as a self-protecting device (like anti-bodies created by an organism) against the pressure for change – the entrenched structures withstand change;
- on the other hand, they can slow, dangerously, the pace of restructuring and adjustment by relaxing financial discipline.

In post-command economies arrears help to preserve, essentially, a *soft-budget constraint syndrome* (J. Kornai, 1980); enterprises have much more bargaining power than in a reformed centrally planned economy whereas soft-budget constraints still operate.[1] In this respect, one can detect a fundamental flaw of the system in transformation, namely the high degree of decision-making power of enterprises when they do not face hard-budget constraints.

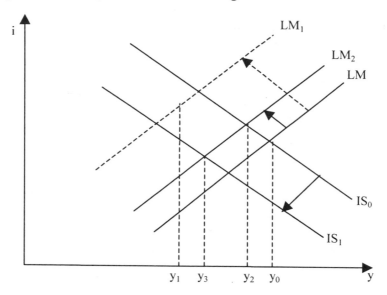

Figure 8.1   Arrears 'soften' shocks and markets

Arrears 'soften' markets – in the sense of relaxing market discipline – and, thereby, cushion against the impact of shocks by moderating the decline of output.[2] The degree of this moderation depends on the dynamic of inflation; the higher inflation is, the less this moderating effect will be. On the other hand, arrears help perpetuate soft budget constraints, complicate monetary policy and slow restructuring (and, thus, preserve resource misallocation). Figure 1, which uses the conventional ISLM diagram, tries to show how arrears moderate output decline once a monetary shock is applied. The tightening of monetary policy would normally mean a shift of LM to LM_1, but due to the growth of arrears, the shift is considerably smaller – to LM_2. Consequently, the decline of output is moderated from y_0 to y_2 (instead of y_1). How durable the LM shift is depends on to what extent and how inter-enterprise arrears will be accepted (or tolerated) by the system.

A way of portraying the softness of markets during transition is to distinguish between nominal net arrears and net arrears, when net arrears are viewed as a measure of system inefficiency. Nominal net arrears take as granted fungibility (mutual convertibility) of receivables and payables which, on a net basis, obscures the degree of loss making within the system. This is illustrated in Figure 1 by a shift of the IS curve from IS_0 to IS_1; the real moderation of output decline is smaller than the nominal one, as depicted by the fact that y_3 is smaller than y_2. The netting out of arrears – not through markets – is partially analogous to an attempt at having multilateralised payments inside the former COMECON trading bloc, a move which was resisted by all member countries because of the different 'hardness' of goods exchanged. Nominal net arrears are smaller than net arrears since they involve transactions, which would not occur were hard budget constraints strictly enforced.

Arrears as 'temporary quasi-inside money'

Arrears are not money creation since, due to currency-constraint, the economy would be brought, sooner or later, to a standstill should prices rise faster than the decline of output and no financial innovation happened that could affect significantly money velocity. It could be argued that arrears, themselves, form a financial innovation,[3] but their *temporariness* as a liquidity means invalidates this argument; arrears are only a temporary substitute for inside money (bank credit). A situation can be imagined where cash and bank credit are used for wage and other currency-demanding payments only, whereas the rest of transactions – which rely on arrears – turn into compensation (barter) deals;[4] it would be a dual monetary system with a demonetised segment of transactions. However, this growing demonetisation would still be subjected to currency-constraint and would have to stop at one point when, either there is a new money injection to support additional money-based transactions (or their nominal growth due to wage increases), or inter-enterprise arrears will start increasing again.

Arrears are inflationary because they allow firms to raise prices and wages without fearing immediate consequences. An intended tight monetary policy – with low credit ceilings and high interest rates – would bring about a brutal drop of output should arrears not provide a 'window of opportunity' for enterprises to escape the financial constraint. However, paradoxically, arrears can also have an *anti-hyperinflationary potential* when they make up a second-worst state of affairs as against a complete accommodative money supply (meant to finance, without restraint, loss-making enterprises and budget deficits). This is, sure, an overstatement for hyperinflation can coexist with growing arrears.

Since they are only a temporary substitute for real money, arrears work to 'endogenize' money supply dynamics in a perverse way. Their growth, related, as both a cause and effect – via inflationary expectations – to rises in prices and wages, makes more binding the cash constraint and magnifies a dilemma for policymakers: either to try to control inflation – ultimately, seen as purely monetary phenomenon – by using, one-sidedly, monetary policy and, thus risk provoking a crash-landing of the economy, or to accommodate money supply to the 'needs' of the economy, a course of action which would maintain the momentum of inflation and would cause hyperinflation.

Strain in explaining arrears

There are several major explanations for the growth of arrears during transition. These include: the state of fuzziness concerning property rights and what it means for enterprise behaviour (S. van Wijnbergen, 1992; M. Khan and E. Clifton, 1992); the set of incentives that shapes behaviour and leads to 'credit market failures' (D. Begg and R. Portes, 1992); financial (institutional) underdevelopment and shortage of information (B. Ickes and R. Ryterman, 1992); the real liquidity crunch following the much higher than expected rise in prices after their deregulation or liberalisation (G. Calvo and F. Coricelli, 1992); and the lack of policy credibility (J. Rostowski, 1992).

Explanations are inter-linked and they pinpoint two foremost features and issues in tackling the arrears phenomenon in the transforming economies, namely, *structure* and *resource misallocation*. Both have put the system under tremendous *strain* once the combination of the internally engineered (by reforms) shocks and external shocks occurred. An outcome of *strain* is arrears.

Structure

Structure refers to the network of institutional arrangements (including rules of conduct that are socially ingrained (D. North, 1981)) and of vested interests (based on material/productive interdependencies and the distribution of property rights) that creates a logic of motion of the system and makes individual enterprises its captives. The vested interests are also the result of the configuration of industry (of industrial structure) as a legacy of the command system – the latter was characterised by chain links, as compared to a market economy which, as a dynamical complex system relies, essentially, on parallel links. This industrial structure, with its extremely high concentration and reliance on chain links, explains the degree of market monopolisation in the transforming economies.

One can talk of a 'power of structure' (a concept quite familiar to business school students), which is well illustrated by the power of debtors over creditors – what Begg and Portes named 'creditor passivity'. This power is not of a conspiratorial nature – the 'cartel' is unconscious – because it rests on the rules of functioning of the system. In this case, creditors, taken individually, find it prohibitively costly to attempt to enforce financial discipline and optimise by desisting from it.

Arrears limit 'freedom of choice' and enhance the 'power of structure'. As argued earlier, arrears are a product of structure. At the same time, they form a protecting device for it and enhance its power. This happens since enterprises, which are caught in the web of interlocked receivables and payables, see the room for potential transactions limited to those that involve the acceptance of arrears; companies that ask for real money as payment will avoid non-liquid partners. Thus arrears limit 'freedom of choice' and, consequently, reduce the variety (K. Lancaster, 1979) and, implicitly, the quality of inputs affecting the quality of output. For certain enterprises – those which do not have a 'defensive survival mentality' – this limitation effect can increase the temptation to escape the trap of arrears and the 'power of structure'.[5]

Resource misallocation

The second feature and issue is the dimension of resource *misallocation*, i.e. the sheer scale of disequilibria – at the new relative prices – that indicates the magnitude of required structural adjustment as compared to the ability of the system to undergo wide range and quick change.

Spread of profitability and dispersion of inefficient enterprises. Command planning, with its inherent impossibility of rational calculation and through forced industrialisation, left a legacy of resource misallocation that was brought, conspicuously, into the open by price liberalisation. The new prices show what was, previously, kept hidden by administrative prices and heavy redistribution of income: a very wide spread of profitability rates and very wide dispersion of units fitting several categories: negative value-added enterprises;[6] inefficient, but, positive value-added units which, in turn, can be split into non-viable and, potentially, viable firms; and efficient enterprises.

The wide spread of profitability rates and the wide dispersion of high divergence in performance enterprises mean that, should market (financial) discipline be strictly enforced, a large number of units would have to go under as a sign of the start of profound reallocation of resources; namely, aggregate output would go down substantially since market destruction is significantly more intense than market construction, in a first stage at least (the so-called J-curve effect). There are two important aspects involved in this process: one is the *scope* of reallocation (dislocation) and, secondly, the *speed* required for maintaining a balance between exit and entry. A plausible assumption is that the larger the scope and the faster the desired speed of the process are, the higher the imbalance will be and tension will build up within the economy. Actually, when we talk about 'low supply-responsiveness' we point the finger at this imbalance.

The problem of the scope and speed of resource reallocation can be posed for an economy operating at any level of employment; any significant change in relative prices would have to bring about resource reallocation. But it makes sense to presume that, the lower the level of employment is, the higher the reluctance will be to undergo change.[7] In this regard, it may be interesting to note the experience with industrialised countries, which had to absorb the oil price shock in the seventies. They had the luxury to undergo the required adjustment at a relatively leisurely pace owing essentially to the quality of the functioning of their economies, their status as world price makers for manufactured goods and the recycling of petro-dollars. Incidentally, monetary policy was also used to delay change, which led to a surge of world inflation.

The post-command economies are fundamentally price takers: they had to absorb a major terms of trade worsening (except the Russian Federation and, probably, Kazakhstan) once world prices started to govern all their trade transactions, and they had to face an almost sudden collapse of Eastern trade following the dismantling of the COMECON arrangements. Additionally, there was a sharp compression of domestic trade and, relatedly, of aggregate supply/demand as a result of skyrocketing information and transaction costs for many enterprises – what Calvo and Coricelli named 'trade implosion' (1992, p. 1) and what I would call, at a more general level, 'network deconstruction'. Due to the extreme fuzziness concerning property rights, it is unjustified to surmise that *X-inefficiency* (H. Leibenstein, 1967), was on the rise in many enterprises – a phenomenon accompanied by pervasive asset stripping. For the transforming economies, the *strain* caused by the magnitude of required resource reallocation, combined with the primitive institutional arrangements and the lack of organisational capital (P. Murrell, 1991), has been compounded by severe exogenous shocks.

Inflation tax and negative real interest rates as implicit subsidies. In a system under substantial strain, there are strong forces that induce a propensity to generate inflation as a way of diffusing tension by spreading out, or putting off, the costs of adjustment. Inflation tax and negative real interest rates are implicit subsidies for those that could not make ends meet financially in a competitive environment. Inefficient enterprises develop a vested interest in raising prices at a faster pace than the dynamics of costs (wages), and, additionally, form a strong lobby in favour of obtaining cheap credit. Their endeavours are made easier since markets are heavily monopolised, a fixed exchange rate – as an anchor and a market disciplining factor – is, almost, a practical impossibility,[8] and the control of money supply is shaky for both technical and political reasons.

The moment stabilisation policy is formulated to combat inflation and monetary policy is tightened, arrears form an escape route for enterprises to continue obtaining credit at no cost and, also, enable them to push prices upward relentlessly. Moreover, inefficient enterprises would clearly view even the diminution of negative real interest rates as a major shock, when it means a substantial cut of the implicit subsidy and brings them 'in the red'.

An analogy can be traced with the situation of the oil-importing developing countries, which, in the aftermath of the oil-price shocks, became heavily indebted by borrowing at highly negative real interest rates; those rates were virtually identical to an invitation to borrow. When interest rates turned positive in real terms on world capital markets a chain reaction was triggered and the world debt crisis of the eighties started to unfold. The basic difference is, however, that whereas domestic firms (in the transforming economies) can run arrears, nations face, essentially, hard budget constraints and are subjected to financial discipline by the international community.[9]

The size of the problem

Analysts have highlighted the relatively lower level of arrears in countries like Hungary, Poland and the Czech Republic, as compared to the Russian Federation, or Romania. Nonetheless, the pernicious effects of arrears bother policymakers in all the transforming economies. It is noteworthy that even where the results of macrostabilisation have been remarkable – like in the Czech republic, where the underlying inflation rate was 6% in 1992 – arrears have shown resilience and have also signalled substantial *strain* in the system.[10] But the question remains: why have the first three countries fared better in this respect? The answer can be pursued by looking at the structure of their economies, their ability to export on western markets and to attract foreign investment, and their size. Furthermore, *structure* is linked with a history of partial changes (that, in some cases, brought about ingredients of market environment), concentration of industry, and the existence of a private sector. Policy credibility[11] can be singled out as a main explanatory factor (J. Rostowski), but it, itself, depends on how much structural adjustment the system can undergo in a period covered by the respective policy. And the *capacity to adjust* depends, basically, on structure and the dimension of *resource misallocation* as initial premises for policymaking.

A paradox is at play here: those who need to be more credible are not (cannot be) because of the magnitude of needed adjustment and the related costs; whereas those who can afford not to undertake similar painful changes (e.g. Hungary) enjoy more credibility due to the, relatively, smaller scale of needed structural adjustment. Granted, a political element has to be factored in as well.

Strain in explaining inter-enterprise arrears – a simple model

In what follows, I use a very simple model[12] in order to underline *strain* in explaining inter-enterprise arrears.

Let us suppose that the output of an agent is an increasing function of market *discipline* visualised as a public good,[13] or as a *positive externality* - as a means for easing the efficient allocation of resources. Were market discipline perfect and resource reallocation fast enough inter-enterprise arrears would not exist; any inefficiency would be promptly penalised. Should inter-enterprise arrears arise however, they would harm creditors, a fact, which would be reflected by their output. Taking as a working hypothesis immediate *resource reallocation,* it can be assumed that the production of agent (i) is:

$$q_i = q + c \cdot g \quad \text{for the agents who do not cause arrears}$$
$$= q \quad \quad \text{for the agents who do cause arrears}$$

Another assumption is that the level of financial *discipline*, (g), – seen as a positive externality – is determined by $n \cdot t$, where (t) indicates whether agents pay their debts, and (n) refers to those who do not cause arrears. A final assumption is that $c < 1 < N$, where $N > 1/c$.

Multiple equilibria situations can be imagined depending on agents' behaviour and the existence of financial discipline as a public good. If agents pay their debts in due time their incomes show up as $q + c \cdot g - t$, whereas if they produce arrears, their earnings appear as simply (q). The decision for an enterprise is to cause arrears if $c \cdot g = c \cdot n \cdot t < t$, or $n < 1/c$, i.e., when the number of those who pay in due time is low. A conclusion would follow: when policy credibility is low, and when financial discipline is widely disregarded, agents are tempted to produce arrears. Conversely, if $n = N$ agent N is stimulated to pay debts since $n = N > 1/c$, as our assumption says.

It would seem that everything boils down to *policy credibility*, to the functioning of market discipline. However, a critical question arises. What is going to happen, and what can be done if the number of those who do not pay is high and, what is even more important, non-payment is the result of the lack of capacity to pay? This means that non-payment is not an opportunistic response to existing circumstances concerning market (financial) discipline, or low policy credibility. Consequently, whichever is the determination of decision-makers to pursue a policy course, the sheer number of those who cannot pay make $n < 1/c$ – and thus, the vicious circle of arrears comes into being.

Moreover, the working hypothesis should be made more realistic by assuming that resource reallocation is slow. In this case, a complete exit of the inefficient but, still, positive value-added enterprises would mean that output is substantially less than if arrears emerge in the system.[14] Consequently, the short-run production function of an agent could be redefined as:

$$q_i = q + c \cdot g \quad \text{no arrears and immediate reallocation}$$
$$= q \quad \text{arrears and no, or very slow reallocation of resources}$$
$$= q - k \quad \text{no arrears and no, or very slow reallocation of resources - the case of an efficient agent}$$
$$= 0 \quad \text{no arrears (full exit) and no reallocation – the case of an inefficient agent}$$

where k indicates the fall of output when there is full *exit*. It is clear that, under the circumstances, the second situation (that includes arrears) appears as a preferred solution for the short term. It should be stressed that the choice of agents is influenced by their – in most cases – wage fund-centred objective function.

Therefore, when resource reallocation is very slow and when the number of those who cannot pay – because of the lack of capacity to pay – is high, *policy credibility* is not necessarily the main factor behind the growth of arrears; the main factor is represented by the large number of enterprises which, at the new equilibrium prices, would have to get out of the economic circuit.

Moreover, since such a huge *exit* is impossible,[15] inter-enterprise arrears emerge as a symptom of *strain* in the system and as a way to diffuse *strain*.

Arrears and exports - is there a relationship?

M. Khan and E.Clifton (1992) showed how arrears developed in Romania as one of the most glaring cases in the post-command economies; at the end of 1991, gross arrears amounted to 1,777 Bln lei, which meant ca. 56% of the GDP valued at December of those year prices. The tremendous growth of inter-enterprise credits should not have come as a surprise if one bears in mind that this country had one of the most distorted economies under command planning.[16] There were, also, an industrialisation drive that blatantly ignored comparative advantages, trade policies that ran counter to the logic of functioning of the domestic economy, and a *sui generis* shock therapy in the 1980s.

The extent of resource misallocation and the extreme repression of consumption – directly, through the squeeze on domestic absorption and, indirectly, by forced substitutions in consumption – led to a price explosion after their liberalisation. This explosion came to a head with the tightening of monetary policy by means of low credit ceilings. After a futile search for other solutions and giving in to political pressure, the Romanian government resorted to a 'global compensation'. Although it was accompanied by sterilisation measures aimed at neutralising the influence of new money injection, the global compensation brought the *moral hazard* problem to the fore.

Arrears resurfaced immediately the following year (1992), in a climate characterised by the imposition of much higher nominal interest rates – in an attempt to make them positive in real terms; the more inexpensive bank credit enhanced the attractiveness of arrears as temporary quasi-inside money. Curiously enough, in spite of an annual inflation rate that approached 180%, gross arrears stood at a level of approximately 30% of GDP by the end of 1992. In 1993 arrears remained at a similar level in real terms. What lies behind this dynamic of arrears is a justified question, bearing in mind that one can hardly talk about substantial restructuring and a dramatic change of the economic environment.

Exports as a side-effect of arrears

It can be conjectured that selective money injections (subsidised credit for special sectors) and more prudent behaviour on the part of enterprises might have caused arrears to grow less rapidly (to be smaller in relative terms). The money injection was used in an attempt to break the 'solidarity' of debtors by favouring those enterprises whose products enjoyed highest saleability (like electricity) and, thus, could exact payment from debtors.

There may be, however, another explanation to the less rapid dynamic of arrears, which is linked with the constraint they imposed on enterprises with growth potential. Arrears, as a temporary substitute for real liquidity, help firms survive, but do constrain the development of enterprises that have the potential to grow. Specifically, in such instances arrears tend to restrain the evolution of enterprises to a common denominator path, a fact which explains why those that can grow try to escape the currency (real liquidity) constraint. Moreover, the way to do it when the economy is starved of domestic liquidity and foreign borrowing is not available is to push up exports. Even when exports seem unprofitable, a *premium on liquidity* can more than compensate the value differential in favour of receipts on domestic sales whose payment is highly uncertain.

As the recent experience of Romania seems to suggest, increased exports can be a side effect of arrears, with the potential to contain their growth. Exports were seen ever more attractive for they enabled growth-oriented companies to do away with the liquidity constraint and avoid the growth-constraining effect of arrears; to escape the 'network trap' and build new chains of reliable suppliers and customers; and to acquire a much prized asset (i.e., hard currency), which preserves both high liquidity and value.

This effect, via exports, was enhanced by the freedom enterprises were granted to hold hard currency accounts. In an inflationary and highly uncertain environment, this freedom has facilitated a tendency toward *dollarisation,* which shows similar features to the process encountered in Latin America (P. Guidotti, C. Rodriguez, 1992). 'The Gresham's Law in reverse' has always been present in command economies, but it seems to have gained 'new currency' once traders were allowed to hold foreign exchange accounts. However, a note of caution is called for here: to the extent hard currency is hoarded (seen only as a store of value) and not used to mediate transactions, cumulated with a very high prudence of banks (that may apply 100% reserve requirements to their foreign exchange deposits) the dampening effect of exports on gross arrears is reduced.

Size of economy and its impact

For a small open economy the relationship between arrears and exports should not come as a surprise. The monetary approach to the balance of payments provides an analytical framework for understanding why arrears can only retard the moment when a reduction in domestic credit would induce an inflow of liquidity (currency) from abroad.[17]

This relationship becomes less clear the larger is the size of the economy. A large economy, which is less dependent on foreign trade and whose output is made up to a considerable degree by non-tradeables – like the Russian Federation – acquires features of a closed economy and the open economy model becomes less suitable. In the latter case, it is questionable that the stimulus for exports will be similarly strong, and, consequently, the implied constraining effect on arrears will be substantially smaller, or negligible. The closed economy argument can be extended by taking into account the degree of 'softness' of output in the transforming economies;[18] this 'softness' impairs their ability to export.

An additional argument for fighting arrears

Empirical evidence and analytical reasoning show that arrears can have a moderating influence on the decline of output, particularly in the context of a sharp tightening of credit policy. It was underlined, however, that this across the board effect impedes restructuring along the lines of comparative advantages by constraining the room of action of firms that enjoy growth potential. Additionally, arrears increase the 'collective lack of knowledge' (Ickes and Ryterman, 1992, p.4) and make it harder to distinguish between good and bad enterprises; they further add to uncertainty, and, relatedly, reduce the propensity for long-term (productive) investment. The latter effect should be considered looking, also, at the *decumulation* caused by excessive wages, which, in turn, are made possible by the building up of arrears.[19]

If we consider the extremely low investment ratios in the transforming economies – a fact that is not surprising under the circumstances – the negative impact of arrears and their resilience has to be of concern to policymakers.

A framework for containing arrears

Arrears cannot be addressed effectively by means of a case-by-case approach that misses the magnitude and the nature of the problem. Moreover, the fight against arrears should not be construed as a campaign in itself; conceptually and operationally, it should be integrated into the overall effort to stabilise and restructure the economy.

If one accepts the argument that the roots of arrears are to be sought in *structure* – so multifaceted – and the *strain* to which the economy is subjected, a conclusion becomes overriding: both *structure* and *strain* have to be targeted by policy. *Structure* means a focus on the property rights issue, and since it is obvious that 'privatisation as the ultimate solution' (M. Khan and E. Clifton, 1992, p. 20; S. van Wijnbergen, 1992) is not at hand *corporate governance* should unavoidably be given an outstandingly high profile. Relatedly, attention has to be paid to developing proper market institutions and to finding ways for eroding the 'power of structure' and changing enterprise behaviour. *Strain,* which mirrors the size of needed resource reallocation, should be approached starting from the truth that 'structural adjustment is a slow process even in a most advanced market-based economy – even when reform is credible' (M. Bruno, p. 753).

Several working principles need to guide efforts in order to formulate a realistic strategy to deal with arrears:

1) First, there is no quick fix to this problem! Arrears are a perverse phenomenon that will persist *as a problem* as long as the economy will have a flawed mode of functioning (i.e., as long as property rights are not clearly defined and markets are not sufficiently competitive). Trying to solve the problem, as a realistic way of stating it, is more a matter of *arrears-containment,* of imagining that there is a moving 'optimum' level that helps the system minimise the costs of structural adjustment and does enhance macrostabilisation. Arrears cannot be eliminated – they cannot disappear completely – since, in a real world, there can be no perfectly competitive markets, which should impose complete hardness of budget constraints. Arrears exist in well-functioning market economies as well and *strain* increases their likelihood to spread.[20]

2) Since the problem is structural, the approach should be holistic, multitrack, looking at the overall mode of functioning of the economy.

3) The approach has to be evolutionary, with the dynamic of arrears seen in relationship with the changing nature of the environment: new, market-attuned institutions, a growing private sector and a less inefficient (i.e., better managed) state sector would most likely reduce the amount of arrears. The policy should strive to increase the level of transparency, to remove the veil on implicit subsidies and enhance the information

gathering and generating-capacity of the system. More transparency would help policy both directly and indirectly (by influencing behaviour).

4)   Government has a role to play. A hands-off policy is unwarranted not only by the sheer scale of the problem, which implies social and political consequences, but also because the state is still the owner of most of the assets and, as such, it has to make decisions about their use.[21] Corporate governance is a code expression for describing the need for a *managerial revolution* in the state-owned sector.[22]

The struggle against arrears – with the caveats underlined above under the guise of guiding principles – involves at least four major domains of action, which all help to deal with both *structure and strain*:

(i) trying to 'break up' *structure* (the solidarity of debtors);
(ii) imposing a disciplining 'straitjacket' on *structure*;
(iii) industrial policy that should reduce *strain*; and
(iv) targeted external assistance.

Trying to 'break up' structure

The goal would be to erode as much as possible the 'power' of *structure*. At least two options appear to be available:

a)   identifying the largest net debtors which, supposedly, are the critical links in the chain of arrears expansion and attempting to insulate them - annihilate their arrears-spreading potential;
b)   trying to undermine the debtors' grip on creditors.

A major impediment in doing this is the big number of large net debtors and their dispersion within the economy. Therefore, policymakers need to restrict the number of firms to those that concentrate a critical mass of net arrears.[23] What such a critical mass means remains, certainly, a subject for debate. Insulation of the worst offenders would need special banking arrangements. An option could be the setting up (or designation) of a bank with a clear mandate of restructuring and monitoring of performance. Such an arrangement would, presumably, considerably relieve the pressure on the other banks by improving their balance sheets. How such a bank will monitor performance and enforce financial discipline depends much on how determined and politically strong the government is, and how capable it is to withstand pressure from the big loss-making units.[24]

The other way – that was partially attempted by the Stolojan government in Romania in 1992 – is to try to blow up the debtors' trap by inducing big creditors to form a strategic alliance against debtors. Those creditors, whose products are *sine qua non* inputs for debtors, would get new finance for their operations to the extent that they force their debtors to pay back by not supplying them with the essential inputs they need.

Hopefully, the improvement of the balance sheets (the stock of bad debts) and the insulation of those that play a key role in triggering arrears (the flow) would help change the set of incentives for banks and, thereby, their behaviour. It would also help to enhance the activity of banks as agents of restructuring; 'the objection that banks do not have the skills to do that right is less compelling than at first sight. The point is not that banks are good at doing this, but that they are likely to be better than anyone' (S. Van Wijnbergen, 1992, p.114). The point becomes even stronger if the giant loss-making enterprises are taken in charge by a special agency,[25] that would work closely with one (or several) especially designed banking units. Nonetheless, the crucial issue of skills remains, and joint ventures with foreign partners, or direct involvement of foreign banks, are more than welcome.

Breaking the 'power of *structure*' from within needs to be complemented by outside action, notably by speeding up privatisation. Private companies face hard budget constraints and they bear, in general, very heavily, the brunt of not being repaid in due time; moreover, they are crowded out from getting credit from state-owned banks. Therefore, the more numerous they are, the more likely they will exert effective pressure on arrears-producing enterprises.

Imposing a 'straitjacket' on structure

The idea here consists of modifying the set of rewards and penalties so those agents optimise in congruence with the thrust of transformation; the 'straitjacket' would be a disciplining device for an economy that lacks a proper structure of property rights. The set of measures should include:
- trying to achieve low[26] *positive* real interest rates;
- turning implicit into explicit subsidies and setting a tight leash on enterprises (hardening budget constraints);
- imposing interest on outstanding debt and taxation of this income;
- penalties for creditors who tolerate non-payment;
- penalties for those who hold hard-currency in their accounts, but run deeply into arrears;
- bonuses and equity-related incentives to those managers who significantly improve the financial state of their enterprises;[27]

-   closing several negative value-added enterprises by using the bankruptcy procedure, in order to show that the government 'means serious business';
-   the demonstration effect can be very powerful for it would signal the resoluteness of policymakers (and, thereby, increase policy credibility) and it would highlight a side neglected in the public debate about bankruptcy, namely, that it does not necessarily entail the physical demise of assets and destruction of jobs.

Such measures need to be embedded in a drive for recapitalising banks and deserving enterprises. At the same time, an income-control policy should be a basic component of the 'straitjacket' since labour markets are heavily monopsonised.

Recapitalisation. There are several avenues, which can be used simultaneously:
-   cleaning up the books of banks by converting their bad debts into government bonds, or by transferring bad debts to a special bank set up to deal with the large loss-making firms;
-   debt-equity swaps that turn banks into core owners, or powerful stakeholders, with clear incentives and a comparative ability to restructure an ailing company and turn it around in the right direction;
-   selling equity in domestic banks to foreign banks, this would, automatically improve the level of skills in the banking sector and would, furthermore, help restructuring and privatisation.

Recapitalisation of viable enterprises can be made by using domestic funds (resulted from privatisation proceeds), foreign direct investment, or external assistance targeted to restructuring.

Recapitalisation means that government *explicitly* takes over bad debts. When external support is not available, it can cause difficulties for the financing of the budget deficit. This becomes more acute when claims on the budget grow (due to rising unemployment, as well) and the tax base diminishes. Therefore, recapitalisation should be undertaken in conjunction with a proper evaluation of how much the budget deficit can be financed in a non-aggravating inflationary way.

Turning implicit into explicit subsidies. A major benefit of this endeavour would be unburdening of monetary policy to pursue its fundamental goal of preserving the soundness of domestic money. Additionally, more pressure would be put on enterprises to trim down their expenditure by knowing that there is a clear financial constraint indicated by the explicit subsidies envisaged by state budget. The goal would be to put into place a combination of *ex ante* (explicit) and some, unavoidable, *ex post* (implicit) subsidies that will increase transparency and help enterprise reform.[28]

A technical issue is 'programming' the dynamic of explicit subsidies when there is a time horizon covering the period of restructuring, or liquidation of various enterprises. This issue is closely connected with reducing *strain* within the system by a gradual phasing out of non-viable enterprises.

Income control policy. The control of incomes (wages) is vital in order to be able to control inflation[29] and, thereby, maintain real balances at a level that reduces the propensity of enterprises to run arrears. How to attain it? Technically, in addition to conventional schemes (like tax-based income), something resembling M.Weitzman's 'profit sharing' scheme (1984) – which would link wages with the dynamics of saleable output – could be thought of. The trouble with profit sharing is that one meets an asymmetry of behaviour on the part of workers: they would share in positive profits, but not in negative profits – the latter signifying lower wages. A way out can be privatisation, with employees' getting a substantial stake in the fate of enterprises. Moreover, a *Social Pact*, like the one concluded in Poland at the beginning of 1993, can involve workers in the management of enterprises – and thereby, considerably reduce the temptation to raise wages uncoupled with saleable output dynamics.

In order to implement macroeconomic stabilisation a consensus has to be found on how to distribute the costs of adjustment. The endowment with resources, as legacy of command planning and hastened industrialisation, can bring fortune to some and misery to others; it lies at the roots of what can be construed as a 'distributional struggle' within society. The very wide range of profitability rates can show us 'who is who' in this contest. In so heavily monopolised and monopsonised economies inflation seems to be practically unstoppable, and a vicious circle can be at work: because of external and internal shocks real national income shrinks, pressure groups ask for and obtain higher nominal wages to keep pace with rising prices, the wage-price spiral is given a further twist, monetary and fiscal policies become tighter, output shrinks further and the vicious circle goes on. This scenario is more plausible the less mobile resources and the less competitive markets are, and when governments are weak and likely to give in easily to pressure from trade unions. 'Stabilisation will come when everybody agrees to share the burden of stabilisation, rather than when a particular group concedes and bears the entire cost' (J. de Gregorio, 1991, p. 146). Thus, achieving a consensus becomes urgent, particularly when market reforms entail wide and increasing income discrepancies.

Industrial policy

Industrial policy can be a major tool for reducing *strain* in transforming economies. Its goal can be described as follows: a gradual phasing out of unprofitable activities in keeping with the capacity of the system to adjust. This capacity is to be related to maintaining a balance between job creation and job destruction, the functioning of a social safety net and adequate retraining programmes.

Under the circumstances of transition from command to market economies industrial policy has been given too low a profile, or has even been neglected, a fact which has crippled economic policy, in general, and stabilisation in particular. Industrial policy can reduce the costs of stabilisation, can help decision-makers deal more effectively with the three major constraints (the foreign exchange gap, the budget deficit, and the low level of savings) in making choices about the trade-off between external imbalance and internal disequilibrium (understood in a broad sense, namely as the degree of unemployment of resources). It can also help in dealing with the 'Big Trade-off' (A. Okun, 1975) that has come into the open in the transforming economies: efficiency versus equality.

It is noteworthy that even the experience of frontrunner countries (e.g. Hungary) suggests the need for such a policy (G. Szapary, 1992). There are many strong reasons to have reservations about industrial policy seen as a means to 'pick winners and losers', especially in an environment with so much uncertainty and lack of transparency. However, in the peculiar conditions of transforming economies, industrial policy should rather be viewed as a *damage control device*. This would aim at allowing a breathing space needed to cope with the high degree of uncertainty and fuzziness about property rights, with the question 'which are the truly non-viable enterprises', and at mitigating the costs of restructuring and resource reallocation. Under the circumstances, industrial policy is about *picking losers among losers.*[30]

On this line of reasoning industrial policy is tightly linked with the action of making subsidies explicit and establishing a time horizon for their ultimate removal. There are two kinds of subsidies involved depending on which enterprises are targeted. Those which are clearly non-viable and their keeping afloat is related to a public budget (resource) constraint; those that are potentially viable and for which some time is needed to ascertain their actual prospects. In the latter case, the same resource-constraint applies. Negative value-added units should be closed without delay for it is less costly to pay workers unemployment benefits and retrain them than to keep such enterprises running.[31] Non-viable enterprises would be programmed for a gradual elimination so that unemployment would be attenuated and its cost redistributed over time. At the same time, authorities would have an easier time in securing resources for a social safety net and for facilitating labour reallocation through training programmes. The time horizon for phasing out non-viable enterprises is related to the advance of privatisation and to securing adequate levels of capital inflows; the more intense is privatisation and the larger are capital inflows (especially those used for long-term direct investments), the easier it is to phase out inefficient activities.

It can be argued that industrial policy slows restructuring, that is a worthy to consider statement if social and political constraints are dismissed. But for the sake of sustaining the process there is solid ground for advocating industrial policy as a way of easing structural adjustment – and at the same time keeping check on arrears.

External assistance

Assistance can be direct and indirect. Direct assistance can be split into three major categories:

- aid that reduces *strain;* for example, financial support that helps the functioning of an effective social safety-net for those affected by economic restructuring;
- aid that improves *structure*, the market-attuned institutional framework of the economy; main areas for action should be the banking system, the management of large (still, state-owned) enterprises, the tax collection system;
- aid that focuses on *structure* by helping markets grow through restructuring and privatisation. This aid should target specific companies and sectors (for instance, agriculture in Romania, or the oil industry in the Russian Federation), and provide *seed capital* for private sector undertakings.

Indirect assistance refers to the evolving international environment. It is unquestionable that rising nationalism in international policymaking, growing protectionism, global economic recession, the level of real interest rates on capital markets do not facilitate post-communist transition and add to the *strain* in the transforming economies. It is very unfortunate that transformation is undertaken in an unfavourable international context whose dynamic, at present, does not give much hope for a substantial change to the better.[32] A concrete example of the distance between myth and reality in the rhetoric of support is the extent of access Eastern European producers have on EEC markets for most of their main export items. Here there is a relationship between needed sectoral adjustment in Western Europe[33] and trade as a weapon for systemic adjustment (transformation) in post-communist Europe. Reducing *strain* in the latter involves increasing short-term difficulties in the former, and the decision on how to deal with such a trade-off cannot be but political. But in a Western Europe still stunned economically by the German reunification blow and with weak governments, prospects for gaining significantly more access on EEC markets are not very encouraging at this point in time.

Concluding remarks

Inter-enterprise arrears mirror the tremendous *strain* under which post-command economies are. The existence of arrears is not a surprise for they can be detected in all real economies, the relatively well functioning advanced market economies included. What is unusual in the transforming (post-command) economies are the magnitude and the effects of arrears, which make up a *structural trap* for stabilisation. In this context, and unless there is a proper embeddedness of monetary policy within the overall policy-mix, the *time inconsistency problem* is much magnified.

The fight against arrears means, essentially, trying to *contain* them to a level that does not undermine efforts to stabilise the economy. Setting up a clearing house, securitisation of inter-enterprise credits, are only temporary, or partial solutions; they do not focus on the main (primary) sources of arrears, which are *structure* and the size of required structural adjustment (resource misallocation). Since dealing with their primary roots will take time, it makes sense to presume that containing arrears cannot be a one shot policy; it is a process that will overlap in time and reflect an evolving environment acquiring ever more traits of a fully fledged market system.[34] The more quickly restructuring and privatisation will proceed, the more competitive markets become and the more mobile labour will be, the less menacing inter-enterprise arrears will be for stabilisation policy and the functioning of the economy.

Containing arrears will help 'stabilise' stabilisation policy. Stabilisation, itself, would have to be understood as a process, most likely, to evince a *stop and go* dynamic including setbacks. It can be surmised that the control of disequilibria during transition will reveal a *stabilisation policy path* moving in tandem with the speed of change of the domestic environment.

Notes

*   Presented at the Conference of the European Association of Comparative Economics, Budapest, 8-10 September 1994. This is a slightly revised form of a paper written during the author's stay as a visiting scholar in the Research Department of the International Monetary Fund. That paper appeared as IMF Working Paper 94/54.

1   '...the soft budget constraint did change its dynamics because individual firms in general strengthened their position vis-à-vis other economic agents as well as the authorities. They no longer have to bargain for new credits or subsidies, or tax relief. Their behaviour can be rather described in terms of *fait accompli*. They do not pay, but non payment is not their problem; it is the problem of those who do not receive their due' (P. Jasinski, 1992, p.32).

2   The moderating influence of arrears on the decline of output can, itself, be moderated by an increase in the demand for transactionary balances. However, this counter-moderating effect has to be judged in conjunction with the reduction of the demand for speculative and precautionary balances.

3   If the equation of exchange (PY=MV) is put in a dynamic form by using logarithms: $\dot{p} + \dot{y} = \dot{m} + \dot{v}$; where $\dot{p}, \dot{y}, \dot{m}$ and $\dot{v}$ are the rates of change of prices, output, money supply and money velocity, respectively. When monetary policy is tightened, $\dot{m} = 0$, and $(\dot{p} + \dot{y})$ is above zero, $\dot{v}$ needs to be positive in order to alleviate the expected decline of output. In this case, arrears appear as if they modify money velocity. If arrears are considered temporary quasi-inside money and velocity is kept constant, the relationship becomes $\dot{p} + \dot{y} = \dot{m}$ (c, a), where c is cash and bank credit and (a) represents arrears. When $\dot{c} = 0$ because of the dear money policy, $\dot{p} + \dot{y} = \dot{a}$.

4   Aside from new money injection, this would be the only way to make the shift of LM to LM_1 durable.

5   This idea is developed in section four, which argues that exports can be viewed as a side effect of arrears, and as a constraining factor on them.

6   See C. Senik-Leygonie and G. Hughes (1992) for an investigation of the size of negative value-added sectors in the former Soviet Union. In Romania, copper and lead mines in the northern part of the country are notoriously known to be negative value-added activities.

7   One reason, for instance, is the smaller tax base for subsidising those who lost their jobs. Therefore, this base has to be taxed more heavily.

8   Due to the highly inflationary domestic environment, in particular, and the very likely scarcity of foreign exchange reserves. In Poland, the temporary relative success in using the exchange rate as a nominal anchor relied on a very substantial devaluation (overshooting).

9   There were signs of a systemic problem and the Brady Plan was, partially, a

policy response to those signs. Almost all major banks needed recapitalisation because of their bad loans to Latin America, in particular. However, the overall policy response remained, essentially, a case by case approach.

10   In the Czech republic 'Many companies are locked in a circle of bad debt caused by unpaid bills from customers... Officials fear that many other companies could be affected if major companies are allowed to go bankrupt' (P.Blum, 1993, p.2).

11   Defining *policy credibility* in post-command economies needs qualification since, with the exception of Poland and Hungary, there is no history of stabilisation attempts. Without such a history, agents react according to entrenched behavioural patterns, and not on the basis of learning about past policy intentions and their eventual reversal. Certainly, when wide range bailouts make up a policy goal reversal stabilisation history starts on the wrong foot and policy credibility is impaired from the very beginning. Still, one can pose the question: under what circumstances is policy credibility a realistic policy trait and what policy choices favour its attainment?

12   Sachs makes use of such models in trying to depict the system (institutional) dissolution in the former Soviet Union (1994).

13   *Market (financial) discipline* emerges as a public good and as a *positive externality* because of collective (generalised) good behaviour. The state does not supply it, though it can influence its production by the enforcement of bankruptcy procedures and the provision of other institutional means. Nonetheless, the state action (policy) of enforcement becomes irrelevant when collective good behaviour is impossible for various reasons, and as it is our contention, because of *strain* in the main.

14   In this case, the damaging effect of inter-enterprise arrears on efficiency is more than counterbalanced by their mitigating effect on the drop of output.

15   Theoretically, a level of foreign aid (or external financing) can be thought of, which should enable a 'big bang exit'. Practically, however, this is more than unrealistic as a policy option, and may not even be the best choice.

16   The Romanian economy was 'one of the most tightly controlled and centralised in Eastern Europe. The Ceausescu regime deprived the country of the experience of any significant economic reform, leaving the administration tied to a Stalinist model that had by that time been abandoned by almost all other countries in the region' (D. G. Demekas, M. S. Khan, 1991, p.8).

17   Arrears, as temporary quasi-inside money, can compensate the reduction of domestic bank credit for a while only; over time, however, arrears become ever more constraining and an inflow of real liquidity (foreign exchange) is triggered.

18   This 'softness' can be looked at as a relative 'absence of ability to transform goods into one another in world markets at the initial world prices' (P. Desai and J. Bhagwati, 1979, p. 359). Often, low exportability (specific for 'soft' goods) can turn into no exportability because of technology and quality-related constraints.

19   As was argued, arrears can, in fact, dichotomise the payment system and make wage disbursement the main (or the only) money-based transaction; this helps

enterprises cope with the upward pressure of wages.

20   'Recession-hit companies now speak of a crisis within a business community unable or unwilling to break free from a vicious circle of overdue debt...The European Commission has just launched an investigation into late payment, which is spreading contagiously throughout the Community' (M. Cassell, 1993, p. 17).

21   Romania's experience is telling in this respect: Law 15 of August 1990, on 'Restructuring of State Economic Units' devolved power by creating confusion as to the owners of enterprise assets. In this way collusion phenomena were encouraged, managers easily avoided management contracts and, ultimately, the attributes of the state – as the owner of the still unprivatised property – were devoid of substance.

22   The 'managerial revolution' that took place in the publicly owned companies (*regies autonomes*) in France, in the 80s, may suggest avenues for action, though the scale and problematique in post-command economies are, comparatively, overwhelming because of the different surrounding environment for the individual companies.

23   In the case of Romania, for instance, a McKinsey study found that the concentration of bad debts is significant within the troubled industrial sectors. Large vertically integrated companies accounting for the majority of the problem dominate the metallurgy, chemical/petrochemical and machine-building industries. The study found that, for the three industrial sectors mentioned, 112 large companies account for 77% of bad debts. Moreover, the three industrial sectors account for 45% of the bad asset problem of all commercial companies, though they comprise only 24% of the lending.

24   The Polish experience is relevant as to this political dimension and the pitfalls of concentrating the tasks into a single agency.

25   Like the State Ownership Fund (SOF) in Romania.

26   Reasons as to why high positive real interest rates are to be avoided are provided by G. Calvo (1991), and A.Bennett and S. Schadler (1992).

27   There are frequent cases when managers favour a worsening of the way enterprises function so that an eventual management buyout is much eased financially. However, there is enough ground to assume that members of the workforce would not stay idle seeing this and would force them out of power; workers operate, actually, as 'managers-monitors'. Therefore, it seems that it would pay managers to accept a deal (with the state as the owner of the enterprise) which would reward them with concrete stakes in the future of the company to the extent they improve its financial standing. Put in a nutshell this philosophy sounds like this: 'why run down a company in order to buy it for nothing and risk losing all (including reputation) by being ousted, instead of turning into an important share-holder (stake-holder) of a, possibly, prosperous company'?

28   A problem could emerge with this conversion. Implicit subsidies are *ex post* and

their size is an uncertain quantity, potentially unlimited. Explicit subsidies are *ex ante* so they are a known, limited, quantity. There is a danger, that, if the economy gets more unstable – because of various shocks, including politically motivated policy decisions – the mix of subsidies could mean both a substantially higher fiscal deficit and very high inflation.

29   'Controls are more likely to be useful, the larger is the desired reduction in inflation, and the more serious is the credibility problem' (P. Persson, S. van Wijnbergen, 1993, p.81).

30   Industrial policy is critical for bridging the gap between the effectiveness of controlling demand and that of stimulating supply. Supply responsiveness is low, endangering the sustainability of stabilisation efforts. Industrial policy should correlate income-control measures with industrial restructuring (including privatisation) undertaken by authorities which process information provided by markets.

31   One qualification is, however, necessary in this respect. When producers of intermediate goods represent these units, the switch to other suppliers could involve non-insignificant costs to certain customers of those producers. However, these costs are a one-time affair, against the flow of subsidising the negative value-added activities.

32   One can compare it with the turnaround of several Latin American countries (Mexico, Argentina, especially) in the 80s, or the progress of Turkey over the same period. One should not downplay, however, the role of surging world markets, driven by a consumption-led recovery of the US economy, in facilitating that transition. This contrasts strongly with the exogenous shocks that have struck the transforming economies.

33   The cases of steel processing industry and of agriculture make the big headlines.

34   '...where distortions have been long-standing, the process of correction can only be gradual...for a *long-run* control over inflation there is no substitute for a comprehensive package aimed at eradicating structural and macroeconomic distortions' (C. Borio, 1990, p. 27).

References

Agenor, P. R.(1993), 'Credible Disinflation Programs', *IMF*, PPAA/93/9.

Aghion, P. and Blanchard, O. (1993), 'On the Speed of Transition in Eastern Europe', Mimeo, March.

Begg, D. and Portes, R. (1992), 'Enterprise Debt and Economic Transformation: Financial Restructuring of the State Sector in Central and Eastern Europe', Center for Economic Policy Research, *Discussion Paper*, No.695, June.

Bennett, A. and Schadler, S. (1992), 'Interest Rate Policy in Central and Eastern Europe: The Influence of Monetary Overhangs and Weak Financial Discipline', *IMF*

Working Paper, August.

Blum, P. (1993), 'Czechs Set to Act on Bankruptcy', *Financial Times*, 17 February, p. 2.

Borio, C. (1990), 'Financial Arrangements, Soft Budget Constraints and Inflation: Lessons from the Yugoslav Experience', *BIS Working Papers*, no. 15, November.

Bruno, M. (1992), 'Stabilisation and Reform in Eastern Europe: A Preliminary Evaluation', *IMF Staff Papers*, vol.39, 4, December, pp. 741-777.

Calvo, G. (1991), 'Are High Interest Rates Effective for Stopping High Inflation? Some Skeptical Notes', *The World Bank Economic Review*, vol. 4, no.1.

Calvo, G. and Coricelli, F. (1992), 'Output Collapse in Eastern Europe: The Role of Credit', *IMF Working Paper*, August.

Cassell, M. (1993), 'The Dangers that Lurk in Delay', *Financial Times*, 23 February, p. 17.

Demekas, D. G. and Khan, S. M. (1991), 'The Romanian Economic Reform Program', *IMF Occasional Paper*, no. 89, November.

Desai, P. and Bhagwati, J. (1979), 'Three Alternative Concepts of Foreign Exchange Difficulties in Centrally Planned Economies', *Oxford Economic Papers*, 3, November.

Gregorio, J. (1991), 'Comment' in R. Dornbusch and S. Edwards (eds.), *The Macroeconomics of Populism in Latin America*, The Chicago University Press, Chicago, pp. 145-149.

Guidotti, E. P. and Rodriguez, C.A. (1992), 'Dollarization in Latin America', *IMF Staff Papers*, vol. 39, no. 3, September, pp. 518-544.

Ickes, W. B. and Ryterman, R. (September 1992), 'Inter-enterprise Arrears and Financial Underdevelopment in Russia', Mimeo.

Jasinski, P. (September 1992), 'The Soft Budget Constraint under Central Planning, under Market Socialism, and in the Post-communist Economies', Mimeo.

Khan, S. M. and Eric, V. C. (July 1992), 'Inter-enterprise Arrears in Transforming Economies: The Case of Romania', *IMF Paper on Policy Analysis and Assessment*.

Kornai, J. (1980), 'The Economics of Shortage', North-Holland, Amsterdam.

Lancaster, K. (1979), 'Variety, Equity and Efficiency', Blackwell, Oxford.

Lane, T. (June 1992), 'Market Discipline', *IMF Working Paper*.

Leibenstein, H., 'Allocative Efficiency vs. X-Efficiency', *American Economic Review*, vol.56, 3, pp. 392-410.

McKinnon, R. (1992), 'The Order of Economic Liberalisation', John Hopkins University Press, Baltimore.

Murrell, P. (1991), 'Evolution in Economics and in the Economic Reform of the Centrally Planned Economies', Mimeo.

Mussa, M. (1993), 'Government Policy and the Adjustment Policy', in J. Bhagwati (ed.), *Import Competition and Response*, pp.73-120, Chicago University Press, Chicago.

North, D. (1981), 'Structure and Change in Economic History', Norton, New York.

Okun, A. (1975), 'The Big Trade-Off: Efficiency vs. Equality', Brookings Institution, Washington DC.

Persson, T. and van Wijnbergen, S. (January 1993), 'Signalling, Wage Controls and Monetary Disinflation Policy', *The Economic Journal*, 103, pp. 79-97.

Rostowski, J. (1992), 'The Inter-Enterprise Debt Explosion in the Former Soviet Union: Causes, Consequences, Cures', Mimeo.

Rostowski, J. (1993), 'Creating Stable Monetary Systems in Post-communist Economies', Mimeo.

Sachs, J. (1994), 'Russia's Struggle with Stabilisation. Conceptual Issues and Evidence', paper prepared for the World Bank's Annual Conference on Development Economics, 28-30 April.

Sachs, J. and Thye Woo, W. (October 1993), 'Structural Factors in the Economic Reforms of China, Eastern Europe and the Former Soviet Union', manuscript.

Senik-Leygonie, C. and Hughes, G. (1992), 'Industrial Profitability and Trade among the Former Soviet Republics', *Economic Policy*, October, pp. 355-376.

Szapary, G. (1992), 'Transition Issues: A Case Study of Hungary', *IMF Departmental Memoranda Series*, October.

Tanzi, V. (1993), 'Fiscal Policy and the Economic Restructuring of Economies in Transition', *IMF Staff Papers*, September, pp. 697-707.

Weitzman, M. (1984), 'The Share Economy', Harvard University Press, Cambridge.

Wijnbergen, S. van (1992), 'Enterprise Reform in Eastern Europe', Center for Economic Policy Research, *Discussion Paper*, no.738.

9 Stabilisation and Exchange Rate Policy in Romania[*]

Economic transformation in post-communist Romania has its own peculiarities, which are linked with the heavy burden of history and the policy vagaries of reforms. In spite of a slow privatisation and little restructuring of big industry, a second round of stabilisation attempts – initiated in the last quarter of 1993 – seemed to be quite successful. From approximately 300% in 1993, inflation came down to 61.7% in 1994, and to ca. 28% (December on December) in 1995. That result was quite interesting for the present author as well since the line of reasoning espoused by him is that inflation reduction and durable macroeconomic stabilisation require doing away with large distortions in resource allocation. The relapse into inflation in 1996 reinforced this line of reasoning, although one can try to explain the derailment through major blunders of macroeconomic policy.

This study tries to present the major traits of the stabilisation efforts while a persistent focus is placed on the role of exchange rate policy. To this end, the period lasting until Q_3 of 1993 is contrasted with the following period when an actual policy breakthrough occurred. Thus, for the first time since the start of transformation positive real interest rates started to operate in the Romanian economy and the flight from the domestic currency was stopped. The surprisingly good response of the economy to the 'policy shock' of 1993-1994 can be explained, basically, by the huge X-inefficiencies existing in the economy and the achievement of a transparent foreign exchange (inter-bank) market, which considerably reduced the information and transaction costs for firms. To this explanation, one can add the coming out of recession of the economy, which started a year earlier. The efficiency gains and the stop of the flight from the Leu enhanced tremendously the stability of the exchange rate during 1994, which further helped stabilisation policy. However, a subsequent relaxation of monetary policy led to too fast economic growth in 1995, which, together with the low autonomous capital inflows, evinced the fragility of the inter-bank foreign exchange market and the limits of the stabilisation policy undertaken at that time. Those limits became obvious in 1996 when inflation was rekindled.

223

Romania's experience shows that macroeconomic stabilisation cannot become durable unless faster restructuring and privatisation – which should help the operation of hard budget constraints – take place. In this context, it can be submitted that restructuring and the imposition of proper structures of corporate governance, on a wide scale, would be unlikely unless Romania achieves a breakthrough in attracting foreign capital as well, preferably foreign direct investment. In any case, it is expected that, because of the *strain* existing in the system, macroeconomic policy will not be able to escape following a 'stop and go' path. The challenge for policymakers would, therefore, be to avoid large amplitudes of policy fluctuations and to build up steadily their credibility.

The first section presents an overview of macroeconomic developments during 1990-1993 and tries to capture the main policy vacillations and dilemmas; the role of the implicit exchange rate brought about by the regime of full retention of foreign exchange is highlighted. The following section deals with the policy breakthrough initiated in the last quarter of 1993 and consolidated in the first quarter of 1994. Developments in 1995 and 1996 are discussed in section three. Section four analyses the nature of the stabilisation policy started in late 1993 and the role played in it by the exchange rate; implications of the regime of full retention of foreign exchange are also analysed.

An overall view: 1990-1993[1]

Internalisation of the external disequilibrium and the extreme overreaction of decision-makers was a major feature of economic policy in Romania in the 1980s. Almost symmetrically, the most salient feature of economic life after December 1989 was the major reversal of the above-mentioned phenomenon: an externalisation of domestic imbalances. What happened in Romania in a relatively short while (1 year) is also unique among her neighbours: from a current account surplus in hard currency of $2.864 billion in 1989 the country moved to a deficit of $1.656 billion a year later (Table 9.1).

The turnaround is astonishing if the size of foreign trade is taken into account – in 1989 exports and imports in hard currency totalled slightly under $10 billion. Thus, the reversal meant almost 45% of the foreign trade turnover in 1989.

The roots of this situation go into the previous decade when a forced and brutal compression of domestic absorption was undertaken in order to pay back the entire external debt of over $ 10 Billion. After December 1989, there was a tremendous *pressure from below* to consume tradeables, to reduce exports, and boost imports of both consumer and intermediate goods. The switch in favour of tradeables was almost instant and hardly stoppable; it was strengthened by a 'shunning of domestic goods' syndrome. Having been starved for years, consumers and producers reacted immediately to the new environment and their reaction forms one side of the story. In 1990, dissaving (the depletion of foreign exchange reserves) primarily financed the boost in consumption. During the following years the expected contraction in aggregate saving was not so severe owing to external financing. Indeed, internal plus external financing accounted for some 20 to 25% of the GDP. The problem was that around half of this financed the increases of stocks (Table 9.2).[2]

However, there is another side of the story that needs to be highlighted. The policymakers complicated the state of the economy by commission and omission. By commission since they practised a brand of populist macroeconomics, faltering in the face of pressures from below, but also lured by the elections held in May 1990. This resulted in high laxity in conceding wage rises[3] and the introduction of the five day workweek, though output was plummeting, the maintenance of wide-ranging price controls and of a much overvalued exchange rate, and mismanagement of the foreign exchange reserves. At the end of 1989 foreign exchange reserves stood at more than $1.7 billion; these went down to under $400 million at the end of 1990. By omission, for one can hardly talk about real attempts to stabilise the economy before November 1990. Trying to sum up one can say that both aggregate external disequilibrium and aggregate internal disequilibrium increased,[4] with micro-disequilibria partially alleviated by substantially increased imports. Policymakers should have been concerned by the fact that production was establishing an import-dependency that was unsustainable in the long run. This became obvious soon.

Events during that year showed a fundamental flaw of the system in transformation: the high degree of decision-making power of enterprises when these do not face hard-budget constraints and enjoy free access to hard currency. The events also made clear the damage caused by an economic policy whose dimension of 'benign neglect' was very high profile. November signalled the beginning of intentions of coming to grips with the large disequilibria by a partial liberalisation of prices and a devaluation of the domestic currency (from Leu 20/$1 to Leu 35/$1). These measures, followed by another package in January 1991, proved to be too little and too late.

Confronted with a free-falling economy[5] (Table 9.3) and unable to contain growing disequilibria (unsustainable trade deficits,[6] rising prices, vanishing investment) an IMF supported stabilisation plan was introduced at the start of 1991.[7] The government could hardly have done otherwise since the looming trade deficits became more than threatening. With the benefit of hindsight, it can be said that, in view of the large external disequilibrium, policymakers were constantly underreacting to the dynamics of the economy.

Why did they underreact? The state of the economy in December 1989 and the high expectations of the population after the 'shock-therapy' of the 1980s, obviously, blunted the resoluteness of decision-makers to move swiftly with a comprehensive austerity programme and comprehensive price liberalisation. Another possible explanation is that the government underestimated the seriousness of the situation for quite a while. Finally, the lack of foreign financing instead of stimulating boldness increased the degree of cautiousness.

A conceptually middle of the road (gradualistic) stabilisation programme took shape which entailed essentially: tightening of the fiscal and monetary policy[8] (although real interest rates remained highly negative), a tax-based income control policy, a new devaluation,[9] and introduction of two-tier exchange rate system (through the initiation of an interbank foreign exchange auctions system in February 1991).

The 'reign' of the implicit exchange rate

The programme was ineffective in stopping inflation; the consumer price index reached 352.2% in October 1991 against the pre-liberalisation moment (in October 1990). Moreover, the real credit squeeze, caused by the very high jump in prices (after their partial freeing) followed by their steadily rising level, affected the output decline. The volume of gross inter-enterprise arrears increased exponentially, reaching a figure approximating 50% of the GDP (measured at the December 1991 prices) at the end of the year.[10] At the same time, the large spread between the two exchange rates persisted, exports continued to be sluggish, whereas the CMEA trade virtually collapsed. The end of the year brought about a 'global compensation' as a means to reduce inter-enterprise arrears. Though the additional credit was mostly sterilised by March 1992, the initiative brought to the fore the *moral hazard* issue. An achievement of the programme was the elimination of the monetary overhang.

At the end of 1991 growing tensions were building into the system because of an overvalued official exchange rate and an excessively liberal trade regime, too low prices for energy and raw materials which favoured their overconsumption, and insufficient inflows of capital to compensate the low levels of saving and the feebleness of investment. The strategic move of November 1991, the unification of the exchange rate,[11] and the introduction of internal convertibility became irrelevant in a short while.

This was basically due to the existence of highly negative real interest rates and the lack of supporting foreign financing. For several months the exchange rate remained unchanged at the Leu 198/$1, a level that meant a growing imbalance between the supply and demand for foreign exchange.[12] Moreover, an overhang of hard currency claims was stockpiling.[13] Many exporters and importers found a way out by practising barter deals, which introduced an *implicit exchange rate* into the functioning of the economy. This rate mitigated the pernicious effects of overvaluation but entailed considerable information and transaction costs. However, since capital flight and insufficient exports were becoming major concerns[14] the whole policy was in need of a major overhaul which, among other goals, should have restored actual internal convertibility.

What came out of the decision-making process in the Spring of 1992 provides a good case study for understanding critical choices faced by macroeconomic policy during transition. Policymakers can be viewed as having been compelled to decide on a mix of short-run disequilibria that should reduce the performance deficit of the economy and deal with major constraints. A line of reasoning was that the recessionary effects of the fight against inflation – that involved austerity measures – could be counteracted by the pulling (multiplier) effect of a policy that would, hopefully, succeed in boosting exports and attracting capital inflows. Increasing exports and restoring internal convertibility appeared as a *must* since the economy was menaced by suffocation on the side of the external balance. The idea of creating an *export drive* was reinforced by the long-run requirements of a sensible reform policy: achieving an equilibrium exchange rate, setting positive real interest rates (which should encourage savings and relieve the pressure on the exchange rate), adopting export promotion measures, and working out an industrial (restructuring) policy that should enable the imposition of financial discipline (the fight against arrears) by distinguishing between 'bad guys' and 'good guys'. The rationale of such a policy was linked with the enormous *strain* in the system, which itself is due to the magnitude of required resource reallocation in a post-command economy.

Consequently, interest rates were raised considerably. Thus, the refinance rate of the National Bank moved from 28% to 80%. The interest rate for credits provided by the National Bank went from an average of 24.6% in April of 1992 to 54.4% in May of the same year; at commercial banks the average rate for credits moved from 27.9% to 55.3% in the same period. Concomitantly, the exchange rate was devalued substantially[15] and exporters were granted full retention rights in order to cope with their mistrust of policymakers and encourage capital return. The full retention measure was thought necessary since enterprises had very vivid memories of what they considered a 'confiscation' of their hard-currency holdings at the end of 1991.[16] As one of the leading Romanian bankers remarked by pointing out the policy credibility issue, 'in Romania the value of 1 USD is 1 USD'. At the same time, Law 76, aimed at enforcing financial discipline and triggering restructuring, was passed by Parliament.

Two major debates revolved around the new package of measures introduced in May of 1992. One controversy concerned interest rate policy. Some argued that in a depressed (declining) economy in which the disinclination to save is on the rise because of the shrinking household budgets, it is counterproductive to raise interest rates in real terms for it would further constrain aggregate demand. They overlooked, however, that the highly negative interest rates were causing a flight from the domestic currency and a rapidly increasing money velocity. Moreover, in Romania's case, the foreign exchange constraint had become so threatening and the capacity for expanding exports was significant enough that it made sense to attempt achieving positive real interest rates. In addition, an additional argument was at hand: domestic investment was so feeble (after 20% in 1990, it reached 12.3% of GDP in 1991, the lowest level since 1945) that bringing in foreign capital was also necessary in order to enhance restructuring of industry and growth resumption.

The other controversy was a Romanian version of the famous confrontation between 'elasticity optimists' and 'elasticity pessimists'. The latter pointed out the structural rigidity and heavy import dependency of the economy and feared that devaluation would only fuel inflation, without provoking a quick and significant improvement of the trade balance. Nonetheless, they seemed to ignore an essential truth which was hovering over the functioning of the Romanian economy: the overvalued exchange rate which had been discouraging exports and had been subsidising imports, under circumstances when the policy-mix was fuelling inflationary expectations. That devaluation was the right move was proved by the dynamics of foreign trade which scored a succession of monthly surpluses after June 1992. A temporary real unification of the exchange rate and the *de facto* disappearance of the black market for foreign exchange – as a fundamental structural achievement in the mode of functioning of the economy – was obtained during the second half of 1992. But the policy turnaround was incomplete and flawed in a key respect: interest rates were still highly negative as a result of a large array of preferential credits and very low deposit rates – the latter maintaining the high propensity to shun the domestic currency and intensifying dollarisation.

Political reasons, connected with the elections of September 1992, stymied the determination of the government to pursue a consistent exchange rate policy. Once the official exchange rate was again kept fixed – at Leu 430/$1 – trade imbalances soon reappeared in October, 1992, and the spread between the official rate and the black market rate resurfaced alarmingly at the end of 1992 (Leu 430/$1 vs. over Leu 600/$1 for the black market rate). In this case, one can see how easily politics can alter economic policy and nullify a structural achievement acquired with a lot of difficulty. As far as interest rate policy is concerned, it was unsuccessful because of inconsistent action and inter-enterprise arrears, which operated as a form of temporary *quasi-inside money*. Though they came down to ca. 25% of GDP at the end of 1992, a clear improvement over the previous year, arrears provided enterprises with costless credit and enabled them to continue putting pressure on the foreign exchange market and prices. As a matter of fact, inter-enterprise arrears – which can be viewed as a defence reaction of a system under much *strain* – *endogenise* money supply in a perverse way and emasculate to a significant extent monetary policy. In essence, arrears mirror structural and sectoral disequilibria within the economy and make up a *structural trap* for stabilisation policy.[17]

For much of the year 1993, highly negative interest rates exemplified a highly inconsistent policy-mix, which was due mainly to an insufficiently tight monetary policy. Thus, money supply (M_2) grew by ca. 140% during 1993. Additionally, the interest rate policy showed incoherence: whereas the official refinance rate of the National Bank was set at 70%, a large array of preferential credits made the weighted average refinancing rate much inferior to it. At the same time, very low deposit rates increased the propensity to shun the domestic currency and maintained the hunger for accumulating foreign exchange. Together with the increase of the money supply, the intensity of inflationary expectations, and the resultant rise in money velocity – see Table 9.4 – showed up in an increased inflation rate for 1993. The increasing demonetisation of the economy was clearly indicated by the evolution of money velocity and the size of the refinancing of the banking system as compared to the dimension of base money (M_0) – see Table 9.5.

The policy breakthrough of 1993-1994

The pace of rising inflation and the persistence of a large unsustainable trade imbalance forced top policymakers to reconsider the policy-mix and undertake some much overdue measures. A real policy breakthrough occurred in the last quarter of 1993 when several critical decisions were reached in order to contain and reverse the dynamics of inflationary expectations, to start remonetisation of the economy and create a transparent functioning foreign exchange market.

The main decision related to interest rate policy; a dramatic rise in nominal interest rates made possible the achievement of positive real interest rates. Thus, the National Bank's average refinancing interest rate grew from an annual rate of 59.1% in September 1993 to 136.3% in January 1994 and stood at that high level for other three months. Commercial banks' lending rates followed suit with a two-month lag, from 77.4% in September 1993 to 99.9% in March 1994. This measure had two major consequences: on the one hand it stemmed the flight from Leu;[18] on the other hand it helped, considerably, the formation of a transparent foreign exchange market and, further, it bolstered a presumed export drive.

Related to the interest rate policy one can raise the following issue: wouldn't it have been possible to achieve positive real interest rates in a different way, so that their probable persistence at (very likely) high levels – which may unduly harm the real economy – could be avoided? For instance, some[19] would argue that a more sensible policy would have been the setting of nominal rates (corrected by a risk premium) in accordance with the levels on the relevant foreign capital markets, and the commitment to change the rates in keeping with the dynamic of the exchange rate. Such a policy, which may sound attractive, presents three major drawbacks.

One shortcoming is that such an alternative policy would not send the right signal to markets concerning the determined anti-inflationary stance of the authorities. This aspect is particularly relevant for an environment characterised by high inflationary expectations and when policymakers have to surmount a big *credibility* problem. By telling agents that interests rates will follow the dynamics of the exchange rate (of depreciation), it is intimated – from the very beginning – that inflation is going to happen. Moreover, and this is where the second drawback appears, the dynamic of the exchange rate may not necessarily adequately reflect that of inflation. For example, should the (nominal) exchange rate depreciation be lower than the inflation rate,[20] agents may not find at all attractive the pledge concerning the change of interest rates in accordance with the dynamic of the exchange rate. Finally, this linkage bans the use of the exchange rate as a nominal anchor.

I think that, under the circumstances prevailing in Romania in the second half of 1993, the 'interest rates shock' was the better available policy. It is true that too high and persistent positive real interest rates can damage the real economy, particularly when the level of *strain* – see note 18 – in the system is very high. Additionally, such a high level may turn out to have a boomerang effect in the sense of sending another kind of wrong signal: that, eventually, the economy will break down under the pressure of too high real interest rates and the inflationary cycle would consequently be resumed. This is why policymakers need to be persistent in calibrating policy so that real interest rates are reduced over time.

But one way or another there was an acute need to get out of the policy conundrum and the way decision-makers read the policy trade-off, and their intuition, made the brutal rise in nominal interest rates the preferred policy choice.

Related to the last sentence one may wonder whether the subsequent shape of the downward path of nominal (and real interest rates) was the proper one taking into the account the dynamics of inflation and of the economy in general; this is an issue which demands a careful investigation in itself. Since the issue of the 'policy shock' is quite important, it will be revisited.

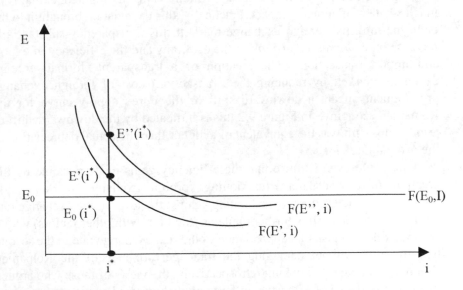

Figure 9.1   The exchange rate system before unification in 1993/94

Another key decision was the substantial devaluation[21] (in several stages) of the official (inter-bank market) exchange rate which made it overlap with the rate prevailing on the grey market; this led to the formation of a transparent foreign exchange market which considerably reduced the entry costs for those in need of foreign monies. The danger posed by devaluation as far as inflation is concerned was much reduced by the existence – previous to devaluation – of the implicit exchange rate which internalised *de facto* many import prices. It should be stressed that, before the devaluation of the official rate, the functioning of the informal foreign exchange market was much enhanced by the full retention foreign exchange regime. This means that big holders of foreign exchange had turned into quasi 'mini-banks' by finding ways of lending hard currency to those in need.

As can be seen in Figure 9.1, the relationship between interest rates and the official rate, E_0, as a quasi-fixed (but adjustable) rate appears as a horizontal axis. At this rate foreign exchange was rationed and used to pay for certain products whose importation was thus subsidised in an implicit way. The usual shape of the curve reappears in the case of the implicit exchange rate, E', which was functioning on the grey market and for the black market exchange rate, E''.

The big devaluation of the Leu (from a monthly average of Leu 1140/USD1 in December 1993 to Leu 1601/USD1 in March 1994) affected only a portion of import transactions,[22] which as was highlighted, explains its much smaller inflationary impact. Practically, this devaluation brought into the open the informal foreign exchange market; this transparency substantially increased the *market integration* of the economy and the efficiency of export and import transactions. The creation of a transparent (formal) foreign exchange market, by reducing the (transaction) cost of foreign exchange procurement, meant a downward shift of the Forex supply curve for the Romanian economy. In Figure 9.2 this is indicated by the downward shift of S to S_1; this shift was the equivalent of a higher than the actual depreciation of the official rate.

One could even surmise that the efficiency gains made possible by the creation of a transparent functioning foreign exchange market made unnecessary a devaluation overshooting against the level of the exchange rate on the grey market – this further explains (together with other factors) why it was possible to register an appreciation of the real exchange rate in the second half of 1994 without damaging the trade performance of the Romanian economy – Table 9.6. Looking retrospectively, the views of those who argued that the importance of a transparent forex market was underestimated by many

Romanian policymakers were validated.

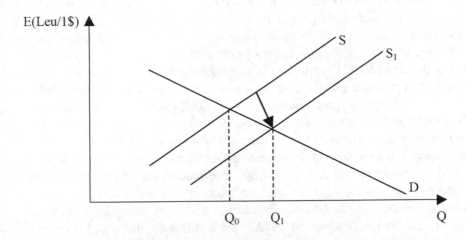

Figure 9.2   The downward shift of the foreign exchange supply curve

Considering the Leu/USD parity in terms of the PPP we can even hypothesise along the following line: to the extent the dynamic of efficiency gains (owing to *learning* and the achievement of the transparent forex market) more than compensates the appreciation of the real exchange rate, the economy can continue scoring better trade performances. In such a case, total factor productivity growth secures a better return in domestic currency for each unit of aggregate national effort. And in view of the very low average wages in Romania (even when compared with other European post-communist countries) and assuming both a shift of and a speedy movement along the learning curve of Romanian companies (exporters), improved trade performances can take place simultaneously with significant rises in real wages. This appears to have been the case for several export sectors in 1994.

The third measure of the policy package consisted of a remarkable putting of the brakes on money creation – via a strict control of base money. Finally, the fiscal stance (a lower budget deficit when corrected by the removal of explicit and implicit subsidies[23]) should be commended since it fits well into the new policy package. All these measures were complemented by a relatively effective wage restraint.

The results of this policy breakthrough confirmed most of its working hypotheses regarding how to fight inflation and the room for invigorating the economy through an impetus to export activity. Inflation came down to an annual rate of 61.7% (December on December) for 1994 and an impressive reduction of the trade deficit was achieved: to - $411.0 million. The economy absorbed surprisingly well the real 'interest rate shock'; in real terms, as a percentage of GDP, aggregate arrears (including inter-enterprise debt) were 23% at the end of 1994 – which was not higher than the figure for 1993 – though one can argue that exports, as a way to get real liquidity, provided a venue for containing arrears. Inventories, overall, did not grow as a percentage of the GDP and the latter registered a positive growth rate. Moreover, gross investment evinced a marked rise – from 13.4% in 1993 to 16.5% in 1994. The functioning of the transparent foreign exchange market and the boost in exports proved an essential conjecture validity: information and transaction costs caused by the lack of market transparency were significant and, therefore, the room for raising exports was substantial. Added to this the effects of depreciation (in the first part of 1994 – see Table 9.6), the world economy coming out of recession, the learning process for Romanian firms, lower oil prices, and one gets a set of explanations for the dynamics of foreign trade in 1994.[24]

The impact of devaluation (depreciation) on the trade balance showed a practically non-existent J-curve effect,[25] which may be seen as a good surprise. But the really big surprise was how well the economy absorbed the shock of high positive real interest rates and of the exchange rate unification – which meant the suppression of most of the implicit and explicit subsidies to inefficient producers.

Thus, according to various estimates, the amount of explicit and implicit subsidies amounted to almost 20% of the GDP in 1992. This figure is not suprising at all bearing in mind the legacy of resource misallocation in a post-command system. Though the figure included cross-subsidisation it did suggest the magnitude of difficulties linked with allocative inefficiency – the possibly large number of firms which would have to get out of the economic game had all subsidies been removed and hard budget constraints strictly imposed. The removal of many explicit and implicit subsidies explains why the budget deficit went up to 4.2% in 1994 – see Table 9.6, with a large part of its financing being obtained from external sources.

The export drive played a major role in pulling the whole economy, but it still could not explain why many enterprises in bad sectors also fared well (or not worse). The more so if one takes into account that arrears did not explode. Several main explanations can be submitted in this respect. One is the existence of important market imperfections – like monopolies that can extract rents and which operate on behalf of bad sectors. Another explanation is the huge 'X-inefficiency' (H. Leibenstein) in the system. This means that micro-efficiency reserves are ubiquitous and, when being under pressure, even firms in the bad sectors can cope with it. Figure 9.3 is an attempt to portray how an economy does cope with enormous strain (Daianu, 1994b).

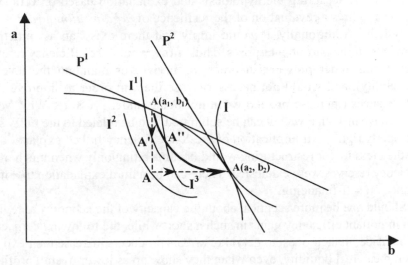

Figure 9.3   Resource reallocation under *strain*

Let us take the simplified case of a two-commodity economy. The initial production combination (a_1, b_1) still reflects the central planners' preferences where the latter is indicated by the price line P_1. Were consumers sovereign, the production combination would be (a_2, b_2) and the price line denoting equilibrium (market-clearing) prices would be P_2. Were resource reallocation frictionless – with no imbalance between exit and entry – there would be no strain in the system; the shift from (a_1, b_1) to (a_2, b_2) would occur along the production possibilities curve. However, friction is unavoidable in a real economy, and furthermore, the imbalance between exit and entry can be considerable; this means that the combination of production A can be much inside the production possibilities curve, which can involve a significant reduction of aggregate utility (from I_1 to I_2). Over time the production combination would have to come ever nearer to (a_2, b_2). How can strain be mitigated? As already implied the most important channels are: the efficiency reserves of producers (X-inefficiency), the elimination of negative value-added activities, inter-enterprise arrears, monopoly pricing, explicit and implicit subsidies, the export of *strain* (by those who are price-makers on external markets, or can delay – restructure – their external payments), and positive exogenous shocks. The action of mitigating factors is depicted in Figure 9.3 by the thick arrow. Here the stress is put on the ubiquitous efficiency reserves, which help enterprises weather the interest rates shock.

However, accepting the hypothesis and explanation based on efficiency reserves requires a revaluation of the resilience of *organisational routines* in the system. Additionally, it would imply that there exists an asymmetrical behaviour on the part of enterprises. Thus, firms would use efficiency reserves when being under pressure in order to survive (or maintain the level of profitability), and would not necessarily use them in order to improve their performances (increase profits) when not being under pressure. Why would they behave in such a way, it can be submitted, can be related to the fuzzy state of property rights. An implication of the X-inefficiency linked explanation is that the pressure for restructuring would become biting only when much of the efficiency reserves were exhausted. There can be a third explanation too: more reliance on self-financing.

Should one be more sceptical about the capacity of the economy to register such important efficiency gains in such a short while, the following conjecture can be made: in their quest to get rid of arrears producers increase their exports, which mean real liquidity, even when they show up as lower overall profits; it is as if to say that they export at any cost. However, an effect of such an export orientation could be increased financial difficulties because of the worsening of the balance sheets, which should cause a rise in the volume of arrears later on although the liquidity situation of some firms may improve. In order to check this conjecture one needs to see what the dynamic of profits was during 1994 and 1995. If profits look worse, it implies that the liquidity motive is still more powerful than profit incentives in the preference functions of many firms.

The relapse into inflation

The year 1995 meant a considerably higher growth rate for the Romanian economy, 6.9%, concomitantly with an inflation rate of ca. 28% (end of year). Those figures even prompted some superficial pundits to talk about Romania's 'joining the club' (meaning the Visegrad Group). The remonetisation of the economy continued, which is indicated by the faster expansion of money supply (+71%) as against inflation – see Table 9.7. Relatedly, money velocity (for the aggregate M_2 which includes hard currency deposits) fell below 5 –

from over 7.5 in 1993 – reflecting a rising money demand.

Unfortunately, economic recovery was driven more by internal demand than by exports. Thus, against the previous year, while exports continued their rapid expansion (by over 20%) imports jumped by more than 30%; this caused the trade imbalance to increase again to more than $1.200 million and put pressure on the foreign exchange inter-bank market.

The renewed sharp rise in the trade (current account) deficit should have caused alarm since Romania relies extensively on compensatory external financing from the multilateral organisations. This means that because of a small level of foreign exchange reserves, relatively small shortfalls of accommodating foreign flows can trigger losses of foreign reserves and, relatedly, confidence crises. Such a confidence crisis occurred in the last quarter of 1995, after several months of reduction of the foreign exchange reserves in the banking system. Consequently, the official exchange rate suffered a fall of ca. 10% in November 1995.

What caused the trade imbalance to sharpen again so much bearing in mind that the real exchange rate did not appreciate in 1995 (though it did so in the second half of 1994), and that major changes of the terms of trade did not take place in that period? One explanation could favour an imports (consumption) binge starting with the last months of 1994, which would, arguably, had been caused by what agents may have perceived as an unsustainable exchange rate. But this explanation would have to reconcile with the fact that, in 1994, the trade (current account) imbalance improved dramatically and the foreign exchange reserves of the banking system (including the Central Bank) increased substantially, which would have indicated, on the contrary, a sustainable level of the exchange rate. On the other hand, maybe, too much stability of the nominal exchange rate is still seen by agents as abnormal and, after a while, they anticipate a depreciation which, paradoxically, may not be asked for by fundamentals. One can also conjecture that some of the improvement in the trade balance, in 1994, was caused by temporary factors.

A more plausible explanation can be related to the higher growth rate of the economy, which spurred imports considerably. The relaxation of monetary policy in the second half of 1994, and continued the following year, enhanced a domestic demand-driven economic upswing in an environment undergoing insufficient restructuring. Consequently, the equilibrium nominal (and real) exchange rate was modified taking other parameters (such as the size of available external financing) as given. The growth of imports was also stimulated by the unusual expansion of hard currency credits which, because of their rates (lower, in real terms, than for leu loans) meant that imports were paradoxically subsidised in their competition with home substitutes. One could also add the operation of an 'inventory cycle' which can be explained by the evolution of real interest rates.

Although signs of too fast growth were obvious in the first half of 1995, policymakers were slow to react and underestimated the trade-offs between the various targets of macroeconomic policy. One can even argue that the seeds of the loss of macroeconomic control, registered in the following year, were implanted in 1995.

The year 1996 made obvious the linkage between the dynamics of inflation and the way the budget deficit is financed. Whereas the programmed consolidated budget deficit was 2.2%, it turned out to be 5.7% (on an accrual basis). What is more significant is that its financing was inflationary via the refinancing of commercial banks which bought an increasing volume of three month T-bills. The size of inflationary financing was augmented by the injection of base money in order to cover the quasi-fiscal deficit i.e., the losses of agriculture and of regies autonomes. Together with the quasi-fiscal deficit, the fiscal imbalance reached 8.4% (on an accrual basis) in 1996.

Moreover, the budget deficit was accompanied by a yawning of the current account deficit – to approximately 7.4% of the GDP, which is a telling indicator of the expansionary policy in that election year. It is noteworthy that, although the growth rate of the economy slowed down to ca. 4.1% in 1996, the trade and the current account deficits increased considerably, as compared to the previous year. These dynamics suggest a worsening state of the economy.

The budget deficit grew at a faster rate in the second half of the year and its inflationary financing caused the monthly inflation rate to increase sharply; thus, in December 1996, the monthly inflation rate went beyond 10%, and for the full year it reached 56.9% (end of the year). The Treasury went increasingly into overdraft in the second half of the year, which was another way of resorting to the Central Bank's financing of the budget deficit – apart from the refinancing of the commercial banks' acquisition of T-bills. In the last quarter of 1996, money velocity was flattening which indicated the coming to an end of the period of remonetisation. How accommodative was monetary policy in the second half of the year is shown by the average monthly rate of expansion of the money supply, which was 6% in that period as against 2.7% in the first half.

The process of remonetisation helped tremendously the efforts of the authorities to subdue inflation, in recent years. This process is indicated by the faster expansion of money supply (M_2) in comparison with the inflation rate. The end of remonetisation is illustrated by the figures for the second half of

1996 when inflation increased faster than the money supply.

Regarding remonetisation, there are several aspects to be singled out. Firstly, this process facilitated the subsidisation of various sectors of the economy (agriculture, energy) from Central Bank's resources. Simultaneously, it allowed the Central Bank to pursue the reduction of inflation. Sectoral financing mirrored the existence of major structural disequilibria in the economy. The size of these disequilibria and their dynamics are illustrated by the structure of the banks' refinancing by the NBR; most of it was made up of directed credit whose share in the whole refinancing was above 50% during 1996. Out of the refinancing, credit to agriculture accounted for about 50%! It should also be said, that this tendency ran counter to the publicly stated intention of raising the share of auction credit in total refinancing and of having markets decide increasingly about credit allocation.

Secondly, remonetisation 'helped' put off dealing resolutely with the two failed banks – Dacia Felix and Credit Bank; more then 1,700 billion lei were injected in both through special credits in the last two years. If money demand had not grown for most of 1995 and 1996, the size of the special credits would have certainly fuelled inflation. This injection was motivated by the lack of an insurance scheme for small depositors, which should have forestalled a run on the banks, a systemic crisis. However, a question springs easily into one's mind: what prevented the setting up of such a scheme earlier?

Thirdly, this remonetisation – which involved the expansion of base money through the increase of net domestic assets, and not through the accumulation of net foreign assets – indicates the unhealthy evolution of the Romanian economy during that period. Ideally, remonetisation should have taken place as an outcome of the rise in net foreign assets (NFA) – as a result of capital inflows, and of net exports – and not, primarily, via base money injections as a way of fuelling an unwarranted expansion of domestic credit. This remonetisation explains, *inter alia*:

a) why the level of refinancing remained extremely high (as a percentage of base money) in the Romanian economy;

b) the deceptive character of the growth of foreign exchange reserves in 1996 (when Romania had several bond issues on foreign capital markets) if one considers that, in the same year, the amount of NFA went down considerably.

Thirdly, it can be submitted that this remonetisation slowed the development of monetary policy instruments, namely open market operations. This is because the Central Bank did not feel the pressure to cope with a surge of liquidity as in the case of substantial capital inflows. Why such inflows did not happen can easily be hypothesised by watching the feeble pace of privatisation during 1994-1996, the functioning of domestic capital markets during those years, and the policy credibility problem faced by decision-makers.

The end of 1996 revealed several worrying tendencies: the very sharp rise in the monthly inflation rate which exceeded double-digit figures, in the last quarter of the year; the sharp rise in the trade (current account) imbalance, although the growth rate of the economy was lower than in 1995 (4.1% as against 6.9%); higher distortions in relative prices due, especially, to the delay in adjusting energy prices and the administrative control of the exchange rate. Overall, the macroeconomic stabilisation programme was losing steam.

Exchange rate vs. money-based stabilisation?

The debate surrounding the policy-package introduced in the Autumn of 1993 regarded the type of stabilisation strategy as well. Some argued that a money-supply based stabilisation would be more realistic owing to factors such as: the lack of foreign exchange reserves; the need to maintain a competitive real exchange rate in order to stimulate exports; and the fear that the other policy alternative may be too constraining in view of the fragility of the Romanian economy and the anticipated political economy of subsequent measures. This policy option advocated a large one-shot devaluation of the exchange rate with its subsequent float[26] in order to maintain a competitive real exchange rate; the latter was supposed to carry the main burden of the balance of payments adjustment via expenditure reallocation.

The other train of thought emphasised the importance of exchange rate stability – at least for a while – for a successful stabilisation. It conceded the need of a large devaluation of the official rate but cautioned against possible negative effects of its floating. One argument used was that, in spite of the not so large share of tradeables in the GDP, what some call the 'dentist efect'[27] is pretty powerful in the Romanian economy.[28] Relatedly, one can emphasise the transparent nature of the exchange rate as a nominal anchor against a monetary aggregate.

As a matter of fact, one can hardly talk about a clearly cut decision as to the type of policy option to adopt, although the main working assumptions could have suggested that a de facto *sui generis* exchange-rate based policy was in the making. Thus, the substantial, but gradual (over a period of several months), devaluation of the official rate was followed by a period of remarkable nominal exchange rate stability over the whole of 1994. This stability was much enhanced by the creation of a transparent forex market and other favourable events, which improved the trade performance of the economy; in its turn, this trade performance unexpectedly allowed policymakers to rely on the benefits of a stable exchange rate.

The effects on the real economy of the high positive real interest rates and the tight credit policy were compensated by the multiplier effect of the export drive and efficiency gains. To this, one should add the inertial accelerating movement of an economy coming out of a big 'transformational recession' (J. Kornai).

It can be submitted, that the type of stabilisation policy embarked upon at the end of 1993 relied on both the control of monetary aggregates (through the money base) and the stability of the nominal exchange rate. This policy was much helped by low capital mobility,[29] which meant that monetary policy retained its effectiveness in terms of determining the size and composition of money supply.

The use of the exchange rate as a quasi-nominal anchor was obviously made possible by the remarkable vigour of exports. Export expansion was so substantial that the Central Bank was able to intervene solidly on the forex market and, considerably, build up its previously very meagre hard currency reserves. It is understood that the initial devaluation of the official rate (less than what was presumed by those who were concerned about the capacity of the economy to carry the burden of adjustment) played a major role in the unfolding of the whole policy.

Some traits of post-command economies, which favour an exchange rate-based stabilisation programme, can be mentioned: no significant history of open inflation which reduces the amount of inertia in the system, and which may help these economies go to the next stage of bringing inflation to a lower level; inflationary expectations are still being shaped since there is no long track of inflation; the policy track of governments is not yet clear, and most of them do not face the kind of credibility problems linked with a long history of policy reversals – though the Romanian experience seems to be contradictory in this respect; and relative low capital mobility, undeveloped financial markets, and reduced integration with world capital markets. Nonetheless, there also can be features which caution against using the exchange rate as an anchor: high inflation differentials; relatively low foreign reserves; high trade and current account imbalances. The latter features should be quite important on the agenda of Romanian policymakers.

The full retention foreign exchange regime and its implications

The foreign exchange full retention scheme was introduced in early 1992 as an instrument to stem huge capital flight; it was also considered as the most effective instrument in view of the growing policy credibility problem faced by policymakers. As it was already mentioned, this foreign exchange regime helped develop the informal markets for foreign exchange and the functioning of a quasi-equilibrium implicit exchange rate.

The immediate results, expected by policymakers, came rapidly into being; capital outflows were stopped to a large extent and the pressure on the official foreign exchange market was partially relieved. On the other hand, the dollarisation process of the economy was officially acknowledged and other consequences burdened the tasks of the decision-makers.

One effect was the complication of the monetary transmission mechanism and the reduced effectiveness of monetary policy. Since the Central Bank authorised some internal transactions to be made in foreign currency, the monetary aggregates had to refer to hard currency holdings as well. Until late 1993, one factor made the monetary aggregates that included hard currency holdings even more relevant: the highly negative real interest rates, which induced agents to hoard foreign currency and, relatedly, stimulated the creation of arrears. The latter phenomenon had intensified as a way to save real liquidity with the purpose of entering the forex market.

The official dollarisation of the economy maintains a high sensitivity to hard currency movements, not necessarily connected with the dynamics of fundamentals. Slight rumours and temporary developments can easily put pressure on the inter-bank forex market. At the same time, since foreign exchange reserves were held by commercial banks and, given the still low quantity of hard currency held by the Central Bank, the latter had little leeway for intervening on the market, in order to prop up the exchange rate when the latter was under pressure. Moreover, a substantial loss of foreign exchange reserves by the banking system (including the Central Bank) could easily trigger a confidence crisis and accelerate the depreciation of the exchange rate. This is what occurred in Romania in the last quarter of 1995.

The regime of full retention asks for much prudence on the part of policymakers, who need to be extremely alert to any sign that unfinanceable trade (current account) deficits are in the making.

If one thinks that post-command environments are seen as highly fuzzy environments, the persistence of high positive real interest rates becomes self-explanatory. Thus, in the equation below,

(1) $i = (E(e)-E)/E + i' + r(z,v)$

r(z,v) refers to the high premium exacted by high inflation and the fuzziness, respectively, of the environment (i' is the foreign interest rate and E(e) is the expected exchange rate).

Even if inflation dynamics would ask for a rapid and substantial fall of (i), the high value of r(z,v) – which is unknown to us but is presumed – may make it impossible. This would indicate quite clearly that in a Romanian – like environment there is an upward bias in the conduct of interest rate policy. In addition, this bias may be contradictory in its effects. High (higher) real interest rates may be needed in order to prevent capital (hard currency) outflows, or an overheating of the economy. Alternately, these rates may discourage long-term foreign direct investment, which may question the stability of the environment over the longer term. Put differently, very high real interest rates can bias the composition of capital inflows towards portfolio funds, which is less favourable to a transforming economy and may even jeopardise a programme of stabilisation. The Mexican lesson is fairly telling in this respect and one would have expected much more debate on this issue among professionals. The experience of Chile – with taxation of short-term movements of capital – may be relevant as to how to deal with such a situation.

How can this bias be counteracted? One way is 'by consequence', in the sense that a highly successful stabilisation policy brings inflation down so much that nominal interest rates follow suit. This would relieve much of the burden of those who carry massive debts. Another way is to practise a more flexible exchange rate policy, but this may have unfavourable inflationary consequences – since it may raise exceedingly inflationary expectations. And finally, massive capital inflows, to the extent they signal the prospects for restructuring and better aggregate performance of the economy, would affect considerably the value of the high premium (r) and, thereby, the size of the real interest rates. Romania finds itself at such a juncture regarding the need for capital inflows and their relationship with restructuring and privatisation.

To conclude, one can argue that the regime of full retention can act as an in-built stabiliser for the functioning of the forex market (in its informal variant) and, implicitly, for the economy as a whole when adverse shocks happen. On the other hand, it does complicate the conduct of monetary policy and maintains a currency duality in the system. This duality is not favourable to bolstering confidence in the national money unless macroeconomic policy reveals much prudence and wisdom and powerful adverse external shocks are dealt with properly.

Final remarks

The Romanian experience with stabilisation and exchange rate policy presents some interesting aspects linked with the pace of reforms and their results. A reason to take a closer look at this experience is that Romania had a fair chance to join the group of transforming economies which were able to subdue high inflation. After 61.7% in 1994, the inflation rate came down to ca. 28% (December on December) in 1995.

That achievement was the outcome of a 'policy-shock' which relied essentially on the realisation of positive real interest rates, tight money and fiscal retrenchment; it was also enhanced by several favourable external factors. It should be stressed that the behaviour of the exchange rate played a major role in this stabilisation. Quite remarkably, the policy breakthrough did not entail a further decline of output, although, in this respect, it can be argued that structural factors – linked with the development of market institutions and 'learning by doing' – were operating. Relatedly, one should think about the fact that output recovery started in Romania one year earlier (in 1993), in spite of inflation of almost 300%, and that economies were bottoming out all over Eastern Europe by that time. The vigour of exports in 1994 gave the image of an export-led economic recovery.

Since industrial restructuring and privatisation did not register significant strides, a big question can be raised: could that stabilisation have been durable in view of the intensity of *strain* in the system? Were a positive answer attempted, then one would have to reconsider the conventional wisdom regarding the possibility of hardening budget constraints in a fuzzy (as far as property rights are concerned) environment, and in which resource misallocation is still substantial. A sceptical answer would stress that monetary and fiscal rigour cannot be maintained for long without causing a build-up of tension inside the system which, sooner or later, causes policy disruptions and instability. A middle of the road answer would argue that the best one can hope for is to embark policy itself on a 'stabilisation path'; that, under the circumstances, 'stop and go' measures are unavoidable and that the crucial issue is how to manage trade-offs, and identify the right 'mix of disequilibria', which should reduce the costs of adjustment (restructuring) intertemporally.

Another big question was brought into the forefront by the evolution of the economy in 1995, when a substantial worsening of the trade deficit happened again. This negative development occurred against the background of a quickening pace of the economy, which grew by an estimated 6.9% in that year. It appeared that an export-led recovery turned into a domestic demand-driven recovery – which underlined the foreign exchange constraint under which the economy operates. In spite of a remarkable further decline of inflation during 1995, the mentioned negative dynamic of the trade balance, under circumstances when the deficit is not yet financed by autonomous capital inflows,[30] questioned the conduct (prudence) of certain macro-economic decisions. The trade imbalance yawned even more in 1996 in spite of a smaller growth rate of the economy – see table 9.1. Likewise, inflation was reignited in 1996 – it went up to ca. 57% – as the government gave up the control of the budget deficit on the eve of elections. The events of 1995 and 1996 underscore the importance of privatisation for inducing autonomous capital inflows and for enhancing restructuring, as well as the danger of 'populist macroeconomics'.

Unless proper concern for macro-equilibria and policy trade-offs is restored and the targeted growth rate is calibrated (managed) adequately, and without a 'breakthrough' in the amount of autonomous capital inflows, macroeconomic stabilisation can hardly be durable. In this respect, one needs to factor in the effects of the political cycle.

The developments of the last couple of years highlight ever again the importance of prudence and wisdom in the conduct of macroeconomic policy, when its positive results are inherently very fragile and are not buttressed by sufficient change in the real economy.

Table 9.1   Current account balance

(in $ million)

	1980	1983	1985	1987	1988	1989
Trade account	-1,534	1,688	1,558	2,436	3,608	2,559
Exports, fob	6,503	6,246	6,156	5,864	6,511	5,965
Imports, fob	8,037	4,558	4,598	3,428	2,903	3,406
Services balance	-865	-766	-450	-211	17	305
Current account	-2,399	922	1,118	2,225	3,625	2,864

	1990	1991	1992	1993	1994	1995	1996
Trade account	-1,743	-1,357	-1,420	-1,128	-411	-1,577	-2.470
Exports, fob	3,364	3,533	4,364	4, 892	6,151	7.910	8.085
Imports, fob	5,107	4,890	5,784	6,020	6,562	9.487	10.555
Services balance	87	-12	-168	-115	-171	-197	-142
Current account	-1,656	-1,369	-1,200	-1,174	-428	-1,774	-2,612

Source: National statistics

Table 9.2   Structure of GDP by final use

	1989	1990	1991	1992	1993
GDP	100.0	100.0	10.0	100.0	100.0
Consumption	70.5	79.2	75.8	76.6	78.3
- Private	58.9	65.9	60.7	61.7	63.7
-Government	11.6	13.3	15.1	15.0	14.6
Investment					
-Fixed investment	29.9	19.8	14.3	14.9	13.4
-Change in stocks	-3.1	10.5	13.7	16.2	14.1
Net Exports of Goods and Non-Factor Services	2.7	-9.5	-3.0	-7.7	-5.8

Source: National statistics

Table 9.3   GDP

(% change per annum)

1978-1981	1982-1985	1985	1986	1987	1988	1989
4.5	4.0	-1.0	2.3	0.8	-5.0	-5.8

1990	1991	1992	1993	1994	1995	1996
-5.6	-12.9	-8.8	1.5	3.9	6.9	4.1

Source: National statistics

Table 9.4   Money velocity

Month

	t	1991	1992	1993
January	1	2.56	4.5	4.41
February	2	2.56	5.66	5.32
March	3	3.18	5.68	5.23
April	4	3.93	5.52	5.54
May	5	3.84	6.14	6.99
June	6	4.05	5.7	6.83
July	7	3.65	4.75	6.46
August	8	4.02	4.51	6.52
September	9	4.31	4.87	6.93
October	10	4.13	5.4	7.73
November	11	3.4	6.13	7.89
December	12	2.87	5.06	6.51

Source: National statistics; Emilian Dobrescu (1994); M2 includes the foreign exchange deposits

Table 9.5   Ratio between Central Bank refinancing and the monetary base

Year	Month	Mo (lei/bill)	Refin. NBR (lei/bill)	Refin/Mo
1992	March	411.7	408.9	0.99
	June	364.5	301.9	0.83
	September	434.7	327.8	0.75
	December	602.4	350.8	0.58
1993	March	674.8	376.9	0.56
	June	728.0	533.6	0.73
	September	1,009.5	1,226.0	1.21
	December	1,299.0	1,541.2	1.19
1994	March	1,520.1	1,936.2	1.27
	June	1,657.2	1965.5	1.19
	September	2,089.0	2,139.5	1.02
	December	3,170.0	2,402.6	0.76
1995	March	2,542.0	2,250.7	0.89
	June	3,097	2,087	0.67
1996	June	4,991	4,338	0.87
	December	7,105	7,312	1.03

Source: National statistics and National Bank data

Table 9.6   Macroeconomic indicators, 1990-96

Indicators		1990	1991	1992	1993	1994	1995	1996
1.GDP (annual change)	%	-5.6	-12.9	-8.8	1.5	3.9	6.9	4.1
2. Unemployment rate (end of period)	%	-	3	8.4	10.4	10.9	8.9	6.3
3.Inflation								
-average	%	5.1	174.5	210.9	290.3	136.8	32.2	38.8
-Dec./Dec.	%	37.7	222.8	199.2	295.5	61.7	27.8	56.9
4.M_2 (end of period)- growth rate	%	22	101.2	79.6	141	138.1	71	66
5. Nominal devaluation								
-average	%	63.7	212.7	303.1	146.8	117.8	22.8	51.6
-Dec./Dec.	%	54.7	728.5	132.9	163.5	55.5	45.9	56.5
6.M_2/GDP	%	55.7	27.4	20.5	13.8	13.3	18.1	20.3
7.Budget deficit[*]/GDP	%	-0.4	-1.9	-4.4	-1.7	-4.2	-4.1	4.9
8.Current account/GDP	%	-8.5	-3.5	-8	-4.5	-1.4	-5	-7.4
9.Real wage index	%	5.1	-19.6	-13.2	-24	-3.2	17	9.3
10.Real exchange index (as against Dec.1991)[**]	%		100	117.1	113.3	102.3	95.5	99.5
- Q1	%			92.1	124.0	114.4	94.2	107.6
- Q2	%			99.3	119.4	108.2	93.6	105.1
- Q3	%			153.9	106.1	97.5	92.5	91.6
- Q4	%			123.0	103.7	94.9	101.6	93.9

[*] State budget
[**] Exchange rate variation deflated by the ratio between Romanian PPI and US PPI
Source: National Bank of Romania

Table 9.7   Remonetisation

(% as against previous year)

	1994	1995	1996
Money supply, M_2	138.1	71	66
Inflation, CPI	61.7	27.8	56.9

Source: National Bank Statistics

Notes

*   Revised version of the paper presented at the conference 'Convertibility and Exchange Rate Policy', Sofia, 22-23 September 1995. Many thanks to Jimmy Iorga, Valentin Lazea, and Jorge Braga de Macedo for their useful comments. The usual disclaimers apply. An earlier version of the paper was published by the *Economics of Transition*, no.1, 1996, pp. 229-248.

1   See also Demekas and Khan (1991) and Daianu (1994c).

2   The stock-building, which averaged almost 15% of the nominal national product, is much above the levels registered by Poland, Hungary, the Czech Republic and Slovakia, where inventory accumulation has ranged from -3% to 3% per year since 1989 – levels consistent with that of most economies in normal years. Valentin Lazea remarked to me that, with a normal rate of stock building (say, of 3% per year), Romania would not have been a net importer. Alternatively, to put it in another way, all of the foreign indebtedness seems to have been lost in stock building. For 1994, the improvement of the current account balance went *pari passu* with a dramatic reduction of inventories.

3   Some would link it with the elections of May 1990. Measured real wages rose by 11% over the period December 1989-October 1990, while output was on the decline; price decontrol was initiated in November of that year.

4   Rising nominal wages against the background of declining output and price controls led to increased monetary holdings.

5   Real GDP fell by 5.6% in 1990 and by 12.9% in 1991.

6   The external trade deficit in hard currency was -$1.743 billion in 1990 and -$1.357 billion in 1991 (table 9.1).

7   In January 1992, Peter Murrell asked me why Romania resorted to an IMF supported plan in view of her excellent external account position at the start of transition. I answered that: a) more important than the stock of external debt are the sustainable flows of imports; and b), under the prevailing social and political circumstances rejecting conditional support from the IMF would have forced

authorities to try to reimpose direct controls, a path-policy scarcely desirable politically and, practically, unfeasible at the time. People too often tend to forget that a Chinese-like solution means 'change strictly controlled from above'. In Romania, the social explosion triggered processes beyond any control.

8   Credit ceilings of 22% were imposed for the year and interest rates (although they remained negative in real terms) were liberalised in April of 1991.

9   From Leu 35/$1 to Lei 60/$1.

10   Eric Clifton and Mohsin S. Khan (1993).

11   At the level of Leu 184/$1.

12   Caused by increasing overvaluation of the domestic currency due to inflation differentials.

13   Because, officially, internal convertibility was enforced.

14   The cash export revenues were by ca. 50% less in February 1992 as against November 1991.

15   From Leu 206/$1 in April 1992, it moved to Leu 226/$1 in May, Leu 304/$l in June, Leu 365/$1 in July, Leu 383/$1 in August and Leu 430/$1 in September of the same year (figures are end of month).

16   After 'the exchange-rate reunification', their claims for foreign exchange were not satisfied adequately by banks and a hard-currency overhang started to build up.

17   For more elaboration on inter-enterprise arrears as a symptom of a system under *strain*, and on *strain* in economic systems see Daianu (1994a, 1994b). *Strain* can be seen as a measure of the required resource reallocation in an economic system which undergoes dramatic changes of relative prices; it can be illustrated by the ratio:

$$J = \frac{\sum p_i^* |q_i^* - q_i|}{\sum p_i^* q_i^*}$$

where (p^*) and (q^*) refer to equilibrium price and quantity values, whereas (p) and (q) correspond to the distorted (inherited) resource allocation. J can be viewed as a measure of aggregate disequilibrium in the system against the vector of equilibrium prices and quantities (see also Richard Portes, 1986). The higher is *strain* (J) the higher is the unemployment that would be entailed by an instantaneous complete resource reallocation. This is a major reason behind the temptation for policymakers to tolerate higher inflation as a way to diffuse tension within a system. From this perspective one can even talk of an 'optimal' rate of inflation taking into account the available amount of non-inflationary (domestic and external) financing of the budget deficit and the need not to fuel inflationary expectations.

18   The leu deposits of households grew dramatically during 1994. The de- and remonetisation of the economy is illustrated by the M2/GDP ratio which was 27.4%, 20.5%, 13.8%, 13.3%, 18.1% in 1991, 1992, 1993, 1994 and 1995

respectively – see table 9.6.

19   Like Jacek Rostowski.

20   Like when there is a substantial inflow of capital, which allows lower exchange rate devaluation.

21   It can be seen that the notion *devaluation*, and not *depreciation*, is used. For much of the period under focus, the inter-bank foreign exchange market was not functioning properly and *rationing* was taking place; this is why the term devaluation is preferred until the market started to operate at market-clearing prices.

22   Especially the big imports of energy and raw materials.

23   The budget deficit was higher in 1994 (-4.2%) than in 1993 (-1.7%), but it meant the removal of most of the implicit and explicit subsidies.

24   The depreciation of the US dollar against the main currencies also helped this process.

25   However, one could argue that the *ceteris paribus* condition hardly applies (owing to the favourable external 'shocks' as well).

26   Though, even this policy option had two variants. One considered the use of a pre-announced devaluation path, which would bring it close to exchange rate based stabilisation. The other variant took floating at its literal meaning.

27   The origin of this expression is the stabilisation experience in Israel in the 80s.

28   This argument refers also to the counter-inflationary implications of the functioning of the implicit exchange rate.

29   This implies a low sensitivity of capital inflows to interest rate variations. Nonetheless, it is more correct to talk about an asymmetric capital mobility since foreign exchange holdings of domestic residents are sensitive to interest rate differentials.

30   Which would presumably enhance the export capacity of the economy.

References

Calvo, G. A. and Coricelli, F. (1995), 'Inter-enterprise arrears in Economies in Transition', paper presented at the Conference 'Output Decline in Eastern Europe-Prospects for Recovery', 18-20 November, 1993, IIASA, Austria, published in R. Holzmann, J. Gacs and G. Winckler (eds.) (1995), *Output Decline in Eastern Europe*, Kluwer, pp. 193-212.

Calvo, G. A. and Vegh, C.A. (1990), 'Credibility and the Dynamics of Stabilisation Policy. A Basic Framework', *IMF Working Paper*, 90/110, Washington DC.

Calvo, G.A. and Vegh, C.A. (1994), 'Inflation Stabilisation and Nominal Achors', in R.C. Barth and C.H. Wong (eds.), *Approaches to Exchange Rate Policy, Choices for Developing and Transition Economies*, IMF, pp.90-102, Washington DC.

Clifton, E. V. and Khan, M.S. (1993), 'Interenterprise Arrears in Transforming Economies: The Case of Romania', *IMF Staff Papers*, vol.40, no. 3, pp. 680-696.

Daianu, D. (1994), 'Inter-enterprise Arrears in a Post-command Economy: Thoughts from a Romanian Perspective', *IMF Working Paper*, 94/54, Washington DC.

Daianu, D. (1994b), 'Explaining *Strain* in Economic Systems: The Case of Post-command Economies', paper presented at the Conference of the European Association of Comparative Economics, Budapest, September 1994 (in Romanian), *Oeconomica*, no.2, pp.5-14.

Daianu, D. (1994), 'The Changing Mix of Disequilibria during Transition: a Romanian Background', *IMF Working Paper*, 94/77, Washington DC.

Demekas, D. G. and Khan, M. S. (1991), 'The Romanian Economic Reform Program', *IMF Occasional Paper*, no.89, Washington DC.

Dobrescu, E. (1994), 'An Econometric Testing of some Monetary Hypotheses' (in Romanian), *Oeconomica*, no.2, pp.15-19.

Kornai, J. (1993), 'Transformational Recession', *Economie Appliquée*, vol. 38, no.3-4.

Leibenstein, H. (1966), 'Allocative Efficiency vs. X-Efficiency', *American Economic Review*, vol. 56, no.3, pp.392-410.

Portes, R. (1986), 'The Theory and Measurement of Macroeconomic Disequilibrium in Centrally Planned Economies', *Discussion Paper*, no. 91, CEPR, London.

Part III

Transformation and External Environment

10   Europe Under a Double Challenge[*]

J Con

Three concentric circles of transition

The year 1989 was a watershed moment in the flow of history as it signalled the start of post-communist transformation in Europe and the end of the cold war. Post-communist transformation marks the close of this century; its assumed and stated goal is to stop the decay of the former communist countries, to transform their non-viable economic systems into well functioning market economies and, eventually, change their political systems into pluralistic democracies. This undertaking is a historical challenge facing Europe. However, a growing malaise engulfing the Continent accompanies this challenge. There are signs indicating that the large European economies have been chronically losing ground in world competition during the past decades, and their dynamics have been featured by diminishing vitality. Additionally, the German reunification and the regional and international implications of the collapse of communism have put exceptional pressure on the direction, speed and accepted patterns of implementing the process of further European integration as defined by the Maastricht treaty. Whereas Eastern Europe (this term is used in a broad, traditional sense here) and the newly established states strive to achieve economic viability in a relatively hostile international environment, the Western European countries appear to be mainly concerned with regaining their vitality. The combination of problems, of a differing nature, faced by the two regions substantially complicates the tasks of policymakers in all the countries concerned.

In a narrow sense, post-communist transition deals with the changing anatomy and physiology of the former command systems. In a broader sense, it refers to the whole array of consequences of the dismantling of communism on the European continent. One telling example is the upheaval of the political establishment in Italy, which was enhanced by the relatively sudden disappearance of the ideological and military confrontation between the two blocs in Europe. The implosion, or the metamorphosis (as in Italy) of the major Western communist parties, is another significant consequence.

Moreover, for Europe as a whole, post-communist transition must be judged in conjunction with trends which had been discernible for more than twenty years – in terms of processes which allow (or do not allow) timely institutional and technological change brought about by internal and external competitive pressures. Thus, an OECD study emphasises that 'the truth is that the culprit is not change, but the rich countries' inability or unwillingness to cope with it'.[1] The same study remarks that '... the industrial countries, especially in Europe, have allowed their economic arteries to harden' for at least the last twenty years.[2]

The double connotation of transition in Europe is not sufficient for grasping the evolution of this continent within the context of the world economy. We have been witnessing a process of redistribution of economic power in the world space with its economic gravity centre shifting steadily and, apparently, inexorably, towards the Pacific Rim. 'The Japan That Can Say No' (Ishihara, 1991) became an open reality in February 1994, when, for the first time in the post-war bilateral relationship, the Japanese prime minister mentioned possible retaliatory measures against eventual unilateral steps taken by the USA.

International economic policy opinion has not failed to take into account the rise of Asian economies. Thus a report by the Bretton Woods Commission (chaired by Paul Volcker), which had been set up to celebrate the 50th anniversary of the IMF and the World Bank, recommends that the voting structures in international financial organisations be changed to reflect the rising power of Asia.[3]

Neither should one forget China, which is seen by many observers as an emerging economic superpower in the next century. The awakening of China will doubtlessly reinforce the process of overall redistribution of economic and political power in the world, with its multitude of geopolitical and economic consequences. Chancellor Helmut Kohl's visit to Beijing in 1993 exemplified not only the new and growing German assertiveness in pursuing its regional economic and political interests, but also signalled the way Germany is looking at the new China.[4]

Likewise, the fact that the Clinton administration had to give up attempts to use the Chinese most-favoured-nation status as a means of political pressure reflects the irresistible power of economic logic in today's world politics. More than ever foreign policy means foreign economic policy. In this respect, let us remember how some Western countries looked at Japan in the aftermath of the oil price shocks during the 1970s – when it was accused of practising single-minded oil diplomacy. Today, even the USA seem to be forced to adopt a similar posture in international relations.[5]

With the benefit of hindsight we can see how unrealistic and misleading a vision can be that proclaimed 'The End of History' (Fukuyama, 1990) by focusing on the demise of communism only. Besides, the clash of ideologies is not over and cannot be left behind in the past – the distinction of left vs. right has defined and will continue to define the political process in all democracies, and it would be very naive to consider that socialist leanings are fading away in the former command societies.[6]

From a certain perspective, ironically, the post-cold war world looks less stable: the proliferation of military and ethnic conflicts, widespread economic recession and trade protectionism, the rise of Islamic fundamentalism, the escalation of nationalism, tribalism and right-wing extremism (neo-fascism) are very worrying signs. We can talk of three concentric *circles of transition* (crisis) in the world: one that comprises the former communist states; a larger one that covers the whole of Europe; and a third one that looks at processes in the world at large.

Trying to define *vitality* and *viability*

In an ideal world of perfect competition, of no significant borders, a preoccupation with 'macro-behaviours' would not be justified. The real world is different. Even arguments put forward in terms of the 'new industrial revolution' and of the tendencies of globalisation of economic activities, which reduce the scope for national economic policymaking, cannot conceal a fundamental truth: the real world is made up of national entities that develop and pursue national goals and have their particular traits and dynamics. Moreover, the real world reveals imperfect competition and shifts in comparative advantages resulting from astonishing catching-up processes and successful institutional design.

There is no shortage of concepts and highly elaborate explanations attempting to capture analytically the differentiated economic evolution of national entities in the global space.

In the late 1970s Charles Kindleberger (1978) talked about the 'aging economy', trying to clarify institutional roots of decelerating dynamics. Some years later, in his book 'The Rise and Decline of Nations' (1982) Mancur Olson suggested that 'institutional sclerosis' was the basic cause of societal decline. He highlighted the development of 'coalitions of vested interests' which capture the public domain and ossify the decision-making process, thereby negatively affecting societal productivity. It is noteworthy that this concept was later used to analyse the economic euthanasia of command systems.[7] 'Overstretch' is seen by Paul Kennedy (1992) as the main explanatory factor behind the collapse of 'great powers' (empires). Put differently, nobody is big enough to enjoy sustainable (permanent) and expanding supremacy unless endowed with celestial vitality. For example, the downfall of the former Soviet Union can be linked with the process of institutional dissolution, fatally speeded up by the virus called *Glasnost.* However, it is indisputable that the Soviet leaders conceived the political opening itself as a means to induce an invigoration of the economic system, which had been overstretched by military competition with the USA.

Michael Porter (1990), using concepts of industrial organisation theory puts the emphasis on clusters of capabilities and on endogenous growth to elucidate the competitiveness of nations. From a different perspective, George Lodge (1990) emphasises the existence of and the need for *national strategies* to achieve, or restore, competitiveness. Alice Amsden (1989) and Robert Wade (1990) reason in the same vein.

Lester Thurow (1993), distinguishes between 'producer' and 'consumer' economies. He argues that the former are most likely to become domineering economic forces in the world because of their institutional and cultural structure which favours saving/investment and the build-up of highly educated human capital. The 'consumer' economies, on the other hand, show a relatively low propensity to save and behavioural short-termism – the latter also being cited as an outcome of inadequate structures of corporate governance. The school of evolutionary *economics* (Nelson and Winter, 1982; Lesourne, 1991) seeks to throw light on the institutional determinants of differentiated dynamics across national economies. From such a theoretical perspective John Cornwall wrote his 'Theory of Economic Breakdown' (1990).

The explanations listed above refer to the developed part of the world economy and are, largely, the intellectual byproducts of the Western anxiety about the dynamism exhibited by Asian economies.[8] One could easily add to this the classical arguments on the congenital malfunctioning and inefficiency of command systems, mainly provided by Ludwig von Mises and Friedrich von Hayek (as protagonists of the Calculation Debate in the 1920s and 1930s) and, more recently, by Janos Kornai (1980). All these theoretical explanations imply two concepts: *vitality* and *viability.*

To put it succinctly, one could say that *vitality* means the sustainability of relatively high rates of competitive economic growth. This also implies the existence of long-term equilibrium in the balance of payments. Competitive economic growth involves intensive innovation (or creative imitation) and a steady accumulation of highly educated human capital. The neo-growth theory (Romer, 1986), with its emphasis on the accumulation of knowledge, externalities and imperfect competition, provides a very illuminating theoretical underpinning to this phenomenon. One could trace this explanation to Gunnar Myrdal's process of 'cumulative causation' and try to identify what allows a poor performer (a poor country) to break the vicious circle, and a good performer (a rich country) to be diverted from the 'corridor' of sustained prosperity.

As for *viability* I would propose the following possible definition: maintaining satisfactory per capita income and an income distribution which does not disrupt the social fabric. In a broad sense, this definition would refer to the entropic degradation of the environment as well.

Both definitions assume a certain stability of the evolution of society; change can be managed, for it is either internally generated (if there are active agents of change), or society has the capacity of absorbing it in a non-disruptive way. Matters become much more complicated in the case of societies which are in the throes of social upheaval, or which are undergoing dramatic institutional and structural change. It is logical to presume that societal transformation, i.e., fuzziness, volatility and institutional fragility accompany large-scale organisational and institutional change. Under such circumstances economic, social, and political stability is more than hard to achieve – it may easily turn into wishful thinking and a policy nightmare.

A viable economy is not necessarily a vital one. The British secular decline is a relevant example in this respect, though one can hardly question the solidity of British society. In fact, there are pundits who fear the spreading of an accentuated 'British disease' – something I would call *civilisation fatigue*,[9] a sort of Spenglerian symptom – throughout the old continent.

Eastern Europe, the first, or inner circle of transition: why is transition so hard?

The general mood has changed dramatically throughout Europe since the end of the 1980s. In Eastern Europe, uncertainty and increasing frustration regarding the pace and results of transition are replacing the euphoria, which followed the collapse of the communist regimes. People are beginning to realise that post-communist transformation is a much more complex and complicated process than initially thought, and that time cannot be speeded up at will.

Defining and enforcing a new structure of property rights, formulating and passing legislation, making institutions work (institutions seen as 'rules enjoying wide social acceptability', in the phraseology of Douglas North, 1981), achieving durable macro-stabilisation via structural adjustment and industrial restructuring, are intertwined prerequisites for attaining economic viability. However, these are time-consuming and painful endeavours.

What is unique about post-communist transformation in Europe is that it implies several simultaneously evolving processes: large-scale institutional change, economic restructuring, structural adjustment and macro-stabilisation, and, last but not least, modernisation. Post-communist transformation lacks the institutional ingredients of a market environment and experiences enormous distortions in the allocation of resources. In this respect, one should not forget that the Asian economies enjoyed the benefits of the golden years of a growing world economy (in the 1950s and the 1960s) and that the boom of several Latin-American countries, in the 1980s, was favoured by a consumption-driven expanding US economy. The current international environment is significantly different and magnifies the shocks produced by the sudden disappearance of Eastern markets. I shall now focus on what I consider to be rather neglected issues in the current debate: understanding the relative backwardness and, in consequence, the institutional fragility of the evolving societal frameworks, and the magnitude of required reallocation of resources.

While the system-related (institutional) dimension of transition is of paramount importance, one can detect a further impulse which has driven the evolution of East European societies through this century; this is the attempt to catch up with the West, an idea which obsessed national politicians during the interwar period and, later, also the communist leaders of these countries. Nowadays this aspiration is reflected in the CEECs' ardent desire to join the EU.

Why is the desire to catch up so strong? One can often hear presumably knowledgeable professionals passing judgements on the transformation process, who seemingly neglect the heavy legacy of backwardness of these societies - a state of affairs which goes back in history.[10] As observed by a keen student of the region: '... Eastern Europe was in some sense economically backward long before it was absorbed into the broader Western world market. This backwardness has roots in the very distant past...' (Chirot, 1989, p.3). Similarly, Ivan Berend (1994, p.110) remarks: 'What is missing in most of these analyses is a deeper understanding of long-term historical trends in East-Central Europe'.[11] However, a note of caution is required. The post-communist societies of Europe are societal entities, which show similar structural traits, but also major discrepancies. The latter can be attributed to the dissimilar pre-communist legacy (the most conspicuous example is Czechoslovakia, which was a leading industrial country during the interwar period) and the different brands of national central planning, in terms of relaxation of direct controls and economic policy choices. The historical differences explain why market institutions vary qualitatively across CEECs and why macro- and micro-disequilibria differed among them on the eve of 1989. Undoubtedly, Hungary, Czechoslovakia and Poland had a substantial competitive edge in starting and managing the process of transition. Unsurprisingly, these countries fared better than the rest in their stabilisation programmes.

Backwardness should be seen as bearing considerably on the potential for overcoming the performance deficit of institutionally poorly arranged societies. On the one hand it points to the lack of knowledge of individuals and of society as a whole and to the constraints obstructing genuine institutional change, and on the other hand it suggests that there is much scope for a system to deviate from what may be conceived as an ideal course of evolution. The stress put on the burden of the past is meant to warn against its dragging effects and the dependency on an unfavourable path from which is not easy to break away.[12] Backwardness makes it harder to overcome the fragility of market institutions in the making, and it enhances the danger that the dynamics of change might get out of control.

It is fair to point out that the high degree of literacy of East European societies, their large segments of well-trained workers, the existence of a numerous technical intelligentsia, and the links with the developed world offered by the information age provide positive counterbalancing factors. Nonetheless, it would be shortsighted and counterproductive to disregard the industrial and cultural distance that separates the East from the West.

The institutional fragility aspect has already been mentioned. Apart from the insufficient analytical attention paid to institutional build-up in the transforming societies in Europe, one must consider the seeds of instability produced by this very fragility. There is a train of thought which argues that as long as property rights are not clearly defined and enforced, durable macrostabilisation will be out of reach (Sachs and Lipton, 1990). This is a relevant line of reasoning although it is incomplete in that it does not take into account the magnitude of the inherited misallocation of resources and the *strain* it causes within the system.

The poor capacity of immature institutions to perform properly can also be mentioned in this context. For example, the debate 'universal vs. specialised banks' is quite relevant to the concerns created by immature market institutions in terms of enhanced instability and uncertainty in the system.[13] From a broader perspective one could raise the issue of the *governance capabilities* of these countries' political and economic élites, namely, the question to what extent they are capable of inducing and managing change (transformation) when so much fuzziness, volatility and uncertainty prevail.

Another issue which, in my view, is not sufficiently highlighted in public debate, is the dimension of the inherited misallocation of resources in Eastern Europe. Here I am referring to the sheer scale of disequilibria at the new relative prices and to the magnitude of the required restructuring compared with the system's ability to undergo wide-ranging and quick changes. What is amazing is the nonchalance of many professionals with respect to the consequences of the magnitude of required restructuring. When one sees Western governments – and their social constituencies – tinkering on the fringes and deeply reluctant to undertake relatively minor adjustments, the *strain* under which the former command economies operate becomes understandable.

The inherited structure of the economies and the misallocation of resources put the decision-making system in CEEs under exceptional *strain* once the combination of internal and external shocks (engineered by reforms or simply triggered by uncontrolled processes of systemic dissolution) had occurred. 'Structure', here, refers to the network of institutional arrangements (including rules of conduct that are socially ingrained) and of vested interests (based on material/productive interdependencies and the distribution of property rights) which creates a logic of motion in the system and makes individual enterprises its captives. Vested interests are also the result of the configuration of industry inherited from the command system.[14] This industrial structure, with its extremely high concentration and its reliance on chain links, explains the degree of market monopolisation in the transforming economies. In this respect one can talk about *the power of structure*, which is well illustrated by the power of debtors over creditors. This power is not of a conspiratorial nature (the cartel is unconscious), because it relies on the system's rules of functioning.

Command planning, with its inherent incapability of rational calculation and its forced industrialisation, left a legacy of resource misallocation, which became visible by price liberalisation and the functional opening of the economy. The new prices show what was previously kept hidden by administrative prices and strong redistribution of income: a very wide range of profitability rates of economic entities. Consequently, one may observe a wide dispersion of units which could be grouped into several distinctly different categories: negative value-added enterprises; inefficient, but positive value-added units (which, in turn, can be subdivided into non-viable and potentially viable firms); and inefficient enterprises.

The wide range of profitability rates and wide dispersion of enterprises with highly diverging performance mean that, should financial discipline be strictly enforced, a large number of units would have to go bankrupt. This would be the start of profound reallocation of resources but aggregate output would go down substantially since market destruction is significantly more intense than market construction, at least during the first stage. There are two important aspects involved in this process: first, the scope of reallocation and, second, the speed required to maintain a certain balance between exit and entry,[15] so that the growth of the healthy private sector should not be unduly impaired. A plausible assumption is that the wider the scope and the faster the desired speed of the process, the higher the imbalance and tension within the economy. Actually, when the 'low supply responsiveness' of transition economies is mentioned in debates, one points to this imbalance.

The problem of the scope and speed of resource reallocation can be posed for an economy operating at any level of employment: a significant change in relative prices would bring about resource reallocation. However, it makes sense to presume that the lower the level of employment, the higher the reluctance to change will be. In this regard, it may be interesting to recall the experience of the industrialised countries, which had to absorb the oil price shock in the 1970s. These countries enjoyed the luxury of undertaking the necessary adjustment at a relatively leisurely pace due, essentially, to the quality of functioning of their economies, their status as world price makers for manufactured goods, and the recycling of petro-dollars. Incidentally, monetary policy was also used to delay change, which led to a surge of world inflation.

The post-command economies are fundamentally price-takers; they had to absorb a major worsening of their terms of trade (except the Russian Federation and, probably, Kazakhstan) once world prices started to govern all their trade transactions. They also had to face a relatively sudden collapse of Eastern trade following the dismantling of the COMECON arrangements. Additionally, there was a sharp contraction of domestic trade and, consequently, of aggregate supply/demand because of skyrocketing information and transaction costs for many enterprises. Owing to the extreme fuzziness concerning property rights, it is not unjustified to assume that X-inefficiency (Leibenstein, 1966) has been on the rise in many enterprises – a phenomenon accompanied by pervasive asset stripping. For the transforming economies, the *strain* caused by the magnitude of required resource reallocation, combined with primitive and fragile institutional arrangements and the lack of organisational capital (Murrell, 1992), was compounded by severe exogenous shocks.

What are the implications of the existence of this *strain*? One is that these economies can very easily become exceedingly unstable, and that their capacity to absorb shocks is pretty low. Another implication is that policymakers face extremely painful trade-offs and that, in most cases, unless sufficient external support is available, the room for manoeuvre is practically non-existent. Basically, policymakers have to sail between the Scylla of high inflation (or hyperinflation, in the structurally more rigid economies) and the Carybdis of huge unemployment, both being highly undesirable politically and socially. Russia provides one of the most dramatic examples of this miserable trade-off: 'Economic chaos could produce a political collapse in at least two ways – through the descent into hyperinflation, or through a catastrophic rise in unemployment not cushioned by a social safety net' (Sachs, 1994).[16]

On this track, it becomes apparent how critical the international environment is for the dynamics of transition. Unfortunately, the international environment is unfavourable and the trends are not encouraging at all. It is unquestionable that the rising nationalism in international policymaking, the growing protectionism, the global economic recession, and the level of interest rates on world capital markets do not facilitate post-communist transformation and accentuate the *strain* in the transforming economies. A concrete example of the distance between myth and reality in the rhetoric of support is the extent of access East European producers have on EU markets for most of their main export items. In this case, there is a relationship between the needed sectoral adjustment in Western Europe[17] and trade as a tool for systemic adjustment (transformation) in post-communist countries. Reducing *strain* in the latter involves increasing short-term difficulties in the former, and the decision on how to deal with such a trade-off cannot be but political. But with Western Europe affected economically by the German reunification blow and by increasingly weak governments, the prospects of gaining wider access to EU markets are not very encouraging at present, in spite of high-level pronouncements and gestures.

East European governments are under strenuous time pressure: for them 'it is raining while the house is roofless'. They cannot afford the luxury of procrastinating, and those who waste time will be heavily penalised. Besides, increasing worries are created because of the depressed levels of output, very low investment ratios and hardly any real wage increase; these are trends, which could undermine the prospects for long-term growth. One should also mention an increasingly intense struggle over the distribution of wealth and erosion of the consensus on a certain kind of societal change, under conditions when large segments of society are made up of losers – phenomena that are not good signs for safeguarding the consistency of and support for economic policymaking. An ever more pervasive social fatigue, coupled with the instability caused by ethnic and military conflicts in several parts of the region, can play havoc with transformation and lead national systems astray.

Path-dependency is a very meaningful expression under these circumstances. A sequence of major policy blunders and unfavourable external shocks can put a system on a trajectory that is misdirected and hard to correct. There is also the 'Russia factor', a variable whose magnitude and dynamics defy predictions – though some would argue that, in spite of all adversities, the march towards capitalism in that country cannot be stopped in the long term (Yergin and Gustaffson, 1994).

One needs also to consider that the degree of instability in the East is amplified by the extent to which the countries of the region feel their security threatened. When military conflicts occur, when borders are questioned, when ethnic tensions heighten, such a feeling is more than justified. All these factors enhance the development of a social and political psychology, which makes the task of working out and implementing sound economic policies much harder.

Western Europe, the second or middle circle of transition: what is behind current pessimism?

Euro-pessimism is not new. This syndrome seems to recur in European history: suffice it to remember the hostile reaction to the international offensive by American corporations in the 1960s. A good barometer of the mood of the political class and of the business community in France at that time was Jean Jacques Servan Schreiber's best-seller 'Le Defi Américain' (1967).[18] One could argue that the 1960s were the decade that gave a decisive intellectual impetus for the formation of companies aiming at developing an international identity, which could enable them to compete with American and, later, with Japanese transnational corporations. One could also say that the 1960s represented a period when the member countries of the (then) EEC started to develop an awareness which went way beyond the initial strategic goals pursued by the Communities (the integration of the former West Germany into pan-European structures and the containment of communism).

The Maastricht treaty and the European Monetary System (EMS) were a response to the syndrome of Eurosclerosis felt so deeply in the late 1970s and the early 1980s. Both were meant to help Europe cope with the globalisation of the world economy and the dynamism of the Pacific Rim. The fight between organicists and constructivists (in Hayek's terminology) was won by the technocracy in Brussels, which argued in favour of a big institutional push: the achievement of the European Union. This vision, however, proved to be limited in the sense of being capable of accommodating – both conceptually and operationally – two shocks: the collapse of communism in Europe and the reunification of Germany.

The de facto emasculation of the EMS (the collapse of the Exchange Rate Mechanism) was a logical consequence of the stress produced within the EU member countries by the economic impact of German reunification and the lack of co-ordination of economic policies. However, this event can be seen as the peak of an iceberg. Rising economic nationalism, lack of policy co-ordination, sizeable and hard-to-contain budget deficits, unusually large and increasing unemployment rates (from an average of 3% in the 1970s to more than 11% currently), non-competitive industrial segments, burdensome welfare nets and restive trade unions are symptoms of what appears to be a lasting disease – and not a cyclical phenomenon.

Especially worrying is the rising unemployment, which creates considerable social and political tension and can harm the functioning of the institutions of democracy. Thus, after the success of the 'National Alliance' in the Italian elections of May 1994, the speaker of the Italian parliament declared that 'unemployment, which led to the rise of fascism and Nazism in the 1930s, poses a greater danger to democracy in Europe than anything else'.[19] It is no wonder then that the main theme of the G-7 Summit meeting in Detroit (March, 1994) dealt with unemployment. An unavoidable conjecture is that rapidly growing unemployment in the East European region poses even greater dangers to the process of building up democratic institutions in the post-communist societies.

Increasingly weak governments and the disenchantment by electorates with their political establishments (a growing 'cognitive dissonance' in political life which can be discerned in the USA and Japan as well!) suggest a serious malaise in Western societies. It is disconcerting to see both left and right-of-centre governments being unable to steer their economies in a way that would indicate resolution and ability to deal with structural problems. The student demonstrations in France in April of 1994 – for many reminiscent of the wave that swept the country in 1968 – and the way the French government had to give in to student demands have more than a symbolic significance. The resurgence, both politically and at the polls, of right-wing extremist parties in many European countries is more than disturbing. Chauvinism, in its most aggressive forms, appears to be spreading all over the Continent. Even in the countries considered to be role models of democratic procedures and religious and ethnic tolerance, right-wing extremism is on the rise (the case of Netherlands is relevant). These trends complement the rise of nationalism and of right-wing extremism in post-communist countries in a very disturbing way.

It is not yet clear what impact these negative trends will have on the process of European economic integration. It would be dishonest, however, not to acknowledge that they create a great deal of unease and concern for the future dynamics of the process. It has always been an open secret that there are disagreements among the member countries as to the final destination of the integration journey. The fear now voiced by many is that, in spite of the further institutional sophistication of the EU and its expansion by three EFTA members, deep countercurrents are at work. There is also a growing sense of unease as to the actual distribution of influence within the EU because of Germany's reunification.

The policy towards Eastern Europe has mostly been reactive. The fact is that the West perceives the Eastern countries as a highly unstable and contaminating zone. In my opinion this policy has been more shaped by the desire for containment, or by an attempt to set up a sort of a buffer zone (with a hard core represented by the Visegrad-group), rather than by an understanding that Western involvement needs to be active and visionary - relying on a philosophy of integration.

The Copenhagen Statement (of June 1993) signalled a significant conceptual breakthrough in this respect. Nonetheless, actual support is still much below what is needed to keep alive the momentum of reforms in the East and secure the stability of the continent. For instance, there are plans in Brussels to undertake large-scale public works projects in order to deal with rising unemployment in the Western countries. At the same time, the similar and more perturbing phenomenon of unemployment could derail reforms in the East. If one also considers the very low investment ratios and the badly needed improvement of infrastructure in the post-communist countries, a logical question arises: why is there no common European strategy to deal with this issue? For, if it is now recognised that sooner or later Eastern Europe (or parts of it) will join the EU, it makes sense to develop strategies together and undertake joint national and regional public works projects in the transforming economies. This would help considerably, it would build up social and political support for the process of economic transformation, and it would help homogenise infrastructure at a European level.

The danger for both the West and the East lies in the inability of policymakers to conceptualise and make operational the intricate connections between the quest of advanced democracies to regain vitality and the quest of the emerging democracies to achieve economic viability. Taken together, the challenge for Europe now is how to speed up its industrial adjustment so as to cope with the trends in the world economy.[20]

A *Grand Alliance* is needed (the third circle or outer circle of transition)

Europe is at a critical juncture in its history. There is a question of identity: how does, or how should Europe look after the collapse of communism in the East? In this regard, the step taken by the EU in May of 1994 to offer closer links with its security arm to nine countries of Eastern Europe[21] can be viewed as another major initiative (after the Partnership for Peace) aimed at defining the post-cold war frontiers and at tying the East more firmly to the West.[22] Jonathan Eyal[23] remarked in this respect: 'The political message is much more important than the practical one at this stage ... Basically, it is now accepted that this is where Europe ends'.[24] This is a fairly bold statement bearing in mind that after the fall of the Berlin Wall in 1989, which can be seen as an ideological, political and social 'Big Bang', Europe has taken the posture of an expanding universe. In my view it is still too early to say where the frontiers of the new Europe are likely to settle. On the other hand, one could argue that Eyal's words reflect a particular vision whose rationale is revealed by a certain logic of development of the European Union. In any case, this political vision needs to be given economic substance and, hence, organic links need to be forged between the West and the East. The West needs to match its rhetorics with more support for the East. A step in the right direction is also the 'partnership' agreement concluded between the EU and Russia, which aims at the establishment of a free-trade zone towards the end of the century.[25] Likewise, Russia's signing of the *Partnership for Peace* accord is a welcome event.

There is much need for *collective strategising*. Though many political leaders have realised the linkage between the quest by Western countries for new vitality and the quest for viability of the emerging democracies, the gap between rhetoric and real action is striking. This linkage can inject new dynamism and do away with European lethargy if it is seen as an historical window of opportunity and if proper strategies and policies are devised.

However, it can also drag Europe down further if the current trends of poor communication, protectionism, shunning and beggar-your-neighbour policies continue.

West Europeans and East Europeans need a *Grand Alliance* – to paraphrase Graham Allison's 'Grand Bargain'. In a broader sense, the Western world needs to structurally embrace Eastern Europe, Russia, Ukraine and other former Soviet republics in order to avoid what Samuel Huntington (1993) suggestively called a possible 'Clash of Civilizations'.[26]

Europe needs vision, wise and bold leadership, and genuine co-operation. In our interdependent continent, strategies of 'sauve qui peut' are dangerous. In a broader perspective, the Western World needs to help preserve an open world economy and provide a conceptual thrust for creating a stable post-cold war world order.

Notes

*   Version of a paper presented at the conference 'Transforming Economies and European Integration', Sofia, 27-28 May 1994. It appeared in R. Dobrinsky and M. Landesmann (eds.), 'Transforming Economies and European Integration', Edward Elgar, Aldershot, pp. 15-31.

1   See Reginald Dale's commentary, 'The way to get the good jobs back' in International Herald Tribune, 3 May 1994, p.11.

2   Ibid.

3   See Alex Brummer: 'Bretton Woods call for rethink on exchange rates', in Guardian Weekly, 19 June 1994, p. 21.

4   It is worthy to note that Chancellor Helmut Kohl returned from Peking with full hands: apart from the nurturing of political relations, economic deals amounting to almost $3 billion were announced. I do not have information about any other European political leader able to achieve something comparable in business terms.

5   In 1994 for instance, President Clinton himself turned into the most effective salesperson for Boeing in the $6 billion Jumbo deal with Saudi Arabia.

6   There are sufficient grounds to expect a resuscitation of socialist ideas, under the ideological guise of social democracy in the former communist countries. In my view, the results of the recent elections in several of the countries in the region are not incomprehensible and do not reflect a temporary swing only.

7   Mancur Olson and Peter Murrell (1991) use the notion 'all encompassing interest' for this purpose.

8   As remarked by James Fallows (1994, p.5), one difficulty for the West in understanding the changes in the world space is that 'Western societies,

especially America, have been using the wrong mental tools to classify, shape, and understand the information they receive about Asia. They try to fit the facts into familiar patterns and categories – and they are hurt and frustrated when predictions derived from these patterns do not come true' (p.5).

9   In a very gloomy tone Zbigniew Brzezinski (1993, p. xiii) says: 'The global relevance of the West's political message could be vitiated by the growing tendency in the advanced world to infuse the inner content of liberal democracy with a life-style that I define as permissive cornucopia... In contrast, outside the richer West, much of human life is still dominated by fundamental concerns with survival and not with conspicuous consumption.'

10   According to A. Solimano, in 1937 the nominal per capita income in Great Britain, Sweden, Germany, Belgium, Netherlands, France and Austria was estimated at $440 in and, $400, $340, $330, $306, $265, and $190, respectively. The corresponding estimates for Czechoslovakia, Hungary, Poland, Romania, Yugoslavia and Bulgaria were $170, $120, $100, $81, $80, and $75, respectively (A. Gelb and Cheryl Gray, 1991, p.65).

11   I espouse the same line of reasoning in my article 'Transformation and the Legacy of Backwardness' (Daianu, 1992).

12   I remember in this respect how baffled were some of my Romanian colleagues when Ken Jowitt stated that 'Latin American countries have been in transition for more than a century' (remark made during the Romanian-American economic round table, Bucharest, 16-17 April, 1991). He referred not only to very erroneous economic policies (Argentina comes easily to one's mind for it belonged to the group of advanced economies before the Second World War) but also, to institutional bottlenecks typical of a certain level of economic development.

13   As Jacek Rostowski (1993) put it, 'The lack of banking skills in the post-communist economies (PCEs) thus introduces a fundamental instability into their monetary systems. Until this problem is resolved, macroeconomic instability will remain hard to attain'. Similarly sceptical is Ronald McKinnon (1991).

14   The command system as a dynamical complex system, is characterised by chain links, in contrast to a market economy, which relies, essentially, on parallel links.

15   When considering this balance Olivier Blanchard and Philippe Aghion (1994) speak of an 'optimal speed'.

16   '...high inflation tends to be dynamically unstable, planting the seeds of even greater inflation in the future. On the other hand, tough stabilisation without large-scale foreign financial support is also likely to fail, if high unemployment and inadequate social support produces political instability' (Jeffrey Sachs, 1994).

17   The steel processing industry and agriculture make the big headlines.

18   'The American Challenge'.

19   Cited by Reuters in the report 'Senate chief blames neofascist', International Herald Tribune, 13 May, 1994, p.2.

20 Hajami remarks (1992, p.3): 'As developmental market economies become successful in industrial development, they begin to compete in the world trade of manufactured commodities. If this speed is too fast and exceeds the capacity of industrial adjustment on the side of advanced economies, it tends to create strong political demand for protectionism. The real danger arises when the protectionism bloc tries to achieve its political goal by escalating economic conflicts to ideological confrontation.'

21 The countries are: Poland, Hungary, The Czech Republic, Slovakia, Romania, Bulgaria, Lithuania, Latvia and Estonia.

22 See Tom Buerkle, 'EU offers 9 Eastern nations a step to security link-up', International Herald Tribune, 7-8 May, 1994, p.2.

23 Director of the Royal United Institute for Defence Studies in London.

24 Cited by Tom Buerkle, op. cit., note 22.

25 See David Gardner (1994).

26 The demographic dynamics suggest that, over the longer term, the *Europeanness* of the USA may alter not insignificantly. This phenomenon may help create an economic and cultural 'bridge' between the Western countries and the emboldened East Asian societies; but it may further stimulate a certain reorientation of the USA toward the Pacific Rim – a tendency that may complicate the multi-relationship with Europe. Thus, Fr. Fukuyama considers that 'There is something in American (as opposed to European) culture that has been stimulated by the dynamism of Asia... There is a kind of cultural creation going on in the business world that is foreign to Europe, and that in time will make America seem more foreign to Europe' (1994, p.4). For the demographically dynamics, and their implications, in the USA see also P. Kennedy (chapter XIII).

References

Amsden, A. (1989), 'The Next Asia's Giant', Oxford University Press, New York.

Berend, I. (1994), 'Annus Mirabilis – Anni Mirabiles?', *Contention*, Winter, No.8, pp.109-28.

Blanchard, O. and Aghion, P. (1994), 'On the Speed of Transition in Eastern Europe', manuscript.

Brzezinski, Z. (1993), 'Out of Control', Charles Scribner's Sons, New York.

Chirot, D. (ed.) (1989), 'The Origins of Backwardness in Eastern Europe', University of California Press, Berkeley.

Cornwall, J. (1990), 'The Theory of Economic Breakdown', Oxford University Press, Cambridge.

Daianu, D. (1992), 'Transformation and the Legacy of Backwardness', *Economies et Societes*, no. 44, May, pp. 181-206.

Davidson, J. Dale and Lord, W. Rees-Mogg (1991), 'The Great Reckoning',

Summit Books, New York.

Dobrinsky, R. and Landesmann, M. (ed.) (1996), 'Transforming Economies and European Integration', Edward Elgar, Aldershot, pp.15-31.

Fallows, J. (1994), 'Looking at the Sun. The Rise of the New East Asian Economic and Political System', Pantheon Books, New York.

Fukuyama, Fr. (1990), 'The End of History', Free Press, New York.

Fukuyama, Fr. (1994), 'For the Atlantic Allies Today, a Fraying of the Sense of Moral Community', *International Herald Tribune*, 6 June.

Gardner, D. (1994), 'EU and Russia close to Partnership Pact', *Financial Times*, 12 May, p.2.

Gelb, A. and Gray, C. (1991), 'The Transformation of Economies in Central and Eastern Europe', The World Bank, Washington DC.

Hayami, Y. (1992), 'Japan and the Model of Developmental Market Economies: A Historical Perspective on the New World Confrontation', paper presented at the World Economists' Congress, August, manuscript, Moscow.

Huntington, S. (1993), 'The Clash of Civilisations', *Foreign Affairs*, Summer, vol.50, no.3, pp.22-50.

Ishihara, S. (1991), 'The Japan That Can Say No', Simon and Schuster, New York.

Kennedy, P. (1992), 'The Rise and Fall of Great Powers', Yale University Press, New Haven.

Kennedy, P. (1993), 'Preparing for the XXI Century', Random House, New York.

Kindleberger, Ch. (1977), 'The Aging Economy', Weltwirtschaftliches Archiv.

Kornai, J. (1980), 'The Economics of Shortage', North-Holland, Amsterdam.

Leibenstein, H. (1966), 'Allocative Efficiency vs. X-Efficiency', *American Economic Review*, vol.56, no.3, pp.392-410.

Lesourne, J. (1991), 'Economie de l'Ordre et du Desordre', Economica, Paris.

Lipton, D. and Sachs, J. (1991), 'Privatisation in Eastern Europe: The Case of Poland', *Brookings Papers on Economic Activity*, no.1, vol. 56, 3, pp.392-410.

Lodge, G. (1990), 'Perestroika for America', Harvard University Press, Cambridge.

McKinnon, R. (1991), 'The Order of Economic Liberalisation', John Hopkins University Press, Baltimore.

Murrell, P. (1992), 'Evolutionary and Radical Approaches to Economic Reform in Eastern Europe', *Economics of Planning*, vol.25, no.1.

Nelson, R. and Winter, S. (1982), 'An Evolutionary Theory of Economic Change', Harvard University Press, Cambridge.

North, D. (1981), 'Structure and Change in Economic History', Norton, New York.

Olson, M. (1982), 'The Rise and Decline of Nations. Economic Growth, Stagflation and Social Rigidities', Yale University Press, New Haven.

Olson, M. and Murrell, P. (1991), 'The Devolution of Centrally Planned Economies', manuscript.

Porter, M. (1990), 'The Competitive Advantage of Nations', Free Press, New York.

Romer, P. (1986), 'Increasing Returns and Long Run Growth', *Journal of Political Economy*, 94, pp.1002-1037.

Rostowski, J. (1993), 'Creating Stable Monetary Systems in Post-communist Countries', Mimeo.

Sachs, J. (1994), 'Russia Struggle with Stabilisation. Conceptual Issues and Evidence', paper presented at the Annual World Bank Conference on Development Economics, April 28-29, Washington DC.

Schreiber, J.J. (1967), 'Le Defi Americain', Denoel, Paris.

Scott, B. (1994), 'Economic Strategies of Nations', manuscript.

Thurow, L. (1993), 'Head to Head', MIT Press, Cambridge.

Wade, R. (1990), 'Governing the Market', Princeton University Press, Princeton.

Yergin, D. and Gustaffson, Th. (1994), 'Russia – 2010', June, New York.

11 Judging Romania's Way in a Comparative Framework[*]

What is unique about post-communist transformation in Europe is that it implies several simultaneously evolving processes: grand scale institutional change (including the unprecedented scale of changing property rights), economic restructuring, structural adjustment and macrostabilisation, and, last but not least, modernisation. The latter forces us to take a look at what makes up a very 'soft' portion of what economists are used to dealing with: the functioning of institutions in economy and the social texture of society. As many social scientists (including economists) would agree it is the quality of institutions that counts, ultimately, for the long term growth differentials of national societies and for their varied lots. For accumulation, and the volume and quality of investment (primarily in human capital) need to be explained in the end and simple macroeconomic parameters do not have sufficient explanatory power to this end. Recent studies by R. Barro, L. Summers, D. Romer, etc. reconfirmed the role of capital build-up for economic growth but this result did not surprise the profession; what needs to be elucidated is what makes a nation accumulate and invest more than others, what role is played by income distribution in it, and why it can achieve dynamic efficiency gains over time whereas others may be plagued by substantial diminishing returns. As M. Olson would forcefully point out economists are quite unconvincing in this respect although they may claim otherwise.

Since the start of post-communist transformation most of the attention of economists has been absorbed by topics like macroeconomic stabilisation, privatisation, trade liberalisation and deregulation, and the analysis has been driven mostly by preferred clichés to the detriment of closer to reality second-best scenarios. Simultaneously, there has been a clear temptation to lump countries together, in various groups, by assuming a direct relationship between preordained results and policies implied by a conventional wisdom in the making. In the vein of the Old Latin saying 'post hoc, ergo propter hoc' similar results were more ascribed to presumed similar policies than to commonalties in initial circumstances and other peculiarities. It suffices to look carefully at the concrete policies in the countries of the so-called Visegrad Group (Hungary versus Poland, for example) in order to support this thesis. Likewise, vicious (and virtuous) circles as sources of economic evolution were frequently neglected. Fortunately enough, a much required soul-searching process among fellow economists is under way and many simplified views (naivités) and some of the unjustified fervour in upholding them seem to be subsiding.

It can be submitted that, in order to explore the future of post-communist societies (their economic dynamic, and social and political stability in the long run), the analysis of institutional change is of paramount importance. Therefore, the fact that economic decline stopped and that economic recovery was ushered in most of the post-communist countries, after 1994, should not be overplayed unless one penetrates the black-box which contains the above mentioned 'soft' portion of society. However, the latter kind of analysis is extremely challenging since economists are not necessarily well equipped to perform it.

In what follows I try to present some issues, which I consider to have been relatively underplayed in the debate on transition. These issues have significant bearing on the 'soft' structure of post-communist society and may provide clues about what lies ahead. Though Romania is under focus, I endeavoured to look at the grand picture and formulate opinions of broader coverage. The first part presents a brief overall assessment. The second part tackles the issue of institutional change against the background of the burden of the past; institutional fragility is also linked with lawlessness and corruption. Part three highlights the implications of the legacy of resource misallocation and the ensued distributional struggle; it touches also upon the magnitude of the privatisation process. Part four looks at the *variety* of capitalism in the region. Finally, a cognitive issue is emphasised.

An overall picture

There is good and bad news about post-communist transformation in Europe. The good news is that, overall, surprisingly much has been achieved bearing in mind the burden of the past – or, otherwise said, the current state of affairs could have been substantially worse. At the same time, a certain kind of *normalcy* is spreading in the area in terms of the functioning patterns of market-based systems. Even the participation rates in the recent elections in most of the post-communist countries can be interpreted from such a perspective. This *normalcy* may be partly at the origin of the apparent declining interest Western public opinion and governments show in post-communist transformation; only lately, the outcome of elections in Russia again made big headlines. It is true, nonetheless, that this diminishing interest can be linked with the mounting domestic problems of Western governments. A necessary qualification is, however, needed in relation to the use of the word *normalcy*; it does take into account what the *realists* – as they can be named – have been saying is most likely to occur, or is achievable under the circumstances. Why the number of realists against that of idealists (optimists) has been much lower, among scholars as well, is a topic less relevant for our discussion, though not uninteresting.

There are some remarkable achievements. One is the Czech Republic's impressive record with stunningly low inflation and unemployment rates. Likewise, the buoyant Polish economy, in spite of the very high unemployment rate, is a proof that institutionally organised expanding markets are getting a good hold on the country's economic body. Economic recovery has been under way in most of the countries of the region.

In general, the formidable expansion of the entrepreneurial sector all over the region is a clear proof of the enormous economic potential that was stifled by the command system. The data on privatisation show that, in spite of many difficulties, this process has registered remarkable advances, in almost all European post-communist countries.

Another piece of good news is the way that the emerging democratic institutions have been able to vent, with relative success – until now –, the frustration of large segments of the citizenry with the costs of reforms and secured, thereby, a surprising degree of social stability. This fact is, in itself, quite encouraging and may seem to give support to those who have argued that history and analogies are not necessarily the best predictor of what is going to happen in Eastern Europe.[1] It is hard not to agree, in this respect, with Valerie Bunce when she says that 'It is the balance between levels of conflict and systemic capacity to adjudicate conflicts, then, and not simply the degree of conflict which should receive our foremost attention in assessing the stability of the new Eastern Europe' (1992, p. 281). But it can be contended with similar validity, that it would be a major mistake to consider that Eastern Europe is endowed with some specific traits which make it relatively immune to what acute social friction entails in the rest of the world. Even in the Czech Republic, which is considered almost a role-model among the transforming economies and which shows an amazingly low unemployment rate – one of the lowest in the world – the pains of economic reforms take an expected toll; they also explain the political ascendancy of the Social Democrats (Milos Zeman's Party).

As in other countries of the region in Romania, too, these pains explain the appeal of political discourses which pledge to cushion the effects of reforms. This propensity of the electorate forced even the Democratic Convention to adopt a political platform with some populist overtones. In a wider context one can speculate that the longer and the more tortuous transition is, and the more distanced from the euphoria of year 1989, the more intense would be the confrontation among brands of populism, at least rhetorically.

The patience (stoicism) of many people (losers) during the last years may also be explained by the big talk of joining the EU and NATO in the near future; this prospect has operated as a kind of 'anchor' for reform policy. For instance, domestic polls and those taken by Eurobarometer and Eurostat show a high desire of Romanians for their country to join the two institutions, which would presumably guarantee economic prosperity and security. Obviously, a question can easily be posed: is this anchor a stable one and for how long can it be relied on?

The bad news, or 'the empty half of the glass' is that lots of people in the region have had a very hard time in coping with the psychological pressure and material difficulties caused by transformation, which is a fact clearly proven by the results of elections in the various countries. Owing to the high expectations entertained by people at large, and by many policymakers, the pace and results of transition are looked upon by many as quite unsatisfactory.

People realise that post-communist transformation is a much more complex and complicated process than initially thought, and that time cannot be compressed at will. Defining and enforcing a new structure of property rights, setting up and making institutions work (seen as 'rules enjoying wide social acceptability'), achieving durable macrostabilisation via structural adjustment and industrial restructuring are intertwined prerequisites for attaining economic viability. However, these are time-consuming and painful endeavours.

In this context, one can try to answer the question: why have post-communist parties fared so well in Eastern Europe? I have in mind the parties which shed their former names and claim to espouse a democratic political philosophy.[2] Part of the answer is linked with the extent of underestimation of the costs of reforms. Another explanation would be that reform programmes that promised to be less painful seduced many people. One should consider also the disillusionment produced by the discrepancy between reality and the portrayal of a market-based system (capitalism) as a perfect society. Instead of talking about the virtues of an emerging society, which can perform in spite of inherent imperfections, a myth has been in the making. Politicians and the mass media should have explained to the citizens of post-communist countries that, as Churchill said about democracy, a market-based system is analogously imperfect but it can deliver on its promises under proper circumstances.

The fact is that, in most of the cases, the left of centre of the political spectrum was pretty much void and the post-communist parties have occupied it for three fundamental reasons: because they wanted that position in view of their professed new ideology; because there was a big vacuum to be filled in there; and because it is in human nature to want power, and especially to wish not to relinquish it. Over the longer term and if the political traditions of Europe (less individualism than in the USA) are also considered, the political future of left-oriented parties in post-communist societies needs to be assessed in a balanced way. Moreover, the quasi-egalitarian ethos espoused by many citizens and the almost subconscious desire of and expectation to be looked after by a paternalistic state reinforces the posture of left-oriented parties, and may induce other parties to ride populist themes in the political debate. This trend is more likely to occur the poorer society is (such as Romania, Bulgaria, etc.) and the higher is the gap between expectations and reality, which may create hurdles for the relatively better off countries as well (like Hungary and Poland).

One needs to mention also, that, in certain cases, the political discourse of the newly emerged democratic parties has met inherently unsurpassable obstacles in selling the programmes of reforms – with their costs – to the public. Lofty ideals, the values and principles of democracy are not sufficient for rallying public support when large sections of the population feel they are left out.[3] As one could say in terms of current French political terminology, post-communist reforms create their own 'exclus'. George Schöpflin pertinently remarked that, the concept of society propounded by some of the new democratic elites 'was curiously like the one Marxists had put forward forty years ago. In their view, society need not be significantly marked by conflicts of interests, nor were there any deep cleavages which called for intermediation and aggregation'.[4]

A highly simplifying and politically counterproductive cliché was, also, frequently used; namely, that the political conflict is between neo-communists and anti-communists (true democrats). This claimed political divide begs one major question: how does it come that so many people voted the so-called neo-communists back in power? Do so many people want 'neo-communism' back? If that were the case our whole analysis and premises about what people dreamed about and fought for under communism would have to be turned upside down. It is my opinion that this cliché, and the line of reasoning that motivates it, are incorrect and cognitively misleading. It is true that former high-ranking officials play important roles in the post-communist parties, which is a fact that adds a moral dimension to the whole issue. However, this fact cannot change the basics of the political equation, and the reality that many voters felt hurt by economic reforms while, at the same time, they espouse a left of centre ideology. Quite confusing can also be the fact that, as in Romania, 'former communists' – as the Western media say – operate all along the political spectrum, which invalidates the notion itself. Of course, in Poland, where the communist party was relatively much smaller numerically than in Romania, the adjective 'former communist' has much more meaning; but even there I would argue that, for many of those involved, the more appropriate term is 'former declared communist'. Things get more complicated when leftism (containing much populism) combines with ultra-nationalism and xenophobia, for the sake of sheer 'power politics' and the preservation of entrenched vested interests – or what is, generally, seen as a process of converting political power assets into economic assets.[5] This combination runs, clearly, against the furtherance of democratic reforms, and it will shape capitalism in this part of the world.

Institutional change and modernisation; the legacy of backwardness

If the system-related (institutional) dimension of transition is of paramount importance, one can detect another meaning, which has defined the evolution of these societies through this century. It is 'the quest for catching-up with the West', an idea which obsessed national politicians during the interwar period and the communist leaderships bent on proving the alleged superiority of their system through forced (Stalinist) industrialisation and modernisation. Today, this quest is reflected by the ardent desire to join the European Union.

Why the quest for catching-up is emphasised? For often one can hear presumably knowledgeable professionals making judgements on the transformation process, while seeming to neglect the legacy of backwardness of most of these societies – a state of affairs which goes back deeply into history.[6] As a keen student of the area observed: '... Eastern Europe was in some sense economically backward long before it was absorbed into the broader Western world market. This backwardness has roots in the very distant past...'.[7] Similarly, Ivan Berend remarks that 'What is missing in most of these analyses is a deeper understanding of long-term historical trends in East-Central Europe'.[8]

A note of caution is nevertheless required. As it has already been underlined, the post-communist societies of Europe are societal entities that show common (structural) traits, but also major discrepancies; the latter can be linked with the different pre-communist legacy and the different brands of national central planning in terms of relaxation of direct controls and economic policy choices. Thus, the former Czechoslovakia, as a leading industrial country during the inter-war period, is a most conspicuous example. Likewise, Romania, with its late Stalinism embodied by Ceausescu's regime and rejection of any partial reforms, is another glaring example. The different histories explain why market institutions vary qualitatively among the national environments and why macro- and micro-disequilibria differed among them on the eve of 1989. Undoubtedly, Hungary, the former Czechoslovakia and Poland have had a substantial competitive edge in starting the process of managing the transition. Unsurprisingly, all these countries have fared better then the rest in their stabilisation programmes, although their recipes were not similar, as some would argue. Not surprisingly, too, Russia and other former Soviet republics have fared worse in this respect.

The stress put on the burden of the past is meant to warn against its dragging effects and an unfavourable *path dependency*, which is not easy to break away from. I remember how baffled were some of my Romanian colleagues when Ken Jowitt, a well known political scientist from the University of Berkeley, said that 'Latin American countries have been in transition for more than a century'.[9] He referred not only to mistaken economic policies (Argentina comes easily into one's mind for it belonged to the group of advanced economies before the second World War) but also, to institutional bottlenecks rooted in a certain level of economic development.

Backwardness makes it harder to overcome the fragility of the market institutions in the making and enhances the potential for the dynamics of change to get out of control. It should be stressed that institutional fragility was very much underestimated by policymakers and their advisers. As Peter Rutland rightly points out by referring to Russia, 'in a travesty of Hayekian logic, it was assumed that market institutions would be self-generating'.[10]

It is true and, at the same time, it is fair to stress that the extremely high degree of literacy of Eastern European societies, their large segments of well trained workers, the existence of a numerous technical intelligentsia, and the linkages with the developed world offered by the 'age of information' provide positive counterbalancing factors.[11] Nonetheless, it would be very myopic and counterproductive to disregard the industrial, cultural, and institutional distance – however varied this is – that separates Central and Eastern Europe from Western Europe.

Institutional fragility has already been implied. Apart from the insufficient analytical attention paid to the institutional build-up in the transforming societies in Europe, one has to consider the seeds of instability produced by this fragility. The poor capacity of immature institutions to perform needs to be mentioned in this context. For example, the debate universal vs. narrow banks (on whether and how banks should be involved in resource allocation) is quite relevant for the concern that immature market institutions create in terms of enhancing instability and uncertainty in the system.[12] And the ubiquity of bank crises in the region tellingly exemplifies this fragility.

From a broader perspective one can pose the issue of the *governance capabilities* of the political and economic elites of these countries – to what extent these elites are capable to induce and manage change (transformation) when so much fuzziness, volatility and uncertainty is prevailing. A possible assessment would emphasise the infancy of institutions and the scarcity of *organisational capital* in these societies; it would also highlight the potential for learning and for catching-up over time. Differently, a sceptical judgement would stress that the very development of institutions would be undermined by the poor quality of 'seeds'. However, one would have to go further analytically in order to differentiate among current and future situations. For instance, governance does not need to refer necessarily to government policy; the term can be broadened. Dorel Sandor, who is a leading Romanian political analyst, pointed at the responsibility which is bestowed on Parliament in this respect – for, apart from those who govern as central government, there are others (members of Parliament) who are supposed to rule as members of the ruling elites. How harsh should then be our evaluation?

One line of reasoning could go along the following way: one should not ask for too much, bearing in mind the burden of the past and other peculiar circumstances. Another line of reasoning could be: the main political players who had no chance until now to test their capabilities in government deserve the benefit of the doubt. And a third view, which is echoed by several high profile Romanian social scientists (A. Teodorescu, A. Mungiu, St.Tanase, etc.), is that the current political elites of the country (including the opposition parties) have not been up to the task and that something different is needed in terms of both vision and policy pragmatism. This thinking prompted the formation by a group of leading members of the Romanian intelligentsia of the party 'Alternativa Romaniei' (The Alternative of Romania) which, however, has not met big resonance in the political electorate until now. I would submit that the main difficulty such a political demarche has faced is threefold: the purported messianistic approach, which is accompanied by a certain implicit intellectual arrogance vis-à-vis other political parties and the rest of society, in general; the challenge of articulating and representing concrete social and economic interests; and the realisation that assessing the political elites' performance against a mythical yardstick is counterproductive. Tellingly enough, 'Alternativa Romaniei' joined the Democratic Convention, in July of 1996.

Organised crime and corruption

A phenomenon, which reflects with much intensity the institutional fragility and the complicated nature and complexity of transformation, is the ubiquity of lawlessness in economic life – the 'blossoming' of organised crime and corruption. There is no doubt that much of it is just an outcome of activities becoming less hidden. It is also true that some of what appears as illegal activity is due to the still very fuzziness of the legal environment, and to the emerged need to privatise contract enforcement when official law enforcement capability is almost non-existent. However, there is also an element of novelty in this field, which, in certain cases, can take frightening forms and proportions. Where bankers, businessmen and journalists are murdered, this has an impact on the social psyche that is not favourable to market and democracy nurturing reforms.

A very detrimental vicious circle can be at play here. Thus, because of institutional fragility (actually, owing to the lack of socially accepted norms and of authorities capable to enforce, and protect them should the need arise) organised crime and lawlessness, in general, do proliferate. Simultaneously, their proliferation undermines the very effectiveness of the budding democratic institutions (see also Susan Rose-Ackerman). Consequently, the so-called 'proto-democratic institutions' are likely to remain in a limbo state for a long period.

One can, normally, pose the following question: what kind of capitalism is being built in the transforming economies? An optimistic answer would be twofold. Firstly, the picture is too multicoloured for justifying an all encompassing answer – the intensity of the phenomenon is different in the various national environments (the Czech Republic is different from, let's say, Ukraine) and, therefore, its consequences and prospects are dissimilar. In fact, different kinds of capitalism are emerging in the post-communist countries. Secondly, the presumption should be accepted that this phenomenon would recede over time in keeping with the unfolding of transformation.[13] A pessimistic answer would highlight the vicious circle mentioned above – as a conspicuous instance of 'path dependency' – and the enhancing factor represented by rising unemployment and poverty among large segments of society, as well as the increasing mistrust of the citizenry as to an apparently impotent and corrupted government bureaucracy. In Romania, this disenchantment is expressed by the saying 'there is much corruption but no corrupted people'. A pessimistic answer would also point out the danger that the tentacles of organised crime would increasingly influence the functioning of institutions, and encroach on the political process, ultimately, in a resilient fashion; something resembling organised crime as a phenomenon in Italy, or in Mexico and Columbia, would come into being, but it would very likely have its peculiarities.

Both Eastern and Western governments should not be complacent about this phenomenon, in the hope that it may prove 'benign' and useful for building up market-based economic systems in the long run.

The magnitude of resource reallocation and privatisation

Another issue which, in my view, is not sufficiently highlighted in public debate is the dimension of the inherited misallocation of resources in Eastern Europe – i.e. the sheer scale of disequilibria, at the new relative prices, that indicates the magnitude of required restructuring as compared to the ability of the system to undergo wide ranging and quick change. What is amazing is the nonchalance of many professionals about the consequences of the magnitude of required restructuring. When one sees Western governments – and their social constituencies – vacillating and deeply reluctant to undertake relatively minor adjustments, the *strain* under which the former command economies operate becomes understandable.

In Eastern Europe, the structure of the economy and its resource misallocation have put the system under exceptional *strain* once the combination of the internal shocks (engineered by reforms, or, simply, triggered by uncontrolled processes of system dissolution) and external shocks occurred.

Structure refers to the network of institutional arrangements, including rules of conduct that are socially ingrained, and of vested interests which are based on material productive interdependencies and the distribution of property rights, that creates a specific logic of motion of the system and makes individual enterprises its captives. The vested interests are also the result of the configuration of industry as a legacy of the command system.[14] This industrial structure, with its extremely high concentration and reliance on chain links, explains the degree of market monopolisation in the transforming economies. In this respect, one can talk about a *power of structure*, which is well illustrated by the power of debtors over creditors. This power is not of a conspiratorial nature (the cartel is unconscious), because it rests on the system's rules of functioning.

Command planning, with its inherent impossibility for rational calculation and because of forced industrialisation, left a legacy of resource misallocation. This legacy was brought, conspicuously, into the open by price liberalisation and the functional opening of the economy. The new prices show what was, previously, kept hidden by administrative prices and heavy redistribution of income: a very wide range of profitability rates and a very wide dispersion of units fitting into several categories: negative value-added enterprises; inefficient, but, still, positive value-added units which, in turn, can be split into non-viable and, potentially, viable firms; and inefficient enterprises.

The wide range of profitability rates and wide dispersion of enterprises with varying performances mean that, should market (financial) discipline be strictly enforced, a large number of units would go under – as a sign of the start of drastic reallocation of resources: namely, aggregate output would go down substantially since market destruction is significantly more intense than market construction, at least in the first stage. There are two important aspects involved in this process: firstly, the scope of reallocation (dislocation) and, secondly, the speed required to maintain a certain balance between exit and entry,[15] so that the growth of the healthy (private) sector is not unduly impaired. A plausible assumption is that the greater the scope and the faster the desired speed of the process are, the higher the imbalance will be and *strain* will build up within the economy. Actually, when 'low supply responsiveness' is mentioned the finger is pointed at this imbalance.

What are the major implications of this *strain*? One is that these economies could easily become exceedingly unstable and that their capacity to absorb shocks is quite low; these economies have a high degree of vulnerability! Another implication is that policymakers face extremely painful trade-offs and that, in most cases, unless sufficient external support is available, the room for manoeuvre is in practice quite limited. Basically, policymakers would have to sail between the Scylla of high inflation (or hyperinflation, in the structurally more rigid economies) and the Carybda of huge unemployment, both results being highly undesirable politically and socially.

Russia and Ukraine provide, perhaps, the most dramatic example of this miserable trade-off. As Jeffrey Sachs pointed out 'Economic chaos could produce a political collapse in at least two ways – through the descent into hyperinflation, or through a catastrophic rise in unemployment not cushioned by a social safety net'.[16] This is a very plausible explanation for the almost negligible official unemployment rate in Russia, which hovered around 2% in recent years. An interesting aspect of Sachs' remark is that it emphasises how an economic policy can collapse when, though it has to cope with a tremendous *strain* in the system and the insufficiency of external support, it goes ahead as if this support was available. This may very likely have been one of the main causes which led to Gaidar's downfall as acting Prime Minister of Russia in the early 90s.

Unemployment rates in the transforming economies are not exceedingly high in comparison with the European levels of the mid-nineties. After a very sharp rise after 1990, they seem to have stabilised around the 1993 level. One should consider also that part of this unemployment disguises the activity of many persons in the unrecorded (shadow) economy. Additionally, the resumption of growth in most of Eastern Europe, in 1994 and 1995, will very probably help contain this phenomenon.

However, there are several factors that provide cause for concern. One is that the yardstick used is itself questionable taking into account the unemployment problem in Western Europe. A second factor is the weakness of safety nets; this problem acquires particular significance in the poorer post-communist countries, where the consequences of a 'new type' of poverty[17] could be extremely serious.[18] And another factor is the fact that the restructuring of large companies – which mostly need to shed labour in order to become profitable – is very slow, or, in practice, not taking place; this means that potential unemployment increases are still very significant unless substantial greenfield investments occur. Thus, John Odling Smee, Director of the IMF European II Department (which deals with the Baltics and the Former Soviet Union) considers that, in most of the countries under his focus, 'The transition will take many years, even decades, especially if one includes the enormous downsizing of heavy industries and the build-up of services and consumer goods industries that will be needed'. The process will involve major disruption and will be painful for those individuals who will lose their jobs. While open unemployment is still relatively low, it is quite possible that 'in some places it will rise quite sharply... Within the aggregate, there will be groups – such as those who lose their jobs and have difficulty finding new employment – for whom hard times are still ahead.[19]

One should also mention an increasingly intense *distributional struggle*, and an erosion of the consensus for a certain kind of societal change in circumstances when many individuals appear as losers – once market forces start to reward people in accordance with merit, effort, good ideas, and inspiration, but also as a result of some worker's misfortune to have jobs in bad (unprofitable) enterprises. These two processes are not favourable for securing consistency of and support for economic policymaking. They also explain why some governments see inflation as a redistributive device when *strain* is extreme. As a leading Russian economist emphasised 'Money is collected from all enterprises and redistributed to the chosen few, and this redistribution cannot be achieved without inflation'.[20]

On privatisation

There is another dimension to this distributional struggle, which needs to be highlighted for its exceptional character in human history, and for its effects on systemic transformation. This is the process of privatisation, which means a massive (total) redistribution of state assets. As we know, economic textbooks take as a *given* the initial distribution of assets among individual private owners; this distribution is almost God given, and it underpins the whole reasoning on how best to allocate resources and to achieve Pareto optimality (highest welfare). In the case of post-communist countries, 'God' has decided to come down from heaven – for what we are witnessing currently is an extraordinary process, without precedent in the history of humankind. In the next few years, much of the fate of tens, if not hundreds, of millions of living individuals (and of their descendants) is going to be shaped by the mechanics and dynamics of privatisation.

Chrystia Freeland, from the *Financial Times*, has captured this process when looking at what is going on in Russia; she says: 'Gang-land style assassinations, of bankers, politicians, and recently of one of Russia's most beloved television personalities, are bloody testimony to the fact that Russia is now absorbed in a strategic competition to determine which families will be rich and which families will be poor for a very long time to come'.[21] What took many hundreds of years in the advanced capitalist countries is supposed to occur, through various procedures (more or less legal), in the post-communist countries, in a snapshot on the scale of history. It is not, therefore, surprising that everything surrounding this process is so highly charged emotionally – why so many hopes, dreams, reckless and ruthless actions, misbehaviour, and delusions are linked to it. All individuals want to be on the winning side, but markets cannot make all happy at once.

The nature of capitalism in the post-communist countries will be decisively influenced by the actual results of privatisation seen as a process. If privatisation results in the development of a strong middle class as the social backbone of the new economic system, stability and vigour will be secured and democratic institutions will develop. Otherwise, the new system in the making will be inherently unstable – like the bad Latin American model[22] – with politics very liable to take an authoritarian route. Obviously, a strong EU anchor would reduce the likelihood for such an outcome.

There is a feature of communism that needs to be emphasised, in order to understand better the social tension engendered by post-communist transformation and the intensity of the distributional struggle. Communism – as an economic system – functioned as a kind of poor and steadily declining (suffering from *economic euthanasia*) but, nonetheless, 'welfare state'.[23] Thus, Janos Kornai, called the former command system in Hungary a 'premature welfare system'.[24] In the spirit of officially proclaimed egalitarianism, its most distinctive trait was job security from cradle to grave, which was accompanied by a full array of other benefits provided by the paternalistic state – in exchange for a total political (ideological) submission. With reference to Russia, *The Economist* made the comment that it 'inherited from Communism a universal system of welfare. This system is an asset as long as it helps to ensure that the poor continue to support reform. The snag is that decent welfare provisions cost a great deal of money. If even rich Sweden is having trouble financing its welfare state, then emerging Russia cannot possibly afford the system it has got'.[25]

The post-communist countries maintain among the most generous social welfare budgets in the world when calculated as a share of GDP; social spending budgets are between 15-30% of GDP as compared to 5-10% in the case of East Asian countries at similar income levels, for similar social programmes.[26]

As in Western countries, where there exist powerful vested interests which oppose economic adjustment, in post-communist countries those who cannot compete on the markets have turned into a strong coalition of interests which can slow down, or even arrest the reforms. This mass of individuals is most likely to fall prey to populist slogans and is obviously inclined to support the left-oriented (mostly, post-communist) parties. Robert Gilpin's observation, that adjustment is very difficult in welfare states, applies *mutatis mutandis* in the case of post-communist countries.

Variety of capitalism?

One can already try to identify different models of capitalism among the post-communist countries, and seek also to speculate on the intensity of Western Europe's vs. Russia's influence in each case. This variety of models has to be judged in a substantive and a formal sense. Formally, all these countries are implementing market reforms, and some of them signed Association Agreements with the European Union. It can be said, also, that these agreements, and the other links with the pan-Western European institutions, have created a sort of an evolution guiding 'straitjacket' – which can be seen as synonymous to the 'anchor'. Nonetheless, post-communist countries differentiate among themselves in terms of the quality of actual institutional development, the quality of macroeconomic fundamentals, and the resultant economic performances. These qualitative differences – many of which are of an intangible nature – are essential when screening the prospects for each individual country.

Countries like the Czech Republic, Hungary and Poland seem to go the Western way, though one cannot – and should not – dismiss possible and quite probably serious stumbling and setbacks on the road (see L. Csaba, J. Hardt). There seems to be a heavy flavour of the German model in these dynamics, not the least owing to the intricate links between banks and enterprises and to the active presence of German and Austrian companies in the region. There is, however, an interesting development connected with the Czech case; the mass privatisation programme, with its ensuing development of capital markets, would have presumably favoured the Anglo-Saxon model of corporate governance which relies on external control (via capital markets). However, major banks turned into essential stakeholders in the most important investment funds, and indirectly, can control a large number of enterprises. One can see, again, the heavy role of geography and history at play.[27] The Baltic countries are, apparently, moving along the Scandinavian model, but with a strong dosage of German financial rigour.

More vacillating, though making strenuous efforts, is Romania, which is burdened by both the effects of delayed reform measures, including privatisation, and the relatively more complicated communist legacy. Romania is at a kind of a crossroads in the transformation process; it will either implement some required changes and, thereby, try to keep pace with the front-runners or will risk losing contact with the Visegrad Group. It should be said, however, that there is a non-negligible probability for Romania to improve substantially her economic performances and, thereby, to keep in the neighbourhood of the Visegrad Group. Nonetheless, in view of the large distortions in its economy and the still slow pace of restructuring, as well as the feeble capital inflows, very much depends on future economic policies.

The danger for Romania, and other post-communist countries, is to fall into the institutional traps of a bad type of capitalism – with cleptocracy, authoritarian politics, ubiquitous corruption, socially damaging growing income inequality and intense social strife. Such an evolution, should it be sealed through an early accession of the Group of Four into NATO and the EU, would accentuate the divide among the European post-communist countries. It may even cause intense disappointment among population at large, whose tolerance for the costs of reforms has been significantly sweetened (until now) by the promises of joining the two Western clubs. This would, clearly, have important consequences for 'high politics' on the European continent and would have implications on the shaping of spheres of influence; it would also fit the logic behind the Copenhagen Statement of June 1993, and reiterated at Essen in June, 1994, which said that the joining of the EU is conditional on actual individual performances.

In a different vein, one could argue that such a policy-accentuated divide is shortsighted to the extent it neglects the different initial circumstances and other geopolitical considerations. For example, could one overlook the bilateral Romanian-Hungarian relationship in view of the precedent created by the 'discipline' imposed by NATO on Greece and Turkey; or could one be oblivious to the growing political assertiveness of Islamic forces in Turkey which reinforces the position of Romania as a potential strong bulwark in the region? Not to mention the fact that Romania is one of the largest and most populous countries of the region. Additionally, one could argue that the best way to fight social and political anomie in Romania and other post-communist countries is via integration and the avoidance of discriminatory gestures. In the case of Romania, I would highlight also that the existence of two major political poles, the Democratic Convention, and the Party of Social Democracy, and the vigour of another alliance (the Social Democratic Union), create prerequisites for precluding a fatal evolution of the political process and the shifting towards blatant authoritarianism. One would also have to mention the role of the independent press in this respect. I dare to say that the leaders of Europe need to pay more attention to the role of icons for social psychology.

It can be stated that the more laggard a transforming country is, and the closer it is to Russia geographically, the more critical for its future is the nature of capitalism in the latter country. Conversely, it can be submitted that the closer is a country geographically to the EU, the more likely it undergoes the influence of the EU 'anchor'. A similar thesis can be submitted regarding the nature of domestic politics, with Russian developments providing a strong demonstration effect, if not direct influence. What are then the prospects for Russian capitalism? As was highlighted above, the new economy is very much market-based, but it is also '«anarchic», predatory, corrupt and oligarchic... unfortunately, the maldistribution of wealth and power is likely to give Russia a rentier economy that fails to provide the competitive dynamism the country desperately needs and its elite expects. It will also make democracy less workable, since it must pit a deprived and resentful majority against a wealthy minority.[28] One danger is populism but the more likely outcome is repression'.[29]

The growing profile of those who advocate a more authoritarian rule in Russia, and the likelihood for it to come into being, can be judged also by the rising number of high-ranking military people (like Aleksandar Lebed) in politics. The temptation of authoritarian rule can be discerned in other post-communist countries as well, but there is, however, a big difference against Russia. This is because, in the latter country military figures are getting increasingly into the limelight of politics and the mood of large segments of the population – who want some 'order' restored – seems to favour their political ascendancy. The comeback of the Communist Party in Russian politics is to be judged in this vein as well.

A cognitive issue: complexity

The analysis of transition needs to recognise the extreme complexity of the process under way. Gross oversimplifications and reductionism of the type 'black vs. white' (with no shades in-between), and the lack of understanding of how interests are socially articulated – particularly in a transition period – cannot but obscure real processes and lead to hasty and inadequate decisions. As a scholar aptly noted, 'The elites failed to understand that society was a far more complex organism than what they had thought, that simple, well-meaning declarations were not effective in politics, that ideas and programmes would have to be sold to the public, and that institutions were necessary for the routinised exercise of power'.[30]

An open and honest debate is also made difficult by what seems to have turned into a kind of non-discussible matter. An entrenched habit seems thus to have developed among some of those who analyse or are involved in the policymaking of post-communist transformation, which does not help a genuine and fruitful exchange of views at all. I refer to the kind of statements and judgements, which seem to ignore completely the existence of trade-offs and dilemmas for any policy, under any circumstances. It is not rare to meet and listen to people who seem to have very hard times in accepting the fallibility of human nature, and the fact that any individual, or organisationally (institutionally) structured thinking has flaws – that there is no such thing as a perfect policy; that they, themselves, or the political or non-political organisations they represent cannot be 100% right in their thoughts and actions.

There are some people who have a very rudimentary view of what a modern market-based system means, and who do not realise that there are variants of real capitalism – that a 'pure' market economy as such does not exist in reality, and that the concept is meaningless without proper qualifications. Besides, 'Imperfect and costly information, imperfect capital markets, imperfect competition: these are the realities of market economies' – aspects that must be taken into account by those countries embarking on the choice of an economic system.[31] The implication is clear in the sense of the stringent need to consider how market economies actually function and maybe, not to succumb to the beauty but the irrelevance of the textbook model of perfect competition.

Such people are blinded to the reality that it is high time to deal seriously with the *fine print* of reforms, and that this involves much more than simple ideological statements and exhortations; that reforms involve unavoidable pragmatism and making hard policy choices based on solid theoretical and empirical knowledge, when one cannot escape facing painful trade-offs and dilemmas.

For instance, one issue that badly needs serious debate is the structure of corporate governance; it is ever more obvious that one needs to go beyond the general statement regarding the necessity of privatisation, and that it is not at all clear what are the best formulae for corporate governance in the transforming economies. On a more general level, it is high time to acknowledge an extremely important fact: the post-communist countries are in a period when the basic constructs of future systems are put in place, and this can be seen as an historical opportunity for designing viable societal aggregates. For example, the future dynamics of the consolidated public budget will very much depend on how its structure is built. At the same time, due to the rush of events and the complexity of the whole process big mistakes can be made. These mistakes can put the evolving systems on a less convenient path; they can create bad 'path-dependency'. This is like saying that the institutional 'QWERTY keyboard layout' of the transforming systems is now being created and one needs to be very careful on which path the lock-in occurs.[32]

It is true that the above described behaviour can more often be met among those who have strong personal and direct political involvement, and who may feel, consequently, more reluctant to be candid and self-critical. In addition, in their case one may try to find justifications, but only to the extent the limits of decent dialogue and transparency are not totally misconstrued and misued. What is puzzling is that such politician's type of behaviour has extended its territory among certain academic people, whose posturing and intellectual masquerading can be quite ridiculous and grotesque.

Overall, this behaviour is mishandling ordinary citizens' interests and feelings and confusing their perceptions of social and political life. For, how else can one interpret the stances that exude, explicitly or implicitly, the slogan 'those who are not with us are against us', which, ironically, fits very much the communist pattern of thinking.

*
*   *

Most of Eastern European governments are under terrible time pressure; for them, 'it is raining while the house is still roofless'. They do not have the luxury of dragging their feet, and those who waste time are heavily penalised. On the other hand, increasing worries are created because of the still depressed levels of output, relatively low investment ratios and real wages; these are factors which can hinder attempts to create viable economic systems, and can undermine the prospects for long-term growth. An ever more pervasive *social fatigue*, together with the instability caused by inter-ethnic and military conflicts in several areas, can play havoc with transformation and lead national systems astray. The diminishing vitality of Western Europe and the latter's inability to provide clairvoyant guidance can only intensify the dilemmas of transition (Daianu, 1996a, b).

Path-dependency is a very meaningful expression under the circumstances. A sequence of major policy blunders and unfavourable external shocks can put a system on a misdirection and a trajectory, which would be hard to correct.

One needs also to consider that the degree of instability in Eastern Europe is amplified by the extent to which the countries in the region feel their security threatened. When military conflicts (wars) occur in the neighbouring areas, when borders are questioned (explicitly or implicitly), when inter-ethnic tensions heighten, such a feeling is more than justified. All these enhance the development of a social and political psychology which makes harder the task of working out and implementing sound long-term economic policies.

Notes

*   Revised version of the paper presented at the annual NATO economics colloquium, Brussels, 26-28 June 1996. This paper relies on the research undertaken while the author was a visiting senior research fellow at the NATO Defence College of Rome.

1   Valerie Bunce, 1992, p. 277.

2   In the post-communist countries, there are still parties which define themselves, politically, in Marxist terms, and even carry the name communist.

3   'For obvious reasons no party has grasped the nettle and explained that the foundation of capitalism does not have as one of its genetic conditions the *just transfer* of material or political resources... It is difficult enough to mobilise society on the promise of greater inequality let alone admit that it will be inherently unjust and will consign one-third of its citizens to social redundancy' (George Kolankiewicz, 1994, p. 47).

4   George Schöpflin, 1994, p.130.

5   See also Ann Applebaum (1994).

6   According to A. Solimano, in 1937, the nominal income per capita was estimated at \$440 in Great Britain and, \$400, \$340, \$330, \$306, \$265 and \$190 in Sweden, Germany, Belgium, Netherlands, France and Austria, respectively. The corresponding estimates for Czechoslovakia, Hungary, Poland, Romania, Yugoslavia and Bulgaria were \$170, \$120, \$100, \$81, \$80 and \$75 respectively (A. Gelb and Cheryl Gray, 1991, p.65).

7   Daniel Chirot, 1989, p.3.

8   Ivan Berend, 1994, p.110. The same line of reasoning is espoused by the present author in 'Transformation and the Legacy of Backwardness' (1992) (chapter 2 herein).

9   Remark made during the Romanian-American economic roundtable, Bucharest, 16-17 April, 1991.

10   Peter Rutland, 1994/95, p.11.

11   Communism mutilated individuals and society and its economic decay was congenitally programmed. Nonetheless, as George Schöpflin remarked, 'The Stalinist revolution introduced the bulk of society to modern working methods; it brought about a major and irreversible population shift from country to town, thereby largely solving the age-old peasant problem; it transformed the country-side; it created or expanded a reasonably competent technical intelligentsia; it greatly expanded the scope of state intervention in society and brought into being a sizeable population that regarded the state as its primary source of protection' (1994, pp. 128-129). In addition, as an example, *The Economist* says: 'Russia is

no longer the undifferentiated peasant country it was when Stalin embarked on his crash-course communism. In 1939 only 32% of the Russian population lived in towns and cities... Now it is 74%... It has 99% literacy rate, 96% enrolment in the secondary education, and a large educated scientific and managerial elite' (7 December, 1991, p.28).

12   Jacek Rostowski, 1993, p.5. Similarly sceptical is Ronald McKinnon (1991).

13   This is the line of reasoning espoused by Jim Leitzel, Clifford Gaddy and Michael Alexeev (1995, pp.26-29); they argue that 'the net impact of organised crime in Russia today is probably beneficial' (p.29), and, that, 'as economic reform continues to progress, the mafia is likely to fade in importance' (p.26).

14   As a dynamical complex system, the command system is characterised by chain links, compared with a market economy which, relies, essentially, on parallel links.

15   Olivier Blanchard and Philippe Aghion speak of an 'optimal speed' by considering this balance (1994).

16   Jeffrey Sachs, 1994, p.1. He further says: '...high inflation tends to be dynamically unstable, planting the seeds of even greater inflation in the future. On the other hand, tough stabilisation without large-scale foreign financial support is also likely to fail, if high unemployment and inadequate social support produce political instability' (Ibid.).

17   According to the World Bank economists' calculations, in the 'observed transition economies, with a total population of 320 million, the number of the poor has increased from 8 million (about 3% of the population) to a conservatively estimated 58 million (18%). There are thus 50 million new poor. More than 40 million of them live in the Slavic states of the former Soviet Union – almost 30 million in Russia alone... The part of the poor increased from 5% to 17% in the Balkans and Poland. In other Central European countries, it increased to only 1%...The part of the poor in Russia has risen from 3% to 21%' (Branco Mihalovici, 1994, p.2). These data, too, can give an idea of the types of capitalism that are evolving in the post-communist countries.

18   Including the potential for the appearance of aggressive extreme-left groups, liable to engage in domestic and international terrorism. The existence of extreme-right (fascist) groups would compound the danger.

19   John Odling Smee, 1995, p.100.

20   Maxim Boycko, 1995, p.88

21   Chrystia Freeland, 1995, p.1.

22   The same journalist, from the *Financial Times*, remarks that 'the increasingly deep divide between the winners and the losers created over the past three years by Russia's traumatic economic and political transformation is emerging as the most important underlying factor in the country's struggle to determine how to move forward' (Chrystia Freeland, Ibid.).

23   In a report from the city of Ulyanovsk, in Russia, Andrew Nagorsky finds that the local authorities' 'old-fashioned welfare-state policies are especially popular

among the poor and elderly' (1995, p.23).

24   Janos Kornai, 1994, p.16.

25   'Russia Survey', *The Economist*, 8 April, 1995, p. 4.

26   Jeffrey Sachs, 1995b, p.2. Though I agree with the main point made by Sachs in this article I think he underestimates the importance of distributional effects entailed by market reforms. Living standards may increase overall and, nonetheless, people may vote against the government if the number of losers in society is high.

27   For a very interesting paper on possible 'organisational modes' developing in the post-communist countries see Masahiro Aoki, 1995.

28   According to a recent opinion poll published by the European Union, 'Three out of four Russians oppose their country developing towards a market economy' (European News Digest, *Financial Times*, 8 March 1995, p.2). Other polls show that 'many Russians feel adrift and bereft of past ideology without anything to replace; they are frightened by crime, inflation and, most of all, the general uncertainty of the future... although a majority of Russians say they would rather have stability and a strong leader than democracy, they also overwhelmingly support freedoms that are, in fact, key elements of democracy: free press, freedom of speech and travel, and regular elections' (Fred Hiatt, 1995, p.1).

29   'Russia is no tame bear', *Financial Times*, 10 April, 1995, p.15.

30   George Schöpflin, 1994, p.130.

31   Joseph Stiglitz, 1994, p.267.

32   The Stanford economists Brian Arthur (1994) and Paul David (1985) are foremost supporters of the 'path-dependency' theory in economics.

References

Applebaum, A. (1995), 'The Rise and Fall of the Communists', *Foreign Affairs*, vol.73, no.6, November-December.

Arthur, B. (1994), 'Increasing Returns and the Path Dependency in the Economy', The University of Michigan Press, Ann Arbor.

Berend, I. (1994), 'Annus Mirabilis - Anni Mirabiles?', *Contention*, no.8, Winter.

Boycko, M. (1995), 'Comments on Russia's Struggle with Stabilisation: Conceptual Issues and Evidence' by Sachs, Proceedings of the World Bank Annual Conference on Development Economics, World Bank, Washington DC.

Chirot, D. (ed.) (1989), 'The Origins of Backwardness in Eastern Europe', University of California Press, Berkeley.

Csaba, L. (1996), 'Economic Reforms in Cooperation Partner Countries', in proceedings of the 1995 Annual NATO Economics Colloquium, 'Status of Economic Reforms', pp.27-39.

Daianu, D. (1996a), 'A Dual Challenge for Europe', in R. Dobrinsky and M.

Landesmann (ed.), *Transforming Economies and European Integration*, Edward Elgar, Aldershot, pp.15-31.

Daianu, D. (1996b), 'Economic Vitality and Viability: A Dual Challenge for European Security', Frankfurt am Main, Peter Lang.

David, P. (1985), 'Clio and the Economics of QWERTY', *American Economic Review*, vol.75.

Freeland, C. (1995), 'Capitalism Exposes the Poverty Gap', in 'Russia Survey', *Financial Times*, 10 April.

Hardt, J.P. (1996), 'A Report Card for Economies in Transition', proceedings of the 1995 Annual NATO Economics Conference: 'Status of Economic Reforms', pp.233-245.

Hyatt, F. (1995), 'A Crisis of Leadership Threatens Democracy In Russia', *International Herald Tribune*, 20 March.

Kolankiewicz, G. (1994), 'Elites in Search of a Political Formula', *Daedalus*, vol. 123, no. 3, Summer.

Kornai, J. (1994), 'Lasting Growth as a Top Priority', *Discussion Paper*, no.7, Institute for Advanced Study, Budapest.

Leitzel, J.C., Gaddy, J.C. and Alexeev, V. (1995), 'Mafiosi and Matrioshki', *Brookings Review*, vol.13, no.1, Winter.

McKinnon, R. (1991), 'The Order of Economic Liberalisation', Johns Hopkins University Press, Baltimore.

Mihailovici, B. (1994), 'A Cost of Transition: 50 Million New Poor and Growing Inequality', *Transition*, vol.5, no.8, October.

Mungiu, A. (1995), 'Romanii dupa '89: istoria unei neintelgeri' (Romanians after 1989: The history of a misunderstanding), Humanitas, Bucharest.

Nagorsky, A. (1995), *Newsweek*, 7 April.

Rose-Ackerman, S. (1996), 'Roundtable Discussion: Second-generation Issues in Transition', in M. Bruno and B. Pleskovic (eds.), *Proceedings of the Annual World Bank Conference on Development Economics*, pp.373-378, Washington DC.

Rostowski, J. (1993), 'Creating Stable Monetary System in Post-Communist Countries', Manuscript.

Rutland, P. (1994-1995), 'Has Democracy Failed Russia', *The National Interest*, Winter.

Sachs, J. (1994), 'Russia's Struggle with Stabilisation: Conceptual Issues and Evidence', Paper presented at the Annual World Bank Conference on Development Economics, 28-29 April, Washington DC.

Sachs, J. (1995), 'Post-communist Parties and the Politics of Entitlements', *Transition*, vol.6, no.3.

Schöpflin, A. (1994), 'Post-communism: The Problems of Democratic Construction', *Daedalus*, vol.123, no.3, Summer.

Smee, J.O. (1995), 'The Baltics, Russia and the FSU Countries: On the Road to a Stable, Market Economy', *IMF Survey*, 3 April.

Stiglitz, J. (1994), 'Whither Socialism', MIT Press, Cambridge.

Tanase, S. (26 March 1996), 'A NATO Border between Romania and Hungary would be Quite Unfavourable to us' (in Romanian), interview for *Curierul National*, p. 15.

Teodorescu, A. (1991), 'The Romanian Economy: The future of a Failure', in O. Sjoberg and M. Wyzan (eds.), *Economic Change in the Balkan States*, St. Martin Press, New York.

12 The European Union and Eastern Enlargement - a compounded challenge*

The European Union is at a major crossroad in its history. The ongoing intense debate on the future shape of the Union goes beyond the foreseen and unforeseen implications of Germany's reunification and the collapse of communism in Europe. *Eurocentrism* is not of much help for coming to grips with the problems facing Europe; one has to embed the European *problematique* into a worldwide context. For what is at stake in Europe now and, in the years to come, needs to be judged against the background of fundamental tendencies in the world economy, which have been under way for almost two decades now. The redistribution of economic power, the emergence of multipolarity in international affairs, the globalisation of financial markets, and the 'new information age' (cyberspace) pose tremendous challenges to the Old Continent. Some even speak of a certain *fatigue* which may have engulfed Western European countries, and which, allegedly, would cause a 'competitiveness problem'. The extremely high structural unemployment in the EU (from an average of about 4% in the seventies to above 11% currently), the crisis of the welfare state, and the burgeoning budget deficits in many countries are symptoms of the problems facing them. While Western Europe attempts to regain economic vigour, the post-communist countries are still struggling to achieve viable market-based economies and democratic polities; the resultant interlinkages form a compounded economic and political challenge for Europe.

While *deepening* is a euphemism for the need to rethink (reengineer) the Union under the current historical circumstances, *enlargement* connotes the exigency of remaking the architecture of the Union by taking into account the changed geopolitical map of Europe. In this new context takes place the process aimed at the creation of the Monetary Union (MU) which, according to a strand of thought, is the means to further the integration of Europe by not slowing down the process to the lowest common denominator. Different 'cultures of stability' (Stabilitätskulturen)[1] and different approaches to political integration clash in the battle for the forging of the MU. Related to the controversies surrounding the MU I would emphasise two issues. One regards the relationship between the MU and the economic challenges facing the member countries. As remarked by the President of the Bundesbank, Hans Tietmeyer, the monetary union is 'no panacea' for Europe's ills.[2] Therefore, the MU should not be seen as a *deus ex machina* that can solve the structural problems of the member countries. The second issue regards consequences of the formation of the single-currency area for the Eastern enlargement of the Union. The formation of a 'hard-core' would have important implications for the future dynamics of the Union and would send several messages. These messages, *inter alia*, are: that there is a multi-speed Union in the making; that 'delinkages' (fractures) are possible, in spite of the avowed commitments to convergence of development levels; that the economically stronger post-communist countries could join a 'soft' area of the Union in a foreseeable future (around year 2002-2004); that cleavages may appear both inside the unified Europe (EU), and between the latter and other European countries, etc.

A big political question is what can be done so that seemingly unavoidable cleavages – in a multi-speed Europe – would not imperil stability and security on the Continent. In this respect, obviously, I have in mind the special case of Southeastern Europe, which is mired in political and economic difficulties, and interethnic conflicts.

This chapter tries to analyse enlargement by looking at the diversity of economic conditions in Europe and at the gaps which separate Western Europe of Eastern Europe.[3] This perspective helps the investigation of major issues and trade-offs involved in the process of enlargement, including the prospects for some Eastern European countries to join an eventual 'hard-core' of the Union. One implied thesis is that the strategy for enlargement, should it internalise political and security related reasons, needs a broader compass; this refers to the construction of a solid pre-enlargement package of measures in terms of the support given to the aspirant post-communist countries.

The diversity of national players (nation-states) and interests

In order to get a better understanding of the motives behind different national policies, a scrutiny of the diversity of national players – nation-states – in European politics is needed. Using the gross, and in a way, traditional, dichotomy between Western and Eastern Europe is highly insufficient for reaching adequate conclusions. Although the European Union operates as a single player, which co-ordinates Western European countries' policies vis-à-vis Eastern Europe, it is useful to try to decipher the process that is conducive to common measures and rules regarding this bilateral relationship.

The first thing one has to refer to is the degree of economic homogeneity among the European countries. There are several factors to be taken into account in this respect: the levels of general economic development of the various countries, the current and the probable state of their economies, and specific sectoral problems – like agriculture for instance.

In Western Europe, which is the part of the rich world with the largest number of inhabitants, one can find an astonishing wide spectrum of development levels; this spectrum is illustrated by the diversity of income per capita. Just think of the differences between countries like Ireland, Greece, and Portugal, on one hand, and Germany and the Nordic countries, on the other hand. In table 12.1, this is suggested by the considerable difference between the income per capita levels in the less rich countries of the EU and the average figure for the Union.

Between the 'rich' and the 'poor' of Western Europe there has always been tensions linked with the size and the structure of aid meant to reduce the development gaps within the EU. The 'poor', obviously, greeted gladly the enlargement of the EU with the new rich members (Austria, Finland, and Sweden), which makes it easier to carry out regional development policy. But the entry of new poor countries from Eastern Europe would increase the competition for regional development funding and, consequently, it is looked upon unfavourably by the weaker members of the EU.

One could imagine also that some of the rich members of the EU, too, could become more cautious about an enlargement of the Union that may tilt the 'balance of power' – in terms of voting power – in favour of the poor countries. For this would affect not only the formulation of the regional development policy, but also the possibility for co-ordinating national economic policies within the EU. However, such a consideration would have to be balanced by the costs of delaying the entry of Eastern European applicants.

The level of economic development perspective can be applied to Eastern Europe as well. As Table 12.1 also indicates, there are significant differences among the post-communist countries, though one has to look cautiously at the available estimates. But much more important is the fact that Eastern Europe is far away from Western Europe in terms of the income per capita; aside from Slovenia, only the Czech Republic approaches the level of the least wealthy member of the EU which is Greece, and only after the purchasing power-parity concept is applied.

The differences among the Eastern European countries, assuming that there is a proper market-related institutional build-up, seem to favour an earlier entry into the EU of the richer countries – like the Czech Republic, Hungary, Poland, Slovakia, and Slovenia.

Table 12.1   Income per capita in several European countries

(in US dollars)

	1993[*]
Albania	999
Romania	2,806
Lithuania	3,110
Bulgaria	4,100
Poland	5,010
Hungary	6,050
Slovak Republic	6,290
Estonia	6,320
Czech Republic	7,541
Greece	8,429
Portugal	9,982
Spain	13,110
European Union average	17,288

* for the post-communist countries the income is calculated on a PPP (purchasing power parity) basis, which means that the figures are higher than the official ones. It can be said that, in general, the figures for the economies in transition have to be looked at with caution, especially when the various sources vary considerably in their estimates.
Sources: Transition Report, EBRD, October 1994, p.7; The European Union Survey, *The Economist*, 22 October 1994, p.4

The state of economies is another factor that cannot and should not be easily dismissed in rationalising the evolution of national economic policies. Can the Spanish government be indifferent to an unemployment rate that has been over 20% in the early 90s? Or take the case of all recent French governments, however their political colour, for which unemployment has acquired an increasing importance, if not the top place among policy priorities. High unemployment complicates the strategic goal of realising the single currency, and also makes many Western governments more distrustful about the competition exerted by the low wage countries of Eastern Europe, particularly in the short run.

Likewise, the state of economies in Eastern Europe will enhance, or not, their intention to become members of the Union. If it is hard for some relatively advanced market economies (like Italy, Spain, and even the UK) to comply with the requirements of economic policy discipline within the EU, it is easy to imagine what could happen in the case of countries that are much more likely to experience relatively high inflation rates, and which are prone to incur large budget deficits in the future owing to powerful social pressures.[4] Is it realistic to assume that Eastern European countries would be able to submit themselves to the financial and monetary rigour of the Union? Or, maybe one has to think that the Union will develop a variable geometry and, consequently, the Eastern European countries will be able to join the 'soft' group at the beginning, or form an even 'softer' group on their own.

But even in such a case, only the best performing Eastern European countries would have a reasonable chance to cope with the competitive pressures implied by membership in the Union – more precisely, by the obligation not to use systematically the exchange rate (devaluation) as a protective device. One should stress, in this context, that the protectionistic stance of the EU vis-à-vis Eastern European countries does not help the latter in advancing their economic reforms, and, further, does not enhance their capabilities to cope with eventual membership.[5] It should be noted that many analyses show that, there is little rational economic explanation for the EU's overall high sensitivity with respect to trade with Eastern Europe.[6] The trade-off involved here is again conspicuous.

Current trends do not induce much optimism concerning the state of European economies. There are two things, which need to be highlighted in this context. One regards the very state of each economy, which bears the impact of continent – and worldwide processes. Europe, as a whole, seems to have been developing a competitiveness problem, which has to be understood in a broader sense – not related to trade only. Secondly, the diverging evolution of European economies makes harder the co-ordination of economic policies, and, therefore, may slow down the integration process along the line of deepening; it may also hamper the enlargement to the East.

The sectoral structure of national economies, too, explains the existence of different sensitivities to external pressures. The case of farming is highly telling in this respect, but one can add other sectors as well, like steel industry and textiles. It is understood that the Western economies, which rely more on farming and other 'sunset' industries, have a higher propensity to ask Brussels to adopt or maintain protective measures, and are more uncompromising in terms of bargaining. If one thinks that the Common Agricultural Policy (CAP) holds more than half of the European budget the strength of the involved vested interests, and why there is such a fierce opposition to the liberalisation of imports from Eastern Europe, become clear. And this is occurring in spite of the widely shared acknowledgement among policymakers that there is an acute need for the revision of the CAP.

From an opposite angle, one could argue that the agricultural trade pressure from the East is, in a way, timely and that this is an occasion to link the two imperatives (opening markets to Eastern European imports and reforming the CAP) through a wide scheme. However, here again an obvious and painful trade-off exists for policymakers which, in order to be solved decisively, asks for strong political leadership and its introduction into a broader policy-package.

The role of geography

Geography is important in Europe and geopolitics plays an important role in understanding countries' specific goals and motives. For instance, in Germany's case, its Eastern neighbours present a strategic interest in all respects and this is why Bonn is supporting speeding up their accession into the EU. As a well known German journalist, who is a foremost expert on European affairs, stated 'the stabilisation of Germany's immediate Central European hinterland is the more urgent task'.[7] Germany can play an additional strong card to this end: its Eastern neighbours are *European* and the EU made a political decisions that they will join the Union, eventually.

Even in pure economic terms, Germany's Eastern neighbours present attractiveness, which compares not unfavourably with the less developed (southern) members of the EU. An article in the leading German journal of foreign affairs notes several assets which make Eastern Europe and, especially, the Visegrad Group a preferred zone of economic interest.[8] These assets are defined as: a development potential which is considered to be 'much greater' than in the peripheral regions of Western Europe, the geographic proximity, the labour skills and the standards of research and training, a structure of production which is 'much more advanced than that of the southern members of the EU', and very low wage levels[9] (see Table 12.2). The same German journalist considers that Central European countries, 'above all the Czech Republic and Slovakia, are Germany's Mexico': 'next door, and with workforces that offer high productivity rates at about one-tenth of German wage levels. Their markets are ideally suited for penetration'.[10] Recent available figures support this outlook. Thus, according to data provided by

Commerzbank, over a third of the merchandise trade carried on between Central and Eastern Europe and the OECD states is done with Germany.[11] The same source mentioned also that, in 1994, Germany's exports to the Visegrad Group countries were DM 28.5 billion, which was 15% higher than its deliveries to East Asia. Concurrently, 9% of Germany's direct investments went to these four economies, up from only 0.5% in 1989. Germany is also the main trading partner of Romania and of other post-communist countries. It is fair to assume that, over the long term, German investments in those countries would grow considerably as well.

One can easily imagine a scenario according to which Germany will expand and deepen economic links with its Eastern neighbours,[12] much to the chagrin of other members of the EU. Should such a dynamic take place it would have many and significant implications for future developments in Europe, for the distribution of economic power and of political influence among groups of countries. Such a scenario would gain in likelihood should the process of European wide integration stumble, or slow down, owing to big conceptual and policy-related differences on the nature of the process of deepening.[13]

Table 12.2   Monthly wages in several post-communist countries (US dollars/month)

	1993[*]
Slovenia	421
Hungary	317
Czech Republic	221
Slovak Republic	201
Poland	194
Bulgaria	114
Latvia	98
Estonia	85
Romania	82
Lithuania	65

* Nominal monthly dollar wages at going exchange rates based on average 4th quarter 1993 earnings
Sources: OECD and IMF data quoted by Transition Report, EBRD, 1994, p.135

The same things cannot be said of the geopolitical and geoeconomic stance of the Mediterranean members of the Union, which fear the competitive pressures of additional low-wage members, and feel to be increasingly under the threat posed by a destabilising northern African fringe. Trade-offs and dilemmas can be easily detected here as well. It is clear that the different perceptions between France, Italy, and Spain on one hand, and Germany and the Nordic countries, on the other hand, regarding the security threats to Europe will be a major contending issue for years to come.

The geopolitics of Europe imply a dynamic of spheres of influence. Though integration is paid lip service by most European governments, the process as such cannot obliterate the search, by the 'primadonnas' of European politics, to carve out their spheres of influence on the Continent. For it would be quite naive to think that the process of integration does away with national foreign policies and goals. Moreover, it can be argued that each member of the EU tries to use the multilateral, Pan-European institutions, to attain its national interests. Alternatively, for the big ones, there is an attempt to 'nationalise' the so-called common foreign and security policies of the EU.

It can be submitted, therefore, that how Eastern European countries' quest for accession is treated depends and will depend also on bargains and compromises reached within the EU and among its most important members. Here one can talk about the role played by what can be called the 'referee-countries'; these are countries which, because of their overall economic and political influence, can influence the decision-making process decisively. De facto, such countries play hegemonic roles which can be expressed more forcefully, or more gently. The USA play such a role within the framework of NATO and clearly, France and Germany play the leading roles in the EU.

It can be expected with a high degree of certainty that Germany, in particular, because of its growing economic power, will get a higher profile in the way decisions are made within the EU. In addition, I would submit that this is going to happen irrespective of how the further construction of the EU takes place. It may thus happen that Germany will be able to pursue more easily its interests within a multilateral framework, than in a Europe of nations which remember vividly the lessons of history. This explains much of what lies behind the debate and conflict on the status and the operation of the future European Central Bank; why Germany opposes France's idea of matching *the Stability Pact* with a political counterweight (*The Stability Council*). Or, should European integration experience strong setbacks Germany would very likely concentrate its energy on carving out what it sees as a 'normal' sphere of influence taking into account its economic and security (strategic) interests. And this is a fact already acknowledged, though sometimes reluctantly, by its Eastern European neighbours – which, one way, or another, feel the need for an anchor which should enhance their stability and prospects for modernisation.[14]

Nonetheless, a major difficulty which a referee-country has in exerting a positive co-ordinating role is that it needs to act in a neutral fashion, as if not having any significant interests of its own, a fact which is quite unrealistic. Certainly, to the extent the hegemon's own interests are perceived favourably by most of the other members of the Community, its co-ordinating role is made substantially easier. However, this would imply that the hegemonic country defines its national interests in a way that internalises the national concerns of the other countries. Is it probable in a period of resurgence of economic nationalism in Europe, and in the world in general?

With respect to the EU, it remains to be seen whether the different political and economic weights of the current members will facilitate the making of fundamental decisions including the attitude vis-à-vis Eastern Europe. Much depends on how prerogatives are split between Brussels and the national governments of the member countries and, also, on the mechanics of and the human touch behind the decision-making process.

One can pose a related question. Is the EU ready to undergo fundamental revisions, which should correspond to the new reality in Europe and to the need of integrating economically and politically the post-communist countries? Likewise, is the EU prepared to move forward viewing enlargement as a way of helping the process of systemic transformation in the post-communist countries by taking into account their current fragility? Is the EU ready to undertake programmes and projects, normally carried out in its poorer member states, which should precede and enhance enlargement? Again, one is forced to return to the conclusion that the big push now cannot take place without strong leadership and a vision, which should encompass the whole of Europe.

By talking about players, non-European actors need to be mentioned. It is clear that continental geopolitics relate to global geopolitics and geoeconomics, and this applies to the competition for Eastern Europe's markets as well. The United States, for example, would not welcome an integration of Eastern Europe into an EU which would make it harder for them to sell their goods and services into that area. The American Undersecretary of Commerce for International Trade was quite blunt in this respect by stating that 'We want to make sure that this does not become some kind of a preferential zone that distorts trade'.[15] I remember also that, some years ago, I was asked by several colleagues from one of the leading American think tanks what I think about a 'free trade area' between Eastern European countries and the USA in view of the reluctance of the EU to open its markets to the emerging democracies.

Without many fanfares and by exploiting opportunities missed by Western companies, major Asian trading nations are taking positions in Eastern Europe through strategic investments. A recent example is Daewoo, one of the leading South Korean conglomerates (chaebols), which invested hundreds of millions of US dollars in industrial domains that range from car manufacturing and ship-building in Romania, to electronics in Poland, and truck-manufacturing in the Czech Republic. In Romania, Daewoo decided to get in after French companies, which were already there, treated, I would say, quite unwisely, their strategic positions.

Although almost all Eastern European countries did sign Association Agreements with the EU and committed themselves to join the Union, the battle for market shares in the post-communist countries includes major non-European players.

The main economic issues

There are several issues which make up the economics of the relationship between Western Europe and Eastern Europe. For the sake of analysis, I will refer to them in the following order: trade, foreign investment, labour movement, and foreign aid.

Let us begin with trade. The conventional wisdom is that the low wage countries of Eastern Europe pose a big threat to several of the weaker sectors of the EU, which is a perception frequently met in the West. This policy rationale is much publicised in the Western mass media and has become part of the public consciousness in Western Europe. The public debate surrounding this issue resembles much that which accompanied the formation of NAFTA, the North Atlantic Free Trade Area. Likewise, the menace to jobs was the stick wielded by politicians, some technocrats, and trade unionists.

What is very likely and much less known is that the European Union has turned a 600 million ECU's trade deficit of 1989 into a 5.6 billion ECU's trade surplus by 1993; this included, thanks to the subsidised exports of the common agricultural policy, 433 million ECU's in farm products.[16] It is true that, in a bilateral relationship, the counterpart of sizeable capital inflows is a considerable trade deficit, and one may think that this is a proper pattern for structuring East-West European economic relations for years to come – as a reflection of a presumed joint effort to build up the economies in transition. However, things need to be seen in a proper light and there are several factors, which indicate that the story is more complicated and not necessarily favourable to Eastern Europe.

Thus, although the Eastern European countries trade more than 60% with the EU, their trade is not exclusively bilateral; this means that they could get capital inflows from other sources as well, which may allow them to run smaller trade deficits with the EU. Additionally and what is more important, the trade deficit in itself does not say much about the potential of Eastern European countries to sell on Western markets. A country can incur the same trade deficit at widely different volumes of its exports and imports. This fact may not be so important for the West, where the economies are operating close to their capacity levels, but it is of vital importance for the East where the level of economic activity is still much depressed; for Eastern Europe an export drive would be tantamount to the revival of their economies through what economists call an export multiplier effect.

Not only are Eastern European countries, currently, more open to trade than their Western partners, but they are a long way from being as sophisticated as the latter in terms of the utilisation of non-tariff barriers. In addition, it is well known that these barriers are frequently a much more serious impediment to trade than tariffs.

A natural consequence of the protectionistic stance of the EU is that Eastern European countries may have to reconsider the benefits of almost total 'unilateral free trade' and try to protect themselves in a Europe where, seemingly, an underlying rule of the game is *'chacun pour soi meme'*, or 'we against them', at least for a while. And this change of heart and policy appears to have already started if one pays attention to the increasing displeasure of Eastern European top policymakers with Western Europe's real actions, and also to the reimposition of higher tariffs in Poland and Hungary. Western European countries need to understand that, for the sake of actual and mutually advantageous integration, adjustment has to occur on a two-way street, and that the current bargaining strength between the two groups of partners does not justify putting the whole burden of adjustment on the weaker partners – on the Eastern European countries.

The discussion about foreign investment concentrates on its impact on domestic jobs in the West. There are some who emphasise that, instead of investing at home, Western companies are running away with jobs towards the low wage countries of Eastern Europe. There are several counterarguments which need to be made in this respect.

One counterargument is that foreign investment can stimulate trade significantly, and the figures indicate clearly that Western Europe has benefited from the functional economic opening between the two parts of Europe. Therefore, one could surmise that, on balance, net job creation was positive in

Western Europe.

Secondly, the capital flows into Eastern Europe have been much under what was expected immediately after 1989. One should remember that, at the start of the post-communist transformation, there were many who feared that this process would crowd out the flow of resources towards the emerging markets and other developing countries. Those fears proved groundless, to a large extent, for two main reasons: the attractiveness of the emerging markets in East Asia and Latin America has not subsided in relative terms; capital judges the overall environment and the latter was viewed as still being relatively less attractive for most European post-communist countries. Data show that, although annual measured foreign direct investment (FDI) rose ten times between 1990 and 1993, they represented ca. 10% of total FDI flows into the developing countries in 1993.[17]

It is no surprise, in this context, that Hungary has been taking almost half of all the external inflows to the region. In her case, one can see the fruits of market reforms which were undertaken well before the demise of the communist regime. Together, Hungary, the Czech Republic, and Slovakia got almost two thirds of the total FDI inflows.

And a final counterargument: it is not higher investment that could provide the main instrument for dealing with high unemployment in Western Europe. The functioning of labour markets, the remaking of the institutional set-up, the redesign of the welfare system, and better education would have to do the primary job to this end.

Labour mobility is a much debated issue since it could turn into highly perturbing immigration for the West and could exacerbate domestic tensions. Whereas some of the Western countries seem to move forward the integration of their labour markets and strengthen the control of immigration (the Schengen Agreement), their fear of potentially uncontrollable inflows from the East is publicly voiced. The argument is clear: the incentives are very high for Eastern Europeans to move into areas which offer them highly superior wages; these incentives would significantly counterbalance the switching costs of moving.

Laszlo Valki and Laszlo Csaba made, nevertheless, a valid point in this respect by referring to the experience of the United States,[18] where an income difference of 1:3 was the threshold which induced substantial movement of people; above that, each percentage of income differential caused 0.026% migration. Their view is that this fact does not support the visions of Eastern European's pouring into the other half of Europe, 'since the differences in standards of living, measured realistically, through purchasing power parity, do not show a larger difference than 1:2.5 or 1:3'[19] – see also Table 12.1.

I would make several additional comments on their worthy observation. First, it does apply particularly to the more developed post-communist countries. Secondly, for the latter there is already a safety valve created by the more favourable treatment of their citizens by the Western neighbouring countries. For example, Hungarians have the right to work in Austria for six months without being asked to hold a work permit. Likewise, many Polish citizens work in Italy or Germany using the informal labour markets. Moreover, the Schengen Agreement is not likely to reverse this trend. Thirdly, one should think also of the distributional effects of reforms on migration; these effects could be quite significant in the less developed countries of Eastern Europe. And finally, I would consider also the potential pressure exerted on labour markets in Eastern Europe by a possible increasing inflow of people from Third World countries; some of the Eastern Europeans countries have turned into immigration countries.

This pressure may stimulate Eastern Europeans to search for work outside their countries. There is information which suggests that this inflow may increase considerably in the years to come, and that Eastern European governments may not be able to stem it. Besides, it appears that organised crime, in its efforts to diversify its activities, has realised the potential and possible gains in this field.

In the longer run, the threat would fade away since Western Europe needs substantial new entry into its workforce owing to its ageing population. There is a need to manage the problem in the short and medium-term.

Aid does raise the eyebrows of many Western officials for a couple of reasons. One is linked with the general development level of Eastern European countries, which would imply a heavy burden for the West in terms of development aid – assuming that enlargement were to occur in a few years. Thus, Richard Baldwin, from the Graduate Institute of International Studies in Geneva, calculated that were the Visegrad Four admitted in the EU this would mean either an increase in contributions to the budget of around 60% or a severe curtailment in EU spending.[20] On the other hand, one could argue that the budget level in itself does not provide a good yardstick. Laszlo Csaba argues in this vein when he remarks that 'on the basis of the EU's present budgetary spending, only about 0.25% of EU gross domestic product is likely to be channelled in annual transfers to new members from the Visegrad Group. In Germany, by contrast, 5% of annual GDP is being transferred to the Eastern Länder'.[21]

Another reason is that development aid to Eastern European countries would severely clash with the current competing claims on the EU budget – with the farmers' lobbies and the big recipients of development aid (Spain, Ireland, Portugal, and Greece).

What lies ahead?

For Western European policymakers the biggest dilemma is, probably, how to proceed with the further *deepening* of the Union. Here there seem to be two clashing perspectives, which are hard to reconcile. Some countries, including France, would rather see a movement towards the creation of the monetary union before any significant political deepening were – if ever – to take place. This suggests a vision according to which deepening would depend on whether governments are able to impose the type of policies which are required by a monetary union – which further means that some progress in terms of economic convergence is needed before the big institutional step forward is undertaken. It seems also that France wants to create the kind of monetary institutional infrastructure which should 'europeanize' (read contain) the increasing influence of the Bundesbank and of Frankfurt as a major financial centre.[22] France would also like to impose its own brand of macroeconomic management, which has a traditional 'dirigistique' flavour. As mentioned in the introduction, one meets here a clash of different 'cultures of stability'.

For its part, Germany stresses that some form of political integration is needed in order to deepen economic integration; this was the gist of the September 1994 paper of Wolfgang Schäuble, who is the leader of the CD parliamentarian fraction. Bonn maintains that it would be very hard to sell to its citizens the idea of giving up the DM, as a symbol of national economic stability and solidity, unless there is a guarantee that economic policies within the Union have the consistency that would secure a similar degree of stability to the common currency. And that, to this end, a political 'straitjacket' – a sort of political integration – would be the only way to discipline policymaking at national level. This reasoning lies very much behind the vision of a multispeed Europe – which argues that the only way to proceed with further deepening is by letting a 'hard core' implement it, and the rest to join at a later stage. However, a 'hard-core' without France would not make much sense and would likely split the Union in a highly destabilising way. Therefore, the crucial question becomes: can France undertake the genuine (sustainable) fiscal adjustment, which should enable her to adopt the common currency by 1999?

Another economic reason for proceeding with a 'hard core' can be the concern that, should some of its members experience some difficulties, Germany would be expected to carry the main burden of assistance. This implies that the more convergent the economic performances of the 'hard core' members are, the easier would be to undertake the expected assistance, which further means that the harder (more homogenous) the core is the better. The *hardness* and homogeneity of the core would also help build up the credibility of the monetary union. It is known that it would be the first time in history when sovereign states agree to give up their national currencies in favour of a single currency, but with retaining independent economic and fiscal policies. Imagine what a blow to the credibility of the whole venture would occur if one of the member countries were to succumb to the pressures exerted by the monetary straitjacket and decided to get out.

One could add also a political reason for Germany's current pushing for some sort of political integration: the possible idea that a common foreign and security policy would make it easier for Bonn to pursue its interests in a multilateral framework – for otherwise, the other European countries would look with much mefiance on any unilateral moves of an increasingly powerful and assertive economic powerhouse.[23]

Contained in the above mentioned dilemma is the choice that pits *deepening* vs. *enlargement* to the East. Germany was shown as the main supporter of an early entry of Eastern European neighbours into the Union, a process that would give an additional rationale for the application of the concept of a multi-speed Europe. However, there are important members of the EU, which oppose a speeding-up of bringing in new members. Between Germany and France, in the main, a strategic decision needs to be made in this respect.

To sum up, one can say that the clash of perspectives is provoked by two sets of reasons. One set regards the different visions on how to integrate politically Europe including the feasibility of achieving common foreign and security policies. This set of reasons refers to the possibility of enlargement to the East as well. The other set of reasons regards different judgements on how to proceed with the deepening of economic integration in view of the diverging performances of the member countries.

A big dilemma for certain Eastern European governments could be formulated in this way: let us assume that the EU decides to let them in, in the near future, and also, that their institutional and legal build-up, as well as the functioning of their democratic institutions, match the provisions of the *l'acquis communautaire*. Does it mean that they will be able to cope with the competitive pressures of the EU environment after the removal of the temporary adjustment facilities, which cover a period of some years only? Can the Eastern European countries benefit – like the member countries of the EU do – on powerful enough safeguards in case something goes terribly wrong? Partially, the same question can be posed for the other side as far as the so called 'sensitive' sectors are concerned; but it is clear that Eastern European countries – particularly the less developed ones – could face infinitely bigger problems should not their low wages and learning potential compensate the considerably inferior overall productivity.

Certainly, one can add the possibility of using the exchange rate as a protective weapon in case they stay outside the 'hard-core' and, therefore, are not subject to the harsh discipline of the monetary union. This would be possible in the framework of an extended application of the concept of multi-speed Europe. Nonetheless, the Eastern European countries would still have to apply strict monetary and fiscal policies in order to avoid being led too much astray in terms of macroeconomic performances; and they would also have to view quite reservedly devaluation, since the latter could fuel inflation in an environment which is already prone to relatively strong inflationary pressures.

In any case, should the EU policymakers internalise broadly defined economic and security interests, a solid package of pre-enlargement supporting measures is required in order to ease the actual process of enlargement and reduce the psychological costs of waiting.[24]

Notes

*	Revised version of a paper presented at the Conference 'The Monetary Union and Implications for Eastern Enlargement', Hamburg, Haus Rissen, 16-17 October 1996. It was published also in S. Bianchini and M. Uvalic (eds.), 'The Balkans and the Challenge of Economic Integration', Ravenna, Largo Editore, 1997, pp. 35-52.
1	See in this respect the suggestively named article 'Torpedos gegen die Zentralbank' (torpedos against the central bank) signed by Gerald Braunberger in the influential *Frankfurter Allgemeine Zeitung*.
2	See his interview in the *International Herald Tribune*, 20 January, 1997, p.1.
3	This traditional dichotomy is used for the sake of simplicity.
4	The Czech Republic is an exception that does not change the broad picture.
5	As two Hungarian scholars remarked 'the petty protectionism' exercised by the European Union against exports from the outside world, but including those from the transforming economies with whom Association Agreements were concluded, gives ground for much concern (Laszlo Valki and Laszlo Csaba, 1994, p.45).

6   See also Jim Rollo and Alasdair Smith, 1993; Riccardo Faini and Richard Portes (eds.), 1995.

7   Josef Joffe, 1994, p.39.

8   See Jürgen Noetzold, 1995.

9   'The wage costs in Poland and in the Czech Republic are roughly 7% of the West German level, whereas roughly 50% of the West German productivity level is achieved' (Noetzold, 1995, p.19).

10   Josef Joffe, Idem.

11   *The Economist*, 14 June 1995, p.12.

12   Into the framework of what Josef Joffe calls a 'Greater Central-European Co-Prosperity Sphere' (1994, p.43). Janusz Stefanowicz, from the Institute of Political Studies of Warsaw, thinks that 'there is a natural and deeply-rooted *Drang nach Osten* of the Germans and nothing will deter them from it' (1995, p.57). The leading Hungarian expert Andras Inotai believes that 'the dynamics of European development are clearly shifting eastwards' (1994, p.78).

13   The post-communist countries need a 'modernisation anchor' and the EU could provide this, in a best-case scenario. But as Andras Inotai remarks 'half-hearted trade liberalisation, delayed answers, and even more importantly, the almost catastrophic lack of a clear forward-looking strategy' reduce this probability (1994b, p.78). Consequently, Inotai conceives of a 'Germany that will be forced to emerge as the main stabilisation and modernisation anchor' (Ibid.).

14   See Andras Inotai (1994b, p.78). For 'the hopes, but also the apprehensions' in the Czech Republic about the increasing role of Germany as a *stabiliser* see Vladimir Handl (1994).

15   Quoted by Tom Buerkle, 1995, p.11.

16   See Survey on European Union, *The Economist*, 22 October 1994, p.14. '...the evidence so far gives some support to those who have argued that the Europe Agreements offered little in the short run to liberalise import policy in the EU and foster export growth from the CEECs' (Riccardo Faini and Richard Portes, 1995, p.5).

17   EBRD Transition Report, 1994, p.122.

18   Ibid., p.57.

19   Ibid., p.57.

20   The EU Survey, *The Economist*, 23 October, 1994, p.15.

21   See Laszlo Csaba, 1995.

22   It should give some pause for thinking the fact that leading British merchant banks (like Warburg, Morgan Grenfell, and Barings Securities) were acquired by German, Swiss, or Dutch financial institutions in the last few years. At the same time the Frankfurt stock exchange is to be modernised in order to become the leading institution of its genre in Europe. What is going to happen with London as a financial centre if Britain decides to stay outside the Monetary Union?

23   I wonder, if a common foreign and security policy is enacted, if France is going

to relinquish its place in the UN Security Council in favour of a seat for Brussels? On the other hand, will the five current members be joined by additional members like Germany and Japan, or by Brussels? However, such a situation would look quite strange, to say the least.

24   Such a pre-enlargement package would include, for example, the financing of large infrastructure projects, which would help homogenise economically Europe. This would be a tremendous aid to a country like Romania.

References

Braunberger, G. (1997), 'Torpedos gegen die Zentralbank', *Frankfurter Allgemeine Zeitung*, 17 January.

Broclawcki, J. P. and Holcblat, N. (1995), 'Reperes economiques pour l'Europe centrale et orientale en 1994', *Le Courrier des Pays de l'Est*, April.

Buerkle, T. (1995), 'US tells EU it wants Eastern Europe kept open', *International Herald Tribune*, 26 April, p.11.

Csaba, L. (1995), 'Time for a Wider Union', *Financial Times*, 9 May.

Daianu, D. (1995), 'A Dual Challenge for Europe', in R. Dobrinsky and M. Landesmann (eds.), *Transforming Economies and European Integration*, Edward Elgar, Aldershot, pp. 15-31.

Daianu, D. (1996), 'Economic Vitality and Viability: A Dual Challenge for European Security', Peter Lang, Frankfurt am Main.

Faini, R. and Portes, R. (1995), 'European Union Trade with Eastern Europe; Adjustment and Opportunities', Centre for Economic Policy Research, London.

Friedman, A. (1997), 'Bundesbank Chief's Blunt View: Europe is too Slow to Adapt', *International Herald Tribune*, 20 January, p.1.

Handl, V. (1994), 'The Czech Perception of Germany: Hopes and Apprehensions', in T. Szemler (ed.), pp. 9-21.

Inotai, A. (1994), 'The System of Criteria for Hungary's Accession to the European Union', *Trends in the World Economy*, no. 76, Institute for World Economics, Budapest.

Inotai, A. (1994b), 'Some Thoughts on Economic Relations between Germany and Central-Eastern Europe, with Special Emphasis on Hungary', in Th. Szemler (ed.), pp.69-87.

Joffe, J. (1994), 'After Bipolarity: Germany and European Security', in 'European Security After the Cold War', proceedings of the 35th Annual Conference of the IISS, *Adelphi Paper*, no.285.

Noetzold, J. (1995), 'European Union and Eastern Central Europe: Expectations and Uncertainties', *Aussenpolitik*, 1, pp.14-23.

Rollo, J. and Smith, A. (1993), 'The Political Economy of Eastern European Trade with the European Community: Why is it so Sensitive?', *Economic Policy*, no.16, April, pp.140-166.

Stefanowicz, J. (1995), 'Central Europe between Germany and Russia', *Security Dialogue*, vol.26(1), pp.55-64.

Szemler, T. (ed.) (1994), 'Relations between Germany and East Central Europe until 2000: Prospects and Policy Options', *Trends in the World Economy* no.75, Institute for World Economics, Budapest.

The Economist, 22 October 1994, p.14.

The Economist, 23 October 1994, p.15.

The Economist, 14 June 1995, p.12.

Valki, L. and Csaba, L. (1994), 'Economic and Social Stability in Central and South-Eastern Europe: Preconditions for Security', in 'European Security after the Cold War', proceedings of the 35th Annual Conference of the IISS, *Adelphi Paper*, No.284, part I, pp.42-59.

Index

W

wage illusion, 181
wage-price spiral, 160, 213
welfare state, 4, 16, 19, 24, 29, 288, 299

X

X-inefficiency, 93, 121, 160, 202, 235, 236, 263